Harold Innis in the New Century
Reflections and Refractions

This collection of original essays explores and expands on the provoca-
tive writings of a remarkable political economist, historian of communication, and cultural theorist. It moves beyond the prevalent view of
Harold Innis as a technological determinist and brings his innovative
ideas to bear on a variety of contemporary issues, such as postmodernism, liberalism, gender, and cultural policy.

The book has three sections: "Reflections on Innis" provides a historical reassessment of Innis, "Gaps and Silences" considers the limitations of both Innis's thought and his interpreters, and "Innis and Cultural Theory" offers speculations on his influence on cultural analysis.
The interpretations presented reflect the changing landscape of intellectual life as boundaries between traditional disciplines blur and new
interdisciplinary fields emerge.

Harold Innis in the New Century is a valuable resource for scholars
and students of Canadian history and political economy, of communications, and of culture.

CHARLES R. ACLAND is assistant professor of communication studies,
Concordia University.

WILLIAM J. BUXTON is professor of communication studies, Concordia
University.

Harold Innis in the New Century

Reflections and Refractions

EDITED BY
CHARLES R. ACLAND AND
WILLIAM J. BUXTON

McGill-Queen's University Press
Montreal & Kingston · London · Ithaca

Legal deposit third quarter 1999
Bibliothèque nationale du Québec

Printed in Canada on acid-free paper

McGill-Queen's University Press acknowledges the
financial support of the Government of Canada
through the Book Publishing Industry Development
Program (BPIDP) for its activities. It also acknowledges the support of the Canada Council for the
Arts for our publishing program.

Canadian Cataloguing in Publication Data

Main entry under title:

Harris Innis in the new century: reflections and refractions

Papers originally presented at a conference held at Concordia
University, Nov. 1994. Includes 1 paper in French.
Includes bibliographical references and index.
ISBN 0-7735-1737-5 (bound).

1. Innis, Harold A., 1894–1952—Congresses. I. Buxton,
William, 1947–   II. Acland, Charles R. (Charles Reid), 1963–

HB121.I6H37 1999   300'.92   C99-900908-7

Typeset in 10/12 Sabon by True to Type

In memory of Irene M. Spry

Contents

Acknowledgments

This collection had its origins in the zeitgeist surrounding the 1994 centenary of Harold Innis's birth. In a collective effort to reflect on the meaning and relevance of Innis's work, various meetings celebrating and examining his legacy took place across Canada. These included a conference that we organized – which focused on Innis as a public intellectual – held at Concordia University in Montreal in November of that year. The sharing of knowledge by participants, chairs, respondents, hosts, and audience members who took part in the symposium made the present volume possible. We also would like to thank the other organizers of "Innis events" as well as Daniel Drache, John Browne, Luc Giroux, Gail Valaskakis, Brian Lewis, Karen Robert, Margaret MacPherson, and the members of a special graduate class on Innis taught by William Buxton at Simon Fraser University during the spring term of 1994.

Funding for our initiative was generously provided by the Joint Doctoral Program in Communication (Concordia University, Université du Québec à Montréal, Université de Montréal), the Department of Communication Studies and the Faculty of Arts and Science (both of Concordia University), Innis College (University of Toronto), the Social Science and Humanities Research Council of Canada, and the Humanities and Social Sciences Federation of Canada.

In preparing this collection for publication we have been assisted immeasurably by the skilful guidance of Philip Cercone, Joan McGilvray, and Susanne McAdam of McGill-Queen's University Press, by John Parry's exacting copy-editing, and by the perceptive comments of two anonymous reviewers. Kim Sawada did an expert job compiling the index, for which we thank her. Finally, it was largely through Robert DeLeski's unstinting efforts that the original material metamorphosed into an integrated text.

Each of us has specific debts of gratitude. Charles Acland is thankful for the years of support and encouragement afforded by the Faculty of General Studies at the University of Calgary. William Buxton wishes to express his heartfelt gratitude to Manon Niquette, whose enthusiasm for life and passion for ideas – which included even joy in the discovery of Innis's thought – helped sustain him throughout the project. Charles Acland wishes to acknowledge the limitless support and encouragement from Rae Staseson, whose creative and intellectual energy is a daily source of inspiration.

Finally, four wonderful children have joined the respective lives of the editors while the volume was in preparation. They are a son and a daughter, Jesse Lee and Océane Niquette-Buxton, and two nieces, Emma and Bianca Acland. Although Innis's intellect was occasionally profoundly pessimistic, we offer these critiques and assessments of his work and thought in the hope that a spark of optimism might be kindled in them and those of their generation – the true inheritors of the next century.

Contributors

CHARLES R. ACLAND is an assistant professor of communication studies at Concordia University. His research is in the field of Canadian cultural studies, and he has published in areas such as film history, taste cultures, and the role of philanthropic institutions in the formation of Canadian culture. He is the author of *Youth, Murder, Spectacle* (Boulder, 1995) and (with William J. Buxton) *American Philanthropy and Canadian Libraries: The Politics of Knowledge and Information* (Montreal, 1998).

ALISON BEALE is an associate professor in the School of Communication at Simon Fraser University. Her work includes the documentary video *Harold Innis: Patterns in Communication* (1990) and the edited volume *Ghosts in the Machine: Women and Cultural Policy in Canada and Australia* (Toronto, 1998). Her articles on Harold Innis and on Canadian and comparative cultural policy have appeared in *MIA/Culture and Policy*; *Continuum*; *Canadian Journal of Communication*; and *Media, Culture and Society*.

JODY BERLAND is an associate professor of humanities at Atkinson College, York University. Her research is in the field of cultural studies, with a particular interest in the geography of communications. Her publications include "On Reading the Weather," *Cultural Studies* (Jan. 1994), and "Radio-Space and Industrial Time: The Case of Music Formats," in S. Frith and T. Bennett, eds., *Rock Music* (London, 1993).

JAMES BICKERTON is a professor of political science at St Francis Xavier University in Antigonish, Nova Scotia. His recent research has been in the areas of parties and elections, regional political economy, and Nova Scotia politics. He is the author of *Nova Scotia, Ottawa, and the Politics of Regional Development* (Toronto, 1990) and co-author of *The Almanac of Canadian Politics* (Toronto, 1995) and *Ties that Bind* (Toronto, 1999). He is also co-editor of the third edition of *Canadian Politics* (Peterborough, 1999).

WILLIAM J. BUXTON is a professor of communication studies at Concordia University. He is the author of *Talcott Parsons and the Capitalist Nation-State* (Toronto, 1985) and (with Charles R. Acland) *American Philanthropy and Canadian Libraries: The Politics of Knowledge and Information* (Montreal, 1998). His current research is on the impact of American philanthropy on Canadian academic/intellectual life, the communications programme of the Rockefeller Foundation, and the history of the social sciences in the United States.

JAMES W. CAREY is CBS Professor of International Journalism in the Graduate School of Journalism at Columbia University. He has published over 100 essays, monographs, and reviews on the history of the mass media, popular culture, and the sociology of communications systems as well as *Media, Myth and Narratives* (Beverly Hills, 1988) and *Communication as Culture* (Boston, 1989). A selection of his writings can be found in E. Stryker and C. Warren eds., *James Carey* (Minneapolis, 1997).

RAY CHARRON lectures in the Department of Communication Studies as well as in the Faculty of Engineering and Computer Science (on issues dealing with the social impact of technology) at Concordia University.

CHERYL DAHL pioneered the development of media and communications studies at the University College of the Fraser Valley in Abbotsford, British Columbia. She still teaches on occasion but recently became the director of Student Services. She has written on social policy, feminist research, the transformation of higher education by new technologies, and the social role of the university.

MICHAEL DORLAND is an associate professor in the School of Journalism and Communication at Carleton University. He is the editor of *Cultural Industries in Canada* (Toronto, 1996) and has recently published *So Close to the State/s: The Emergence of Canadian Feature Film Policy* (Toronto, 1998).

KEVIN DOWLER is an assistant professor in the Mass Communication Programme at York University. He has published a number of essays addressing issues in Canadian art and culture.

DONALD FISHER is a professor of sociology in the Department of Educational Studies and co-director of the Centre for Policy Studies in Higher Education at the University of British Columbia. He has written on such topics as philanthropy, the historical development of the social sciences, and academic-industry relations. His publications include *The Social Sciences in Canada* (Waterloo, Ont., 1991), *Fundamental Development of the Social Sciences* (Ann Arbor, 1993), and (ed. with T. Richardson), *The Development of the Social Sciences in the United States and Canada* (Stamford, 1999).

SARAH FORTIN is a doctoral student in political studies at McGill University.

ALAIN-G. GAGNON is a professor of political science at McGill University, where he also directs the Quebec Studies Program. He has published extensively on politics in Quebec and Canada, including, most recently, (ed. with M. Sarra-Bournet) *Duplessis* (Montreal, 1997) and *L'Almanach politique du Québec* (Montréal, 1997).

JANE JENSON is a professor in the Department of Political Science at the Université de Montréal, where she teaches comparative politics and Canadian politics. She has published on women and politics, citizenship, and political economy.

MICHÈLE MARTIN is a professor in the School of Journalism and Communication at Carleton University. Her publications include *Hello Central?* (Montreal, 1991) *Communication and Mass Media* (Scarborough, Ont., 1997) and *Victor Barbeau, Pionnier de la critique culturelle au Québec* (Sainte Foy, 1997).

HEATHER MENZIES is an adjunct professor of Canadian studies and women's studies at Carleton University, Ottawa. She is the author of seven books, including *Whose Brave New World?* (Toronto, 1996) and *Canada in the Global Village* (Ottawa, 1997).

RICHARD NOBLE is an associate professor of political science at the University of Winnipeg. His research is in the field of political philosophy, with a focus on the Enlightenment. Among his publications is *Language, Subjectivity and Freedom in Rousseau's Moral Philosophy*

(New York, 1991). He is currently writing a book on the values of tolerance and free expression in liberal political theory.

DANIEL SALÉE is professor and principal of the School of Community and Public Affairs at Concordia University. His research is on the political economy of Quebec. He has written and edited a number of books including (with G. Bernier) *The Shaping of Quebec Politics and Society* (Washington, 1992) and (with H. Lustiger-Thaler) *Artful Practices* (Montreal, 1994).

LIORA SALTER is a professor at Osgoode Hall Law School and the Faculty of Environmental Studies, York University. She has written extensively on the relationship between scholarship and public policy. Her books include (with D. Wolfe) *Managing Technologies* (Toronto, 1990), *Mandated Science* (Dordrecht/Boston, 1988), and (ed. with A. Hearn) *Outside the Lines* (Montreal, 1997).

KIM SAWCHUK is an associate professor of communication studies at Concordia University. She writes frequently on art, culture, and technology and is co-editor (with B. Burns and C. Busby) of *When Pain Strikes* (Banff and Minneapolis, 1999) and (with J. Marchessault) of *Wild Science* (London, forthcoming).

IRENE M. SPRY (1907-1998) was professor emeritus of political economy at the University of Ottawa. Her publications include "The Tragedy of the Loss of the Commons" in I.A.L. Getty and A. Lussier (eds.), *As Long as the Sun Shines and Water Flows* (Vancouver, 1983). She was honoured with a festschrift: D. Cameron ed., *Explorations in Canadian Economic History* (Ottawa, 1985). Professor Spry died just before this volume went into production. Her long and distinguished career – marked by passionate scholarly engagement – stands as an inspiring point of reference for intellectuals and social activists.

JUDITH STAMPS is a visiting lecturer in political theory and media studies at the University of Victoria. She is the author of *Unthinking Modernity: Innis, McLuhan, and the Frankfurt School* (Montreal, 1995).

ANDREW WERNICK is a professor at the Centre for Theory, Culture and Politics at Trent University. His publications include *Promotional Culture: Advertising, Ideology and Symbolic Expression* (London, 1991), (ed. with M. Featherstone) *Shadow of Spirit: Religion and Postmodernism* (London, 1994), and *Auguste Comte and the Religion of Humanity* (Cambridge, forthcoming).

Harold Innis in the New Century

Harold Innis: A Genealogy of Contesting Portraits

WILLIAM J. BUXTON AND
CHARLES R. ACLAND

In a letter to his long-time friend and former mentor, Frank H. Knight, dictated from a hospital bed while fighting the cancer that would claim him some six months later, Harold Innis remarked: "I do think that some civilizations or even generations think, e.g., as regards time, in quite different ways than others and that they work under conditions which assume that time is different to them than to others. I could say the same about space but am not up to an elaborate reply."[1] Responding to Knight's reflections on the "*one-sidedness* of communication" as a "partial clue to the universal tendency to *centralization*,"[2] Innis suggested that "this one-sidedness seems to lead to monopoly and to general corruption and bureaucracy to the point that it is eventually burned out ... The problem seems to be that of working out a sustained attack on the factors responsible for the one-sidedness."[3]

This exchange was undoubtedly occasioned by Innis's election to the presidency of the American Economics Association which required him to prepare an address for the Association's annual meetings to be held in December 1952. As Innis's former mentor, and as his immediate predecessor as president (and a fellow economics renegade), Knight was an appropriate sounding-board for Innis's concerns. Yet it is striking that issues related to economics were judiciously avoided in their exchanges. Innis and Knight discussed primarily the links among culture, communications, monopolies of knowledge, and intellectual present-mindedness. All of these matters were evidently on Innis's mind as he struggled to prepare his presidential address. His deepening illness prevented him from going beyond preparing a draft, and his death kept him from delivering the talk.

Nevertheless, the draft version was read at the meeting and published in the *American Economic Review* in 1953 as "The Decline in the Efficiency of Instruments Essential in Equilibrium." Reflecting this rather cumbersome title, the paper sketched out "the problems inherent in the pulp and paper industry as related to the production of information for purposes of trade and the efficiency of the price system." It also traced the rise of newspapers and advertising as forms of communication and bearers of information (1953, 21). Yet as his son Donald attested – based on a number of discussions about the address during the summer of 1952 – his father was not able to produce in written form what he really wanted to say – namely, an elaboration of the "idea that America's strongest tradition is that she has no tradition." He meant by this that "a tradition which consists of keeping oneself to oneself in both space and time is more stultifying than the traditions which Americans are trying to avoid" (D. Innis, 1953, 23). This slavish devotion to an escape from tradition had meant "a concentration on immediacy. The range of interests and means of expression of modern American culture are severely limited by her refusal to be interested in any media of communication which have been used before. America's tradition will make it very difficult for her to go beyond the narrow range of interests which she has set for herself, but until she goes beyond these limits her culture must retain the difficulties which it now has" (25).

Donald Innis noted that his father's critique was closely aligned with his despair and anger at trends in American higher education.

It is only in specialized fields that professors can act as authorities. For the body of culture which is common to all citizens there are no authorities and all opinions are of equal value. No matter how carefully and objectively a study of society may be done, anyone is free to dismiss it as just another idea. The freedom of thought which is so dearly loved in America can become freedom from thought ... It made [Harold Innis] feel angry and frustrated to hear the purveyors of education and information insisting on the importance of freedom of the press and of communication while using this same freedom to channel minds into the thin layer of contemporary froth which is the subject of study in American books and schools. My father felt that it would be very difficult for Americans to realize the nature of their predicament. He did not see any method of escaping from a trap in which the media of communication are the stronghold of a dogma. (23–4)

As his other writings from the same period reveal, the point of these comments was not simply to impugn American culture and intellectual life; Harold Innis viewed developments in the United States as the culmination of a process of change taking place in the world since the nineteenth century. As Havelock (1981) described these sentiments with reference to Innis's essay "A Plea for Time" (in Innis 1952a), "he castigates the present-mindedness of our culture, the lack of predictive intelligence induced by the technologies of the modern media; our increasing inability as he saw it to grasp the importance of duration in time as opposed to extension in space. These matters are part of his intellectual legacy, even if coloured in this particular context by some ill temper" (D. Innis 1953, 25).

As Innis himself indicated in a letter to Knight, he had come to rely heavily on his former colleague Havelock for guidance and inspiration in the final year of his life.[4] This is abundantly clear in his enthusiasm for Havelock's preface to *Prometheus Unbound*, which the author described as a myth about a "conflict between the short range intelligence exercised by men of power, represented by Zeus the tyrannical overlord, and the long range intelligence employed by the intellectual, embodied in Prometheus the Forethinker" (Havelock 1982, 40–1). Innis was very taken by Havelock's analysis, which he incorporated into his preface to *The Strategy of Culture* (1952b), restating Havelock's position in his own terms: "Intellectual man of the nineteenth century was the first to estimate absolute nullity of time. The present – real, insistent, complex and treated as an independent system, the foreshadowing of practical prevision in the field of human action – has penetrated the most vulnerable areas of public policy. War has become a result and a cause of the limitations placed on the forethinker. Power and its assistant force, the natural enemies of intelligence, have become more serious since 'the mental processes activated in the pursuit and consolidating of power are essentially short range'" (41).

In his final years Harold Innis was thus passionately absorbed with the crisis of contemporary culture as it related to intellectual life, human action, and mass communications. Yet after his death a much different image of Innis emerged. He came to be viewed primarily as a committed and dedicated scholar, whose work on economic history, with particular reference to Canada, would be his most lasting legacy. Rather than emphasizing his concern with how the intellectual could combat the present-mindedness and the calamity that it was engendering, commentators largely confined themselves to encomiums about his contributions to academic life, within an English-Canadian context.

His former colleague Donald Creighton noted that Innis "was always ready and willing to promote the interests of scholarship, both national and international, and to defend the unfettered pursuit of truth whenever and wherever his championship was required ... His ideal was the pursuit of truth but never its promulgation as dogma" (1952, 405–6).

W.A. MacIntosh provided a focused assessment of what this scholarship entailed, namely, "the field of Canadian economic history," in which Innis "worked most exclusively, intensively, and fruitfully" (1953, 185). "The work which Innis did from 1920 to 1940 will stand as his most lasting work ... His later work is suggestive and will stimulate further inquiries in the field, some of it will bear fruit. But it differs from his earlier work, in that there is not beneath it the massive base of research which will make *The Fur Trade in Canada* and *The Cod Fisheries* works to be consulted in the next century and beyond" (193).

Another former colleague, W.T. Easterbrook, analysed Innis's reflections on economics and economic history. In tracing Innis's "search for perspective in economic thought," as it evolved over four phases, Easterbrook claimed that his reflections on economics ultimately gave way to what could be best described as "a philosophy of history" (1953a, 291). This orientation, suggests Easterbrook, underpinned Innis's investigations during the fourth and final stages, when he began to examine "the character of communications" as it related to "questions of power and stability, to nationalism, and to ancient and modern concepts of time" (300). In effect, "interest in the spatial aspects of communications now gives way to concern with time concepts and the possibility of avoiding the fatal disease of bias by attainment of a balanced view of time and space as a condition for survival." Rather than dismissing the communications phase, Easterbrook commends it as indicative of "the increasing range and maturity of his thought" and "his search for what he termed 'an integration of basic approaches' as an offset to the fragmentation of knowledge which destroys prospects for understanding among peoples and nations" (303).

While emphasizing Innis's work in communications, Easterbrook's account also might have contributed to suspicions about its value. By framing his analysis in terms of Innis's contributions to economic thought and by periodizing his career into four stages, he suggested that the work in communications represented a speculative and philosophical departure at odds with his earlier, more solidly grounded work in economic history and political economy.[5] Moreover, by maintaining that Innis came to study communications as an extension of his earlier analysis of staples, Easterbrook implied that the later work did not have an integrity of its own but could be fitted into his empirical work on Canadian economic history.[6]

Such an interpretation appeared to guide the decisions of the special executors' committee that oversaw the publication of Innis's hitherto-unpublished writings. In addition to Creighton and Easterbrook, it included S.D. Clark; Innis's widow, Mary Quayle Innis; and their son, Donald Innis. Its mandate was to "supervise the collection of Innis's papers, and to decide which of these ought to be published" (Christian 1980, xvii). Mary Quayle Innis was responsible for selecting material to be placed in Innis's papers, deposited at the University of Toronto Archives. As A. John Watson noted, this process of filtering by Quayle Innis and other members of the committee distorted the collection (1981, 5). Personal items were largely omitted, and the correspondence is scattered and incomplete.[7]

The committee was also highly selective in choosing works to be published or republished. As Brian Shoesmith points out, with its bias towards economic history and political economy, the committee largely neglected communications, a subject with which Innis had become pre-occupied in his final years (1993, 126). Indeed, this inattention contributed towards failure to publish the massive "History of Communications" manuscript (Innis, undated). Mirroring MacIntosh's assessment, the committee evidently did not believe that the lengthy and densely documented work in this new field met Innis's previous standards of scholarship. Undoubtedly, the suspicion about communications stemmed in part from the growing notoriety of Marshall McLuhan at the University of Toronto. Given that Innis's ideas about communications had come to be closely associated with the controversial views of McLuhan, it was not surprising that the committee did not believe that his unpublished writings in this area should be made readily available.

Indeed, McLuhan's own views of the "later Innis" may have contributed to the committee's reluctance. According to McLuhan, "the early Innis working with the insights and methods developed by Mead, Clark, and Veblen was acutely conscious of the inter-penetration of the economic and social life." By contrast, "the later Innis turned to study archaeology and anthropology where any separation of economics and society was meaningless, and where he could make use of simpler societies as working models on which to base a critique of our total civilization" (1953, 390). "Once he had crossed that bridge to the network of information and ideas he never turned back to the merely economic network. Classical economics had ceased to exist for him except as an historical phenomenon."

McLuhan argued moreover that the "later" Innis, in breaking away from economic inquiry, "inevitably adopted a discontinuous style, an aphoristic, mental-camera sort of procedure which was indispensable to his needs" (388). In effect, the inability of readers to "find what he was driving at" was "no accident": "The later Innis had no position. He had become a roving mental eye, and intellectual radar screen on the alert for objective clues to the inner spirit of our time" (392). McLuhan's assessment very possibly contributed to the committee's view that the writings in communications would do nothing to enhance Innis's academic reputation.[8]

Donald Creighton reinforced this image of Innis in a biography that appeared in 1957. Describing his colleague at the peak of his "authority and influence," Creighton noted that the "place he had made for himself was unique," in that "he had become the chief repository of academic information, the principle confidant of academic secrets, the accepted interpreter of academic opinion, and the final arbiter of academic disputes" (Creighton 1957, 130).

Creighton chose the term "academic" to describe Innis's myriad activities not merely for alliteration; it provided the leitmotif for his narrative of Innis's career: "a great Canadian scholar" who wished to help preserve "the university tradition, the tradition of scholarship, of learning and teaching," which he saw as "a vitally essential element of western civilization" (107–8). While this description of Innis is not without foundation, it can be called into question. Rather than exploring how Innis viewed this civilization, why he believed that university scholarship was critical for its survival, and what this meant for Innis's activities as an intellectual, Creighton provided little more than a narrative of Innis's scholarly career and interests. The memoir creates the impression of a prototypical "ivory tower" academic, whose main goal was scholarship for its own sake, with little regard paid to its public meaning or consequences.[9] This vocation, Creighton maintains, was linked to Innis's commitment to Canadian nationalism.[10]

Creighton had little to say about Innis's late-blooming concern with communications, which had "led him further and further away from Canada into researches and speculation which, in his view, touched at the heart of modern problems, but which obviously did so in a general and philosophic fashion" (1957, 138). This dismissal was evidently supported by the executors' committee, which oversaw the publication of *Essays in Canadian Economic History* (1956a). This volume, as stated by S.D. Clark in the preface, was thought to "represent the best of Innis's scattered writings in Canadian economic history" (vi).[11]

As the committee predicted, it was Innis's "staples approach" that had the greatest immediate impact on scholarly work, as evidenced by new studies of Canadian economic development in the dozen or so years after his death.[12] Indeed, by the early 1960s, Innis's work on communications, originally seen by McLuhan as such a departure from his early writings, was rather thought to be continuous with them. McLuhan now argued that the media of communications could best be seen as a form of staple, whose intrinsic characteristics led it to have a particular effect on human sensibility and perception (1960). In this sense, his view of Innis largely converged with that of Easterbrook, who made a contribution to the same volume (*Journal of Economic History*).[13]

It was not until 1964 that the committee saw fit to publish any of Innis's writings in communications. But rather than making available the "History of Communications" in a readable form, it chose to republish *The Bias of Communication* (1964a) along with new versions of *The Cod Fisheries* (1964b) and *The Fur Trade in Canada* (1964c). An anticipated further volume never materialized (Shoesmith 1993, 127).

Reflecting the apparent rapprochement between McLuhan's views of Innis and those of the executors' committee, an introduction by McLuhan accompanied the reissue of *Bias*. That his former colleague would be chosen to this task supported the widely held view that Innis's writings on communications foreshadowed McLuhan's rather than having their own integrity.[14] With McLuhan's own reputation and celebrity reaching their apogee in the 1960s, it was difficult for Innis's work on communications to receive the attention that it deserved. Rather, reflecting the periodization of Innis's work prepared by Creighton and Easterbrook, communications became a code word to describe the final phase of Innis's work. At the same time, Innis appeared to have fallen out of favour in two of the areas in which he forged his original reputation – namely, economics and economic history, neither of which showed much interest in Innis's later work (Neill 1972, 121; Patterson 1990, 49). However, the "Innisian" tradition of political economy fared little better. Ian Drummond, for instance, a member of the Department of Economics at the University of Toronto (which had broken off from the original Department of Political Economy) dismissed Innis as having little relevance to contemporary economic analysis and stated baldly that his later writings were remote from the concerns of economists (1987, 857–8). Many economic historians echoed the sentiment. Mel Watkins (1963) observed that interest in staples theory by Canadian economic historians was on the wane (51). Hugh Aitken (1977), who had championed the staples approach, now derided Innis's work in Canadian economic history as based on "myth" rather than on "measurement." As he noted, "The staples thesis, in the hands of Innis and his school, provided a rationale for the existence of the Canadian nation. It helped to make what had happened understandable and what existed acceptable. It placed Canada in historic time, so that you could see it whole and believe that you comprehended it. The myth has now lost its power, as all myths eventually must if they are not continually refreshed and reinterpreted. What takes its place is a matter of some importance, to Canadian and to all who wish them well" (1977, 105).

Along similar lines, W.J. Eccles (1979) severely challenged Innis's work on the fur trade, in an attack that was met with little rebuttal by economic historians.[15] In effect, as economics and economic history in Canada became increasingly dominated by quantification and neoclassical modelling, the Innis tradition of staples analysis and institutional economics came to be seen as speculative and insufficiently rigorous.[16] To be sure, political economists like Mel Watkins (1963, 1977), Ian Parker (1977), Abraham Rotstein (1976), and Robin Neill (1972) continued to work within an Innisian tradition. But the field of economics was clearly moving elsewhere, and the work of these thinkers came to speak more to other audiences than it did to members of the economics profession per se.

Interest in Innisian political economy had moved from the mainstream to the margin, to radical political economy and to Canadian analysis more generally. In these fields, Innis's writings became a resource for dealing with the development of a left-nationalist political economy[17] and the formation of an identity for the emergent field of Canadian studies.[18] In the wake of McLuhan's rise to prominence, the putative connection between the two thinkers came under closer scrutiny. A number of American scholars reached the similar conclusion that Innis's work on communications differed from McLuhan's in fundamental ways.[19]

More generally, subtle shifts occurred in the interpretation of Innis in the late 1970s – occasioned in part by the twenty-fifth anniversary of his death. Major reassessments challenged some of the prevailing assumptions about Innis's legacy. A special issue of the *Journal of Canadian Studies* (vol. 12 no. 5 [winter] 1977) – while concentrating on the implications of Innis's work for the nascent field, also included examinations of his contribution as an intellectual. A. John Watson noted that interpretations of Innis had been dominated by "two frames of reference corresponding to the two main phases of Innis' intellectual activity" – "the 'staples approach' of the 'early' Innis and the communication studies of the 'late' Innis." Thus "Innis becomes the victim of the very specialization in the social sciences that he warned about." Watson suggested that this form of "intellectual schizophrenia" was largely accepted because it "provides the built-in coherence that goes with a specialized branch of the social sciences, be that economic history or communications theory." In an effort to reconcile the two frames of references, Watson proposed greater attention to Innis's "philosophical approach," which began to emerge in the 1940s, as evidenced not only in Innis's increasing concern with the humanities but in his intense interest in classical scholarship (1977, 45–6).

Watson's refutation of the "early"-versus-"later" dichotomy found echoes in the issue. Tom Cooper stressed "the unknown Innis," or "the man behind the mask," in terms of "what he meant by what he said, who he was when alone, what his inner feelings and thought processes were like [and] how his mannerisms and attitudes changed with age and circumstance" (1977, 111). In gaining a glimpse of "the whole Innis," claimed Cooper, one could understand how his early observations and later explorations were interconnected and of a piece (117).

Leslie Pal, challenging McLuhan's depiction of "the later Innis" as primarily "a communications theorist," argued that it was a mistake to "focus too narrowly on the simple biases of media and their presumed results." Rather, the "major themes of his communications works ... such as the relationship between learning, public opinion, force and religion, or the requirements of liberty," were already present in the 1930s, when "he wrote and thought as much about universities and scholarship as he did about staples" (1977, 32). Rather than divorcing later from earlier concerns, it would be fruitful to think of Innis more in terms of a "political theorist" concerned with understanding how communications within empires were linked to humanistic scholarship, public opinion, and the production of knowledge.

Pal's view of Innis complemented that of William Christian[20] who took issue with the widely held view that Innis was a supporter of nationalism.[21] Christian noted that while Innis may have been a nationalist in the weak sense of loving his country, "he was opposed to nationalism as a programme or an ideology, and even more strongly opposed to the exclusivist and intolerant spirit which that doctrine usually incorporated" (1977b, 70–1). Christian's "inquisition of nationalism," along with a number of the other contributions to the volume, called into question many of the prevailing assumptions about the nature and meaning of Innis's work.

The following year, the Department of Communication at Simon Fraser University, in conjunction with the Department of Continuing Studies, organized a conference entitled "Harold Adams Innis: Legacy, Context, Direction."[22] The resulting book was guided by the editors' perception of a "need for an inclusive assessment of the Innis legacy, one that would involve an examination of his work as comprehensive scholarship, not merely as a set of artificially fragmented contributions to specialized academic disciplines" (Melody, Salter, and Heyer 1981, x). True to these goals, a number of chapters probed how one could draw on Innis's work to explore the intersection of communications and culture with domination and dependence.

Shortly thereafter, two fine dissertations – written by A. John Watson (1981) and Thomas Cooper (1979) – were submitted to the University of Toronto. Both works, foreshadowed by the authors' contributions to the special Innis issue of the *Journal of Canadian Studies*, reassessed Innis's life and work. Watson drew particular attention to how Innis addressed the colonized and marginal stature of academic life in Canada. Through a painstaking analysis, Cooper demonstrated the degree to which Innis's career was intertwined with that of McLuhan. The link between Innis's biography and his intellectual concerns received further emphasis in Eric Havelock's (1982) memoir of Harold Innis, published a quarter-century after Creighton's. Rather than focusing on Innis as an "academic," Havelock examined him as "the philosophical historian," fully realized in Innis's last five years, when he was immersed in studies of communications. Havelock's analysis showed how Innis's concern with communications was inherently related to his reflections on how monopolies of knowledge could be countered through alternative forms of intellectual practice.

Havelock's memoir reinforced the trend to search for common ground between Innis's early and later writings and to examine his attitude to modernity, as revealed in trends towards increased state power, nationalism, and the ascendancy of space-biased forms of communication (Kroker 1984; Wernick 1986; Collins 1986; di Norcia 1990; Stamps 1995). Other works have illuminated a range of issues related to Innis's work, including his contributions to geography (Barnes 1993; Randall and Ironside 1996), international relations (Cox 1995), northern studies (Evenden 1998), and social science method (Comor 1994; Dudley 1995).

This attention, while expressing respect for an eminent scholar, also betrays some degree of bewilderment about his actual contribution. The demonstration of high regard for Innis's work sometimes has the same enthusiasm as an obligation to visit a relative one doesn't really like.[23] None the less, his name continues to come up, showing that there is a consensus that he initiated something important, though the consensus-makers may not be sure what. For example, an issue of *Continuum: The Australian Journal of Media and Culture* – vol. 7 no. 1 (1993) – was titled "Dependency/Space/Policy: A Dialogue with

Harold A. Innis." The theme, according to the editors' introduction, arose "when one editor wrote to the other inquiring about the current place of Harold A. Innis in North American communications and cultural studies." Articles in the issue explored "the broader applications of his approach," despite an almost-apologetic observation that Innis was "thoroughly tied to the Canadian context" (6). The matter is introduced not as an authoritative reading of the theorist but as a tentative questioning of whether or not Innis remains of interest and to what extent he has wider resonances.

Despite some confusion about how Innis's legacy can best be appropriated, researchers are increasingly attracted to his writings. There is something about his work – its intellectual breadth and theoretical shifts – that lends itself handily to reinterpretation. Our ongoing research on the history of intellectual *and* cultural life in Canada (Acland 1994; Acland and Buxton 1994, 1996; Buxton and Acland 1998) had already shown us that Innis influenced intellectual practice and organization in Canada in a manner not fully recognized or appreciated. The centenary of Innis's birth on 5 November 1994 provided an occasion for further reflection on the meaning and significance of his legacy.

To this end, through the coordinating efforts of Innis College at the University of Toronto, conferences took place throughout Canada, addressing diverse topics for which Innis's writings were considered pertinent, ranging from monopolies of knowledge to art and money. Such a set of meetings is itself testimony to the relevance of Innis's thought to the contemporary world. Within the framework of this celebration, we organized a conference entitled "Harold Innis and Intellectual Practice for the New Century: Interdisciplinary and Critical Studies" (1994).[24] Organized under the auspices of the Joint Doctoral Program in Communication (Concordia University, Université de Montréal and Université du Québec à Montréal), it brought together participants from different backgrounds and interests to reflect on the meaning and relevance of Innis's thought to today's world. We tried to include not only Innis specialists but those who might look at his work with a fresh eye and illuminate aspects of his work previously ignored. It was at this conference that the chapters in this volume first appeared.

The conference took place in a period of attacks on Canadian universities, most visibly in the form of funding cuts and various austerity measures. With increasing force through the early 1990s, many universities have felt under siege from a rhetoric of "doing more with less." Many have seen this translate into a deterioration of teaching and research conditions and believe that the drive to a more "flexible" university, responsive to the demand of an educational marketplace, is counterproductive to intellectual life and, in the extreme, an infringement upon academic freedom.

However manifested, the forced restructuring of Canadian universities was a sign that a simmering anti-intellectualism had finally boiled over. It was the editors' view that Innis's commentaries on intellectual work might inform our present situation, if only to shine a light on the urgent need for a sustained critique of it. It was with these changes in mind that we took as a general conference theme the place of intellectual practice in a fast-approaching new century. That sense of urgency and expectation concerning scholarly life in Canada, as well as a broader examination of the contemporary era, forms the core of the present volume.

THE COLLECTION AT A GLANCE

As with earlier commentaries on Innis, the present collection represents – to paraphrase Hegel – our times apprehended in thought. In an era of globalization, resurgent nationalism, identity politics, and new technologies of communications, Innis speaks to us in ways that would not have been possible in the past. The interpretations offered also reflect the changing landscape of intellectual life. As the boundaries between traditional disciplines such as economics, political science, and history blur, as new interdisciplinary fields such as communications, Canadian studies, and cultural studies arise, the discipline-bounded angle of vision also begins to lose its focus. Moreover, as it becomes increasingly evident that knowledge is at the centre of struggles for power, authority, and control – especially as we see that talk of the information society refers in fact to the emergence of an information *class* – academics must reflect on how the ideas they produce have a bearing on social and cultural transformation.

These concerns were certainly on Innis's mind in his last years, as he became increasingly disconsolate about the trends towards present-mindedness and space-biased communications that he witnessed (Buxton 1998). In search of a corrective, he thought about how intellectual and cultural life could be revitalized. Arguably, running through many of the chapters in this volume is the impulse both to engage with Innis's intellectual legacy and to draw on his work to address current problems and issues.

It would be misleading, however, to emphasize only the continuity in this volume. Innis's multiple incarnations, sometimes in full conflict and contradiction with each other, are amply represented. For each author and essay, Innis's work and ideas serve as a point of departure for challenges to orthodoxies about Innisian scholarship and explorations of broader intellectual engagements. The organization of the book has the modest goal of highlighting some of the friction and debate, thus capturing the liveliness of interdisciplinary and critical research today.

The volume presents three sites of engagement: the historical reassessment found in part I, "Reflections on Innis"; the limitations of Innis's scope (and of some of his interpreters) in part II, "Gaps and Silences"; and the speculation about his influence on cultural analysis in part III, "Innis and Cultural Theory." In part I, chapters 1–4 treat Innis's own intellectual context, and chapters 5–8 focus on the politics of intellectual practice. In part III, chapters 13–16 deal with Innis's relation to critical theory, especially theories of the modern and the postmodern, and chapters 17–20 explore the uses of "Innisian" analysis for the study of cultural practice and policy.

In order to reassess the currency of Innis's writings, many of this volume's authors found it essential to examine in detail the thought and context that shaped his views. The first four essays of part I examine how Innis built on and appropriated particular traditions in developing his central themes, as well as the relationship between his work and his experiences. A number of works have examined aspects of his biography, including his rural Baptist upbringing (Creighton 1957; Gauvreau 1996), his war experience (Gwyn 1992), his time at the University of Chicago, where he encountered the work of Thorstein Veblen and the Chicago School of Sociology (Stark 1984), and his publishing initiatives (Campbell 1995). The second half of part I includes essays that examine how Innis's thought and practice fused Canadian, British, and American sources.

Richard Noble in chapter 1 draws attention to the eighteenth-century roots of Innis's views on freedom within the "Whig" tradition of political thought, associated with David Hume, Adam Smith, and Edmund Burke. Innis understood liberty as a realm of non-interference, guaranteed by a set of cultural, legal, and political institutions. As Noble persuasively argues, Innis believed that these institutions – universities, the judiciary, common law, parliaments, and related practices – were grounded in what remained of the oral tradition. They served as antidotes to the predominant tendency towards space-biased communications and the attendant features of centralization and loss of collective memory. The oral tradition made for a flexible and vigorous intellectual culture, which was anti-dogmatic and open-ended. Freedom could be best preserved by autonomous institutions, which balance both the highly centralized authority of the central government and the monopolies of knowledge based on space-biased technologies. Threats to those same institutions, conversely, could result in a state of imbalance and overemphasis on space bias, which is precisely what Innis saw unfolding.

In chapter 2, Judith Stamps complements Noble's analysis with a detailed discussion of the way in which Scottish Enlightenment ideals had come to pervade Canadian education prior to Innis's time. While Noble bases his account on a close reading of Innis's writings, Stamps provides an account of the educational system in Canada around 1900. She shows how various elements combined to form a body of thought that informed Innis's thinking, including Scottish common-sense philosophy, historicism, and dialectics. True to the heritage of Thomas Reid and Canadian Hegelians, Innis espoused an approach characterized by organicism. For instance, his analysis of staples echoed Andrew Seth's claim that "every object carries us necessarily beyond itself." Like Noble, Stamps takes us to Innis's central preoccupation with orality, but by a different route. As she points out, the oral tradition, and its basis in dialogue, served as an antidote to modernity; it enhanced cultural memory, and a sense of history, and it promoted empathy and a tolerance for ambiguity in meaning.

Michael Dorland (chapter 3) examines Innis's views on the link between religious and political life in Canada. Mirroring some of the themes addressed by Noble and Stamps, Dorland examines Innis's analysis of how the Canadian state, as a rump of the Gallican church, preserves its authoritarian character. Drawing on Michel Foucault's account of governmentality, Dorland suggests that Innis considered aspects of absolutist statecraft to have been preserved in a sedimented form in Canadian state institutions, making for a very limited public sphere. In light of Innis's critique of the authoritarian state as a purveyor of monopolies of knowledge, this state of affairs accounts for Innis's dismay at the lack of public life in Canada during the 1930s and for his support of regionalism and public discussion as a possible corrective.

James Carey in chapter 4 explores the complex relationship between Innis and the Chicago School of Sociology, demonstrating how Innis was able to extend and develop its frame of reference by "grounding it more firmly in the geography and economics of the continent." One explanation of this convergence of thought, argues Carey, can be located in the changes occurring in early twentieth century Chicago, still reinventing itself after the great fire of 1871 and a massive shift in immigration patterns. The new Chicago offered an ideal testing ground for the innovative approaches, being developed at the University of Chicago, to the study of urban community life. Always the "Second City" to New York's dominance, Chicago came to be a major urban centre through its connections to the resources of the midwest and the financial markets of the east. Carey argues that Innis had found a congenial milieu in which to formulate a critical response to Frederick Turner's frontier thesis, counterpoising it with the metropolitan thesis. This line of argument would become highly influential in Canadian historiography for understanding hinterland-metropolis relations.

These claims about the development of Innis's thought encourage us to look beyond his academic output in particular realms, such as political economy and communications. Instead, we should view him as someone wrestling with the onset of modernity – particularly its Canadian variant – and seeking to define a form of intellectual practice that could serve as a counterweight to the associated monopolies of knowledge. These conceptions of the backdrop to Innis's thought dovetail with considerations of his stance as an intellectual, seen here in the second quartet of essays in part I.

As a former colleague of Harold Innis – and someone who was very much influenced by his ideas – Irene M. Spry provides a fascinating account in chapter 5 of his style of work and his research. According to Spry, Innis believed that the notion of *homo economicus* was useless; economic problems should be viewed within the broader context of human experience. Economists needed to understand geology, biology, botany, human customs, culture, religion, technology, and politics in order to address economic problems. Thus Innis wanted economists to visit the actual settings of problems that they were seeking to understand. This method inspired Spry, who undertook field investigations, travelling to the prairies and the Rocky Mountains to do work on Canadian energy resources and on the Palliser expedition. Spry also shows how Innis promoted scholarly publications in the social sciences, in the *Canadian Journal of Economics and Political Science*, *Contributions to Canadian Economics*, *The Encyclopedia of Canada*, the Canadian-American Relations series, and the Frontiers of Settlement series.

Cheryl Dahl and Liora Salter (chapter 6) examine Innis's definition of the public intellectual and the role of the university. They point out that Innis's scepticism about whether social scientists could retain their integrity if they became too involved with boards and commissions relates to the need for a university environment that would protect the intellectual from biases. Based on their reading of Innis, they challenge the widely held notion of the polarization of sciences, because it assumes a clear dichotomy between the intellectual and the public. They point out that the dangers that Innis detected are present today: the way intellectual work could become irrelevant, could be measured against an unrealistic picture of science, and could become predictable and thereby normless. In their view, Innis shows that scholarship should promote sympathetic imagination and expand the horizons of the public domain.

Innis's support of academic communities is well brought out by Donald Fisher (chapter 7), who points out that Innis was the primary "boundary-worker" in the formation of the Canadian Social Science Research Council in 1941. In making sure that the council was in the hands of social scientists, and separated from other fields and from the state, Innis was acting on his conviction that centralized authority represented unpalatable monopolies of knowledge. Accordingly, applied or policy research done for the state or private interests served to create "short-term, space-biased information," which supported these dominant interests. Fisher notes that Innis advocated a "philosophical approach," carried out by researchers who were interdisciplinary, "flexible, open-minded, and reflective." Fisher's account of Innis's views on academic freedom corresponds to the form of freedom that Noble detects in Innis's writings on political life. Just as political freedom entailed limitations placed on centralized authorities, academic freedom meant protection and isolation from dominant and controlling tendencies, or "pure" as opposed to applied research.

While Innis felt that those working in universities should not be involved in active policy-making, he still believed that academics had a role in social and moral life. His approach to intellectual practice, as Michèle Martin and William J. Buxton (chapter 8) point out, can be usefully contrasted with that of his contemporary in Quebec, Victor Barbeau. While Innis was wary of the modern media as being space-biased, Barbeau thought a critical, journalistic critique the possible basis for progressive social change. These differences, Martin and Buxton argue, reflect the two men's respective contexts and traditions. Whereas Innis's Baptist upbringing led him to be suspicious of monopolies of knowledge, Barbeau, with the Catholic church in Quebec as his frame of reference, held that monopolies of knowledge were necessary for social engagement and social advancement.

Accompanying the shift towards examining Innis's intellectual practice has been closer consideration to his views on culture and cultural production. While Innis's influence on communication studies has been profound, especially its introduction and maintenance a strong link to the humanities, his significance for cultural analysis has been less thoroughly examined. The essays appearing in part III move in that direction. The authors of chapters 13–16 reassess Innis's thought in light of cultural and critical theory. Charles R. Acland (chapter 13) demonstrates that Innis's work constitutes a rich legacy for cultural studies.

To be sure, culture for Innis was not something to be enjoyed or used for diversion. Yet he was concerned about the increasing depravity and impoverishment of culture, especially in terms of collective life. As Acland notes, Innis shared with Canadian cultural nationalists of his time the view that industrialism had severely distorted American culture and threatened Canada's as well. Unlike his contemporaries, Acland emphasizes, Innis was profoundly ambivalent about nationalism and critical of those cultural nationalists who helped develop, for instance, a monopolistic publishing industry. Innis, moreover, offered a critique of international media imperialism and, in so doing, showed how this phenomenon was linked to knowledge and ideas as well as to the economics of cultural industries. Reexamination of the debates concerning the appropriateness of Innis's concepts for Marxist analysis leads Acland to suggest that Innis's thought had strong affinities with cultural theory and in particular offers insight into the analysis of core–periphery relations.

How did Innis consider issues of space and time in relation to culture? As Andrew Wernick (chapter 14) demonstrates, Innis's conception of time in relation to the mass media differed fundamentally from Marshall McLuhan's. Indeed, as he points out, McLuhan's well-known introduction to *The Bias of Communication* (McLuhan 1964a) has served to obscure the meaning and significance of Innis's writings on communication. Above all, by emphasizing Innis's concerns with the values of tradition and continuity, McLuhan has played down Innis's insights into the interrelationships of timesense, education, knowledge, and self-corrective practice. What Wernick offers is an "Innisian" response to McLuhan's criticisms, showing how Innis's concept of time advances a much more believable and compelling critique of modern time sensibility and linear time than McLuhan's commentary suggests. For Wernick, it follows that Innis cannot be categorized as a "conservative anti-modernist" (to use Habermas's phrase), as McLuhan's account implies. Unlike McLuhan, Innis never forgot that time was being constructed by industrialism. Nor does Innis exhibit nostalgia for Greek culture; he was concerned with the present and how to encourage and cultivate oral resistance to space-biased communications.

While Wernick draws on Innis to criticize aspects of postmodernity, Ray Charron (chapter 16) detects some postmodern elements in Innis. In a manner similar to thinkers such as Lyotard, Innis claims that ancient Greece created ways of thinking that have led to the exclusion of alternatives from Western thought. Moreover, as Charron points out, there are striking parallels between Innis's critique of writing and that offered by Jacques Derrida. While Innis, according to Charron, does not address problems in Western metaphysics in the same way that postmodern thinkers do, he shares their concern with the community as the final arbiter in disputes and arguments. Like Rorty, for instance, Innis sees conversation as the ultimate context within which knowledge is to be understood. Charron suggests that Innis shares both a pessimism and a certain expository style with postmoderns. This convergent view of the fragmentary nature of knowledge is expressed in a common writing style that invites the reader to participate in creating meaning in the text. At the same time, Charron suggests, Innis, with his concern to recover the oral tradition, advocated a reliance on oppositions that is at odds with postmoderns, and deconstructionists in particular.

Jody Berland (chapter 15) finds merit in Innis's notions about space, which converge with some of the claims made by postmodern geography. Like Acland, Berland looks at how Innis's thought can illuminate a key issue within current discussions about space – the margin. As she notes, Innis emphasized the role of European imperialism in producing a new geography of colonial space. Colonial space was traversed space, that which "has been mapped and shaped by specific imperial forms of knowledge and interest." Innis's contribution, argues Berland, is to demonstrate how communications serves to mediate between imperial strategies and the transformation of space. But what Innis fails to deliver is the space of everyday life in which forms of emancipatory politics can take place. All the same, he comes to terms with the current destabilization of the relationship between place and identity.

Other authors in part III have explored the implications of Innis for a discussion of cultural policy. Here, Innis's work is seen as an ideal starting point for a critique of the mechanisms that administer knowledge in the cultural realm, with specific consequences for the experience and production of space and time. The later essays in part III explore the correspondences among Innis's theories, arts administration, and cultural practice.

Heather Menzies (chapter 17) examines the manner in which popular practices oriented towards time – in relation to community – become appropriated and commodified by corporate and state interests to administer and control territory – Innis's control of space. She sees the internet as a site of contestation between popular groups and corporate interests. Does it represent a breakthrough towards cooperation and sustainable coexistence, grounded in an emergent worldview? Or will the earlier space-binding tendencies reassert themselves? While the internet started in communitarian terms (as Menzies demonstrates was the case with women's groups), this impulse came under intense pressure from forces emphasizing transmission and control.

Recent developments underscore this trend. In Canada, the push towards the so-called information highway comes from those subscribing to a space-biased view of communications – in particular, through the federally funded CANARIE program. While the fast-forward hype of the internet and the information highway are leaving popular groups behind, Menzies believes that marginal groups can use the technology to break the corporatist monopoly and ultimately to reassert the time-binding nature of communications in the face of dominant space bias.

As Kevin Dowler (in chapter 18) notes, Innis believed that if Canada was to resist the commercialism of American media, some form of state protection was necessary – a sentiment that echoed the Massey Report (Canada 1951). Dowler shows that Innis's perspective was informed by his early studies, which saw the centralized state as crucial in building an infrastructure for economic activity. The building of a communications infrastructure set in motion forces that in turn imperilled Canadian sovereignty. This situation made it imperative to create a civil society and culture to compensate for the dependence that had developed. It is within this context of "government ownership, a weak civil society, and security against American mass culture," argues Dowler, "that cultural practices in Canada emerge." Through close attention to Innis's early writing, Dowler claims, one can begin to understand how culture and cultural policy have taken the direction that they have in Canada.

Alison Beale's account (chapter 19) of culture and cultural policy in Canada fits nicely with Dowler's. She notes that in this context, art and culture have been at odds with one another. The arts, as traditionally practised in Canada, while conservative in orientation, still permitted active engagement with cultural material. In the new era in cultural policy ushered in by the Massey Report (Canada 1951), the Federation of Canadian Artists (FCA) favoured a network of community arts centres, an initiative that was never acted on. Given the membership of the Massey Commission, it was not surprising that the notion of "community arts" lost out to "flagship cultural palaces." Art and artists, as Beale suggests, can be seen as points of resistance to the control of state rationality, underscoring the claims made by Dorland and Dowler. Further, the ideas of Innis about the penetrative powers of the price system shed light on how cultural policy has become biased towards the support of cultural industries rather than cultural practice. In line with Innis's dismay about academe's role in establishing monopolies of knowledge, Beale chides contemporary academics for becoming clever about cultural policy, while largely ignoring how their own knowledge has become bound up in the price system. She looks to artist-run centres as alternative ways of conceiving production, distribution, and consumption, in Innis's spirit of encouragement of humanists in the universities to balance the economistic direction of culture.

Kim Sawchuk (chapter 20) finds similar tendencies within the practice of art itself. While Innis never dealt with art and aesthetics directly, his fragmentary notes in *The Idea File* (1980), as well as other writings, reveal that he saw artistic practice as linked to the materialities of technology and power. Innis's ideas, according to Sawchuk, can shed light on the increasing entanglement of art and technology. Like Menzies, she believes that Innis's insights can help us puncture some of the discourse around the technological sublime. She addresses the claim that the fusion of art and technology represents a point of liberation. Her method is not that of Innis, who made large-scale generalizations on the basis of classical references. Rather, she pursues a variant of the early Innis's "dirt research," investigating the phenomenon from the inside out, exploring "the structural relations designed into the works that act as indicators of larger patterns." In doing so, she discovers "connective affinities" between Innis's ideas and the work of two Canadian media artists, Nell Tenhaaf and Kathy Kennedy. Their art engages with the hardware of "neocybernetic capitalism" and, in a manner consistent with the spirit of Innis, provides critiques of the limitations and unstated premises of these technological forms, through a "subtle unravelling of effects." Their artistic engagement serves to call into question common claims about technological interactivity. One does not really interact with a feedback loop; real choice and the open-endedness of dialogue are missing.

While most of the chapters in this volume either flesh out the contextual determinants of Innis's thought or seek to extend his ideas into previously neglected areas, the essays in part II explore the reasons for and implications of Innis's failure to address crucial issues and questions. As Jane Jenson (chapter 9) points out, like most male thinkers of his time and place, Innis largely ignored the place of women in political economy or economic development. This oversight is symptomatic of a more general difficulty with his theory – his lack of attention to the role of human agency in making and shaping the course of history – echoing a point made by both Acland and Berland. His approach has little to say about the space between the structure of the economy and the practices of everyday life. Drawing on feminist scholarship on the economic and social history of the fur trade, Jenson demonstrates how gender relations served as crucial points of mediation and communication between colonizers and colonized, thereby making possible the production and trade of the fur staple.

As Daniel Salée (chapter 10) and Alain-G. Gagnon and Sarah Fortin (chapter 11) note, while Innis has been canonized within the English-Canadian world, his ideas have failed to generate much interest in Quebec. To be sure, as Gagnon and Fortin point out, there was a certain following for Innis at the Université Laval. As the centre for the "modernizing" tendency within the social sciences, the Faculté des sciences sociales at Laval, under the direction of Père Georges-Henri Lévesque, made a point of sending its students to universities outside Quebec for postgraduate training so that they could return to teach at Laval and contribute their knowledge to the curriculum. These students included Albert Faucher and Maurice Lamontagne, who both studied at the University of Toronto with Innis and became supporters of Innis at Laval. That Innis was held in high esteem at Laval is indicated by the honorary doctorate he was awarded there in 1947. As Gagnon and Fortin argue, one could explain Laval's receptiveness to Innis in terms of that institution's general openness to influences from outside Quebec, which included also the Chicago School of Sociology and the Rockefeller Foundation.

Otherwise, they stress, the influence of Innis in Quebec has been negligible. By comparison with English Canada, economic history emerged relatively late as a field. Moreover, while Canada outside Quebec had a number of commissions – for example, Rowell-Sirois (Canada 1940) – examining economic problems and drawing in the social sciences by the 1930s, this sort of activity was not at all encouraged in Quebec. It was not until the Quiet Revolution that there was intervention in the economy, which in turn led to formation of commissions of investigation. These served as a catalyst to the development of the social sciences in Quebec, much as their counterparts did elsewhere in Canada during the 1930s. As Fortin and Gagnon argue, accompanying the growth of the social sciences of Quebec in the 1960s came diversification and fragmentation, a trend that did not lend itself to the reception of Innis's ideas. Fortin and Gagnon draw attention to features of Quebec historiography that were at odds with Innis's perspective. The concern of Quebec historians with the national question and with family and rural life made them unreceptive to broader, more structural approaches to the study of economic development.

Daniel Salée (chapter 10) examines the lukewarm reception to Innis in Quebec from another angle – the lack of "fit" between Innis's ideas and those of Quebec intellectuals. Echoing Fortin and Gagnon, he notes that during the pinnacle of Innis's career in the 1940s, when English-Canadian academics had largely become secularized, academic life in Quebec was still under the sway of religious thought. Yet there were the glimmerings of change in the tradition of Esdras Minville at the École des Hautes Études commerciales, which examined economic and social policy. According to Salée, Minville's reformist, interventionist stance was at odds with the more withdrawn intellectual stance of Innis. Salée also reveals why the new political economy tradition, based in part on a left-nationalist appropriation of Innis's ideas, found little resonance in Quebec. Québec political economists looked instead to French structuralist Marxism for their inspiration. Salée suggests a deeper reason for the indifference to Innis – his lack of experience of internal colonialism.

As James Bickerton (chapter 12) notes, the response to Innis in the Maritimes has been similarly unenthusiastic. However, while most Quebecers have seen Innis and his followers as irrelevant, Maritime intellectuals have perceived their thought on staples theory as misguided, if not pernicious. This current of thought took shape in the early 1970s as part of a challenge to conventional beliefs that the Maritime region owed its lack of development to geography, technological change, and an inability to respond to change. In this context, the ideas of Innis, and those who developed his ideas on staples, appeared to have contributed to wrong-headed thinking and policy, buttressing claims that the decline of the Maritimes was necessary and inevitable because of geographical and technological factors. The writings of S.A. Saunders (1984), considered a "disciple of Harold Innis," were taken to task for the picture they drew of the Maritimes in relation to central Canada. The staple theory, according to Maritime thinkers, sought to explain regional development in terms only of resource endowments and the working of the market economy in the primary sector.

As Bickerton points out, such impressions are based on slim evidence, and even the criticized articles of Innis do not bear out such a reading. Moreover, Innis produced a great body of material of relevance to the Maritimes. Indeed, Innis was a true "Scotia-phile" who was invited to served on the province's Jones Commission (Nova Scotia 1934). In contrast to the advocates of the new Maritime political economy, Innis did not believe that industrialism would improve the situation; he felt that the golden period had taken place prior to Confederation, when culture and technology were in balance. He felt that confederation was not a defeat but rather a defensive strategy, and he had great admiration for the far-sightedness of those supporting Maritime interests between the wars. Hence it is difficult to make him out to be simply an apologist for central Canadian hegemony.

The work of Innis can be seen as both figure and ground to current shifts in intellectual and culture life. On the one hand, while his writings spanned several conventional fields, they found common ground in a concern with modernity as related to monopolies of knowledge and the producers of ideas. They thus provide insights into today's predicaments. But Innis's writings do not yield this wisdom easily; they do not speak for themselves. Reading Innis almost obliges one to connect his thought to other perspectives and points of view. This means, in effect, filling in, elaborating his ideas, relating them to particular phenomena or situations. The work of Innis becomes less like a repository to be mined for ideas than a theoretical shunting point for refracting and juxtaposing various perspectives.

If there is any theme that conjoins the essays in this volume, it is the spirit of reading Innis in a fresh and creative way and resituating his thought and practice through an exploration of novel links and comparisons. To do so means less paying attention to Innis's ability to help bridge the claims of a particular field or discipline and more examining how his ideas relate to some of the issues and concerns that confront us at this historic moment.

NOTES

1 Harold Innis to Frank H. Knight, 11 May 1952, Harold Innis Papers (IP), University of Toronto Archives (UTA), B72-0025/11 (06). Material from the Innis papers has been published with the permission of the University of Toronto Archives.

2 Frank H. Knight to Harold Innis, 15 May 1952, IP, B72-003/005 (16).

3 Harold Innis to Frank H. Knight, 21 May 1952, IP, B72-003/005 (15).

4 Ibid.

5 Writing of Innis's "new venture" of studying "the history of media of communications," Easterbrook noted that he (Easterbrook) "expressed misgivings at the risks involved in this move into the large and complex area of communication systems." Innis replied "that in spite of the imperfections which were certain to be present in this working in strange territories, experts might put right what was wrong, much more important, that it was high time that localized monopolies of knowledge held by antiquarians and others were broken down" (Easterbrook 1953, 10–11).

6 Easterbrook reiterated this view in 1960, 562.

7 In terms of organizing the material, Christian notes that the original processing of the "Idea File" was less than ideal: "The committee had Mrs. Jane Ward, for long Innis's assistant in the Department of Political Economy at Toronto, prepare a version for typing, and subsequently had it microfilmed for limited circulation." As Christian points out, "this version did great violence to the text, since it reorganized the material under a series of alphabetical headings. The consequence of this reorgani-

zation was to lose completely any notion of the chronological span of the material, covering about eight years" (Christian 1980, xvii–xviii). Christian's judicious and carefully editing of the text represents a most welcome effort to reveal the letter and spirit of Innis's work.

8 Mary Quayle Innis's assessment of her husband's later writings was undoubtedly influenced by the opinions of George Ferguson, editor of the *Montreal Star* and long-time friend of the family. In particular, she sought Ferguson's counsel when she was deliberating about how to proceed with publication of the "History of Communications" manuscript. In an address of 4 November 1965, "Harold Innis and the Printed Word" delivered at the Innis College dinner, Ferguson held (4–5) that "when [Innis] started his communications project he had bitten off a much bigger mouthful than he could digest in a mere decade of time." He claimed further that "communications ... was the least developed of the various subjects upon which Harold Innis spent his life." (University of Toronto Pamphlets "F," UTA)

9 That this image of Innis has survived intact is evident in one of Michael Valpy's "Street" columns in the *Globe and Mail*. He notes, "To a considerable degree ... the detachment of our contemporary Canadian academic community from political involvement derives from his attitudes and efforts" (1994).

10 Creighton's bias towards centralized nationalism has been clarified by Graeme Patterson (1990, 80). This slant perhaps accounts for his reading of Innis, which may well have affected the outlook of the publication committee.

11 That the committee chose to frame the volume (Innis 1956a) in terms of "the economic history of Canada" underscores the image of Innis's legacy that it sought to convey. While most of the essays in the volume deal nominally with economic history, they also cover a broad range of communications, culture, and power, perhaps most evidently in "The Penetrative Powers of the Price System" and "The Church in Canada." The reader edited by Daniel Drache (Innis 1995a) provides a badly needed corrective.

12 See, for instance, Fowke 1957; Buckley 1958; Caves and Holton 1959; Aitken 1959, 1961; and Watkins 1963. Innis-style concerns figured prominently in an issue of the *Journal of Economic History* (Dec. 1960). The articles by McLuhan and Easterbrook both addressed Arthur Cole's (1959) text *Business Enterprise in Its Social Setting*, which applied Innis's ideas to the history of entrepreneurship. Moreover, a discussion of the social basis of the market was framed in terms of Innis's notion of "the penetrative powers of the price system."

13 Easterbrook and McLuhan had both taken part in a communications group at the University of Toronto, which may have contributed to the convergence of their views.

14 This impression was reinforced in the most recent edition of *The Bias of Communication* (1991). While McLuhan's introduction has been dropped in favour of one written by Paul Heyer and David Crowley, his name, as Roman Onufrijchuk (1993) describes it, has been "boldly retained on the cover – below the title, almost by way of a subtitle – 'The classic Canadian work on communication by the man who inspired Marshall McLuhan'" (43).

15 The critique of Eccles's article and the spirited defence of the Innis tradition provided by Hugh M. Grant (1981) were informed more by the championing of general principles of political economic analysis than by claims for the accuracy of Innis's depiction of the fur trade.

16 Robin Neill (1991) notes that, beginning in the 1950s, Canadian departments of economics became "more oriented towards centres of excellence in the United States" and that respondents to questions he posed about their orientation "after 1979 tended to be part of an undifferentiated North American profession" (220–1).

17 See, for instance, Daniel Drache 1978 and Mel Watkins 1977. This effort to try to find common ground between Marx and Innis was severely contested by David McNally, among others; see, for instance, McNally 1981. That the ideas of Innis have found a firm place within left-nationalist political economy in Canada is evident from the attention his staples thesis is given in many of the chapters in Clement and Williams (1989).

18 See, for example, Ralph Heintzman 1977, 1–2, 118–21. This article introduced the special issue of the *Journal of Canadian Studies* (1977). Heintzman notes that "the current revival of interest in Harold Innis could not be more opportune. For one thing it coincides with, and in part reflects, the growth of concern for 'Canadian studies' in general. In this context, the name of Innis serves as a beacon and an inspiration" (1). See also Hutcheson (1978).

19 See, for instance, Carey 1967; Kuhns 1971; Czitrom 1982.

20 In an article published the same year, Christian also addressed Innis's views on political theory. Innis's later writings, as he pointed out, were not simply about the history of communications, but rather "represent a heroic attempt to draw attention to the perilous decay of Western civilization and to direct its intellectual resources to a contemplation of the conditions necessary for its preservation and resuscitation (1977a, 41).

21 In addition to Donald Creighton, this interpretation could be found in the writings on Innis of J.B. Brebner 1953, Carl Berger 1976, and Daniel Drache 1969.

22 It took place at Simon Fraser University, 29–31 March 1978.

23 We can see this sentiment in the occasional misnaming of Innis. Two recent examples include a misspelling of his name in Hartley 1992 and an article that mistakenly names him Claude Innis, coupled with an erro-

neous description of his relationship with Marshall McLuhan as one of professor–student (Geiger and Newhagen 1993).

24 Subsequent interviews with a number of participants in the conference (conducted by David Cayley) provided the basis for "The Legacy of Harold Innis," originally broadcast on CBC Radio's *Ideas* on 6, 13, and 20 December 1994.

PART ONE

Reflections on Innis

1 Innis's Conception of Freedom

RICHARD NOBLE

My intention in this paper is to expound Harold Innis's conception of freedom and to offer an interpretation of its significance for his thinking about politics and culture. I want to claim that Innis regarded freedom as a substantive or defining value of Canadian society, and one that was, along with Canada itself, under threat in what he termed the "modern crisis" of Western civilization. For Innis, Canada's continued existence as a democracy and a nation depended on its ability to preserve and foster freedom through its cultural and political institutions. This paper explores what Innis meant by the term "freedom," the question of why he believed it to be under threat, and the types of cultural and political measures he thought necessary to effect its preservation.

I also argue that Innis's conception of freedom is best understood against the background of the "old," or conservative Whig tradition of political thought – the eighteenth-century British tradition of political thinking associated with David Hume, Adam Smith, and Edmund Burke. This tradition and particularly the conception of freedom that it fostered, formed the normative background of Innis's political thought.[1] This style of thought strongly influenced both his critique of contemporary societies and his proposals for their reform. Focusing on his conception of freedom brings the normative basis of Innis's liberalism sharply into view, especially his well-known assertion of the value of the stability achieved by a balance of space and time biases in modern societies.

Previous commentators on Innis have noted the negative value of this notion of stability as a bulwark against imperialism (Watson 1977, 55–6) or as the necessary means of staving off an apocalyptic collapse of Western civilization (Whitaker 1983, 824). This essay suggests that Innis also made a positive, or prescriptive case for the value of stability, which explains, among other things, why we should think of him as a liberal political thinker. Innis thought that stability in Western nations depended on their maintaining (or acquiring) the cultural and political conditions necessary for liberty. I attempt to show why that concept of liberty is central to his critique of Western societies and that we can understand the political dimension of his thought better if we grasp what he meant by the idea and how he thought it could be preserved and promoted.

I began by claiming that Innis had a Whig conception of liberty, which drew on the "old," or conservative Whig tradition of Hume and Burke. This conception has three distinguishing features. First, it sees the individual's liberty as an area of non-interference that is consistent with and indeed guaranteed by law. John Locke, who made a vital contribution to this idea, points to the need for reconciling liberty and law. Freedom is not "a liberty for every one to do what he lists, to live as he pleases, and not to be tied by any laws; but freedom of men under government is to have a standing rule to live by, common to every one of that society and made by the legislative power erected in it, a liberty to follow my own will in all things where the rule prescribes not, and not to be subject to the inconstant, uncertain, unknown, and arbitrary will of another man" (Locke 1947, bk. 2, ch. 4, para. 26). The claim here is that freedom can reliably exist only when the law creates and maintains a civil culture in which individuals are protected from the arbitrary wills of others. This argument is central to the Whig tradition, because it reconciles (however inadequately) the negative conception of liberty, as non-interference, with the requirements of social order (A. Smith 1931: 4, 40–3).[2]

The eighteenth-century Whigs extended Locke's argument with respect to law to include moral and political conventions that have evolved (gradually and unconsciously) over time. Burke argued that liberty was possible only in a society in which traditions or habits of morality had taken root. "Men are qualified for civil liberty, in exact proportion to their disposition to put moral chains upon their appetites" (Burke 1881: 4, 51–2). Freedom requires not only that we be law-abiding but that we be acculturated or socialized to uphold voluntarily the moral standards of our community in our everyday behaviour. Moral self-restraint inclines us to obey the law and also to treat each other with respect and civility; both are necessary conditions of civil liberty.

Yet these "moral chains" could not, as Kant demanded, be the self-imposed dictates of human reason. According to Hume, "Morals excite passions, and produce or prevent actions. Reason of itself is utterly impotent in this particular. The rules of morality, therefore, are not the conclusions of our reason" (Hume 1965, 457). If passions, which are most often self-regarding, are always a stronger motivation than reason, then law and custom are necessary bulwarks against our tendency to interfere with each other's freedom in pursuit of our own good. Freedom inheres in specific historical and cultural conditions – in customs, conventions, and institutions that have evolved gradually over a long period.

The second feature of the Whig conception of freedom is that the proper institutions and practices afford us, as members of a given society, an area of non-interference in which to pursue our own good. This notion sharply distinguishes the Whig conception of freedom from the social contract tradition represented by Rousseau and Kant. For the latter, freedom derives from some aspect of human nature, such as reason or natural goodness, and as such imposes universal standards of right upon human social organizations (Rousseau 1968, 1, 55; Kant 1970, 133). On this view, individual freedom becomes a standard of justice for *all* societies. Its advocates tend to want it encoded in written constitutions, in order to ensure that it remains the substantive ordering principle of society. However, for Whigs such as Hume and Burke, freedom is contingent on a nation's historical experience.[3] Its nature and extent depend on the institutions and practices that have evolved over that nation's history, and these may vary substantially.

The third feature of this conception of freedom is the view that our liberties are best preserved by a system of government that divides and balances power among the executive, the legislative, and judicial branches of government. Again, this idea is found in Locke (1947, ch. 7, paras. 142–8), but it became an article of faith among eighteenth-century Whig supporters of the British constitution. There were generally thought to be two advantages to dividing legislative and judicial power. First, it subjected those who made the law to its authority, thus ensuring the rule of law rather than of human beings (Hayek 1960, 173). If liberty requires law for its protection, it must also require an independent judiciary that can enforce the law. Second, division of power, *if* properly balanced, kept one group or set of interests in society from dominating all others. King, Lords, and Commons in Britain were seen to represent different orders of society; and their proper balance in the legislative process meant that law would be directed at the good of society as a whole rather than at the good of the faction in control of the machinery of government (Hume 1903, 43–6).

Innis's conception of freedom ought to be understood against this background. In general terms, Innis conceived liberty as a sphere of non-interference made possible by specific types (and configurations) of cultural, legal, and political institutions. He was, in this sense, an older kind of liberal: one who regarded liberty as a virtue of certain types of civil association rather than as a universal right derived from the very nature of human beings. Innis also believed that freedom was a substantive human good: that its presence or absence was a measure of a society's balance and stability, a measure of its ability to produce conditions in which humans can flourish. However, like his Whig predecessors, he did not believe that freedom should be conceived solely in terms of equal rights for individuals, particularly if this meant, as it did in the United States, equal rights guaranteed by a written constitution.

This is not to argue that Innis's idea of freedom is identical to an eighteenth-century Whig conception. There are important differences. For instance, Innis associates liberty with cultural traditions and historically evolved institutions for reasons other than epistemological scepticism or reverence for traditional wisdom. For Innis, liberty in the overwhelmingly space-biased cultures of the West is to be found in what remains of their oral traditions. Innis grounds our liberties in the institutions and cultural practices that preserve the oral tradition: universities, the judiciary, common law, parliaments, and the conventions and practices associated with them.

In order to understand this, we need to consider Innis's distinction between oral and written traditions. Innis argued that communications technologies are always biased towards either space or time. At the conclusion to *Empire and Communications* (1950) Innis claims: "Monopolies of knowledge had developed and declined partly in relation to the medium of communication on which they were built and tended to alternate as they emphasized religion, decentralization, and time, and force, centralization and space." This gives us a sense of the formative effect of communications technologies on societies, and also of the social characteristics Innis associated with the two dominant forms of bias. Time-biased civilizations tend towards institutional decentralization, an emphasis on the sacred, and efficiency at solving problems of continuity. Their instability arises from their inability to solve problems of space. Space biased civilizations, in contrast, emphasize institutional centralization, imperialism, and efficiency at solving problems of space. Their instability arises from their neglect of the problems of time. Balance is the key to stability. "Large-scale political organizations such as empires ... have tended to flourish under conditions in which civilization reflects the influence of more than one medium and in which the bias of one medium toward decentralization is offset by the bias of another medium towards centralization" (211).

Two other features of civilizations resulted from the bias of communication. All societies, Innis claimed, develop either oral or written traditions of communication in relation to the monopolies of knowledge that predominate in them. These traditions in turn shape the character of that civilization: the kind of knowledge it produces, its culture and political life, and thus its prospects for balance, stability, and freedom.

Innis believed that Western democracies were in danger of losing their oral traditions of communication and intellectual inquiry and that this constituted a serious threat to the balance and freedom. The overwhelming space bias of contemporary Western societies arose largely because of the inventions of paper and printing and the consequent rise of writing as the basis of intellectual activity and communication (Innis 1951a, 130–1). Innis believed that modern societies were obsessed with the present, and consequently with the need to extend their control over space. This in turn leads to the centralization of political power, the imposition of cultural uniformity, and conflict between states arising from nationalism and imperialism (1951a, 211). It also leads to a loss of individual freedom.[4]

In the modern world then, writing supports monopolies of power biased towards space and is therefore part of the problem of Western civilization. Innis blames newspaper writing for a great many evils, including the virtual destruction of the oral tradition, the intellectual impoverishment of our culture, and support for vested interests (1951a, 82, 138). Freedom of the press, as Innis sees it, has undermined the cultural conditions necessary for meaningful freedom (and democracy). He quotes Clarence Darrow to the effect that "our independent American press, with its untrammelled freedom to twist and misrepresent the news, is one of the barriers in the way of the American people achieving their freedom" (187). Innis saw mechanized mass communications as a product of the written tradition. It had so debased our intellectual and civic culture that freedom and democracy were in danger of becoming illusions useful for little more than upholding commercial and political elites (139).

The oral tradition, by contrast, represents the antidote that can restore balance to our currently unbalanced civilization. Innis believed that the oral tradition was primarily a legacy of ancient Greek civilization (1951a, 41; 1950, 67; Watson 1977, 45–53). His idealization of Greek civilization illustrates a number of the crucial features of the oral tradition. The Greeks, he claimed, adapted the Phoenician alphabet to the requirements of their already well-established oral tradition. The result was a balanced cultural tradition of astonishing artistic, intellectual, and political creativity (1951a, 40–1). Innis claimed that the source of Greece's tremendous influence on the West was its oral tradition. The Greeks managed to avoid developing monopolies of knowledge based on written sacred scripts, and so their intellectual culture was not chained to the rigid and dogmatic finality of *written* truth.

The Greeks sought truth through discussion or dialogue, which method was the main source of their intellectual creativity and power. They understood the world through an open-ended and flexible process, which sought truth without expecting to find a final version of it. For Innis, Plato's writings represent the last gasp of this oral tradition. "The power of the oral tradition persisted in his prose in the absence of a closely ordered system. Continuous philosophical discussion aimed at truth. The life and movement of the dialectic opposed the establishment of a finished system of dogma. He would not surrender his freedom to his own books and refused to be bound by what he had written" (1950, 69).[5] We are now in a position to understand Innis's preference for the oral tradition and its relevance to freedom today. He believed that writing had a tendency to lead to dogmatism and monopoly, both of which restrict the freedom of inquiry necessary for artistic and intellectual progress. It does so by imposing a kind of closure around arguments that would remain open in the oral tradition. Once an argument or position is written, it acquires a spurious finality, which more often than not leads to the dogmatic defence of that position, rather than further inquiry (1980, 157). This situation stifles intellectual freedom because it forecloses the open-ended dialectic fostered by discussion and debate. The search for truth, which Innis believed crucial to our freedom, becomes the defence of dogmatism mounted by monopolies whose power depends on their control of knowledge and truth (Innis 1945, 305).[6]

The dominance of writing in the form of mass communications has another, more sinister effect on freedom. Innis had witnessed the successful use of newspaper and radio to manipulate the minds of millions of people on both sides during the Second World War. The manipulative power of mass media undermines individual responsibility by removing the need to think for oneself. This in turn destroys the civic culture of democracy and renders freedom illusory. However, in Innis's view such manipulation would be impossible in an oral tradition, which requires open-ended and mutually respectful dialogue between actual human beings in order to reach conclusions about actions with moral or social consequences. "The printing press and the radio address the world instead of the individual. The oral dialectic is overwhelmingly significant where the subject-matter is human action and feeling, and it is important in the discovery of new truth but of very little value in disseminating it. The oral discussion inherently involves personal contact and a consideration for the feelings of others, and it is in sharp contrast with the cruelty of mechanized communication and the tendencies we have come to note in the modern world" (1951a, 191).

For Innis, then, there is a connection between the oral tradition and liberty. The oral tradition fosters a flexible and vigorous intellectual culture, which preserves intellectual freedom in a civilization increasingly dominated by dogmatisms (85).[7] It also fosters a civic culture in which individuals must exercise their own judgment, rather than abandon it to the mindless propaganda of their ruling elites.[8] The oral tradition decentralizes in an age of obsessive centralization. It does so by creating cultural conditions in which the reigning monopolies of knowledge and power can be questioned and resisted. However, Innis also believed that our space biased society was dominated by a written tradition. What then of the oral tradition and the balance and freedom that it might afford us?

Innis believed that remnants of the oral tradition were contained in our most ancient (and consequently time-biased) institutions. Universities, the common law, the court system, parliaments, and even churches were vestiges of the pre-modern era and to some extent embody the oral tradition that gave rise to them. These institutions and the practices connected with them are crucial to Innis's conception of freedom for three reasons. First, they protect spheres of non-interference in which the individual is free to act. Second, they foster a civic and intellectual culture in which that freedom can contribute to re-establishing the balance between space and time. Third, they act as counterbalancing institutions that check the tendency of power in the modern world to centralization and monopoly.

To illustrate this, I want to consider Innis's analysis of the effects of the "modern crisis" on Canada's political system. One of its primary effects, as we might imagine, is a pronounced centralizing of power in the Canadian state. The reasons he adduces for this are numerous, but they derive mostly from the lack of countervailing powers to balance those of the federal cabinet and its bureaucracy. Both the Senate and the Supreme Court lack the power and prestige to balance the power the cabinet derives from its control over the Commons (1946, 248). In addition, party discipline has focused power in the hands of a few ministers and in turn increased the power of the professional, and in effect, unaccountable civil servants who serve the cabinet. The Union Government during the First World War reduced the critical effectiveness of the opposition, leaving a small, dictatorial oligarchy of federal politicians and their deputy ministers with virtual control over the machinery of government (1946, 249).

Such centralization was reinforced by developments in Canadian political culture. Amalgamation of previously independent newspapers led to a decline in the quality of public debate about government policy, further exacerbated by the advent of radio (1946, 248–9).[9] Furthermore, the character and autonomy of Canadian political culture were under considerable threat from American imperialism. American commercial and political monopolies were making serious inroads into Canadian culture, economy, and politics. Innis believed that this change undermined Canadian liberty. For example, power was centralized within the Canadian federal system. Canada responded to the American threat to its independence by developing imperialist policies towards its own hinterlands (1952a, 69). The hysterical anti-communism of the American popular press in turn fed this tendency and restricted Canadian liberties (70). Indeed, Innis suggests that there is no longer much to choose between Canada and Soviet Union: "The political shape of Canada began to assume characteristics similar to those of Russia. A politburo in Canada comparable to and paralleling that of Russia effectively diverts attention from its character by pointing to the dangers of the politburo in Russia" (72).

Innis was far from sanguine about Canada's ability to preserve its autonomy as a nation or the liberties inherent in its traditions and institutions. He saw the monopolistic features of the Canadian state – its highly centralized political and bureaucratic elites, its one-party dominance, and its militarism – as at least partial consequences of American imperial influence. For Innis the genius of this influence was its painlessness. Canadians were under the spell of American imperialism largely without knowing it, because of the overwhelming influence of American mass communications and propaganda. The U.S. propagandists were promoting their imperialist ambitions as the triumph of freedom and democracy in a world under threat from communism. Innis saw this practice as a tissue of lies that threatened the existing, and substantial, freedoms of Canadians. "Neither a nation, nor a commonwealth, nor a civilization can endure in which one half in slavery believes itself free because of a statement in the Bill of Rights, and attempts to enslave the other half which is free. Freedom of the press under the Bill of Rights accentuated the printed tradition, destroyed freedom of speech, and broke the relations with the oral tradition of Europe" (1952a, 128).

Clearly then, Innis did not believe that Canadian freedoms depended on his fellow citizens' becoming more like the Americans, especially if this meant acquiring written constitutional guarantees, which he regarded as a fatal departure from the oral tradition. They impose dogmatic and inflexible 'truths' on society, which tend to reinforce monopolies of power. The U.S. Bill of Rights was Innis's favourite example. By guaranteeing press freedom as an absolute right, the U.S. constitution had granted its commercial and political monopolies licence to debase its civic culture and made the United States an aggressive imperial power. It was Innis's view that Canada should avoid this problem at all costs. But if it were to preserve its independence and individual liberties, it would have to balance the forces of centralization, uniformity, and mindlessness with institutions and customs grounded in the oral tradition.

Innis thought that both political and cultural institutions would have to be involved in this strategy. At the political level, the courts and the provincial legislatures (parliaments) had to be reinvigorated to offset the monopolistic power of the federal government. Innis conceived this situation in classic Whig terms. Liberty depends on a balance of powers. "Freedom in Canada rests on the tenuous support of the Privy Council [JCPC] and on continued struggle between the provinces and the Dominion. The weakening of Parliament and the dictatorship of the Cabinet or of a small group of the Cabinet, and the present unanimity of all parties on expansion of state control weaken the prospect of continued freedom" (1946, 132–3).

Innis saw the courts as an important counterbalance to the space-biased, presentist policies of the Canadian state. The judiciary had its roots in the oral tradition of the common law and was thus concerned with continuity. Its procedures also reflect the oral tradition; testimony, rules of evidence, and cross-examination all involve the dialectic of discussion and remain open-ended and flexible with respect to truth (1952a, 52–3). Most important, however, the courts must be capable of subjecting the legislative branch to the common law. Innis quotes Sir Edward Coke, the seventeenth-century English jurist, to the effect that Parliament's authority is ultimately circumscribed by the common law. "'When an act of Parliament is against

common right and reason, or repugnant, or impossible to be performed, the common law will control it, and adjudge such act to
be void'" (48).

Innis believed that this overruling could occur in Canada's existing
political system, without the elaborate written guarantees of an
American-style constitution (76). He favoured the parliamentary
approach to a balance of powers over the American constitutional
approach, because he thought the common law more flexible and more
oriented towards sustaining continuity. This gave the British tradition
greater stability and balance than political systems founded on written
constitutions (127–8).

The courts in a common law system also protect freedoms. They do
so by means of their procedural conventions and also by enforcing the
criminal and civil law. Their historically evolved procedures protect
the individual's right to a fair trial, freedom from arbitrary arrest, and
the right to seek counsel. By enforcing the civil and criminal law, the
courts shield us from arbitrary incursions into our freedoms by others.
They also protect individuals from the arbitrary will of the state, by
subjecting the legislative branch to the common law (and legal conventions) of the community. However, they do not uphold freedom in
the form of absolute constitutional or human rights. Though Innis
believed that we were likely to move closer to the American system of
written constitutional guarantees for civil rights, as indeed we have, he
was not happy about it. He argued that it would make our constitution less flexible and as a result more prone to revolutions or other
drastic changes (76). Innis was profoundly sceptical of freedoms
understood as abstract rights guaranteed by written constitutions.
These rights have no roots in the oral tradition and consequently pose
an acute problem of continuity. They do so because they are written,
and therefore dogmatic assertions of abstract right, which pre-empt
the various claims that a society's continued existence (or common
good) imposes on its members. As Innis saw it, the American system
of constitutionally guaranteed individual rights was too inflexible to
balance those rights against the common good. Like Burke and Hume,
he tended to favour the more concrete liberties that had evolved over
the course of the community's practical historical experience. The
common law and conventional practice provide a legal framework in
which economic, intellectual, religious, and political liberties can be
exercised in a way consistent with the continued life of the society.
Furthermore, because these liberties derive from the oral tradition,
their exercise can help in the recovering of a balance between space
and time.

In Canada, the courts were central both to combating the federal government's monopoly of political power and to protecting individual liberties. Innis also believed that the provincial legislatures could help counter-balance Ottawa's power. He advocated greater provincial powers, on the general principle that decentralization would balance and limit the power of monopolies (1946, 132, 248–50).

Of the cultural institutions necessary for restoring balance and protecting freedom in Canadian society, by far the most important for Innis was the university. Innis saw it as one of the last great bastions of the oral tradition. As such, it was crucial to the rebalancing of space and time, and also an important source of liberty. However, Innis also believed that it was under assault from all quarters; that its continued autonomy and integrity were in serious question, and that this was a major threat to the West. "[The university] must continue its vital function in checking the dangerous extremes to which all institutions with power are subject ... The trend of the social sciences in response to the demands of the new bureaucracy has been toward increasing specialization. And this has threatened the universities. The university must deny the finality of any of the conclusions of the social sciences. It must steadfastly resist the tendency to acclaim any single solution of the world's problems at the risk of failing to play its role as a balancing factor in the growth of civilization" (141).

We have already noted that Innis believed the oral tradition to be under siege in the space-biased West. Universities were no exception. Internally, their traditional emphasis on time-biased studies (the humanities) was being replaced by ahistorial natural and social sciences aspiring to universal (or final) truth (65; 1951a, 191–2). Externally, governments and their agents – boards of directors – were demanding commercially relevant vocational training and research. Innis saw these attempts to twist the time-biased scholarship of traditional universities to the imperatives of space biased commercial and political monopolies as a serious threat to liberty. "We stand on a small and dwindling island surrounded by the flood of totalitarianism. Universities supported by the state have seen the disappearance of freedom of speech and freedom of the press, to say nothing of academic freedom" (1946, 73).

The threat to university autonomy and the oral tradition it upholds has serious political consequences. The loss of academic freedom means the disappearance of the liberty to engage in scholarship that has no immediate 'use-value' in our space-biased, utilitarian culture. For Innis, this was precisely what made it valuable. Because of their traditions, universities provide disinterested, non-specialized knowledge, which challenges the existing monopolies of power and knowledge. It therefore counterbalances the space-biased commercial and ideological propaganda put about by the mass media and the monopolies that control them.

Traditional universities also train citizens in the oral tradition to exercise critical and independent judgment, which leaves them less subject to manipulation by their ruling elites. Innis argued that if democracies are based on the idea that people can make up their minds, universities should inculcate character and judgment, not overwhelm students with "facts disseminated with paper and ink, film, radio and television" (1951a, 203). Traditional, humanities-based universities can educate citizens to think independently of the bias of their culture. In this sense, the freedoms that inhere in universities are central to the long-term balance and stability of a society.

Innis did not think, however, that the liberties that universities provide should be the right of all citizens. He was generally opposed to the notion of universities as agents of greater social equality; in fact he argued that their ability to serve the common good depended on their liberties being restricted to the few. In respect of the intelligence and training required for leadership, Innis believed that democracies should be strictly meritocratic. "Any community has only a limited number capable of sustained mental effort. According to biologists they may be found in all regions and all strata. A democratic society can thrive only by the persistent search for its greatest asset and by constant efforts to conserve, to encourage, to train and to extend it" (203–6). Innis insisted that finding the 'best brains' to educate requires a fair and effective recruitment system, divested of its current middle-class bias.

But the idea of "fairness" here is closer to Aristotle's principle of proportionate equality than Rawls's "difference principle." For Innis, the liberties of universities are justified by what they contribute to society, and so only the best and brightest should have access to them. Natural intelligence, not one's equal right as a human being, is what creates entitlement to them. This was the basis of Innis's opposition to adult education. He argued that the admission of students on grounds other than academic excellence (such as need or past discrimination) would erode traditional time-biased research and result in lower standards and more vocational forms of study (210–12). Thus "affirmative action" admission would be inappropriate unless it could be shown to attract the 'best brains.'

For Innis, what qualifies people for the liberties provided by universities is the ability to assist in the university's primary social function – the restoration of balance and stability. The just distribution of such liberties is the one that enables the university to continue to make this contribution. If we extend this line of reasoning to other institutions in society in which freedoms inhere, such as parliaments, we have at least the potential of a profoundly unequal distribution of liberty. Innis wrote, however, in a social context in which class distinctions were both more sharply defined and more obviously determinate of post-secondary educational opportunities than they are today. In such a situation, a meritocratic principle of justice would have seemed progressive to many.

I have argued that Innis's conception of freedom should be understood in terms of the British Whig tradition. He understood freedom as something that inheres in a society's institutions, and in the social and political environment they foster, rather than in our humanity or certain essential features of it. Innis believed that our freedoms were grounded in the institutions and conventions that continued to embody the oral tradition in our predominantly space-biased culture. Individuals experience freedom in their daily lives because these institutions and conventions protect them from the morally arbitrary interference of other citizens, or the state, in their self-chosen projects. The freedoms thus afforded us are not so much rights (though they could be described as such) as they are simply a matter of being left alone to do what one wants within the limits prescribed by the conventions or institutions that embody them.

For Innis, such liberties do not override the fundamental interests of society as a whole; nor are they universalizable, in the sense that they need logically apply equally to all persons in society. The justification for an individual's liberty to do what he or she wants is based on the rule or institution that provides that liberty. In so far as this rule or institution is grounded in the oral tradition and hence helps to restore balance to a space-biased culture, the liberties it provides are justifiable. Innis's defence of liberty was, like Hume's, a form of indirect utilitarianism (Grey 1989, 96).[10] Freedoms are justified because of their links to the oral tradition and to the social good that it promotes. Yet this is not to suggest that they were of lesser importance to Innis. As I have shown, he thought freedom a necessary (though not sufficient) condition for achieving balance and stability in Canadian society.

Innis did not, however, accord individual liberty priority over the common good. By grounding it in institutions and practices embodying the oral tradition, Innis tied individual freedom to a conception of the broader social good. He was quite willing to restrict liberties he believed to be harmful to that good, and not solely because they impinged on the liberties of others. This stance explains his profound opposition to a constitutionally guaranteed right to freedom of speech, which he believed reinforced the dominance of space bias and its monopolies. Innis's conception of freedom has a similar implication for equality. Because he did not ground liberty in our nature as persons, it did not follow for him that liberties should be distributed equally. In so far as the equal distribution of a freedom contributed to balance in a political system, Innis would be bound to support that distribution. But if it did not, as one might argue in the case of the right to vote, he would recognize no moral or logical obligation to support its equal distribution.

Innis's political vision was a complex one. He regarded liberties grounded in the oral tradition as substantive moral values, because they were a necessary condition of a social order in which human beings could flourish. He also believed that these liberties were under threat – from American imperialism and from the centralizing and anti-democratic nature of space-biased culture.

The solutions he advances are piecemeal and unsystematic, but on the whole they reflect the Whig tradition. For Innis, freedom is best preserved in Canada by the existence of autonomous institutions able to balance the highly centralized authority of the federal government and combat the monopolies of knowledge and communication that propagate space bias. Universities, churches, provincial parliaments, and the common law all have a role to play in decentralizing power and restoring the balance between space and time in our culture.

NOTES

1 My claim here is that the "Whig tradition" formed a general background or framework through which Innis thought about politics and political theory. Thus while many commentators have traced his well-known distaste for authority and monopolies of power to his background and experiences (see Judith Stamps below, chapter 2), my claim is that Innis used the Whig tradition, and particularly its conception of liberty, to articulate these personal intuitions into a more or less systematic theory.

   The reasonableness of this interpretive claim lies primarily in the reading I provide of Innis's writings and in the extent to which this reading helps to illuminate Innis's political thought. It does not rest on a historical reconstruction of Innis's intellectual context. Nevertheless, it seems to me that Stamp's very careful elaboration of the influence of Scottish Enlightenment philosophy on the Canadian university curriculum lends credibility to my entirely non-contextualist account of Innis's political thinking.

2 Smith, whom Innis frequently invoked as a champion of economic liberty, follows Locke in arguing that the benefits of economic freedom can be reaped only within a framework of law.

3 Burke writes: "It has been the uniform policy of our constitution to claim and assert our liberties as an *entailed inheritance* derived to us from our forefathers, and to be transmitted to our posterity – as an estate specially belonging to the people of this kingdom, without any reference whatever to any other more general or prior right" (Burke 1955, 37).

4 A feature of the overwhelming space bias of modern culture was its presentism, which threatened individual liberty. "This contemporary attitude leads to the discouragement of all exercise of the will or the belief in individual power. The sense of power and the instinct for freedom have proved to costly, and been replaced by the sham independence of democracy" (1951a, 90).

5 This is a somewhat eccentric reading of Plato, whose epistemology is generally associated with the claim that all knowledge derives from immutable Forms or Ideas, which are both absolutely true and knowable through the dialectic.

6 "It is the search for truth, not 'truth,' that makes men free" (Innis 1945, 305).

7 One of these dogmatisms is instrumental rationality, which may destroy the university and render those trained in it incapable of exercising judgment based on proportion and balance.

8 Innis writes of Canada: "The development of advertising and mass propaganda masquerading as education compel the consent of the governed" (1946, 143).

9 See also Innis (1952a): "Those on the receiving end of material from a mechanized central system are precluded from participation in healthy, vigorous, and vital discussion" (102).

10 Grey argues that Hume's defence of liberty is indirectly utilitarian. Hume's thesis "is that rules of justice conferring liberty-rights on individuals are defensible or justifiable in terms of their tendency to promote utility (96)."

2 Innis in the Canadian Dialectical Tradition

JUDITH STAMPS

In the nineteenth and early twentieth centuries, Canadian universities taught two sorts of philosophies: Scottish Common Sense and Hegelian dialectics. The former was dominant until the 1870s and continued to be taught until past the turn of the century. The latter became prominent after 1875 and remained so into the 1920s.

Continuity between the schools of thought was provided by two elements. The first was a homogeneous, overtly Protestant culture, strengthened in academe by a reverence for philosophy – until the First World War, a required subject at all Canadian universities.[1] The second was the large number of Scottish and English teaching recruits to Canadian universities who brought with them the aforementioned philosophies. Earlier Canadians studied the writings of Thomas Reid and his followers; later ones, the Christianized Hegelianism of T.H. Green and Edward Caird.

Broadly speaking, the earlier philosophy was individualist, and so emphasized perception, while the later was collectivist, and concentrated on institutions. But because of the cultural continuities between them, the transition was gradual, creating a kind of layering effect. The quality of this change stands in contrast to the tradition in Europe, where the transition from the individualist Hume and Kant to the collectivist Hegel and Marx was revolutionary. As in Europe, interest in Hegelian philosophy ran parallel to, and intertwined with, the emergence of social science.

American higher education followed a pattern that was similar but set earlier. There the Scottish Common Sense school reigned until the mid-nineteenth century (T. Martin 1961), and Christianized Hegelian thought, until just before 1900 (Goetzman 1973). The U.S. timing undoubtedly reflects the earlier onset of industrial and urban life; social science is fundamentally a response to "modern" living. After 1900, American education became progressively more secular, individualistic, and, predictably, "scientific." The German influence was also more immediate in the United States than in Canada: between 1870 and 1920, thousands of Americans did graduate work in Germany, taking advantage of its pioneering efforts in the social sciences; many returned home to teach (Herbst 1965, 1-10). Some, like the scholars of the early Chicago school, were highly sensitive to the wider implications of modern life and thus offered critiques of the liberal values associated with it.

Running intermittently through these philosophical traditions was the theme of communication. In Scottish Common Sense, it took the form of concern with the universal aspects of language. As such, it was part of a linguistic defence of subject–object monism – the idea that certain perceptions could be taken as true without question. In the later, Hegelian tradition, study of language took a historical turn that stressed the specific, cultural constitution of meaning. In the United States, early Chicago school theorists Charles Horton Cooley, John Dewey, and George Herbert Mead illuminated the social, institutional essence of all human interaction.

Harold Innis, Canadian political economist, communications theorist at the University of Toronto from 1920–1952, and a focal point for the thoughts expressed in this chapter, is an interesting and unique representative of these traditions. In his undergraduate years at McMaster University, he was deeply influenced by James Ten Broeke, a Hegelian educator with a special interest in language. Like others of his generation, he also drew on the work of nineteenth and twentieth century German philosophers. Key examples for Innis were Ernst Cassirer, Werner Jaeger, and Thorstein Veblen, an American-born theorist who specialized in German philosophy.

Innis had a passion for empirical study, not unusual for a mid-twentieth century North American theorist. But his passion had a difference that has left him little understood. The standard empiricism of his day, still largely with us, was based on the notion of "pure fact," an approach that shunned intangible objects of study, especially ethics. Innis resisted this route: he placed ethics at the centre of his empirical work. This approach was more akin to Hegelianized Common Sense theory than it was to trends since the 1950s – a good reason to reacquaint ourselves with it. Reacquaintance will make his insights clearer.

Innis, however, was not merely a follower. He used his situation at the heart of a culture peripheral to Great Britain and the United States to develop new insights based on the concept of marginality, which gave his studies a unique dialectical twist. This chapter explores the influences described above, with emphasis on dialectical theory, and identifies Innis as a Canadian dialectician.

THE INTELLECTUAL BACKGROUND

We begin by looking at key aspects of dialectical analysis, considering first its role as an alternative to certain kinds of dualism. Scottish Common Sense philosophy was counter-dualistic in significant ways, so exploring this dualism will help us to see its place in Innis's intellectual heritage.

Dialectic did not begin as anti-dualist. As defined by Plato, its originator, it was part of a worldview that cheerfully divided idea from matter, universal from particular, and space from time, classifying only the first member in each pair as real and thus worthy of study. In this system, truth was ideal, universal, and spatial in the sense that it was static. This theory would have remained of little more than antiquarian interest had it not included an interesting dynamic element: dialogue. Plato believed that truth emerged progressively through conversation. It emerged when participants shared opposing views – theses and antitheses – and arrived at new and more correct ones – syntheses.

But this theory was problematic. How could speakers having a real conversation be said to be moving towards a preordained, static truth? We expect preordained truths from machine processes and applied mathematicians; from conversationalists, a certain open-endedness. Dialogue and the dualism that divides the static (or spatial) from the dynamic (or temporal) are surely among the oddest bedfellows in Western thought.

Oddness notwithstanding, the idea of improvement through a thesis, antithesis, and synthesis has remained central to all conceptions of dialectic. Not so for oral discussion, as can be seen from the modern heirs to dialectical thought. Hegel's renowned theory of dialectic featured interacting movements in history, but not conversation. A response to Hegel – Marx's work, equally renowned – featured interaction among social classes but no analysis of dialogue. None the less, both theorists had attempted to resolve the space–time problem by historicizing dialectical theory. Neither entirely succeeded: Hegel failed because he posited a given (and so timeless) "end of history"; Marx, because he posited a given (and timeless) bearer of truth in the form of the proletariat.

But their failures were useful because they point to an interesting feature of temporality: adequate theorization may well require subject-matter that resists space–time dichotomy. As we see below, communication, as developed by Innis, is an ideal candidate for such a subject. In order better to understand this point, we turn now to the Scottish Common Sense theorists' contribution to the subject of language.

Canadian students of social theory today are taught a historical sequence that begins with the Scottish philosopher David Hume, advances through Kant (a key responder to Hume), and proceeds through Hegel, Marx, and beyond. Canadian students of an earlier era, however, learned a different sequence, through which Innis's work can more easily be grasped. In it, Humean philosophy was followed by a now-little-known, non-Kantian response in the form of Scottish Common Sense. This approach was less dualistic than was Kant's: it did not separate matter from mind, faith and feeling from reason, and human subject from world as object. It achieved such holism in part through an appeal to language. To understand the context of this appeal, we must look briefly at the work of Hume.

A self-styled sceptic, Hume set himself the task of determining the "proper" objects of philosophical study – the things that could be determined to be true. He began by rejecting the Platonic faith in the search for conceptual essences such as goodness, beauty, and justice. For him, only tautological statements, such as mathematical equations, could make claims to truth (Hume 1979, 171). Correspondingly, other statements, regarding matters of fact or moral judgment, could make no such claim. Hume defended his view by appealing to the logical axioms of identity and difference: he noted that tautological statements were the only kinds of statements that could not be denied without self-contradiction. One could not deny that two and two made four, for example, because doing so would entail denying that two and two were two and two. Further, in any case, humans are unable to imagine two twos that do not add up to four. By contrast, other kinds of statements can be denied rationally. It is not self-contradictory, for example, to deny that there are birds in the world. Moreover, we could certainly imagine a birdless world. By the same token, it is not self-contradictory to deny that some acts are morally wrong.

Since Hume believed his approach to be thoroughly rational, he concluded that factual and moral claims had no rational ground. They were grounded rather in habit or custom (56). We are accustomed to claiming that birds exist and that there is right and wrong in human actions. But since to be accustomed is a far cry from knowing, such claims will never satisfy the philosopher as seeker of knowledge.

Hume's scepticism, if accepted, had far-reaching implications. One could not "reason" that there was an external world: denial of this world did not entail contradiction. One could not "reason" that events had causes. Externality and causation, for Hume, were only useful assumptions. Purportedly, this theory put an end to centuries of cloudy speculation on the nature of reality. It did not, however, put an end to dichotomous thinking. Like its speculative forebears, it divided matter from mind, or reason, since by its rules one could "reason" only in purely analytical, or non-empirical ways. It divided subject from object, since it rendered the thinker uncertain that there was an objective world; and it divided reason from ethics, since the rules for empirical claims applied equally to moral ones. In the process, it quantified philosophical language and thought, leaving them static.

Immanuel Kant, best-known answerer to Hume, accepted this dichotomous view. He agreed that there was no certainty about the existence of perceived objects; they might be there, and they might not be. But he rejected the idea that perceptions of externality resulted from custom or habit. He argued that they resulted instead from in-built mental categories – filters that organized sensual experience. That being the case, human beings had no choice but to perceive certain physical qualities. Without the categories, Kant argued, sensory input would be chaotic, and thought, impossible (Kant 1982, 111-18). But clearly, given them, one was never sure of a real world that possessed the qualities perceived.

For Thomas Reid (1710–1796), Scottish philosopher and educator at the University of Aberdeen, this response would not do (Seth 1899, 76–119). To show why, Reid pointed to a dimension of Western philosophy left unquestioned by his predecessors. He noted that from the seventeenth century onward philosophers had accepted a problematic theory of ideas, according to which humans are never immediately aware of the world around them. They are aware only of ideas or mental pictures. Descartes had taken this stance when he had adopted thought as the hallmark of being. Later theorists, critics of Descartes included, had not questioned this theory. But, as Reid pointed out, this neo-Platonic view, once assumed, did not permit a convincing reunion of mind and body. Only a non-dualistic theory could serve as a solid basis for knowledge.

Reid's version of such a foundation reflected a religious sensibility and a keen awareness of the implications of scepticism. He argued that human abilities to reason and to perceive had been designed by one creator; they had "come out of the same shop," so to speak. To mistrust one kind of ability was thus to mistrust both. If we could not trust a sense telling us of an external world, we could hardly trust the thinking that ascertained mathematical claims (Lehrer 1989, 18). Besides, Reid noted, belief in an external world was a fact of nature, comparable to belief in our own sensations (Stewart 1845, 22). If we doubt the existence of objects, we must equally question that of the attending sensations. Such a position was absurd, and, in any case, no one held such doubts. Hence trust for the faculties had to be regarded as a first principle (Lehrer 1989, 18).

Reid also adduced a cognitive theory that stressed the interrelation of the objective and subjective worlds. He noted that to interpret something as an idea of an object – a sign of some external thing – we had first to have a concept of such an object (Lehrer 1989, 14–17). Otherwise, nothing (no idea, no smell, no sensation) would appear a sign of anything. So, for example, we could not interpret something as external to us unless we first had concepts of externality and of a self against which it could be defined. For Reid, this meant that there are some signs and some features of objects of which we must have innate and correct conceptions. The innate conceptions corresponded to Hume's list of unknowables and were similar to Kant's innate conceptual categories as described above (Lehrer 1989, 20). They included the idea that there is an external world; that it has specific qualities; that we are distinct, conscious subjects; and that we have certain moral duties. But they did not, as with Kant, imply a dualistic concept of the world.

Reid buttressed these arguments with an appeal to language (Lehrer 1989, 40–1). Language, he argued, was a set of signs that humans share by a consensus on general meanings. They could have arrived at such a consensus, historically speaking, only through some original, gestural language that involved pointing to and imitating objects. Clearly a gift of God, this first language had given rise to a series of secondary, spoken ones. Moreover, each of these included terms distinguishing the self from other objects – ample evidence that the distinction was not imagined. Reid argued that modern life placed too much stress on formal, scientific language, suppressing awareness of its gestural predecessors. Closer attention to the latter, still preserved in art, might lead to better appreciation of the commonsensical – that is, essentially correct – perceptions of the world.

Thus Reid avoided the dualism of previous philosophers. By stressing the shared dimensions of the human and the non-human world, he tied subject to object and body to mind. At the same time, he linked reason to the more bodily oriented concepts of intuition and faith. Sociologically, this focus made the theory more congenial to those who wanted to preserve a religious outlook: Reid called the built-in or constitutional principles of the human psyche "the inspiration of the Almighty" (Lehrer 1989, 70). Undoubtedly, this was part of its appeal to Canadian and American educators.

The Common Sense legacy paved the way for a social or institutional understanding of knowledge, and its religiosity was also a spur to empirical study. The inherent faith in perception carried with it a lack of interest in examining alternative metaphysics. Unlike the speculative Kant, early North American Christian scholars were generally happy to concentrate on studying the natural world. Not surprisingly, they found their model in Francis Bacon, the scholar who studied science in order to reveal the workings of God's laws.

Still, despite its counter-dualism, the Common Sense tradition lacked a true historical dimension. Its theorists did not regard perception in historical or developmental terms. Nor did they view it as a dynamic process. They posited in-built concepts, or the potential for activating them, but no tendency for selective perception. This outlook left no room for a theory of class or culture-specific consciousness. Similarly, these theorists had only a limited historical analysis of language; they emphasized the universal aspects of communication. Historicization was thus the next step towards a dialectical analysis of culture.

Historicization of Common Sense philosophy came about largely through contact with the historicist movement in Germany. By the 1870s, a number of Canadian universities had begun to teach philology, the German historical approach to the study of meaning; German authors featured prominently in the texts used. At the same time, a Hegelian movement, prominent at the universities of Oxford and Glasgow, found its way into Canada, imported through people and books. Students of this movement were recruited to teach at Canadian universities. In Canada, one of the most prominent was John Watson of Queen's University (Armour and Trott 1981). A protégé of the Scottish Hegelian Edward Caird, Watson arrived at Queen's from Scotland in 1875; his prolific scholarship was to influence Canadian thought for the next half-century. Other students included George Paxton Young of the University of Toronto and, as seen above, James Ten Broeke of McMaster University. From the 1880s through the 1920s, the Canadian philosophical curriculum was dominated by Hegelian texts. The works of Thomas Hill Green, founder of the movement at Oxford, were universally read; Watson's writings on Kant and other essays were standard fare; and Hegel was required reading everywhere.

Hegel's outlook was historical, organic, and dialectical. For Hegel, history was a series of syntheses of opposing ideas, in which ideas and syntheses alike were moments in a single, transcendent consciousness seeking expression and self-awareness. The ideas in question stemmed from three distinct levels of community: family, society, and state. For Hegel, these were interactive parts of a single organism animated by a self-actualizing world spirit. In this dialectic, it was the state that constituted the synthesis – the highest expression of human ethical life.

One can hardly exaggerate the influence of this philosophy on the West. It was the basis for Marx's concept of alienated labour and has been foundational to many modern socialist movements. It influenced Canada's Social Gospel movement, designed to make God's rule a material as well as a spiritual reality. It is also central to the liberal concept of self-actualization as a human goal. Though steeped in Christian thought (Hegel had begun university as a theology student), Hegel's philosophy was not primarily Christian. Hegel saw Christianity as an important moment in the developing world spirit, but one surpassed by the philosophy that comprehended the spirit as a whole.

By contrast, North American Hegelians, like their Scottish Common Sense predecessors, were solidly Christian: they taught a Christianized version of Hegelian dialectics. Thomas Hill Green adopted Hegel's theory but rejected the hierarchy that placed philosophy first (Nettleship 1906, 126). For Green, Hegel's real message was that "there is one spiritual self-conscious being, of which all that is real is the activity or expression, and we are related to this being not merely as parts of the world which is its expression, but as partakers in some inchoate measure of the self-consciousness through which it at once constitutes and distinguishes itself from the world; and that this participation is the source of morality and religion" (Nettleship 1906, 126). In dialectical fashion, we participate in two antithetical realities: we are God and not-God, divine and material. These moments come together in our self-understanding, which is realized in an ethical and religious life. Followed with variations by North American theorists, this theory inspired a reverence for the state – or at least for the state's potential to actualize such a life – coupled with an institutional, non-individualistic mode of analysis.

Canadian theorists stressed yet another element of Hegelian thought: its organicism. Andrew Seth, a turn-of-the-century Scottish philosopher who taught for a time at McGill University, described this emphasis as a fusion of Reid's and Hegel's philosophies. The resulting theory involved recognition that no object, considered in itself, was intelligible. Situating his description in the context of a critique of Hume's scepticism, Seth put the point thus: "So far is it from being true, as Hume says, that there is nothing in any object, considered in itself, which can afford us a reason for drawing a conclusion beyond it, that the exact contrary might be formulated and defended. The mind is incapable of considering any object in itself; every object carries us necessarily beyond itself, and forces us to recognize its connection with other objects" (Seth 1845, 56–7). Given this condition, he continued, one could not sensibly deny knowledge of an external world: what made objects intelligible was clearly their being part of a universal that joined them to other objects. For Christian Hegelians, this outlook entailed defining objects in a way that illuminated their relatedness to the world around them. As we see below, this type of definition was central to Innis' work.

Hegel's organicism, however, did not involve much emphasis on perception or communication. These further foci, taken up later by Innis, were provided by two other developments in German scholarship, equally imported to North America. In psychology, then taught largely under the rubric of philosophy, the works of the German philosopher Wilhelm Wundt became widely taught. Wundt had developed a dynamic theory that saw perception as a creative synthesis of perceived elements. Emphasis on communication was advanced by the Higher Criticism in theological studies, also inspired by Hegel. This movement stressed critical, historical interpretation of the Bible, calling for close textual analysis of scripture. Higher critics assumed that the culturally specific linguistic understandings and motives of the authors were the key to deriving their true meaning.

From one perspective, the change from Scottish Common Sense to Hegelianism was not radical. Philosophers of both persuasions agreed that perceivers stood in an organic relation to perceived objects, mediated by a shared universal (a shared God) in which they participated. Both rejected scepticism. Hegelians added a historical dimension: for them, perceivers interacted with the world, changing both it and their own perceptions in the process. Both schools maintained a religious, idealist outlook and yet emphasized empirical study. But the earlier group focused on the laws of the natural world; the latter more the social one.

Still, in another way, these schools were quite unalike. Each belonged to a distinctive set of economic and political conditions. Thomas Reid and his followers, situated in the mid-nineteenth century, found currency in the age of British free trade policy. Although causal lines are difficult to trace in these matters, it should come as no surprise that they were proponents of free trade. Of course, their views were unlike the individualist concept of free trade popular today. North American theorists of the nineteenth century presupposed a uniform, Christian culture, which they believed could be sustained through higher education. Their support of commodification thus did not extend to ethics. Moreover, their theory was qualified by an Aristotelian faith in agrarian values. In his widely used economics text, Francis Wayland, revered American proponent of Common Sense theory, argued that God had designed the world to favour the agrarian life. This could be seen from the large number of labour-saving innovations in trade and manufacture as compared with agriculture. For Wayland, this was God's way of keeping most of his subjects in the healthiest of occupations (Wayland 1870, 47–50). Still, because of these beliefs, Common Sense theorists developed no significant critique of the market and held a negative view of the state.

By contrast, the historical theories popular later in the century coincided with a parallel move towards protection in trade – in Canada, with the National Policy. At least in one case, causal lines are not difficult to see. When in 1888 the University of Toronto was set to hire a professor of political economy, the key concern was the prospective scholar's view on protection. In those days, professorial appointments were made by order-in-council, and the Ontario cabinet was keen to avoid hiring a "free-trader." W.J. Ashley, well versed in, and sympathetic to, Germanic historicism, was the welcome choice (Drummond 1983, 18). Under his guidance, the curriculum of the department developed a strong historical orientation, which it maintained throughout Innis's years there. In terms of theory, the historical outlook coincided with the organic style of definition described above; in terms of policy, with belief in a positive state designed to help its citizens reach maximum self-development.

INNIS

For Harold Innis, this heritage was mediated by a devout Baptist upbringing: his parents had hoped that he would become a minister (Watson 1981). He attended two Baptist universities: McMaster and Chicago, for his undergraduate and doctoral studies, respectively. The Baptist experience provided insight into three topics relevant to Innis's later work – oral communication, a grass-roots approach, and the role of history and moral vision. First, Baptists comprise one of the so-called dissenting denominations: in contrast to Anglicans and Presbyterians, they have never been an established church. Their method of outreach has thus been personal and oral, carried out by travelling ministers and enlivened through revival meetings, which have always distinguished Baptists from their cooler Protestant fellows.

Second, the grass-roots approach was necessary for economic and numerical survival: a non-established church must learn to rely on its own resources. In turn, this necessity had implications for Baptist attitudes towards the state, a point equally relevant to Innis's work. Denied official status, Baptists cultivated the virtue of church–state separation. They nurtured a strong distaste for public funding of any religious undertaking, which included education, since in the early days schools, colleges and universities were invariably confessional. Acadia and McMaster, Canada's key Baptist universities, remained privately funded for much longer than did other Canadian universities (Longley 1939). This rendered their educational tasks difficult and their survival precarious. Their endurance under these circumstances underscores the strength of their anti-statism and the oral culture that kept it alive.

Third, this religious background also highlighted the importance to human community of history and of a moral vision. Innis ultimately rejected religion, but he retained its intense focus on ethics, which led in turn to a historical style of analysis. Innis was especially interested in the declining role of ethics in the social sciences. He saw the decline as symptomatic of modern life, bereft of long-term, historical concerns and correspondingly overwhelmed by short-term or, as he put it, spatial ones. Decreased appreciation for ethics goes hand in hand with declining appreciation for history: both constitute long-term concerns. This issue tied in closely with Innis's interest in communication: he came to see the decline as rooted in the history of Western media. He saw its apogee in the present-minded and amoral mechanized press, and he concluded that the bias of modern media threatened the survival of the West.

These Baptist refinements of Canada's intellectual tradition came together in the teachings of James Ten Broeke, Innis's Hegelian teacher of psychology. Ten Broeke's work stressed ethics and oral communication, topics he explored by studying natural language. In keeping with Baptist anti-statism, he developed these ideas via the individual – particularly perception. But like a Hegelian, he did so in a non-individualist way. It is a fair guess that his teachings had a strong influence on Innis, since Innis kept the notes he took in Ten Broeke's classes – something he did not do for other courses.[2] In addition, Innis was happy to call one of his texts *The Bias of Communication*, an effort to answer questions on perception raised by Ten Broeke.

Recruited to McMaster in 1875, the same year that brought John Watson to Queen's, Ten Broeke was a product of the U.S. Hegelian movement, trained at Yale. Ten Broeke believed that Hegel had produced a foundation for holistic, Christian thinking that was more solid than Plato's or Aristotle's (Armour and Trott 1981, 354). He set out to pass this foundation on to Canadian students. As he saw it, the strength of Hegel's dialectic came from the light that it shed on the interactive nature of human knowledge. No mind, he pointed out, could express more than a part of the world. Humans could share a world only because they share language (355). By sharing language, they share in the many formulations possible and hence in perceptions other than their own. It followed that perceiving and knowing were social rather than solitary activities.

Ten Broeke extended this theory of language to his religious outlook: he defined God in terms of what it meant to use the word "God." In the Hegelian spirit, he also stressed self-actualization: the word "God" expressed the human need for life in its fullness, the belief in God expressed the strength of the human conviction that such a life was possible, and the difficulty of defining God was the difficulty of explaining this need adequately (359). In his later work, Innis developed this idea by showing that the media available for expression help foster or suppress awareness of these needs. Innis's key question, posed initially by Ten Broeke, was: "Why do we attend to that to which we attend?"

Like Ten Broeke, Innis shunned an individualistic approach to perception: he was especially interested in the effect of institutions on perception. He learned much about this kind of analysis from the work of Thorstein Veblen, a Kantian scholar and specialist in German economic theory (Innis 1956a, 17–26). Veblen had once taught at the University of Chicago, and during his residence there Innis studied his writings intensively. Veblen's ideas included a scathing critique of modern individualism, in the form of an attack on "psychological hedonism" – the individualistic theory of psychology dominant in Veblen's day and still common today. First expressed overtly by eighteenth century theorist Jeremy Bentham, this ahistorical theory reduces human behaviour to simple movements towards pleasure and away from pain.

Since Veblen was also an economist, he commonly encountered psychological hedonism as part of price theory (Neill 1972, 23). According to that theory, the prices that confront us in the marketplace reflect the usefulness or pleasure-giving qualities of the items offered. Similarly, the articles that we acquire reflect our true desires. How we spend our money and what there is to spend it on are good indicators of pleasure and utility. Obversely, money not spent and products not available provide neither utility nor pleasure.

Veblen countered that market purchases are governed by historically developed ranking systems that assign prestige to certain commodities. People do not purchase things with pleasure or utility in mind, he argued; they buy to emulate the lives of those who can afford the highest-ranking commodities. The driving force behind these purchases is vulnerability to humiliation and a corresponding need for social acceptance (Innis 1956a, 20). We learn from Veblen that market values are never simply the product of individual perceivers carrying out rational calculations of utility. Rather, historically developed rules set the boundaries for what choices can be made. Innis continued his own work in a similar vein: he came to see communications media as the boundary markers of social perception.

In Canada, the collectivist tradition described above often found expression as a positive theory of the state, especially among left Hegelians, for whom collectivism meant provision of a broad range of social services to educate people morally and intellectually. The most prominent example of this outlook around the turn of the century was the Social Gospel movement, foundational to the CCF. Salem Bland, a leader of that group, was educated in Hegelian thought through his contact with John Watson at Queen's (McKillop 1979, 219–21). His colleague J.S. Woodsworth had studied Hegel with Edward Caird (223). Hegelian ideas were equally to be found in the *Grain Growers Guide*, which Innis had read since childhood.

But Innis did not follow the left Hegelian path. Like his Baptist fore-bears, he distrusted the state. This feeling was strengthened by his experiences of the First World War and of empire as it affected Canadian life. For Innis, the state was an institution saturated with party politics – a dangerously present-minded force unable to perceive the larger implications of its policies. It was an institution, moreover, that liked to eat academics, as shown by the academics drawn into public service during the Second World War. To Innis, this whole situation created a deadly imbalance, correctable only by the long-term concerns of a relatively disengaged scholar. To demonstrate the approach required, he set out to show that all large concentrations of power (states included) had self-destructive, empire-like qualities and that the power centred in Western media had created perceptual distortions that fostered war.

Clearly then, Innis chose to work out his theories in a non-statist fashion. Like his Baptist predecessors, and specifically like James Ten Broeke, he maintained an interest in perception: he set out to determine what had shaped Western consciousness. He was also drawn to analysis of the oral tradition, which had sustained Baptist educational institutions. Through this study, he came to believe that mechanized, dangerously centralizing media could be offset by institutions that promoted dialogue. This interest was enhanced by Innis's university teaching environment. The University of Toronto has always had a substantial Classics department – easily the largest in Canada – and scholars examining the effect of alphabetization on the oral civilization of ancient Greece. Innis consulted their work and so chose to study oral communication via Greek civilization, aided by his reading of the German philosophical writings of Werner Jaeger, Friedrich Nietzsche, Ernst Cassirer, Sigfried Kracauer, and Hegel. These foci yielded an institutional analysis centred on communications media and the institutions affected by them.

They also led to a holistic approach to definition similar to that outlined by Andrew Seth, noted above. This practice was evident beginning with Innis's early days as an economic historian. His special interest was Canadian political economy, on which he concentrated for the longest and most influential part of his career. It was during this time that he came to understand relations among history, culture, and ethics and lay the basis for his later study of how those relations were affected by the development of Western media.

Consider Innis's approach to history. Early Canada was cultivated as a source of staples – a set of unprocessed materials such as fish, fur and wheat. The standard classical economic theory of his day saw these staples as commodities. As such, they had a quantity and a price. For Innis, this view falsified Canada. The things that Canada sold to foreign markets in its colonial days had price and volume, but these were not their significant features. Each staple had to be worked in a manner specific to its material make-up, which included the attending social and geographical conditions.

Fur, for example, had to be extracted with the help of the Native population, which alone knew how to make mass extraction workable. These extractions in turn required trade goods as a medium of exchange: ships loaded with such goods had to be sent to Canada. They also had to remain until the exchange was complete. Since this process could take up to six years, it required high levels of long-term finance. To facilitate exchange, trading posts had to be established, and, since these stored goods, forts were needed to guard them. Thus fur could be traded only under highly stable and centralized conditions. And fur's qualities helped to shape the economic and political landscape of its home setting.

Two elements here demonstrate Innis's dialectical method. The first was his use of holistic definition. For Innis, each aspect of the staples economy was coextensive with and implied all the others that affected and were affected by it. Fur was coextensive with the animal from which it was extracted; the animal, with its habitat (Canada); the habitat, with the people who knew how to work and survive in it; and those people, qua large-scale trappers, with the trade goods they demanded in exchange. This organic way of seeing the world was integral to the thinking developed by Thomas Reid and carried forward in distinctive forms by Canadian Hegelians. It recalls Andrew Seth's claim that "every object carries us necessarily beyond itself."

The second element was Innis's emphasis on culture as a historical phenomenon. Innis understood that classical economics was faulty because it was profoundly static. It presupposed something that it never attempted to demonstrate: that all markets were alike. This in turn implied that all historical developments were alike. Innis especially resented the importation and common use of classically oriented British and American textbooks in Canada. From the classical standpoint, of course, it matters not a bit that Canadians studied economics – their own included – from foreign texts. But for Innis, this practice marginalized Canada. His own theory was an attempt to show how destructive this practice was. At stake was the specificity of Canadian culture, a culture visible only through the holistic lens provided by an Innis-style approach to economics.

In his later work, Innis turned this organic and historical approach to the larger philosophical themes touched on by the early scholars discussed above. He came to believe that the ahistorical and relativistic attitudes embedded in classical theory had their roots in Western consciousness. For many reasons, he chose to examine these themes via media. North American education, which since the days of Scottish Common Sense theory had stressed empirical method, made it likely that Innis would approach this subject concretely. In terms of focus, he demonstrated the influence of James Ten Broeke, who had shown that studying linguistic meaning can illuminate human desire and that perception can illuminate the direction of that desire. We saw, too, that Innis's Baptist heritage inclined him towards a perceptual rather than a state-centred approach and that its oral character provided a basis for his interest in dialogue. Innis had already had occasion to criticize one medium – the textbook – and he had developed expertise in holistic analysis, aided by his reading of Veblen's institutional theories. These influences came together in a dialectical philosophy of consciousness.

To develop this philosophy, Innis, like his Common Sense and Hegelian predecessors, addressed dualism directly. Keeping his focus on language, Innis set out to show that Western dualistic consciousness had developed as a function of dominant communications media. He did so by contrasting two kinds of media – spatializing, or space biased, and temporalizing, or time biased. Employing his organic form of definition, Innis argued that the bias of any given culture resulted partly from the bias of its dominant medium.

Innis argued that a time-biased culture is dominated by a medium that is heavy – in the most literal sense, massive. Conceived holistically, this massiveness has cultural implications that can, like a staple, be seen by examining its qualities. Hieroglyphics chiselled in stone were one of Innis's examples. The definition of this medium included the requisite hours of labour for transport (in this case, a great number, for obvious reasons) – and of labour in learning both the script and the technique used to inscribe it in stone. These latter elements are also time-consuming, making stone culturally as well as physically heavy.

This heaviness has social and political implications – also part of this medium's definition. Stone and hieroglyphics are destined to be governed by a select group, since a lengthy apprenticeship is required to master them. Moreover, it will be a durable group, since chisellers of stone do not work for short-term goals. So where stone is the dominant medium we are unlikely to find social equality. The physical force needed to transport and work stone requires access to masses of unskilled labour (Innis 1964a, 94). When we add the primitive technologies available in the ancient West, we can see that stone provides a material foundation for a series of overlapping dualisms: the separation of skilled from unskilled labour, of intellectual from physical labour, and of an elite political leadership from those who are led. All these elements define stone and hieroglyphics – media that underpin time-biased dualism.

By contrast, a space-biased culture is dominated by a medium that is light, or relatively non-massive. Here we take paper and the alphabet as our example. Since paper is light, it is relatively easy to transport. The technique used for writing takes little time to master, and so it is time light. The same can be said of the script itself. Together, they define a medium whose use requires little investment of time.

Like heaviness, lightness is defined organically in terms of its cultural consequences. Paper and an alphabet are ideally suited to be mass media. The short period needed to master them makes it unlikely that one would find them limited to a small group. Simplicity and portability also favour a geographically expansive society, since one can use them to administer wide areas (33). Administrative expansiveness in turn favours war: military conquests make more sense when one can hope to control the areas won. So expansiveness, both administrative and military, are part of the definition of paper.

The space bias will also tend to induce present-mindedness. Scribes will become a civil service, and states will dissolve into military technique. State leaders will value uniformity and administered sameness as represented in the state's military and its systems of orthography. Their time will not be the time of enduring tradition but rather that of technique. This condition will produce a peculiar form of cultural stasis that identifies reality with the moment, thus locking the culture into an eternal present. Such a society is likely to develop a spatial philosophy, crudely materialistic, which will identify the objective with the purely material.

For Innis, the West had begun with a temporal bias and had ended, in the modern age, with a spatial one. Central to modernity was a relativist view that marginalized ethical claims by denying them status as objective knowledge. We will remember that David Hume had expressed such a view. Theoretical critiques of Hume by Scottish Common Sense philosophers and Hegelians were from this standpoint critiques of modernity. Battling relativism in values (the view that moral values are never objective) has long been a Canadian tradition.

That tradition also included a holistic form of empiricism – one that encompassed moral values. Innis, for example, saw that one had to counter not only sceptics such as Hume but crude empiricists – key bearers of spatial bias. We saw above that this bias identifies reality with the "purely material" – the visible, tangible, and measurable. The classical economic theory that Innis had battled is a key example of this outlook: it reduces commodities to price and quantity – that is, to what one can measure and see. But Innis added something more to this insight. Following his longstanding interest in perception, he argued that such reductionism was not only spatially but visually biased.

Innis demonstrated these points in his analysis of the press. He focused on perception here by contrasting visual and oral experience. For Innis, the newspaper made possible and permissible a dichotomous division of public from private interests. This division affected its engagement with moral issues in two ways. The newspaper touted itself as the quintessence of objectivity, and it did so primarily by visual means. It promoted the simplistic idea that seeing is believing, even where seeing was a matter only of reading print. At the same time, it did nothing to promote awareness of the interpretive thought processes behind the printed word. This practice pushed the invisible and immeasurable world of philosophical thought – the only world capable of revealing bias – into chronic obscurity. It also worked against the invisible realm of ethics.

For Innis, the results were evident in the new sensibilities of press owners, journalists, and editors. In keeping with the liberalism of the day, they presented their product as a vehicle for public education. Yet it was clear from the shallow, sensationalist quality of parts of the press that this concern went little beyond the immediate goal of manipulating readers (Innis 1964a, 138). This shallowness demonstrated that, with respect to the social good, outward façade took precedence over less visible substance. The stress on window dressing was part of a visual bias that undermined the basis for moral truth. It was, in short, part of the definition of a medium whose disintegrative effects on individuals were paralleled by a disintegration of the society as a whole.

Though this condition had become prominent in the era of the press, its course had not ended there. For Innis, it had progressed to deeper levels with the invention of the movie camera. The camera had emerged in a world that already worshipped the visible word in print. It was thus easy to convince people that the new visuals were objective representations of reality. The result was a peculiarly modern frame of mind known as photo-realism – the naïve belief that the camera (and indeed the eye) cannot lie. The seriousness of this naïveté was proportional to the medium's increased range of nuance and ability to manipulate. Its perverseness first became evident in its use as a tool for propaganda during the Second World War. Innis noted that in Germany films taken on site at the front and shown in theatres afterward had convinced German citizens of the superiority of German arms. In his view, this was not a localized phenomenon: it was a symptom of a spatial drift in Western thinking, a perceptual malady underlying modern dualism.

To counter this dualism, Innis returned to a central element in his Baptist heritage: the oral tradition. He argued that the key antidote to modernity was dialogue. Dialogue had three features that made it helpful in this way: it enhanced cultural memory and thus a sense of history; it promoted empathy and thus a reverence for values; and it promoted tolerance for ambiguity in meaning. In taking this theoretical route, Innis moved beyond his intellectual heritage to create a new, sound-based (anti-visual) theory of knowledge.

As noted above, Innis developed this theory on the model provided by ancient Western oral traditions. Of particular interest to him was that tradition's effect on memory. In the oral tradition, cultural wisdom was stored in, and communicated through, epic poetry. The epic was designed to be memorized; its formal elements – stock phrases, characters, and rhymes – had evolved so as to allow its burden of information to be retained and recalled. Together, they created a way of communicating that induced an ongoing concern with remembrance. An educational system that concentrated on training the memory enhanced this effect. It placed value on traditional knowledge and on those who, as accomplished reciters, became its best carriers. In the world of the epic, history was the recited and highly valued human story (Innis 1964a, 105).

First, such education worked on the deep structures of thought: it injected a fluid time-sense into reciters and listeners. Epics contained their material in dramatic story form, and so reciters had to become actors. They conveyed their information dynamically through characterization. As in all dialectical interactions, this practice helped to structure reciters' own thinking. Reciters and listeners came to internalize and imagine the world in the dramatic spirit of the epic: temporal communication produced a temporal imagination (Innis 1964a, 106). This tradition fostered a real human sense of time, for characters in a storyline do not follow the rhythms of factory clocks, and it was broadly inclusive: it invited both the listeners' emotional involvement and memorization, for listeners could become reciters in their own right. By contrast, the passive orality encouraged by media such as the modern radio did little to encourage such development. The radio invited no responsive articulation and was not inclusive, since listeners were rarely announcers or programmers (191). For Innis, the oral spirit was essential to proper dialogue.

Second, the oral tradition was also essential to Innis because of the mimetic identification that it encouraged between speakers and listeners. Basing his analysis on Nietzsche's work, Innis (1964a) argued that the oral tradition enhances listeners' empathy or mimetic identification with speakers (71–2). In that tradition one communicates to absorb and remember rather than to distance and criticize. Discussion has some of these qualities too, since it calls for consideration of the feelings of others (191). For this reason, a tradition of public discussion sets an empathic tone for its society. Once firmly established, Innis thought, such a tradition might be sustainable even in the presence of alternative media. For him, such balance was essential to a concept of knowledge that included values.

Third and finally, dialogue also has a wonderful capacity to tolerate ambiguity in meaning. It has a looseness that allows participants to make adjustments in the meaning of their terms. This frees them from drawing hard lines – from defining things in ways that exclude other people. For Innis, an example is the inconsistency characteristic of oral decision-making in Western polities. These polities have a tradition of discussion based on precedents rather than on written statutes. Terms are left loose: specific meanings emerge through local decision-making. This process leaves room for adjustments that suit particular times and places (Innis 1952a, 120) and hence for discussion of values. But

Western thinkers have too frequently viewed this ambiguity as a sign of weakness in logic. Innis responded by calling for a new logic that acknowledged values (1964a, 102).

Through his unique history of media, Innis also developed his own version of dialectical theory. For Innis, dominant media comprised what he called monopolies of knowledge, monopolies of the kinds of knowledge entailed by the media in question. Innis pointed out that monopolies always invite attacks from marginal groups. These attacks can be violent, but they need not be. Violence can be avoided if such movements can be understood dialectically, as a way in which knowledge emerges in the world.

One of Innis's historical examples was his description of how the Aramaeans, developers of an alphabet, also came to invent historical writing. The Aramaeans, outsiders to an empire, were denied access to learning the dominant imperial medium – hieroglyphics. Unable to retaliate physically, they responded by developing a script easier to master than the one denied them. Since they were refused spatial power, they sought a time-centred form of power. Their tactic was to invent written history, a practice that gave them a measure of control over time. And thus this dialectic of marginalization and retaliation resulted in a historical innovation of major proportions. It had given the world a new form of knowledge. This was Innis's sense of how dialectic worked.

Though this example did not feature friendly relations, Innis believed that, given opportunity for dialogue, dialectical processes could be peaceful. He understood that all forms of knowledge and all related media create margins. Life tends toward monopoly, and so one cannot eradicate monopoly. Instead, one must incorporate it into a theory of change and then develop methods of communication that enhance its creative possibilities. Dialogue offers hope not only because it counters dichotomies but because it is a model for a creative approach to margins. Speakers in a conversation, especially one involving widely differing viewpoints, represent natural margins in relation to one another. Innis believed that understanding this process could revolutionize the concept of communication: it could de-emphasize the ideal of logical agreement and emphasize instead the dialogical, dialectical interaction of competing marginalities as helpful and innovative contributions to knowledge.

This was Innis's contribution to the Canadian intellectual legacy. It shunned dualisms and stressed communication. It emphasized history, dialogue, holistic definition, and open-ended development. It was distinctively Canadian because it grew out of Innis's intellectual background and his theory of Canada's development. But to grasp the significance of Innis today requires placing him in a larger Canadian historical context. The foregoing thoughts attempt to show one way in which this can be done.

NOTES

1 All references to early university curricula are based on archival research that I have conducted at six universities across Canada: Acadia, Dalhousie, McGill, McMaster, Queen's, and Toronto.
2 Harold A. Innis, "Mental Notes," n.d., Harold Innis Papers, University of Toronto Archives, B72-0003 27 (36).

3 "The Expected Tradition": Innis, State Rationality, and the Governmentalization of Communication

MICHAEL DORLAND

Les peuples se ressentent toujours de leur origine. Les circonstances qui ont accompagné leur naissance et servi à leur développement influent sur tout le reste de leur carrière.

— Tocqueville [1835]

The physiognomy of a government can best be judged in its colonies, for there its characteristic traits usually appear larger and more distinct. When I wish to judge of the spirit and faults of the administration of Louis XIV, I must go to Canada. Its deformity is there seen as through a microscope.

— Tocqueville [1856]

What appears below is an argument about the historical origins of Canadian state formation and their influence on the present. The argument orients itself in relation to certain observations of Harold Innis, particularly in his writings of the mid-1940s concerning the relation between church and state in Canada – that is to say, on the delimitation of the realm of the symbolic order in a society and on the control exercised by institutional bodies, such as church and state, over the extent of the symbolic order. In texts such as "The Church in Canada" (in 1956a)[1] and *Political Economy in the Modern State* (in 1946),[2] Innis made an underappreciated contribution to the understanding of the history of cultural, as opposed to economic, development in Canada. By "cultural," I understand that which precedes, contains, or interacts with economic development – the cultural, organizational, or ideological contexts that give shape to particular forms of economic action.

Thus in "The Church in Canada," for example, Innis observes: "Students of cultural development in Canada have failed to realize the extent to which religion in English-speaking Canada has been influenced indirectly by the traditions of the Gallican Church in Quebec" (1956a, 384). One realizes soon enough that Innis here is talking about something more than religion. He continues: "Nor do we appreciate the significance of the political background of the France of Colbert and Louis XIV. State and Church under an absolute monarchy in France was State and Church under an absolute monarchy in New France" (384). This has been a favoured thesis of English-Canadian and American historians since Parkman (Dumont 1993, 357).

Innis, however, goes on to draw out some of the implications, pushing them further than other historians had done:

Great Britain ... succeeded in the second Empire to a greater extent than is generally realized because French bureaucracy had become solidly entrenched in New France. It was this bureaucracy which enabled the British to govern New France and which enabled Canadians through governmental activity to develop their natural resources by construction of canals, railways, hydro-electric power facilities, and other undertakings. It was this bureaucracy in Church and State which was reflected in the place of Quebec in Confederation and in turn of English-speaking provinces. Clemenceau once remarked that England was a French colony gone wrong. He might have felt that in Canada the French colony had followed expected traditions. (1956a, 384)

There are many intricate leaps in this passage. Innis is suggesting, it seems to me, that key aspects of European absolutist statecraft are preserved in sedimented form in Canadian state formation, political organization, and culture. The absolutist state and church shared a common form of organization – bureaucratic rationality. This common factor determined the trajectory of Canadian institutional history; for it allowed the state to dominate the church; this in turn permitted the British, through the church, to govern New France; on a more general plane, of the same order of domination, it enabled Canadians to develop their natural resources by the construction of canals and other channels of transportation/communication, and it determined Quebec's place in Confederation.

For Innis, the bureaucratic rationality of the Canadian state thus has its roots in an unbroken continuum reaching back to the early modern emergence of the European, absolutist state. As a result of such an unbroken continuum (the famed absence of a revolutionary tradition), Canadian institutions developed in conditions of "relative stability" and "continuous repression." The relative stability of large-scale forms

of social organization evolved hand in hand with a repressive symbolic culture of highly formalized, unimaginative "ecclesiasticism" or
Puritanism, for "the arts of *suppressio veri, suggestio falsi*" have been
particularly evident in "our literature, in our art and in our cultural
life" (Innis 1956a, 386). Innis saw the cramped public sphere of the
time of his writing as characterized by political leadership – the domination of politics over other discursive forms; supine public opinion
and the hazards of public expression; and the settling of all great public
questions on the basis of personal prejudices – in a word, "the fundamental corruption of Canadian public life" (1956a, 386). But – his
principal point – the forms of organization and the means of expression are complementary; the Canadian state remained absolutist, with
grievous consequences for public life.

This argument, or at least some aspects of it, though not usually
referred back to Innis's insights of the mid-1940s, finds evocation
today in the work of Canadian historians of state formation. Bernier
and Salée (1987), for instance, comment on the "strange" silence of
contemporary political science as regards the history of the Canadian
state yet note that "in many respects, state power as exercised today
continues practices that date to the nineteenth and *even* the eighteenth
centuries," which they trace back to "a *remarkably pure* model" of the
absolutist state (101, 128, emphases added). Resnick (1990) has also
commented on the paucity of theoretical work: "In this country,
writing about the state (and indeed civil society) has barely proceeded
beyond square one" (152). If some of these lacunae have been filled by
Greer and Radforth (1992), few anglophone writers have matched
Fernand Dumont's (1993) attempt to extend the historical framework
back to the seventeenth century and argue for the sedimentation of
past practices into the present day. Except perhaps for Innis.

I try next to contextualize Innis's approach by way of two hypothe-
ses. First, what Innis is attempting becomes much clearer if read
through the prism of Foucault's theories of governmentality. Second, in
the light of that theory, the "corruption" of the Canadian public sphere
appears as an aspect of the limited extent of the development of civil
society – that is, of the extent and duration of the symbolic order and
the resulting truncation of forms of public expression.

FOUCAULT, GOVERNMENTALITY, AND
THE THEORY OF POLICE

The nature of early modern bureaucratic rationality – Foucault's "governmentality" – preoccupied Michel Foucault in the late 1970s and,
since then, his students in Britain, France, and Italy (see Burchell and

Miller 1991). For Foucault, following Meinecke (1957), what distinguished the early modern state (sixteenth century) was the emergence of a form of rationality particular to itself: *raison d'état*. *Raison d'état*, which the seventeenth-century German academic statist Hermann Conring called "the polar star of modern politics," is the modern form of governmental rationality as an autonomous rationality. As historian Étienne Thuau has written, it is a form of reason "born of the calculation and ruse of men" and makes of the state "a knowing machine, a work of reason"; the state ceases to be derived from the divine order of the universe and is henceforth subject to its own particular necessities" (Thuau 1966, 9).

In the international system of states that took shape in late-sixteenth-century Europe, *raison d'état* in effect bifurcates into two distinct logics: an external form, governing relations between states (what German political theorists would term *Politik*), and an internal form governing relations between the state and its "subjects." It might be more accurate for the latter to speak of relations between the state and its knowing arts of exercising power within a field of intervention crystallizing in a concept of "economy." In Foucault's words, "To govern a state will therefore mean to ... set up an economy at the level of the entire state, which means exercising towards its inhabitants, and the wealth and behaviour of each and all, a form of surveillance and control" – German *Polizei* (Foucault 1978, in Burchell 1991, 92).

If police theory (or policy science) developed in its most systematized form in the numerous seventeenth-century German principalities grappling with the problems of governance, it would constitute a substantial pan-European body of literature increasingly disseminated throughout the seventeenth and eighteenth centuries (and resurfacing in American sociology in the late nineteenth century). Police theory was the theoretical distillation of reflection "formed by the institutions, processes, analyses ... the calculations and tactics that allow the exercise of this very specific albeit complex form of power, which has as its target population, as its principal form of knowledge political economy, and its essential technical means apparatuses of security" (Foucault 1978 quoted in Burchell 1991, 102).

For Foucault, police theory was the outstanding manifestation of early modern rationality within the workings of the state. Power is no longer based on a legalistic conception of justice (divine or natural) but instead becomes rational, on the basis of a logic proper to itself. The function of a rational politics is to guarantee that there be "communication" between humans. As Foucault states it: "As a form of rational intervention exercising political power over men, the role of politics is to grant them something more than mere existence; and, in so doing, to give the state a little more power. This is achieved by the control of 'communication'; that is, the common activities of individuals (labour, production, exchange, comforts)" (Foucault 1979, 29).

In eighteenth-century France, Gordon observes in his commentary on Foucault, urbanization and police are almost synonymous. One formulation of the objective of police was that of organizing the entire royal territory like one great city. Public space, bridges, roads, and rivers are prominent among the objects of police attention. "[T]his physical infrastructure of connection and mobility is seen by police theorist Jean Domat as the means whereby the policed city can function as a place of assembly and *communication*, a term whose meaning embraces all the processes of human intercourse, exchange, circulation and cohabitation within a governed population" (quoted in Burchell 1991, 20). However, the aims of the early modern state were still shaped by ethical, religious, and political considerations (just as contemporary Canadian politics remain far more entangled with religious, ethnic, and linguistic considerations than with class). To the extent that accumulation was not yet an end in itself, the aims of the state derived from a conception of innate human sociability. Thus the ruler could conceive of himself or herself as the prudent manager of a large-scale household modelled on the classical *oikos*. In this still-limited sense, economic action was the prerogative of the state, and economic order flowed from the prudent direction of such action. The individual subject had no independent initiative, nor interests potentially or autonomously productive of order. As historian Keith Tribe states, "Humanity confronts the state as 'population,' a subject mass to be regulated, enhanced and supervised" (Tribe 1988, 27–9). As a result, the concepts of society and polity are synonymous: one cannot exist without the other, and they are as such conceptually indistinguishable.

It would not be a great leap to the assumption that social order was owed uniquely to governing activity and that the proper concern of government was "the happiness" of a population. As an innately social being, a creature of wants and needs – of commerce, broadly understood – human beings could attain happiness if their needs were properly administered, and this goal could be ensured only by good government (*gute Polizei*). Thus the primary task of the ruler was to ensure the numerical sufficiency of the population, that it had the institutions necessary for its subsistence (such as academies and entertainments), the regulation of prices, the proper punishment of crime, the prevention of disease, and similar social policies (Tribe 1988, 29–33). The "policying" of society implies infinite, ever-extending networks of regulation. As Foucault put it, "police oversee everything that regulates society ... It is life itself that is the object of police: in whatever is indispensable, useful and superfluous. It is the responsibility of police to make it possible for men to survive, to live and improve themselves" (Foucault 1979, 31). As Tribe observes, "Unlike a legal order which defines transgressions and prescribes punishments, *Polizei* remained a prescriptive model of social order" (Tribe 1988, 31).

POLICING CANADA: THE NATIONAL INSECURITY STATE

Contra Innis, Eccles has argued that "for the better part of two centuries war, and the threat of war, was one of the great staples of the Canadian economy" (1987, 124). Mirabeau had once remarked that the primary industry of Prussia was war, and the same could be said of New France. In this perspective "it likely would be found that the military establishment runs the fur trade a close second in the economic mainstay of the colony." But, Eccles continues, it was not only the economy that was affected by this establishment. The whole fabric of Canadian society – of Canadian culture, as it were – was imbued with the military, or police, ethos (1987, 110).

It is from the perspective of a social fabric saturated with a military ethos that one has to consider the police powers of New France's intendant. The intendant was the most important official, responsible for civil administration, justice, finances, and development of the economy. As Lanctôt remarks, "il possedait le droit de faire seul les reglements de police generale" (1971, 139). Originally a military appointment – in France, intendants had been sent to the provinces to strengthen the royal power against the nobility – the intendant in the colony would, by the 1660s–1670s, end clerical authority in civil affairs. As well, military operations – paying, feeding, clothing, and billeting troops; supplying them with arms and munitions, amd with hospitals; allocating materials and labour for work on fortifications; and transporting and arranging supplies during campaigns – depended on the intendant (Eccles 1987, 112).

The first representative organs of public opinion in the colony were the "assemblées de police" – an initiative of the royal governor. According to Lanctôt, "Ce fut Frontenac qui en eut la première idée. Dans ses reglements de police de mars 1673, il etablit qu'à l'avenir, il se tiendrait, tous les six mois, une assemblée publique où tous les habitants du pays pourraient se trouver pour communiquer leurs vues sur la culture des terres, les entreprises et les commerces ... et regler le tarif des marchandises, les conclusions de l'assemblée devaient être mises devant le gouverneur qui, à sa discretion, pourrait en faire l'objet d'une ordonnance pour le bien public" (1971, 144). Frontenac's initiative seems to have met with opposition from Versailles, unwilling to tolerate anything equivalent to the estates of France.

Lanctôt, however, cites evidence of police assemblies of the citizens of Quebec as of 1677, dealing principally with issues of municipal administration (cf. Greer and Radforth 1992), and the preoccupation with the policing of "well regulated communities" can also be found in the representations of the merchants of Quebec City and of Montreal to the legislative council after 1760. Thus in a report of January 1787 to the legislative council's Committee on Commercial Affairs and Police, the merchants of Montreal (who include James McGill, Benjamin Frobisher, and Thomas McCord) reveal not only the specific interaction of commerce with police but the all-encompassing nature of this approach to governance, intertwining commerce, communication, and education. "One of the first things necessary to the facility of commerce is good roads, a subject which perhaps comes more properly under the head of Police than of Trade but in the instance at present to be spoken of, these two objects are so intimately connected as to render the consideration under either applicable to both."

Here the domain of police extends from building a jail in the district of Montreal, through prohibiting importation of slaves (but keeping "the few Negroes and Indian slaves already in servitude"), to regulating roaming cattle, improving and keeping in repair roads and bridges, regulating beggars and vagrants, providing for "helpless Foundlings," regulating weights and measures, and creating municipal charters for Quebec City and Montreal. Finally, "the surest and best means of obtaining a cheerful and dutiful obedience to the laws and Government from Subjects in general" is by establishing public schools and seminaries for the education of youth "for the purpose of enlarging the human mind, conciliating the affections of all His Majesty's subjects ... to render this a happy and flourishing Province."[3]

The civil administration of New France and later that of the "Old Province of Quebec" in the early years of British rule constituted a police state in Foucault's sense:

The sum of means which need to be put into practice in order to ensure the "public good" in a way which goes beyond the maintenance of peace and good order is, in general terms, that which in Germany and France is called the "police" ... Understood in this way, the police extend their domain beyond that of surveillance and the maintenance of order. They look to the abundance of population ... to the elementary necessities of life and its preservation ... to the activities of individuals ... to the movement of things and people ... It can be seen that the police force is the whole management of the social body. This term "body" should not be understood in a simply metaphorical way, for it deals with a complex and multiple materiality ... The police force, as an institutional grouping and as a modality of intervention, takes charge of the physical element of the social body. Quoted in Armstrong 1992, 194

If one keeps in mind Eccles's point about the lasting significance of the military deviation of Canadian economic development towards security ends (economist Hugh Aitken's "defensive expansionism"), one can begin to appreciate Westley Wark's characterization of Canada as "a national *insecurity* state" (Wark 1992, 286).

INNIS, CHURCH, AND STATE:
THE EXTENT OF THE SYMBOLIC ORDER

Let us look in greater detail at some of Innis's specific points. First, English-Canadian historians have tended to emphasize and be impressed by the direct, unbroken influence of French absolutism on the institutional development of the colony more than have their Quebec counterparts, who are more sensitive to the responses of the local environment (Dumont 1993). Innis is categorical: "State and Church under an absolute monarchy in France was State and Church under an absolute monarchy in New France." Innis sees religion in Canada, whether Catholic or Protestant, as "Erastian" and is therefore "largely concerned with the development of organization" (1956a, 384). For Eccles, in contrast, Erastianism begins "to creep in," but only after the French crown takes over administration of the colony in 1663 (1987, 29). Both scholars characterize relations of state to church in Canada as Erastian, though Eccles views that relationship as historically specific and incremental, whereas Innis sees it as ahistorical and generalized (which is perhaps why he bizarrely refers to the church in New France as "Gallican"). Hastings, in his 1912 encyclopedia article on "Erastianism," comments on the term's "notorious fluidity" and "the contradictory judgments of historians and political philosophers" in "estimating the quantity or the quality of the Erastianism that has actuated the great makers of Church history" (1912, 359).

We may follow Figgis's (1900) "simpler definition of Erastianism as the theory that religion is the creature of the State," though the term originated in the disruption in the established church of Scotland in 1843. Thomas Erastus wrote aiming "to prevent the evangelical churches becoming what one of them claimed to be in Scotland and actually became in Geneva, a *societas perfecta*, with all its means of jurisdiction, complete and independent" (in Hastings 1912, 355). Quebec's Catholic church would in 1875 also define itself as "a *societas perfecta*," as an original society, distinct and independent of civil society, to which it is superior "par son origine, par son étendue et par sa fin," as a result of which "l'État est dans l'Église et non pas l'Église dans l'État" (Dumont 1993, 225), Innis's characterization of Canada as Erastian is perhaps of limited use, for church–state relations have not been fixed and immutable throughout Canadian history but have been fluid, changeable, and negotiated.

Writing on church–state relations in the seventeenth century, Guy Rocher distinguishes two periods. Prior to 1660 came the phase of the "comptoir," a form of social organization established in a new land for purposes of commercial enterprise, in which the church was "primarily a missionary church" (1957, 271). From 1660 to the end of the French regime – the period of the colony – the Church was increasingly subordinated to the Gallicanism of a civil administration overwhelmed by Versailles. However, it does not follow that the later "servitude" (G. Lanctôt) of the church made it Gallican, as Innis would have it. If the civil administration adopted Gallican principles in respect of the church, "the clergy of New France ... remained outside the gallican movement of thought which characterized the French clergy ... under Louis XIV" (Rocher 1957, 282).

Rocher finds four types of Gallicanism in France (that of the bishops under Bossuet, a theological form, and royal and parliamentary variants). But France's Gallican Declaration "was never signed by the bishops in New France, and was never made official in the colony" (282). In Rocher's terms, the church in New France was never Gallican but remained "devoutist" – embodying a mixture of mysticism and action, an asceticism of life and a moral rigor; anti-intellectual; ultramontane and greatly concerned with orthodoxy (85–6). It is precisely this devoutism that Innis claims is a result of the Erastian character of religion: organizational development marked by a repressive symbolic culture of ecclesiastism.

The religious project of the French Church in the New World was, as Dumont has recently argued, profoundly utopian: the establishment of an autonomous theocracy, separate from the surrounding society, modelled on the recreation of the apostolic church around the ideals of poverty, community, and mission (Dumont 1993, 40–6). Delâge (1991) sees the deployment of the religious apparatus as a crucial component of the entire French strategy of colonization: as the ideological mechanism by which the French empire will compensate for its economic backwardness vis-à-vis Holland and England. For Delâge, the archaic production structures of a still predominantly feudal French economy join the missionary and the merchant in a symbiosis of mutual need. The survival of the missions depends on that of the fur trade (1991, 129), just as the later survival and growth of church organization always depended on the annuities and gratuities of the royal budget. Dumont sees an irreconcilable conflict between evangelization and commerce, which he argues will never be reconciled (1993, 41).

The theocratic utopia was short-lived – shattered after 1663 by the rise of the state and the fur trade (Delage 1991, 334) – but produced a compensatory myth of glorious collective origins and the promise of a radiant future that informed later Québécois historiography. As Dumont puts it, "les utopies présentes à l'origine ont retrouvé plus tard le statut de mythe" (1993, 57). Most significant, "Bien avant que survint la Conquete anglaise de la Nouvelle France, cette société a subi un traumatisme de l'enfance qui devra faire appel dans l'avenir au travail compensatoire de l'imaginaire" (57).

As Rocher suggests, the debate between church and state was part of a larger conflict over symbols of authority, from rules of precedence to economic policy. After the complacent period of the *comptoir*, post-1660 Quebec is marked by a number of such symbolic conflicts. "They resulted from a larger system of symbols which discriminate between [social] functions at different levels" (1957, 314). What was at stake was a struggle over symbolic control that presages the emergence of civil society as a plurality of social subsystems. If by the end of the French regime the church had indeed been reduced to "servitude" (in Lanctôt's image), or to "an inferior and dependent position" (in Rocher's terms, 349), it would under British rule rapidly regain "une surprenante liberté, qui devient de plus en plus grande et finit même par acceder à une indépendence totale" (Lanctôt 1942, 5). Parkman was not entirely wrong in his famous conclusion to *The Old Regime*: "A happier calamity never befell a people than the conquest of Canada by the British arms" (1888, 401).

INNIS, CIVIL SOCIETY, AND PUBLIC EXPRESSION

What then is left of Innis's argument? Not only was the church in Quebec not Gallican, but Innis's postulation of an essential Erastian-ism needs qualification. Furthermore, if his initial premises are dubious, what happens to the rest of the equation – the relationship between governmental activity and the development of transportation/communication networks, and the place of Quebec and the English-speaking provinces in Confederation? But perhaps what Innis is saying here amounts to this: it is not the specific details that matter as much as it is grasping the general tendency, which is one of duration. And the general tendency here is *always* Erastian, always one of political and organizational domination for control of communication – but in the *police* sense of the term. It does not really matter whether one is talking about state or church, for both act in the same manner, as totalitarian institutions that have no sense of their limitations, that interfere thoughtlessly in people's lives through the fanatical manipulation of both dogma and data. Institutions of social action (whether of state, of church, or of education) have become means of social surveillance and the enforcement of conformity. They have lost their interest in ideas, in philosophy, in long periods of intense training and the development of character. And one could sustain this line of argument by further reference to the texts of this period; for example, Innis's wondering "whether ecclesiastical Christianity has not tended to suppress the Greek point of view ... and to overemphasize the Hebrew point of view" (1956a, 390). But let me instead refer only briefly to two passages from "The Church in Canada" (in 1956a) before putting my own suggestion as to what Innis was really talking about.

The first and well-known passage is the one where Innis writes of the "constant surveillance" to which the Department of Political Economy at the University of Toronto was subjected, as a result of which "I am largely compelled to avoid making speeches in public and to resort to the careful preparation of material to be made available in print. In most cases this involves writing in such guarded fashion that no one can understand what is written or using quotations from the writings of authors who stand in great repute" (1956a, 387). He provides a specific instance of this discursive strategy on the same page, in the section entitled "Church Weaknesses," where he states that the church has not been sufficiently philosophical and follows this with two quotations, both from his beloved Mark Pattison. The first reads: "This absence of a professional public, and not the restraints of our formulairies, seem to me the true reason why a real theology cannot exist in England. Every clerical writer feels himself bound to decide every question of criticism or interpretation in favour of the orthodox view. It is demanded of him by public opinion that he shall be an advocate and not a critic. Science or knowledge cannot exist under such a system; it requires for its growth the air of free discussion and contradiction" (cited in 1956a, 388). Innis is drawing our attention here to the limited existence of civil society itself, as the locus of a symbolic or rhetorical culture not dependent on the institutions of social action.

Innis's is indeed a conception of civil society. In its contemporary (and possibly ideal-typical) form, the recent return of the concept in political theory means by "civil society"

a normative model of a societal realm different from the state and the economy and having the following components: 1) *Plurality*: families, informal groups, and voluntary associations whose plurality and autonomy allow for a variety of forms of life; 2) *Publicity*: institutions of culture and communication; 3) *Privacy*: a domain of independent self-development and moral choice; and 4) *Legality*: structures of general laws and basic rights need to demarcate plurality, privacy, and publicity from at least the state and, tendentially, the economy. Together, these structures secure the institutional existence of a modern differentiated civil society. Arato and Cohen 1992, 346

To the notion of publicity one would want to add Thomas B. Farrell's observation: "Rhetoric is the primary practical instrumentality for generating and sustaining the critical publicity which keeps the promise of a public sphere alive" (1993, 199).

If we can see in Canadian state formation and institutional development significant *survivals* from the early modern absolutist or police state, what we are left with is an insufficiently differentiated society, whose dominant institutions substitute themselves for the whole – as Foucault put it: "The police force takes charge of the physical element of the social body" – in which the demarcation of that social body into separate spheres (polity, economy, and culture) remains arrested. The forms of subjectivity represented by art and literature – by a rhetorical culture – are inherently and always problematic, as in the questions "Why Canadian literature/film, etc.?" and "Why waste taxpayers' money on artworks?" And the forms of public expression are not guaranteed autonomy but remain under scrutiny of the institutions of social orthodoxy and police.

THE LIMITS OF POLICE THEORY

Classical police practice foundered in the course of the transition to an international, capitalist market economy, as the realm of the economic achieved greater differentiation in the late eighteenth century and the study of national wealth increasingly demarcated civil society from the state. As a result, the study of economic processes became the study of the self-regulation of civil society (A. Smith 1986). The cataclysmic enormity of the transition to a market economy hardly needs restating (Polanyi 1944; Marx 1967; Taussig 1981). But the scale of economic transformation need not have inhibited the development of civil society and its differentiated institutional and cultural forms; quite the contrary. For the police state, however, negotiating such transformations is more difficult: the technologies of power have created profound dependencies.

Since the early 1970s Canada has seen an inversion of the logic of state rationality, away from internal, prescriptive policy to external, more legalistic forms of interstate rationality. For a country with Canada's backward linkages (a statist culture, small domestic market, undercapitalization of a cultural infrastructure dependent on subsidy – in short, a weak civil society), such transitions are extremely painful. If some academic analysts agree that globalization of markets necessitates rethinking traditional interventions of the state in the marketplace of goods or of ideas, one of these dimensions would have to be that of the relation of the state to civil society (Raboy et al. 1994). But an account of this kind would first entail, as John Keane (1988) has argued, rethinking the concept of civil society as an alternative venue for participation in the public sphere not mediated either by the state or by the market. At the very least, this new approach would require a better comparative historical understanding of the emergence of civil society.

If all industrialized societies have experienced complex tensions between the spheres of economy and culture in the definition of the symbolic order, Canada offers particular articulations of these tensions. Ostry claimed that "the cultural issue in Canada is more complex and requires more attention as a continuing political problem than is the case in other countries" (1978, 27). I have attempted above, through Innis, to provide a possibly more pertinent perspective, because the Canadian police state blocks the emergence of civil society. One might look again at Canadian discourses as experimental forms of "currency," as nodes of sociability, aimed at establishment of a civil economy of symbolic exchange. Such an approach would better explain the shifting grammars that emerged within the symbolic order during the transition to commodity exchange. One might just begin with the recognition that much of the discourse of Canadian cultural development has taken the form of what Innis called "panic literature rather than exhaustive studies of the field as a whole" (1956a, 89). But it is precisely those more thorough studies that are required. And until these are produced, or their skeletons unearthed from the archives of the state, we cannot even begin to say, as Innis could: "I am sufficiently humble in the face of the extreme complexity of my subject to know ... that I am not competent to understand the problem much less to propose solutions" (78).

NOTES

1   Originally published in *The Time of Healing*, twenty-second annual report of the Board of Evangelism and Social Service (Toronto, 1947), 47–54.
2   Originally published in *Proceedings of the American Philosophical Society* 87 (1944), 323–41.
3   National Archives, Ottawa, RG 1, E1, vol. 9, Quebec Legislative Council, E, Part II, 194–230.

4 Innis 'in' Chicago:
Hope as the Sire of Discovery

JAMES W. CAREY

The development of communications is rapidly transforming the world from small undifferentiated, symmetrical units of spatial distribution into the highly centralized and specialized axiated pattern ... The world is fast becoming a closed region organized on the axiated pattern, in which centers and routes are gaining precedence over boundaries and political areas ... Routes rather than rims are becoming the subject of stressed attention ... The expansion of Western civilization is a result of the development of transportation and communication.

— R.D. McKenzie 1927

When Marshall McLuhan described Harold Innis as the preeminent descendant of Robert Park and the Chicago school of urban sociology, he clearly got it wrong (McLuhan 1964a, xvi). As I have argued elsewhere (Carey 1989), such a designation diminished Innis's achievement; he was much too original a scholar to be anyone's direct descendant. Still, none of us writes in a vacuum, and, as Whitehead remarked, everything of importance has been said before by someone who did not invent it. So where do we situate Innis? As the quotation from R.D. McKenzie makes apparent, Innis-like statements can be found throughout the work of Chicago scholars, and the more I have pondered his formidable texts, the more I have become convinced – but discovery is the child of hope – that his experience of Chicago, at a particular moment in the intellectual and economic history of the city, can help us decipher and interpret the meaning and import of his work.

That is essentially the argument I want to make: not that Innis was a member or descendant of the Chicago school but that Park and John Dewey and their cohort and students provide the most illuminating and useful framework for an exegesis of Innis's work, at least for those of us working in the United States.[1] After a brief introduction, I pursue this thesis through some history of Chicago, an outline of its urban sociology, a characterization of how Innis grounded that sociology more firmly in the geography and economics of the continent, and an examination of his concept of monopolies of knowledge.

INTRODUCTION

Eric Havelock (1981, 254) described Harold Innis's premature death as a "minor disaster in the long history of the human understanding." Innis's death was a catastrophe for the politics and scholarship of North America. His immense moral presence was lost at a time when it could have provided a desperately needed corrective to the dangerous excesses of the Cold War. Furthermore, his passing cut short and endlessly delayed the development of our understanding of communications in relation to urbanization, the contemporary economy, and the modern state. Following his death, the study of communications had a premature suicide, at least in the United States, cut off from the broadly historical and interpretive social sciences and absorbed into a narrow and confining psychologism.

But what was the natural trajectory of his scholarship? He was headed somewhere with his analysis of communication, but scholars have never been able to agree on the precise direction and destination. Can we agree, however, that his work was self-consciously etched deep into the geography and history of North America? That he was a scholar of place, despite his incessant wandering through ancient empires and foreign kingdoms? That he was a certain kind of liberal, though hardly of the utilitarian sort, one in tune with the tradition of civic republicanism? If so, the attempts to assimilate him to the more hostile vocabularies of European social theory, first Marxism and more recently Foucault's analysis of power and poststructuralist literary theory – positions wildly out of touch with the hard surfaces of North American life, mute on central questions of geography and economics – seem at best unfortunate.

I realize that these are large and tendentious assumptions and they can hardly be substantiated in one essay. Moreover, establishing their believability is compromised by the fragile and fragmentary nature of his work on communications, which was written against time, in his last years, when declining health, political urgency, and administrative overload accentuated the normally elliptical character of his writing. His principal teacher at the University of Chicago, and one of the great economists of the interwar years, Frank Knight, noted of Innis that "he always wrote more than he knew. But he always caught up."[2] Not always. He may have caught up in economics, but his final illness prevented the natural catching up in communications, and we are left to follow out the lines of his inquiries while struggling through the enormous obscurity, absences, silences, and ellipses of his final writings.

But let us begin with what is beyond dispute. Harold Innis was born in 1894, a year after the historian Frederick Jackson Turner announced the closing of the frontier in a landmark paper delivered at the Chicago Columbian Exposition (Turner 1920). In an essay taking stock of Thorstein Veblen, Innis savaged the frontier hypothesis as notably wrong-headed. The year Innis died, 1952, the first pocket-sized Sony transistor radio was produced, video tape invented, and U.S. federal policy creating a national television system became official. In his lifetime, we moved from an urban, international, newspaper culture to a suburban, televisual, and progressively global society. A fully developed worldwide communications system came into existence, national in organization but international in reach. However much the historian, he had something of the presentist in him: he sought to understand his own country in his own time, to connect, in C. Wright Mills's happy phrase, biography to history (Mills 1958).

Innis came to intellectual maturity in the years following the First World War in Chicago, the most representatively American city of the era.[3] His time in the city coincided with the development of a distinctive Chicago school of sociology, which proposed an ecological framework based on the analysis of communication as the key to urban industrial life. This project was not solely an academic one, for the same intellectual impulses were found in many institutions of the city, the most famous of which were Jane Addams's Hull House and the architectural offices of Lewis Sullivan (Duncan 1965). While Innis's time in the city was not great, though long enough to wed a fellow student, Mary Quayle of Evanston, Illinois, and finish his degree, he absorbed the fundamentally ecological outlook of Chicago's intellectual culture.

By his nature unromantic, he abjured the frequently sentimental impulse of Chicago culture, its tendency to lurch into the natural history of Lamarckian evolutionary theory. The union of this intellectual culture with Innis's relentlessly empirical attention to economics and geography led him from the outset to see the complex metropole–hinterland relations engraved into this ecology. He understood eventu-

ally that routes of trade were more than corridors of capital and commodities but also routes of culture. His historical archaeology of such
routes did not lead him, as was fashionable, particularly during the
1930s, to cast his analysis in the internationalized vocabulary of the
times, the use of which would certainly have brought him greater fame.
Rather he stayed close to the common sense knowledge of the oral tradition within which he was raised, which hovered close to the land and
was bonded to the temporal order of the seasons. He stayed close to
the hard surfaces and local knowledge of North American life and its
democratic traditions, which were the product less of theory than of
the concrete experience of living.

If this description has merit, I think it appropriate to bind Innis, generously I hope, to my own purposes and to place him in conversation
with other U.S. scholars, historic and contemporary, who share something of this outlook, such as John Dewey, Clifford Geertz, R.D.
McKenzie, Robert Park, Richard Rorty, and Michael Walzer. This is
not an easy task, and I can merely make a beginning here. W.H. Auden
wrote an essay that Stuart Adam called to my attention in which he
describes a poem as a contraption with a person hidden inside. Innis's
prose is also a contraption – an infernal quotation machine of indirect
speech – with its author elusively hidden within it. His work is both
formal and chaotic, alternately disclosing and disguising the argument
he seeks to register. While this characteristic gives him the quality that
Charles Cooley (Cooley 1927) advised us to seek in a conversational
partner – someone constantly stimulating and never more so than
when we disagree with him – it makes interpretation at once difficult
and dangerous.

THE CHICAGO SCHOOL

When Innis arrived in Chicago to begin his doctoral studies in economics in the summer of 1918, a few months before the end of the
First World War, the city was at the end of a long cycle of growth that
had begun with the great fire of 1871. The fire burned away not only
the city's buildings but much of the crust of its beginnings as an outpost
of the fur trade. News of the fire's devastation radiated out over the
telegraph and rail lines that invisibly connected the city to a wider
national and international community. The conflagration publicized
the community as only a natural disaster can, and to the surprise of
Chicagoans offers of aid and expressions of sympathy radiated back
over the same lines.
    Chicagoans realized for the first time that they were living in a

network, not just a city. Twenty years later a more menacing truth of the telegraph and rail system hit home when the depression of 1893 radiated along the same lines, revealing that Chicago had become silently integrated into a national and international system of markets that rose and fell to the rhythm of distant, invisible, and unknowable forces. Time and space had been eclipsed, fulfilling the dream of nineteenth century romantics, adventurers, and imperialists – often the same people – but the conquest had calamitous as well as romantic consequences.

The city's new, invisible relations may have been accepted, but they were hardly understood in either intellectual or common sense terms. The "booster" talk, often taken as so much afflatus, contained a truth, however exaggerated and overweening, when it wrapped the city in metaphors of empire: the new Paris or Rome or Athens of the prairie. Chicago was concretely understood, however, through the romantic metaphors of the landscape which were commonplaces of the time. Raymond Williams (1973) has taught us to see the dichotomy of the country and city as an inheritance from the nineteenth-century romantics, who in turn learned it from the pastoral poets stretching back to Virgil. This tradition, particularly in its American version, always has been ambivalent about its subject, sometimes emphasizing the pastoral nature of the landscape framed as a place without human intervention in order to contrast it with the fallen city – the site of human labour, a disordered presence within an otherwise idyllic arcadia. Just as often the terms are reversed, and the landscape is identified with the small town, the suffocating babbitry of an enclosing bourgeois civilization, and contrasted with the freedom, sophistication, energy, dynamism, and opportunity of an open urban civilization. But however rendered, these images disconnect the city and the country; they place the city here and the country there, representing them as alternative rather than complementary and interdependent human terrains.

Following the fire of 1871, Chicago began an ambitious project of reconstruction that was at once physical and cultural. The city was physically raised to hold back the waters of the Great Lakes. (We were reminded of this a few years back when the underground tunnels gave way to the waters, revealing a submerged Venice.) The entire city was also pivoted ninety degrees, diverted from a north–south pattern, a rim clinging to the lakefront that was a legacy of its past as a trading outpost. It was shifted to an east–west orientation, an axiated form of organization, with new routes of movement running outward in long rail lines to the basins that the city drained of staples for purposes of national and international trade. Along its new axes, the middle classes that arose to develop the trading empire moved their residences west also, into new suburbs; they became, in Richard Sennett's nice phrase, "families against the city" (Sennett 1970), as a transformed country-side became adjacent but disconnected small towns. The city went through a zoning mania, a riot of segregation, as a desire for spatial purity overtook the civic imagination.

The winds of the social change that blew across the American land-scape around the turn of the twentieth century found particular reso-nance in Chicago, where they were less impeded by conservative resis-tance, by the drag of a long-established class and class-based institutions. Black migration was unleavened by a pre-Emancipation Black bourgeoisie. In the city, labour was less constrained by tradition, and violence and conflict reached new intensity in the Haymarket riots and the Pullman strike. Chicago was a centre of the social movements that swept the country: progressivism, populism, middle-class profes-sionalism, the civic-reform and the better-government movements, and women's suffrage. New movements in art and architecture, literature and music developed with a more indigenous feel, as they were dis-connected from or in open hostility to European centres of culture (Duncan 1965).

This depiction hardly does justice to the city, of course, and is intended merely to suggest allusively that Chicago presented a chal-lenge to the mind as well as to the body, to the imagination as much as to the physical energy required for construction and reconstruc-tion. Here was the first major American city that developed outside the immediate shadow of New York, but whose growth depended on the corridor of trade that tied it to the New York port and to New York's centres of finance and capital, which underwrote that trade. The city lacked an immediate, unmediated connection to Europe but it was invisibly connected to the other side of the world. It was gen-erating new or radically modified patterns of social relations, aes-thetic forms, and linguistic styles, and therefore we should not be sur-prised that new forms of journalism and intellectual culture arose there to try to take account, however indirectly, of this new civiliza-tion on the prairie.[4]

Much of that culture arose, not so incidentally, in the university where Innis completed his education, the University of Chicago. The institution was almost as new as the new city itself; it arose within urban, commercial life and was the last founded of America's major private universities. In 1893, fittingly enough the year of the Columbian Exposition, the new campus arose adjacent to the fair, the midway of one becoming the southern boundary of the other. It was the product of new oil money laundered through an old institution –

Standard Oil meets the Baptist church – and achieved greatness in a typically American way: it bought it. William Rainey Harper, its first president, scoured the country for eminent teachers and lured them not only with the promise of a new Delphi but with salaries that doubled what was being paid elsewhere. Unlike the older universities of the east coast – increasingly estranged presences in an urban environment, disdainful of the ethnic and commercial character of urban life – Chicago was from the outset an integral institution of the city, taking on the challenge of its problems and crafting an intellect of place. John Dewey was among the founding members of the faculty, where a new American sociology, distinctly different from Old World patterns of social theory, grew in relation to the new American philosophy of pragmatism.

The hallmark of Chicago social thought was its emphasis on communication. While its practitioners were not indifferent to or unaware of what Innis would later call the "spatial bias" of modern communications, they initially exploited another meaning of the term. They sought to conceive communications in a way that pragmatically advanced their interests in American democracy, which they recognized was under threat from the vast concentrations of corporate power that fuelled the growth of the city and from the disorder engulfing the city at the high tide of immigration and social change. As the Chicago sociologists were, like Innis himself, largely products of small-town, pre-industrial, though not pre-commercial, North American settlements (Otterville, Ontario, will do as well as Burlington, Vermont, or Red Wing, Minnesota, as an image), they reached into that experience for the terms and ideas with which to grasp and reform the urban life that challenged their understanding as adults.

Their comprehension of communication is best captured through an off-hand remark by the late psychologist Carl Hovland. He observed that in the United States communication is a substitute for tradition.[5] In the absence of a shared inherited culture, communication had to accomplish the tasks of social creation and integration that were elsewhere the more automatic by-products of tradition. There was no shared traditional culture available to people who were forming new communities and institutions on the frontier or in the western regions, a formation that typically preceded rather than followed the westward migration of federal agents. In the absence of a shared sentiment, these communities could be organized and held together only through discussion, debate, negotiation – in a word, communication. Social order was neither inherited nor unconsciously achieved but actually hammered out as diverse people assembled to create a common culture and to embody culture in actual social institutions. This attitude looked towards the future, not the past, as the source of social cohesion: the meaning of things, the character of social relations, and the structure of institutions had to be actively created rather than merely drawn out of existing stocks of knowledge and culture.

Communication, at least in the nineteenth-century United States, was an active process of community creation and maintenance. Small towns were not places for isolated individuals. Freedom was not a mere negative product of removing restraints or leaving people alone. Freedom required, first of all, the institutions – government, courts, schools, churches, public houses – of civic and civil life. It required as well, more subtle cultural creations: modes of conduct, styles of speaking, forms of address, instruments of social control and ostracism.

It is this unromantic view of the sheer necessities of social life that led to Dewey's oft-quoted line that "society exists not only by transmission, by communication, but it may be fairly said to exist in transmission, in communication" (Dewey 1916, 5). Communication, in Dewey's sense, referred to the activity of creation and imagination, not merely transmission and control. He grasped as the fundamental American experience the creation of communities, institutions, and cultural forms among people who were as new to each other as to the land they sought to inhabit. To this foundational activity they gave the name "communications" and installed it as the distinctive and unique part of the achievement.

The first site of this process was on the frontier, where strangers came together and had to negotiate a world out of diverse and conflicting cultural resources. They had to create actual physical communities: build towns and the institutions of local life. This project occupied a full century as the nation expanded west and south. It was carried out by groups of strangers who did not necessarily share a common background, experience, or tradition; they constituted and inhabited little worlds made more or less autogenetically. By making a revolutionary break they oriented themselves to the future, not to the past, to posterity, not to tradition, and this made them unusually reliant on explicit processes and procedures of debate, discussion, negotiation – mutual sense-making in radically undefined situations.

It is this sense of communication – of community building, of communion – that gives the word a certain weight in American culture. This creative aspect of culture has an antinomian counterpart. The ceaseless creation of communities out of need, desire, and necessity was accompanied by a ceaseless attempt to escape from the authority of what had been created. Americans are for ever building a "city on a hill" and then promptly planning to get out of town to avoid the

authority and constraint of their creations. Both the creation and the
escape – the organization and disorganization, to use the terms of
Chicago sociology – involve intense episodes in sense-making, in the
formation and reformation of human identity.[6]

The network of communities painfully created in the nineteenth
century was dismantled during the turn to the twentieth as the frontier closed and the cities that now dominated the culture burgeoned
through multiple forms of immigration. A second phase of community creation followed along the ecological frontier of urban life. This
second wave, which involved the simultaneous destruction and transformation of older patterns of living and settlement, was also a
radical and creative cultural achievement. The urban milieu, the
centre of a social drama in which a national society revealed itself,
was the scene of parallel change: the creation of a multitude of micro-
urban worlds fuelled by three forms of immigration. The first was the
emptying out of rural areas, as migration from the farm and small
town accelerated. The second was the Black diaspora from the rural
south. The third was the international migrations, which largely had
the city as their terminus and filled these spaces with new and
unusual faces.

The city was the site of conflict and accommodation as these new
groups struggled with one another to occupy urban turf. New forms of
racial, ethnic, religious, and class communities were created in the
cities simultaneous with attempts to give institutional and cultural
shape to these new urban containers. The creation of ethnic communities was the crucial event of this phase, and W.I. Thomas and Florian
Znaniecki's *The Polish Peasant in Europe and America* (1984) was the
single most important study of the phenomenon.

Ethnic communities were not merely transplants of intact cultures
from the Old World to the New. In fact, ethnic groups were formed in
the diaspora. The Irish, Italians, Jews, and Poles, even African Americans, were in significant ways creatures of the New World of the American city. Distinct people identified with different regions, speaking different dialects or languages, were formed, partly by self-identification
and partly by social imposition, into self-conscious groups, aware of or
made to accept a common heritage and fate. Again, these groups
created new institutions of neighbourhood life – newspapers, entertainment centres, churches, hospitals, orphanages, poor houses, and
family and burial societies, along with distinctive patterns of social
interaction, ethnic and social types, new forms of language, and particular types and styles of popular art.

The Chicago sociology of symbolic interactionism provided the conceptual tools to understand and analyse the new world of the city or,

better, the many worlds of the city. Chicago sociologists examined the city, census tract by census tract, and showed how the whole adhered through the interaction of its parts. Symbolic interactionism was ideally adapted to a fluid social structure undergoing radical change as new groups struggled to carve out ecological niches within the city and to transform the physical boundaries dividing its sectors and groups into symbolic forms that identified both the self and the other. It was a sociology particularly adapted to conditions of change and contingency.

One recognizes here the genesis of an expressive and interpretive theory of culture. To use a contemporary phrase of Stanley Cavell, culture and communication are a process of "wording the world together." Common words had to be found to create and express a common world. And, in the absence of a common means of communication, there cannot be a common world. Theory and action are indissolubly linked in community creation.

The views of the Chicago School were backed by the new biology and natural history, which allowed them to see community creation not as an aberration, outside history, but as an adaptation within natural history to a concrete set of circumstances, an adaptation consonant with the goal of bending inherited notions of democracy to new circumstances. Democracy they conceived not as some temporary aberration within that history but as part of the evolution of intelligence itself. That intelligence was best represented by science, not understood as some arcane and privileged method, but as the creation of an institutional structure, a form of communication, in which intelligence could best function to achieve its purposes: the free adaptation to and control of circumstance. In short, they emphasized that side of communication involving creation and preservation of culture and social institutions rather than the mere transmission of intelligence. They gave this understanding a peculiarly democratic and scientific twist, however, for it was understood as a process involving the widening of shared experience and the growth of systematic intelligence.

Recognition of this continuous and ceaseless process of community creation and recreation gave rise to a peculiarly Americanized version of the theory of mass society. Its European counterpart charted a transit from *Gemeinschaft* to *Gesellschaft*, from organic to mechanical solidarity, from feudalism to capitalism. U.S. history and experience lacked one pole of this contrast. The product of revolutionary circumstances on a "virgin continent," and lacking a feudal tradition, it was never a *Gemeinschaft* society, never one of status or mechanical solidarity. Without a point of origin in traditional society, it could not have a destination in a mass society.

Instead, the Chicago School suggested that societies go through recurring, even ceaseless cycles of social organization, disorganization, and then social reorganization, in which existing patterns of social interaction and relations, social institutions and forms of life, even forms of individual identity, are broken down and dispersed. What follows is a moment of mass society, when social disorganization reigns, when identities and relations are in flux and change. However, this phase itself is never permanent, for the social system is reorganized and restructured. New identities emerge, and new patterns of social relations, usually quite surprising and unpredictable, are forged.

It was in this context that symbolic interactionism emerged as a social psychology of urban life, a means of charting the complex inter-actions of these urban worlds. The new communications technologies of the 1890s were one of the forces creating social disorganization: a moment when established routines, institutions, and identities ceased to offer enough structure for the conduct of social and psychological life. Disorganization was a temporary state, however. Eventually new identities, new routines, and new institutions would establish them-selves and take on the illusory permanence and stability of those recently displaced.

The social may have gone opaque at the moment and resisted repre-sentation, but the very opaqueness of the society inspired the intellec-tual and cultural work necessary to map and configure a new urban world. Out of it came the structures of ethnic, racial, occupational, and class groups, the new "progressive" institutions of the economy and polity, and the new routines of love, marriage, and child-raising that were the predominant features of the "modern." The ethnic and other groups were creations of a process of symbolic interaction, and to understand these formations required a sociology of border crossings, of migration across the semi-permeable membranes of social life that constituted the disorderly fronts of urban living.

The first major burst of energy in urban sociology occurred in the 1920s, with Robert Park and Ernest W. Burgess. In crafting an ecolog-ical framework for viewing urban life, they drew on, among others, Herbert Spencer, in order to understand competitive relations among human groups. Competition, they argued, "invariably tends to create an impersonal social order in which each individual being free to pursue his own profit ... invariably contributes ... to the common welfare" (Park and Burgess 1924, 507). "Together with geographers, these urban sociologists viewed this market competition as resulting in unplanned regularities in urban land use patterns and thus as genera-tive of a social map of concentric zones moving out in waves from a central business district. These zones were considered to be naturally segregated areas of location for a diverse human population" (Feagin 1989, 74). Moreover, the urban sociologist felt that these segregated zones ensured a common welfare or generalized public interest.

However, in the decades following Park and Burgess, mainstream ecologists abandoned the interest in the public welfare, substituting for it a resurrected faith in the "invisible hand." Ecologists were then free to concentrate on broad demographic trends (for example, the statistical analysis of metropolitan deconcentration) rather than on the mapping and analysis of urban zones and the interactive processes that integrated or segregated them. For mainstream ecologists, competition, conflict, and accommodation still take place within a "framework of rules approximately the same as those advocated by Herbert Spencer – with room for social evolution, enterprise, and the survival of those most fit to survive" (Scott Green, quoted in Feagin 1989, 75).

Eventually the central insights of Chicago sociology were abandoned, giving way to an uncritical acceptance of a self-regulating market system, a pervasive technological determinism, a playing down of inequality, and a structuralist approach, de-emphasizing human actors and classes of actors. The central problem of inquiry became the decultured adaptation of a population to a changing environment and a merely mechanical interest in social equilibrium. Mainstream ecologists frequently viewed the functional complexity of cities as determined by transportation and communication technologies. They explained changes in urban form by some type of technological transformation, particularly shifts in rail and automotive transport systems. They largely ignore the political economic history and decision-making context that result in the dominance of one type of transport over another, one mode of communication or social interaction over another.

Mainstream analysts tend to see city patterns as inevitable, even as efficient and neutral. Park and Burgess, however, went beyond the strict laissez-faire view of later ecologists to argue that the growth of population, communication, and organizations in cities had so increased mutual interdependence that some state intervention was necessary. Park and Burgess had a Darwinist view of the urban scene, but a reform variant, which accepted the necessity of an independent state adjudicating conflict and protecting essential values. The reason for this emphasis is that Park and Burgess argued that in periods of rapid population growth competition is converted into conflict and the expansion of judicial and other governmental institutions is necessary to mediate this conflict. In short, later work in urban ecology transformed the outlook of the symbolic interactionists into something closer to the neoclassical individualism in opposition to which they actually developed their understanding of community life. This shift in turn obscured both their connection to and their continuity with Harold Innis and, even more, his distinctive additions, modifications, and transformations to the sociology of the Chicago School.

INNIS'S REFORMULATIONS

One immediately senses the fundamental revisions and additions that Innis made to both Chicago history and the Chicago School of Sociology. Indeed, my characterization above of that history and outlook would have been impossible without my reading it through Innis. It provides us with one way of describing the decisive importance of Innis's scholarship. In the first phase of his work – the staple theory and the economic history, which emphasized metropole–hinterland relations through commercial and trade activities involving commodities such as fur, cod, timber, and pulp – he not only produced an indigenous Canadian history but corrected and completed the displaced relations of country and city common to thought in Chicago and in much of Europe. In his initial concentration on but one aspect of communications – the spatial bias of long-distance transmission – he was, borrowing a lesson from his mentor Thorstein Veblen, attacking the frontier hypothesis, which undergirded Chicago thought. You could not have frontiers without backtiers. The energy of a civilization could be found not in its margins but rather at its centre.

Next, and confronting the long political crisis of the twentieth century, the second phase of Innis's work, which we identify as distinctively about communications, reached back to Dewey and the Chicago group to determine the relations among the instruments of communications necessary to the achievement of equilibrium.[7] The spatial bias of modern communication he thought of as distinctively disequilibrating, and so he turned to the conditions of social life that permitted balance, innovation, and creativity. These conditions he found, like Dewey, in the oral tradition[8] – that is, in the process of symbolic interaction through speech. The issue surrounding communication emphasized by Chicago scholars – the creation and preservation of culture and the elaboration of institutions necessary to civic republicanism – is the shadow cast across Innis's historic archaeology of the oral tradition, monopolies of knowledge, and the relation between space-binding and time-binding communications media.

Innis developed what later became a staple of Canadian historical writing – the metropolitan thesis. Despite the relatively similar settlement histories of Canada and the United States, most American historians of the west continued to follow Turner's emphasis on the region's rural aspects. Even where they focused on cities, they rarely emphasized the city–country relationship. Canadian historians, in contrast, have more or less rejected the Turnerian frontier notion and have pursued a thesis that accepts in effect the booster conception of the city but transvalues its meaning.

Metropolitanism implies the emergence of a city of outstanding size to dominate not only its surrounding countryside but other cities and their countrysides. The entire metropole–hinterland area is organized by the metropolis, through its control of communication, trade, and finance. Together they form one economic and social unit, focused on the metropole, that regulates trade with the world. Beneath the central metropolis were smaller cities, playing similar but less extensive roles, since "the metropolitan relationship is a chain, almost a feudal chain of vassalage, wherein one city may stand tributary to a bigger center and yet be the metropolis of a sizable region of its own" (Careless 1954, 17).[9] The relationship between the metropolis and the hinterland was homologously reproduced in the relations of smaller cities and institutions.

Innis, in rejecting Turner's analysis, turned his attention to the issues that concerned him most – the metropole–hinterland relation within Canadian history and, at the national level, the relation of Canada to the metropolitan nations, Britain and increasingly the United States. While Montreal might be a metropole city of a vast region beyond, Canada was a hinterland country, which furnished staples to another metropole. The staples formed then both distinctive regional cultures within Canada and a distinctive national culture as well.

This same analysis, projected southward, explained Chicago's distinctive role in American life. It shattered the complacent view of the separation of rural and urban, frontier and city, metropole and hinterland and revealed these relations as knitted together by a long-distance, spatially biased system of communication centred in New York. It showed how the United States developed via an imperial competition among cities – Boston, New York, Philadelphia, Baltimore – for dominance of the west and how the history of Chicago could be explained only by taking literally its complaining self-description as "The Second City." It grew as an outpost of New York and was decisively shaped by inter-urban competition, which created the corridor of communication and transportation joining it to New York. Chicago was the western outpost of a metropolitan economy centred on Europe and the American northeast. The streets of Chicago were the place where products of different ecosystems, different though interdependent economies, different though interdependent ways of life, came together and exchanged places.

In the United States an artificial corridor had to be built, for there were no natural ones like the St Lawrence. So it was built by rail and canal, lock and dam, national highway and country road. It was a corridor of relatively cheap transport, which appeared like a fault line across the diverse staple zones of the American west. The railway, canal, and telegraph broke radically with geography, for they made possible the straightest possible line, a geometrical route through areas with high market demand and low operating costs. They operated pretty much independent of climate, invulnerable to mud and snow, and therefore evened out the seasons, which controlled the rising and falling of economic cycles with temperature and precipitation. They straightened time by controlling time zones and substituted the regularity of mechanical time for seasonal time, merged night and day, winter and summer, wet times and dry times. When one entered a railway car or the telegraph system, one went into an environment separated from the outside world, with its own sense of time. Wherever the railway and telegraph extended, frontier became hinterland. And as people prospered in the hinterland, they became more dependent on nameless, faceless institutions: grain elevators and railways. Chicago was the critical link that bound east and west into a single system, and it grew to metropolitan status less by being central than by being peripheral.

Turner chose to see the frontier as a rural place, the very isolation of which created its special role as a cradle of a distinctively American democracy. This view is not totally wrong, but it obscured much that Innis had to rescue. Against Turner's romantic view, Innis showed how the country would not be there without the city in which to sell its crops and products; the city would not be there without a countryside to feed it. These relations had gone invisible and were scorched over by ideological work. This invisibility served finally to isolate human life from the physical and cultural ecosystems that sustained it. Innis's analysis of staples revealed the marginal nodes where adherent tangents were formed and the products of two distinct ecosystems met and were transformed.

Allan Eckert's series on the relations of the Native Americans and the European settlers devotes one volume to Chicago and intelligently entitles it *The Gateway to Empire* (1983). If the mantle of world's greatest city was to pass from London to New York, then it would be driven by western trade. New York needed an interior city that it could control and would be its gateway to the staples beyond: hardwoods from Michigan and Wisconsin, ore from the Mississippi basin, crops from the prairies. If Chicago was to be a tributary of New York, then it in turn would act as a great catch basin, drawing 700,000 square miles of western territory into its feeder system and concentrating it at its mouth. The natural landscape had to be transformed into a spatial economy. Nineteenth-century American life was in a way "a tale of two cities" – metropole New York and its Chicago hinterland. We can now see that the metropole–hinterland relation between the United States and Canada was reproduced in the U.S. system of cities, most dramatically in the relation of New York and Chicago. Western cities came into existence when eastern capital created remote colonies in landscapes that contained few people. Frontiers were thereby linked to backtiers and to an international system of cities. Chicago and New York were end points of a trunk communications system, and the principal problem of communications was to link them closer together in space and coordinate their activities in time.[10] Chicago in turn attempted to draw hinterland cities into the same relation and to stave off competition from other hinterland cities such as St Louis and Milwaukee.

The frontier may have been the outer edge of a wave, but it was more than a tidal flood of migration; it was also the extension of market relations into the ways in which humans used land and each other. The penetrative power of the price system, not the extension of democracy, was the major force in national expansion, though if one emphasizes the latter one must not demean the former. In a thinly settled country, effective markets – able to compete with the denser markets of Europe – required the extension of physical markets beyond rimmed and identifiable places. Everywhere and nowhere markets were created, bound together not by face-to-face trading relations but by the spatial bias of modern media. The relations engraved in the physical, symbolic, and media ecologies of North America by this activity lasted through the age of television and started to become unhooked only in the 1970s, with the emergence of satellite technology.

The 1890s, as was said, marked the closing of the frontier. This meant, from Innis's standpoint, that the United States had been fully enclosed in space. First of all, the expansion of the railway and telegraph had connected the major cities into a national system of transportation and communication, and then, in the late nineteenth century, the vacant spaces were "backed and filled," hooking "island communities" into a national society. This process everywhere met local resistance, but the "system was the solution," and communities everywhere were either integrated into it or circumvented by it and left to die.

The closing of the frontier represented larger closings and transformations. Space was enclosed in two senses: first, the nation was enclosed, reaching its manifest destiny as a prelude to a leap beyond its own borders in imperial expansion. Second, space was enclosed institutionally, as national networks of communication invaded the space of local institutions. That is, local institutions of politics, commerce, and culture were reconfigured as end points or nodes in national structures. Local political organizations became outposts of national parties; local business became elements in chains; local newspapers, lectures, performances, concerts, and educational institutions became stops on a national circuit. They lost their autonomy and increasingly their local identity.[11]

Time was also transformed and opened as a new frontier. Time was, first of all, standardized into a national grid, so that everyone was on the same clock of awareness. The telegraph organized and controlled time zones so that organizations and activity could be coordinated nationally. But new "times" were also opened as commercial and other forms of activity broke into the sabbath and then upward, via the electric light, into the nighttime. It began with the Sunday newspaper invading the sabbath. Eventually, nationally produced communications would occupy every space and every time: every office, home, street, city, and institution; every time, sacred and secular, seasonal and annual, daytime and nighttime. One would never be out of earshot or eyeshot of national media. This imperialism of images spread the representation of the national into all geographical times and spaces and into all cultural times and spaces as well. The system represented an imperative that every social time and space should be filled by commerce and communications. The national system, the system of the modern, was, for "advanced" nations such as the United States, formed in the 1890s, and subsequent developments in communications – motion pictures, radio, television – from this perspective were protracted and relentless mopping-up operations – perfections in what Innis would call the spatial bias of modern media.

These changes produced a crisis of representation; they raised the disorienting spectre of an unknowable society lacking the terms or vocabularies necessary to ingest these changes into consciousness. The maturing of the wire services, the growth of national magazines, the development of national retail organizations and catalogue sales, rural free delivery, national advertising and marketing, and national political parties all had the effect of eclipsing the local, of terminating the existence of self-contained island communities. Urbanization, industrialization, the maturing of industrial capitalism (with increasingly international connections), the closing of the frontier, the eclipse of agriculture as a predominant way of life and, with it, the country town as a cultural force were the events of Innis's lifetime that demanded explanation.

I have elsewhere suggested (Carey 1996) that one way of keeping the contributions of Innis and the Chicago school clear is to recognize the three distinct ecologies that were knitted into the spatial phenomena they were examining. First, in a purely physical ecology, the landscape was technologically inscribed via communication and transportation and social groups formed settlement patterns, whether in the city or in the country, by radiating over the networks. Second, there was also a symbolic ecology, as the struggle and competition among these groups – which at one level was strictly physical, the struggle for space – were transformed along a series of symbolic fronts: the naming, identification, and characterization of the groups that constituted this symbolic ecology. Indeed, the pastoral language of the country and the city, along with the derivative epithets describing the inhabitants thereof, was evidence of the formation of these fronts.

Third, a media ecology overlay both of these processes, as newspapers, magazines, and eventually radio and television stations became articulated to and disarticulated from the underlying physical and symbolic struggles. The city, for example, was at one level a purely physical world, but it contained an imaginative world of social relations as well. Each group in the city had to struggle to find and maintain an ecological niche – literally a bio-spatial home. Each group had to know, understand, compete, name, and struggle against other groups inhabiting contested physical and symbolic space. The media overlay these baser ecologies, creating yet another imaginative world of the city, one articulated to and integrated with the national community.

The communities of the city were in every case transmuted or diasporic communities. Some were formed out of the physical diaspora of migration – nationally and internationally. Others were formed by imaginative diasporas – cosmopolitans and the new professionals who lived in the imaginative worlds of the national societies of medicine and law and journalism and the new imaginative worlds of the city: the art world, the fashion world, and so on. These diasporic groups were twisted and knotted into one another within urban life – given form by the symbolic interactions of the city and the ecology of media that reported on and defined these groups to one another, fostered and intensified antagonisms among them, and sought forms of mutual accommodation.

INNIS ON MONOPOLIES OF KNOWLEDGE

I have tried to emphasize throughout this essay that the Chicago school recognized, albeit at times somewhat dimly, the interdependence created by the mechanical extensions of communications on this continent. However, it viewed these extensions in a natural history framework and therefore was not particularly attentive to the industrial, financial, and trade relations that shaped this social formation. It focused instead on another issue – how to transform the great society created by transportation and communication into the "Great Community" (Dewey's phrase). How could interdependence be transformed into mutuality?

The Chicago school placed unusual hope and reliance on the new media of communication in effecting this transformation – a crucial error, I think – and for a model of the process it brought forward images of communication formed both in the small-town United States and the urban villages of the new cities. This framework, however, led it to keep intact certain distinctions – between country and city, between speaking and printing, for example – that had to be transcended. Dewey, for example, was aware of the need for modern discourse communities to be rooted in the activity of speech and discussion, of the ways in which a healthy public life, through the newspaper and magazine, had to articulate into a vibrant community life at the local level.

But because he saw these forms as separate historical phases or separate phases of a singular social process, he did not emphasize what became central to Innis – namely, the need to maintain speech as a vital counterbalance to print, to check off the bias of one medium with the bias of another: to see the oral tradition as a source of countervailing power to the spatial bias of print. These were not continuous worlds but had to be maintained as distinct and antagonistic. Innis's view on these matters can be best illustrated through the notion of monopolies of knowledge. To carry that analysis forward, I want to borrow, paraphrase, and twist about a remarkably similar argument that one finds in the later writing of Paul Feyerabend (1978), if only to state the argument in a form more congenial to contemporary times.

In carrying through his analysis of staples, Innis stepped outside the mainstream of neoclassical economic thinking. He understood the latter as the knowledge of the metropole, knowledge developed with a particular purpose: the governance of a large-scale, integrated network. This knowledge came into necessary conflict and contradiction with the knowledge of the margin or periphery, which was developed in place rather than space. There were therefore at least two economies and two distinct forms of economic knowledge: one was a tradition forged on the ground, as it were, in direct experience and struggle with the recalcitrant realities of geography, crops, commodities, seasons, cycles, weather, in the direct encounters of survival and development. At Chicago, and earlier, he encountered something quite different, economic science, which was at best an abstraction from the knowledge of direct experience and at worst an expropriation and displacement of it. One of his inspirations, Thorstein Veblen, had abjured economic science for rather more direct and immediate observation of what we would today call the phenomenology of everyday economic life. Veblen attempted to produce an economics of place, and so would Innis, though his place would be Canada.

Innis did his dissertation in economic history, but when he returned to Toronto he took up the struggle with economic science by asking whether we can disestablish economic science in favour of a body of knowledge more particular and circumspect, grounded in the direct experience of North America. Innis's answer, I believe, was that economic science – the abstract science of the metropole, divorced from the on-the-ground experience of the hinterland – had to be removed from the life-centres of Canadian society.

Let me rephrase his argument, following Feyerabend. Canadian life has been marked by the interaction of two traditions of knowing. One is the tradition of science and reason – a global, universal, well-articulated, familiar set of intellectual practices, but thin in the sense that it describes this continent superficially. This knowledge paralleled or was part of the same impulse that led to the discovery or imagination of the continent. Just as North America had been understood in the voyages of discovery as a new geographical continent – blank, featureless, and abstract, without indigenous knowledge – so too it was available to form an entirely new continent of knowledge – the real North America of knowledge – by the long-distance application of skill and abstract study.

This new continent of knowledge encountered in Canada, as elsewhere, another tradition. It is local rather than global, particular rather than abstract - a thick, well-articulated set of practices. It arose not in generality or abstraction but on the ground in experience, in thousands on thousands of adjustments and adaptations made by Canadians (and before them Native North Americans) to the conditions of living on this continent. This second kind of knowledge – let us call it, following Clifford Geertz (1983), local knowledge – was viewed by the high science tradition as mere opinion, unsecured by any foundation – in fact not any kind of knowledge at all. Local knowledge did not come packaged in either the methods or the cosmology or formalities of real knowledge

Paul Feyerabend (1978) calls the first kind of knowledge the observer tradition, for it asks about what happens and what is going to happen, about the laws or rules that formulate happenings. The second, or participant tradition asks other questions. What shall I do? How shall I live? Shall I support this or that? Shall I simply forget about it? Let us call the first tradition a spatial-print tradition, for it is formulated with sufficient generality that it can not only move about in space but it has no particular space as its reference point. Let us call the second an oral, or time-biased tradition, because it exists in place rather than in space, has continuity of development over time, and does not travel very well.

A fruitful tension and interaction between these traditions shaped nineteenth-century life, but in the twentieth century the relationship became increasingly detached and unbalanced. The Empire of Reason took over the life-centres of society and economics. While church and state had been effectively separated, science and the state were increasingly joined at the hip, so that observer knowledge increasingly gained state legitimation.

Innis recognized that the observer tradition saw itself not as a tradition at all but as something objective, independent, in the nature of things. It came to monopolize thought and the channels and instruments of communication erected in its name, and, as it assumed that position, it increasingly tyrannized over and delegitimated the participant tradition. It did this by reinstituting the distinction between knowledge and opinion. It delegitimated the knowledge one gets from what William James called "acquaintance with" – immersion in the concrete particulars of a way of life – in order to legitimate "knowledge about," gained from books, formal study, and abstract reasoning.

If the participant tradition resisted, if it did not accept the gifts offered by the observer tradition, then certain "interpretations" were developed to describe the participant tradition: commentators emphasized the psychological meaning of the knowledge, its social functions, the existential temper of the culture, rather than its factual claims and ontological implications. Local knowledge, it was held, expressed the needs of members of society; it functioned as social glue and revealed basic structures of thought, but it did not contain knowledge. This term was reserved for observers. Because local knowledge was taken to be divorced from critical thought, observers could have it both ways: they could pose as understanding friends of the local tradition without endangering the supremacy of their own religion – formal science.

This was the situation that Innis sought to overcome with his notion of a monopoly of knowledge. He did this ethnocentrically by developing the staples theory and by insisting on the integrity and formative power of the oral tradition. And he tried to create genuine interaction between the two traditions by developing the following arguments.

First, the oral tradition – local knowledge – could flourish only if all traditions, including observer science, are seen as temporary, make-shift operations and not as intrinsic or lasting constituents of thought and action. He hoped to counter the view of economic science that saw itself not as a tradition at all but as the revelation of reason itself. However, if reason were itself a tradition, it could not be an arbiter of tradition. A free society gives all traditions equal rights, and it creates protective structures to ensure these traditions by maintaining a balance between the biases of what Innis metanomyically called "speech" and "print."

His studies led to a search for ways of strengthening local knowledge and the oral tradition, for I believe the following reason. In speech or conversation we never make the mistake that we are encountering reason or science as an abstract and disembodied force. In speech we encounter talk, the fusion of the speaker and the speech; we encounter people struggling to articulate views, to outer their inner thoughts. One never loses the speaker in the speech, the very phenomenon that print disguises and which can be recovered only archaeologically.

CONCLUSION

Let me conclude by emphasizing again the happy relation I am insin-uating between Dewey and Innis. I have formulated Innis's arguments in what is today frequently called post-philosophical terms. By doing so I want to emphasize that both Dewey and Innis shared a certain scepticism about the neurotic quest for certainty at the basis of the observer tradition. Both men direct us to the overriding issue of cul-tural policy as it attends communications. How are we to avoid monopolies of knowledge? How are we to prevent one tradition of our understanding from dominating all others? How are we to main-tain and manage the interactions between the observer and partici-pant traditions? How can we developed protected structures that do not guide and manage interaction but leave it open to a full play of creative imagination?

The tradition of symbolic interactionism that John Dewey spawned insisted that reason and practice entered history on equal terms and that a free society is one in which all traditions have equality and equal access to centres of power. A pragmatic philosophy – and I realize I have here slowly transformed Innis into a pragmatist – can flourish only if we view our knowledge not as guaranteed and foundational, but as a temporary and make-shift adaptation to the world; not as a lasting constituent of thought and action, but as things we make up as we go along. The only foundation I can find in Innis is the same singular foundation I find in Dewey: the end of scholarship is to secure the republican forms of political democracy, which alone guarantee the possibilities of scholarship. Fortunately, civic republicanism secures much more, particularly a form of communication that is an end in itself, the very name of liberty, and a means to a yet-greater end, the achievement of a genuinely common life.

NOTES

1 Actually, McLuhan is quite circumspect in pointing out the differences between Park and Innis, which makes his conclusion on descent seem unwarranted. About all that Innis and Park have in common, on McLuhan's account, is an interest in social control and an emphasis on processes of communication. On my interpretation, Innis should be situated relative to the Chicago school rather than as a member or descendant of it. I trust this clarifies, even it does not dispel, F.M. Stark's claim (1994, 131-3) that I place Innis in the Chicago school or argue that he incorporates its basic positions. I can find no evidence, for example, that Innis used or was influenced by the social psychology of communication developed by G.H. Mead; but see Innis 1980, 128, 181.

2 The remark was reported to me indirectly by a retired economist from Columbia University, Donald Dewey, who had also been a student of Frank Knight.

3 Distinctively American because Chicago was deep enough in the interior to attenuate the culture and social structure of the east coast, which had a more European cast. However, Chicago was none the less close enough to New York that its quasi-colonial status was still engraved in its way of life. Chicago was a point at which two ecosystems – one constituted in European capitals, one hatched on the frontier – met and merged.

4 The best analyst of this period in Chicago and the United States was the late Hugh Duncan. His book *Culture and Democracy* (1965) is a remarkable and remarkably underappreciated description of the city's art, architecture, journalism, literature, urban form, and economic organization. Also see a text that I rely on heavily below – William Cronan's *Nature's Metropolis* (1991).

5 For an elaboration consistent with the argument, see Duncan 1965 along with Benson 1951 and the development of Benson's position in Elkins and McKitrick 1954.

6 I lay out a similar argument to a somewhat different end in Carey 1996.

7 "Reached back" is too active a verb and must be explained. I am merely suggesting that the first phase of Innis's work was an attempt to displace the frontier hypothesis as a governing framework for understanding the

economic and political ecology of North America. The second phase, the one identified with communications, was something much more. It was a search for the spiritual basis of civilization. Here Innis needed an understanding of communication that was much more extended and nuanced than the one that governed his economic studies.

8 Dewey's views on the oral tradition are most accessible in *The Public and Its Problems* (1927).

9 The discussion that follows is indebted to the exceptional historical work of William Cronan (1991).

10 The geographical trunks and tributaries largely held to their nineteenth-century shape through the age of television and were fundamentally modified only after the deregulation of jet travel and the launching of satellites for broadcasting and point-to-point communication.

11 I develop this argument further in two related papers, Carey 1993a and 1993b.

5 Economic History and Economic Theory: Innis's Insights

IRENE M. SPRY

Since I had the privilege of working with Harold Innis for a number of years, I have been asked to record my memories of him as a person and as a colleague. My first and overwhelming impression is of how hard he worked. After a full day at the university, he would take home a bundle of books and arrive next morning having mastered their contents.

He expected his colleagues and his students to work equally hard. This accounts in part for the difficulty many of us had with his lectures. He assumed that everyone would have done all the necessary reading. However, his classroom style intensified the problem. He tended to talk to his notes and not to his audience, so much so that a group of especially brilliant students, including the late A.F.W. Plumptre,[1] waited on him to explain that they could not hear what he was saying. They reached an agreement with him as to clearer communication; this worked well.

Innis's handwriting was as inscrutable as his lectures were. It was the despair of the department secretary. Luckily, I was sometimes able to interpret almost-illegible passages, perhaps because my own writing was equally unintelligible.

His writing style was in many cases equally inscrutable. He told me once that he had modelled his style on that of Thorstein Veblen. A friend gave me a clue when she told me that one should begin by reading the conclusion of *The Fur Trade in Canada* (Innis 1930) and then go back to the main text. The same could be said of his history of the Canadian Pacific Railway and other works.[2]

Despite his unrelenting scholarly labours, Innis always found time to help students and young colleagues. When my work on sources of energy in Canada took me all over the country, from Yukon to the Maritime provinces, he gave me introductions to friends he had made in his own field-research travels.

He taught me that it was useless to ask engineers and farmers questions in economic jargon; I had to learn to talk to them in their own language. As he had shown in his own research, it was essential to go and see the actual setting of the problems that one was struggling to understand – the geography, geology, biology, botany, meteorology, human culture, customs, religion, and technology, in fact, the entire context of the economic problem. This approach stood me in good stead in my later work on sources of energy in Canada[3] and also in my work on the Palliser Expedition. For the latter I traversed the prairies and the southern Canadian passes through the Rocky Mountains. In addition, I have tried to pass on this wisdom to my students.

Innis insisted on my reading such works as the writings of Egerton Ryerson. He discussed the importance of peripatetic Methodist preachers in Canada's development. He made it clear that the concept of the "economic man" was useless, as indeed he had shown in his own writings. Not that he ignored the work of other economists or documentary sources – his office was piled with stalagmites of books and papers. Any visitor had to wait for a chair to be cleared before it was possible to sit down. It did not seem conceivable that he could know what was in the piles, but he did. Once, when he was ill and had to stay at home, he phoned the secretary to ask for a document. It was in the third pile to the right of the door to his office, half-way down. She found it exactly there.

Innis consulted and used the work of past and present writers, such as Alfred Marshall and John Maynard Keynes. He was well aware of the emerging theories about monopolistic competition.[4] However, he would not accept holus-bolus other people's patterns of thought, such as those of the classical theorists and Karl Marx. He was intent on working out his own ideas, based on his careful observation of what actually went on in the industries that he studied.

In this endeavour, he was alert to the dangers of biases. He warned me about the funding of a book about Ontario Hydro written by a well-known academic, but financed by the notorious American advocates of private enterprise in the production and distribution of electrical energy. When biases could not be eliminated, they should be declared. He thought that a scholar's responsibility was to remain uncommitted to any political party or special interest group, so that he or she might keep as clear as possible from biases. He was prepared to serve on royal commissions and to speak at gatherings of political parties, but he considered that it was a betrayal of academic responsibility to take a job with the government or a firm or to advocate a particular policy. He did not think that we knew enough about how the economy – or society – worked to allow social scientists to propose prescriptions for the solution of problems, though he did himself propose a number of possible improvements in his preface to *Problems of Staple Production in Canada* (1933).

Notwithstanding his tireless and serious scholarly work, he had a splendid sense of humour. Being a woman, I could not join my colleagues at lunch in the University of Toronto's Faculty Club, which was then in Hart House, but I heard many tales of Innis's humorous quips at faculty lunches and heard similar amusing comments in my own encounters with him. Once, when I found him plying a pair of scissors and pot of paste, he commented "the tools of the trade"!

He loved to get out into the country to pursue country activities. A colleague, Vincent Bladen, had a small farm at King, north of Toronto. On visits to the Bladens', Innis would arrive with an axe to help with woodcutting chores. His farming background perhaps explains his insistence on the necessity of seeing economic problems in the whole context of human experience. In his *Problems of Staple Production in Canada* he is described as "Associate Professor of Economic Geography." His works abundantly reflect his interest in geography, as did the part he played in securing the appointment of Dr Griffiths Taylor as professor of geography (Dunbar 1985, 161–2). Besides the geographical basis of economic life, Innis believed that economists had to understand geology, biology, botany, human customs, culture, religion, and technology, as well as politics, if they were to understand economic problems. His own various studies of Canadian industries show how effectively he lived up to this belief. His books on the CPR, the fur trade, the Atlantic fisheries, and the mining industry are well known.

His work on the pulp and paper industry never reached publication as a book but appeared as an article in *The Encyclopedia of Canada* (Innis 1937, vol. 5, 176–85). The conclusion of this article makes it clear that this study was leading him into his later work on communications. I shall leave the analysis of this aspect of his work to others who are better equipped than I am to deal with it, along with other facets of his wide-ranging investigations.

The whole matter of the staples approach to Canadian economic history has been widely discussed, so I will not discuss it here, but I must mention another article in the *Encyclopedia of Canada*, on labour, written in cooperation with Betty Ratz (now Mrs Jack Hearn) (1936, vol. 3, 353–64).

This article was followed by another, included in *Essays in Canadian Economic History* (1956a), which summed up Innis's reflections of Canadian labour in relation of the country's whole economic development (176–99). This included not merely farm and labour organizations, but also fluctuations in the demand for labour, the mobility of the workforce, and other aspects of the availability of workers. In his first book, *A History of the Canadian Pacific Railway* (1923), there is little or no discussion of labour problems, while the amount of attention that Innis gave to this matter increased in his later studies of staple industries.

Besides publishing his own seminal books and articles, he promoted other scholarly publications in the social sciences. He was instrumental in the appearance of the *Canadian Journal of Economics and Political Science*, which followed the publication of *Contributions to Canadian Economics*. The *Encyclopedia of Canada* and the *Canadian–American Relations* series owed much to his assistance.

Despite all these achievements and his work as head of the Department of Political Economy and as dean of the School of Graduate Studies and other contributions to the affairs of the University of Toronto, he remained most modest. In his major works he wrote of attempting to understand the problems he discussed. He never felt that what he had written was the final word on a subject, and he mentioned gratefully that as an economist he received enlightenment from "a large number of individuals engaged in the mining industry" (1936b, 171).

Besides being modest, Innis always seemed to me shy.

It is impossible to remember Harold Innis without remembering his charming and brilliant wife, herself a noted author.[5] She never looked more than fifteen years old, even when she was dean of Women for University College. She once described to me how she compiled an index for one of her husband's books – in those pre-computer times. She said that for days the whole dining-room was covered with slips of paper, which she later assembled into the index. It must have been an agonizing job. Without the indexes, it would be difficult to track down all the riches contained in Innis's works.

What I wish to emphasize here is the contribution that Innis has made to economic theory as a result of his observations of what actually happened in the major industries that he examined. Readers frequently have difficulty in grasping his ideas as he uses portmanteau words and phrases – for example, "rigidities," "overhead costs," and "virgin resources" – to compress a variety of circumstances and ideas into one short phrase.

To begin with "rigidities." In his various studies Innis revealed a number of types of "rigidities." Some of these are the result of the character, fluctuations, and limitations of nature-given resources. The catch of fish, the fur harvest, the cut of lumber, the wheat crop, and the production of minerals and of hydro-electric power all depend on what nature provides in the way of resources and climate. When codfish stocks are exhausted, when the fur cycle is at its nadir, when the white pine forests have all gone, when an ore body or oil or gas reserve is used up, would-be producers are face to face with the ultimate rigidity – that imposed by nature and the rate of exploitation.

The character of the resources provided by nature is also subject to another kind of rigidity – that of the manner in which a resource can be used. In some cases, if a resource is to be used at all, all of it must be used. If a water-power site is to be harnessed to its full capacity, it must be developed totally at once. Another rigidity imposed by nature is that of joint products. If the ore in a mine is extracted, the cobalt as well as the silver must be brought to the surface; the copper, lead, and zinc must be dug out, as well as the gold and silver in a complex ore body.

Yet another type of rigidity is that resulting from an imbalance in productive capacity and an uneven rate of use of that capacity. The outstanding case is that of an imbalance between inward and outward freight demands. The case of the "coffin ships," carrying human freight to Canada on the return voyage of lumber ships, is well known (Innis 1956a, 146–7), but Canadian history is replete with other instances of such imbalances. An early case was that of the Atlantic fishery, in which outgoing vessels had to sail in ballast (141). This called for regulations against dumping ballast in a harbour (142, footnote 2) – perhaps the first anti-pollution provision in our history. A much later case concerned the problems created in Yukon by heavy and bulky inward traffic in provisions and supplies in general and the compact and valuable outward cargo of gold (1936b, 254).

Freight imbalances were not the only type of rigidity creating unused capacity. The wheat economy required heavy outward shipments of grain and substantial transport facilities in a short harvest season, leaving a lack of traffic at other times (1956a, 151). Other seasonal rigidities exist because of climatic problems – notably, the freeze-up of the seaway and Montreal harbour.

A type of unused capacity results from daily or weekly (as well as seasonal) fluctuations in the demand for energy. If the peak load is to be met, there will be unused capacity in off-peak periods. When a high flow of water can all be used in a hydro-electric plant, the total capacity of all the turbines and other equipment cannot be put to work in low-water periods.

In all these instances great efforts have been made to find some means either of reducing the maximum capacity required, and so the surplus productive capacity, or of using otherwise-unused capacity, as with the human cargo on the coffin ships.

These efforts have acted as a stimulus to Canada's economic development. The coffin ships brought new settlers to the country that was to become Canada, while the fishing ships that plied between England and Newfoundland bringing more men on board than were needed to work the ship began to leave men to winter in Newfoundland. Many of these men were drawn off to New England to man that colony's year-round fishery, lumber and shipbuilding industries, as well as its overseas trade.

In both these cases, an unbalanced cargo led to shifts in Canada's population. The seasonal peak load of grain shipments, combined with the lack of agricultural opportunities on the Canadian Shield, provided an incentive to develop mines in the Pre Cambrian rock north of Lake Superior. The surplus power potential in the Lac Saint-Jean area of Quebec resulted in the development of the aluminum industry at Arvida. The excess power potential not required by the pulp and paper industry was absorbed by the production of aluminum. Thus the Canadian economy experienced a stimulus to expand and to diversify.

Some of these problems of unused capacity arise from natural rigidities, and some from the construction of costly and durable equipment, which provides continuous productive capacity for which there is only intermittent and often uncertain use, which cannot be foreseen.

In other cases productive capacity has to be installed initially at the capacity that was expected to be required eventually, while the demand could be built up only by degrees, as with an electric-generating station.

These problems of inflexible productive capacity and limited or fluctuating demands are paralleled by financial rigidities. Building a railway costs a great deal of money, which may be provided either by risk-takers, who are prepared to invest their money in the hope of a future satisfactory return, or by lenders, who, by buying bonds or by making other sorts of loans that carry fixed financial obligations, put up the necessary funds on the basis of a contract for repayment and for the payment of interest at a fixed rate. Projects such as the construction of canals have been financed by governments, which incurred debts that had to be discharged. Enterprises funded by private bond-holders may be forced into bankruptcy, with the bond-holders assuming ownership or disposing of it to some other owner. Government-financed enterprises, however, cannot escape from rigid financial obligations in this way. The result may be inflexible charges, levied in the hope of securing sufficient returns at least to cover the guaranteed interest payments.

The combination of rigid productive capacity and rigid financial obligations creates the problem of "overhead costs," which are frequently mentioned by Innis. These may range from heavy initial outlays required for some specific line of production by means of a specific type of advanced technology. The difference between economists' use of the term *cost*, to mean the sacrifice of some alternative possible return, and business people's use of the term, to denote outlays of any sort, including payment of financial obligations, perhaps accounts for some of the difficulties arising from the term *overhead costs*. It does not seem to me that Innis disentangled this issue or the difference between the expenditure necessary to make available a particular productive capacity and the rigid continued availability of that productive capacity without any further expenditure or sacrifice of any alternative possible use.

The result of these two kinds of rigidity has thus been a third type – rigidity in charges for the services of those rigid productive capacities and the rigid financial obligations. In Innis's studies of the history of the Canadian Pacific Railway and of the industries about which he wrote, all these types of problems became evident, as did their results. Among these were the emergence of monopolies and monopolistic competition. Innis noted that Champlain, disturbed by the disastrous effects of unfettered competition in the fur trade, became the first promoter in Canada of a monopoly (1930, 30–1). He discussed the pressure towards centralized control in industries with a continental sphere and the competitive pressures characteristic of maritime industries, notably the Atlantic fisheries. Even in this case, however, competition was never perfect. The nation-states concerned enforced mercantilist and naval policies, while wars – and piracy – meant that "other things" were never "equal."

This brings us to Innis's insistence that an economic analysis that might illuminate in the case of a large, well-established metropolitan centre might be totally inappropriate for a new country that was a hinterland of a metropolis, especially one that relied on the exploitation of nature-given resources and their export (1956a, 74–5). The classical and neo-classical economists tacitly assumed perfect competition with smoothly adjustable demand and supply. They envisaged facile responses to changes in the conditions of production and of market situations, making the attainment of equilibrium in each market – even general equilibrium – possible, and hence the proper focus of economic analysis.

Innis pointed out that smooth adjustments were not and are not characteristic of economic activity in Canada. Marshall's dictum that "natura non fecit saltum" was conspicuously untrue of Canada. The completion of a transcontinental railway line, the coalition of the Hudson's Bay Company and the North West Company, the Treaty of Utrecht, Napoleon's continental system, the abrogation of the British Corn Laws and Navigation Acts, the Fraser, Caribou, and Yukon gold rushes, and the completion of huge power plants were all enormous leaps. Some of these, such as the drought of the 1930s, were acts of nature, not merely human interventions. Sudden and violent disturbances in the conditions of an economy, whether natural, political, technological, or in markets, were more usual than any trend towards equilibrium. We should be studying what Innis called "cyclonics," not purely abstract and unrealistic ideas of equilibrium (1956a, 293). We should be analysing monopoly and monopolistic situations, not rare conditions of perfect – or nearly perfect – competition. We should, moreover, be thinking about the interplay of economic and political forces as well as all the other natural and human factors that shape economic processes.

One fundamental misconception was put right by Innis as a result of his study of Canada's economic history. Many commentators have held that Canada became a nation in defiance of geography. Innis showed clearly that the fur trade and the wheat economy developed not in defiance of geography, but as a result of the basic east–west pull of the commercial empire of the St Lawrence. Only now, when new politics and new industries – pulp and paper, minerals and the automotive industries – are substituting a southward pull for the original east–west axis, are we Canadians coming to grips with the economic changes that caused Harold Innis to reflect sadly: "From colony to nation to colony" (405).

NOTES

1 A.F.W. (Wynne) Plumptre (1907–1977), BA, University of Toronto, MA, Cambridge University (England); author of many articles and books, notably *Central Banking in the British Dominions* (1940) and *Canada's International Financial Policies, 1944–1975* (1977). He taught in the Department of Political Economy at the University of Toronto, and during the Second World War and subsequently he served, among other public appointments, at the Wartime Prices and Trade Board, NATO, the Department of External Affairs, the Department of Finance, and the International Monetary Fund, in Washington, DC. From 1965 to 1972 he was principal of Scarborough College, University of Toronto.

2 For a list of Innis's publications, see Ward 1953.

3 See my articles in the *Encyclopedia of Canada* (Biss [Spry] 1936; 1937), later reproduced and updated in *The Encyclopedia Canadiana* (Spry 1958a; 1958b).

4 The work of Joan Robinson and Edward Chamberlin was drawing attention to monopolistic competition. For Innis on Marshall, see Innis 1956a, 274 and 280; in reference to Keynes, Innis wrote, "the emergence of vested interests (i.e., the legitimate right to something for nothing) under capitalism has reduced the value of economic theory based on Adam Smith and increased the value of economic theory adapted to nationalism. To extend the thesis of Mr. Keynes as to the influence of rising prices of literature, it may be said that they tend to correspond with free will

systems of economic thought" (1956a, 272). See also Innis 1956a, 124, footnote 2; Innis 1934, 4, footnote 2.

5 Mary Quayle Innis was a graduate of the University of Chicago and received honorary degrees from Queen's University and the University of Waterloo. As author and editor, she had produced a number of distinguished books, including M.Q. Innis 1954 and 1967. She served for a time as dean of women at University College, University of Toronto.

6 The Public Role of the Intellectual

LIORA SALTER AND CHERYL DAHL

It is rare today to hear discussions about the public role of the intellectual. Yet this theme, which was taken up extensively by Innis, does echo in contemporary debates. It is cast in a new language, captured by such phrases as "the relevance of the university," "the popularization of science," and "the use of science for policy making." Would Innis have recognized such treatments as reflecting his own preoccupations? We think not. This paper explores what Innis meant by the public role of the intellectual, comparing it with current variations on his theme and offering a commentary on their shortcomings. We argue that much is lost in the current renditions and that a return to Innis's version is overdue.

We begin by laying out Innis's conception of the public role of the intellectual, illustrating how it was connected to his preoccupation with the issues of bias and objectivity, the corruption of the university, and the potential for intellectuals to resist this corruption. We then deal with three of today's variations on Innis's theme. One variation, captured in the phrase "accountability and relevance of the university," has, at different times in recent history, been the rallying cry of both left and right. Omitted from the analysis in both instances, however, is an adequate explanation of how accountability is to be rendered. Innis's answer to this question was clear. The university was accountable and relevant, he indicated, when it spawned reflection and dialogue. How far from today's often-vacuous discussions of accountability this answer seems.

A second variation is captured in the phrase "the popularization of science," which generally means the dissemination of science (of intellectual work) to an allegedly ill-informed or less sophisticated public. Innis would have had no patiece with this approach, nor with today's discussion about the "popularization of science," because this discussion is premised on a demarcation between the intellectual and public domains, which, in his view, actually undermines the public role of the intellectual.

However, with respect to the third variation, the intellectual as contributor to public policy, Innis did have much to say, and most of it was critical. His critique is as apt today as it was when he wrote it. It is time to return to Innis's formulation.

INNIS ON THE PUBLIC ROLE OF THE INTELLECTUAL

It is not surprising that questions about the public role of the intellectual were often debated in the years between 1920 and 1945, especially given the Great Depression, the rise of fascism, and the Second World War. There were few intellectuals employed in Canadian universities at the time, and those who could claim some knowledge or understanding of contemporary social problems were still fewer. The social sciences were just emerging in the arts faculties, and there was little funding for research from other than policy-related sources (Ferguson and Owram 1980). Thus the incentives for intellectuals to become involved in public matters were many. Innis joined the debate. He focused his attention on policy making – the interactions between governments and intellectuals – rather than on politics. He had little doubt that intellectuals should be engaged with the major problems of their time but was deeply sceptical about the ability of social scientists to retain their integrity as they rushed to serve on boards and commissions (though he too served) or give policy advice. His position seems contradictory. It can be understood only if we link his comments on policy making and the university to his more scholarly work on bias and objectivity, communication, and culture.

Bias and objectivity were among his central concerns. Innis developed his concept of bias in relation to the problems of objectivity in the social sciences. He recognized differences between natural sciences (which he believed could be objective in the conventional sense) and social sciences, which were inevitably infused with values and the unpredictability of human behaviour. He sought to identify an approach for the social sciences that would incorporate some elements of objectivity and generate something akin to social laws.[1] His solution was that social science should take as its subject matter "the sediment of experience," or "bias" (Pal 1977, 33). As Westfall later claimed, Innis "tried to solve the problem of bias [i.e., objectivity] by making the problem [i.e., bias] itself into a part of the solution" (Westfall 1981, 43). There are regularities in the way that biases affect culture, Innis noted. Furthermore, bias is invariably tied to other social processes. Social sciences should address the relationship among culture, bias, and these social processes. To study bias, Innis argued, one might reasonably begin with institutions, which represented "cumulative bias."[2]

Problems concerning objectivity were not entirely resolved for Innis by making the study of bias central to the subject matter of the social sciences. The intellectual (i.e., the social scientist) was also affected by bias, being also a product of a culture shaped by social forces. No one could stand entirely outside his or her own culture, he noted; there could be no complete escape from bias.[3] But Innis's discussion of objectivity did not run aground with this assessment. The university could provide a setting for the type of reflective work necessary to gain perspective on bias – one's own as well as the biases of others. Indeed, the primary function of the university administrator was to protect the intellectual from the influences of government and industry so that all biases could be put into perspective and consequently better understood. All institutions embody particular values and interests, of course, and they encourage the development of particular kinds of knowledge. The university was no exception in this regard. But, by contrast with the orientation of governments and industry to space and power, the university could support the intellectual in his or her search for complex forms of knowledge, oriented towards the benefit of the society as a whole, and involving a long-term perspective (Innis 1946, 103–44; 64–71; 72–82).

The university was familiar ground for him. He had no illusions about the possibility of corruption, of intellectuals or of the university.[4] He also emphasized the negative consequences of the disciplinary specialization usual in intellectual work within universities. The social process is highly complex, Innis said, and any academic discipline necessarily privileges some questions over others, some factors over others (1936a).[5] Disciplines are themselves "biased." Consequently, objectivity in the context of intellectual work must mean not only scholarship sheltered from demands (including self-imposed demands) of those seeking quick answers to the perplexing problems of the society, but also open-mindedness on the part of the intellectuals themselves. He called this desirable perspective "the philosophical approach," by which he meant, among other things, that intellectuals' search for knowledge should remain open-ended, that they themselves should remain sceptical, that their orientation should be towards the needs of the culture, broadly defined, and that their focus should be on knowledge as opposed to information or data.[6] In other words, notwithstanding the negative side of disciplinary specialization, Innis believed in basic research because it best represented what society at large needed from experts. In this context, disciplinary specialization had a particular meaning. It was no different from the demands of government and industry for research with a narrow focus, inasmuch as it would require the intellectual to lose sight of objectivity (Innis 1946, 128). Disciplinary specialization and direct engagement in policy making both undermined the public role of the intellectual.

In discussing the "philosophical approach," Innis owed a good deal to the classicists, as Watson has argued (1977). "The philosophical approach" was also rooted in Innis's method. Abstract categories or theoretical schema had little attraction for him. Indeed, as McLuhan concluded, the later Innis "had no position," no grand schema or abstract system at all; instead he cast a "roving mental eye." All his work displays "a mistrust of abstract systems as a means of achieving prediction and control of practical problems" (McLuhan 1953, 392).

Innis began each of his studies by amassing enormous numbers of facts, by developing a painstaking catalogue of details. He then sought to identify the connections, the ways in which different factors were related, often drawing (in his later work) on classical literature. "Sympathetic imagination, disciplined by and controlled by the comparative study of peoples and cultures" was how Cochrane had described the task to be done (Watson 1977, 48). Innis agreed and adopted it as his own "philosophical approach." Basic research characterized by such an approach could provide a different perspective from that offered by disciplinary specialists, governments, and industry. It could provide the balance of perspectives necessary for democratic life.[7]

In this way, the approach was not divorced from public life, but neither was it intended to persuade or to resolve public policy problems. As Innis said, "[t]he task of the social scientist is to discover" (1936a, 408). Intellectual work required its practitioners to admit that they did not have answers, even in the face of expectations – from the public, policy makers, and other "intellectuals" – to the contrary. There could be no definite truths in the social sciences (even though something akin to objectivity was possible), and any search for them would only foster an arrogant concern with concrete and practical issues to the exclusion of a much more productive (albeit only in the long term) philosophical approach (Innis 1946, 103).

From the classics as well, Innis derived his definition and his commitment to culture. Culture was bound up in the interplay of power and knowledge: the need for order, stability, and continuity and, as well, for innovation, dialogue, and creativity. In dealing with culture, he was preoccupied with the problem of balance and moderation. Media associated with territorial expansion needed to be balanced by media associated with continuity, he said. Power was important (empires were inevitable, in his view, and they fostered stability), but creation of knowledge was equally valuable because the creative impulse was central to any successful society (empire). Rigidities (monopolies) in either sphere were to be avoided.[8] When monopolies of power and of knowledge were aligned, Innis argued, freedom was destroyed; fanaticism, disintegration, and chaos might well follow. Anything that undermined balance (rigidities, monopolies of knowledge in particular) was to be decried (1946, 103). Freedom, by which Innis meant something akin to the flourishing of culture, and democracy were both threatened when "a monopoly or oligopoly of knowledge is built up to the point where equilibrium is disturbed" (1951a, 3–4).

Much of Innis's discussion (especially of communication and media) may have centred on classical conceptions of culture, freedom, and democracy, but his chief interests were clearly in his own era. In 1944, Innis pointed out that a basic condition of freedom was the division of power. He argued: if the quality of society rests on decisions of government, and if government in turn reflects popular opinion, and if popular opinion in turn reflects the content of the mass media, then a dangerous monopoly of knowledge was being established. Mass media were problematic because they were spatially biased to support power to the exclusion of knowledge and because they increasingly controlled the terms and forums for public discourse. But governments themselves were part of the problem. Innis quoted Lord Acton: "Government by the whole people, being government of the most numerous and powerful class, is an evil of the same nature as unmixed monarchy and [it] requires, for nearly the same reasons, institutions that shall protect it against arbitrary revolutions of opinion" (1946, 103).

The few institutions that did offer alternative viewpoints and a balance of perspectives were being eroded, in part by the overpowering influence of the mass media. Intellectuals assume a critical role in such an analysis, for they represent the best hope for retaining the sense of history, the tradition of free inquiry (including into the problems of bias and freedom of expression), and the oral tradition necessary if balance – i.e., democracy and culture – were to be possible.

Innis's vision of the public role of the universities and intellectuals was idealistic, but it was not naive. Innis had little doubt that intellectuals could be sidetracked from their public role by accepting another version of a public role – for example, by engaging directly in policy making. He had no doubt whatsoever that universities could be, and were being, sidetracked for many reasons. "The culture of western civilization, the values that have permitted and encouraged the development of knowledge, is threatened when the university becomes drawn into the sphere of monopoly," he said (1951a, 190). This also occurs, as we noted above, when concern for the immediate and practical takes over – when knowledge is fragmented by disciplinary specialization, when conservation of knowledge takes precedence over its creation, when knowledge is falsely equated with information, or with the proliferation and accessibility of information, and when the temptation to abandon intellectual work for other social priorities, or even for budgetary reasons, overwhelms basic research and/or the philosophical approach.

The public role of the intellectual was being diminished, but more seriously – because Innis believed that that role was important and influential – a loss of values was occurring. Indeed, in his most despairing moments, prodded by current events, Innis talked, not unreasonably, about the potential collapse of Western civilization, which he attributed in part to the retreat of the intellectuals and to the erosion of the university, in contrast to the growing influence of fanatics, whose ranting could no longer be balanced by reflective inquiry and thought.

To speak of the public role of the university and of the intellectuals was akin to a call to action in the face of a crisis (Watson 1977, 49). Their role was to encourage the development of sources of centralized power (today we might call it a critical mass of work) in order to counteract the centralization of power in the state and the ever-more-penetrating influence of mass media on its citizenry. Intellectuals could challenge bias (in this case, monopolies of knowledge) directly by studying social processes and institutions. Consequently Innis's was a very different notion of politics than his contemporaries' or even our own. The university could provide an environment as free as possible from the biases of the various institutions that form the state, so that its intellectuals could continue to seek out and explore other perspectives (Innis 1951a, 27). The focus should be on moderation, especially of the tendency towards extremism and fanaticism, which were so evident in Innis's time and resulted in part from the spatial bias and character of the mass media and from the skewing of the relationship between power and knowledge towards an unhealthy emphasis on power. The university should reject the idea of making public policy decisions on the basis of public opinion, but it should do so by fostering a questioning attitude on the part of policy makers, citizens, intellectuals, and students. The university was the only place, Innis believed, where the monopoly instituted through the press and radio was not yet fully realized (1951a, 61–91).

How might the university be a source of resistance? Surely for Innis, as well as commentators on universities today, this is a crucial question. Innis's view – and it remains applicable to some extent today – was that the universities could remain a site where Western civilization was preserved. This was what he meant by resistance. The university could play this role because of its traditions, which were products of an earlier time. The university maintained an oral tradition, he said, and with it an emphasis on history and the humanities. The values espoused by the university were those that characterized Greek civilization. Tolerance, an open-minded attitude towards truth seeking, flexibility, reflexivity, a "philosophical approach" – all these characterized the university (and ancient Greek) ideal. As Innis put it, "Her traditions and her interest demand an obsession with balance and perspective – an obsession with the Greek tradition of the humanities" (1946, 64).[9]

As we said above, his may have been an idealistic view, but it was not a naive one. Innis had no doubt that the ideal of the university and the intellectual was being eroded by "overwhelming demands of (university) administration," by "larger numbers of poorer students," by emphasis on training and professional education, etc. (1946, 128). The ability of the universities and of intellectuals to resist the forces of modern culture was being weakened; the freedom that arises from access to a multiplicity of monopolies was being eroded, and people were being left defenceless, without the historical or philosophical basis to make informed decisions. It was the task of intellectuals to sustain historical and philosophical work, and of the university to make it possible:

We have assumed that government in democratic countries is based upon the will of the governed, that people can make up their minds, and that every encouragement should be given to enable them to do so. This implies that the state is concerned with strengthening intellectual capacity, and not with the weakening of that capacity by the expenditure of subsidies for the multiplication of facts. It also implies that adults have been so trained in the educational system that they can choose the facts and reach their own decisions. We should, then, be concerned like the Greeks with making men, not [with] overwhelming them with facts disseminated by paper and ink, film radio and television. Education is the basis of the state and its ultimate aim and essence is the training of character. (1951a, 203)

Not only was the student in danger of being robbed of the intellectual experience that would adequately prepare him or her to make the decisions of a free individual, but what was being substituted reinforced all the negative characteristics of the newspaper and radio. In the final analysis, for Innis, the public role of the intellectual was undermined much more seriously than was the case when intellectuals simply became engaged in the pragmatic worlds of policy making, advertising, or industry, however undesirable this might be. It was being undermined when intellectual work, and the university itself, fell prey to the spatial bias represented best (but not exclusively) by the mass media, when intellectual life was stymied because the role of the intellectual in fostering democracy and culture disappeared from view.

Not everyone could or should become an intellectual in the conventional sense of being a scholar, Innis believed. The specialized knowledge of the university-employed academic would also always remain important. But every student could and should be taught the value of good scholarship by participating in the oral tradition of the university, which encouraged respect for truth, evaluations of bias, multiple perspectives, tolerance, and scepticism. Everyone could assimilate the major values of intellectual life, even if few were actually scholars. Knowledge was, in Innis's view, essential to the preservation of democracy; therein lay the public role of the intellectual.

CURRENT CONCEPTIONS OF THE PUBLIC ROLE OF INTELLECTUALS

There is no less concern today than in Innis's time with the public role of the intellectual, even if the debate is now couched in quite different terms. Nowadays intellectuals and the universities are on the defensive, forced to justify their existence or at least their continued levels of funding. Surprisingly, given this situation, two highly idealized notions of intellectual work abound both within and outside the university. The first is a utopian version of the claim that science and technology bring significant benefits. In this conception, enlightenment, progress, rationality, and intellectual work are tied into a single bundle of ideas said to underpin the current age, the "new economy" that will spawn yet further development. The second is a dystopian view of science (and of all conventional intellectual work more generally), as being at best a socially constructed edifice of "knowledge" constituting power and authority. These two profoundly conflicting views – sometimes held by the same individuals – create a kind of hothouse atmosphere for discussion, one so emotionally and theoretically charged that it obscures the practical problems inherent in the public role of the intellectual.

It is useful to step back from both views and to focus directly, as Innis did, on the more pragmatic dimensions of the issue. This discussion is often cast around three themes – the relevance and accountability of the universities the popularization of science, and the role of science in the making of public policy.

The University as "Relevant" and "Accountable"

An excellent example of how the intellectual's public role is linked today to the relevance and accountability of the universities occurred in 1994 in the Roundtable on Science and Technology, sponsored by the Canadian government and intended to produce a white paper and specific policies regarding research funding.[10] Virtually every time that research was mentioned at the roundtable, it was in the context of how research could be translated immediately into social – or, more probably, economic – benefits. Accountability was the synonym for efficiency and control, and senior university and government people, no less than their industrial counterparts, spoke readily of getting "better bang for the buck." It was also a synonym for budget cutting. It is all too easy to reiterate Innis's critique of such short range instrumental thinking in light of current debates about relevance and accountability and, in doing so, to lose sight of the core of Innis's notion of the public role of intellectuals.

Furthermore, it is not surprising that single words, such as "accountability" and "relevance," could take on such ideologically laden but different meanings in public debate. One can argue about the social values underlying each meaning, but decoding meanings can easily become a superficial task. What gives the concepts their power is not simply the values that motivate the speakers, but the methods of putting the ideas into practice that follow from each of the various meanings. Obviously there is a strong reactionary undercurrent in the debate about the public role of the intellectuals and universities, which was reflected in the Roundtable's proposals to increase relevance and accountability through new controls on research and on budget cutting. Yet preoccupation with accountability and relevance is neither new nor necessarily reactionary. This same preoccupation was evident in Innis's time. It was also a theme in the politics of the new left in the 1960s, and it reflects both left and right politics today.

In fact, even for conservatives and certainly for others, any call for accountability, whatever its meanings and origins, poses difficult problems.[11] Even if consensus could be reached among the multitude of constituencies within and outside the university about proper public roles, it would still be unclear how accountability or relevance could or should be delivered appropriately. Those of a conservative bent seem preoccupied with efficiency, but even their schemes run aground when efficiencies have been achieved. There seems to be no satisfying the urge for accountability, even when the most stringent controls and cuts have been made.

But the left has no easier time dealing with accountability as anything more than a social value and an abstraction. The left's preoccupation is with governance, not efficiency, but specific proposals for change are difficult to come by. For example, several years ago, a seminar series at York University on democratic administration, designed specifically to deal with accountability and relevance, came to naught when its participants could not resolve such basic issues as whether elections or recall of officials were necessary and how unions fit into the picture, especially in institutions with shared governance.[12] It was unclear to participants what constitutes shared governance and where cooptation begins. Much attention was given to "the new social movements" as possible exemplars and as champions of accountability and relevance (i.e., as popular movements). But granting the premises that the democratic impulse lies outside the university (with the public itself) and that it is expressed through new social movements (a view that Innis might well have disputed vigorously, faced as he was with the example of fascism, which was in part a popular movement), it was entirely unclear how these new social movements play out their public role when faced with the problems of governance.

It does little for our analysis to hearken back, as is often done even when new social movements are being discussed, to a glorious age when the university was uncorrupted by inappropriate demands. Even assuming that commentators agreed when this golden age occurred, universities have always been beholden to others for public approval and for funding, as Innis was quick to point out. Moreover, the outside world has always made demands on intellectuals, drawing them away from exclusively scholarly endeavour, a point also noted by Innis.

Innis might well have claimed, and historically he would have been right, that it has always been possible to write a "political economy of the university," to indicate how universities are made beholden to particular constituencies and interests. Further, Innis often observed how intellectuals themselves also eagerly offer advice to anyone who is inclined to pay attention. Innis was more conscious of the ties that bind the university and the contradictions attending the public involvement of its intellectuals. Furthermore, he did not feel much nostalgia for an imaginary historical past so much as he posed an ideal, which was – or could be – represented in some measure by the intellectuals and the university. He drew this ideal from a reading of classical times to be sure, but it would have been useful even had there been no classical golden age.

For Innis, the ideal was as follows. Relevance should mean the opposite of today's meanings. Universities, and intellectuals working within them, should be relevant precisely because they are in an almost unique position – that of being one step removed from the pressures of pragmatic existence and governance. Virtually every other domain is characterized by a preoccupation with results, while those within the university can turn to the examination of bias, to longer-term perspectives, and to debating the full dimensions of public issues. What makes the university, and its intellectuals, accountable and relevant should be their capacity to act as a counterforce to the single-minded pursuits undertaken elsewhere. Especially in the face of politics increasingly based on public opinion polling and the mass media, the contribution of intellectuals – their "relevance" – should not be minimized, for where else might the monopolies of knowledge be challenged and dislodged?

The modern analysts, whatever their politics, look outside the university in searching for accountability and relevance. They look to the public funders, to the boards of governors, to the various public clients and constituents of the university and its research. Their preoccupation is to find the right constituencies and the appropriate audiences for intellectual work. By contrast, Innis found relevance and accountability *in* intellectual work and in the universities. The public role of the intellectual, for Innis, is to be intellectual. The public role of the university is to offer the venue for intellectual work. This does not imply a retreat to an ivory tower; on the contrary, in Innis's view, intellectuals and universities were and should be engaged in public issues. Relevance and accountability meant to him being engaged in the public debate on the basis of the particular skills, expertise, and approach characterizing intellectual work. It meant taking advantage of the unique opportunities afforded by intellectual work and the universities to enter the debate and extend it accordingly. More on this point below.

The Popularization of Science (and Intellectual Work)

In many debates today, to speak of the public role of the intellectual is to speak about the popularization of science (Hilgarten 1990). This too runs directly contrary to Innis's view, but to understand why it is necessary to delve quite deeply into the current debates in the literature on the popularization of science. After all, Innis did not reject the notion that intellectuals might be asked to, and properly respond to demands to, speak publicly about their work. He himself often wrote for non academic audiences. He was concerned, as noted above, only that the result not be simply a recasting of intellectual work to be more in tune with the immediate needs and demands of the politicians and the public. As noted above, Innis's view was that intellectuals would enhance the democratic debate by functioning – and speaking – as intellectuals.

The current literature on the popularization of science, varied as it is, envisions something quite different – "science culture," "science literacy," media coverage of science, and so on. In all of these approaches, the premise is that scientific knowledge (i.e., all intellectual work within the universities) should not be the sole prerogative of those who carry the mantle or authority of science, or even of those with scientific training or expertise.[13] The public should also become expert, or at least as expert as its lack of rigorous training will permit. Innis would have agreed. The rationale found most often in the literature, however, is one of an implicit contract. About this contract, Innis would have had profound doubts. The contract is as follows. Intellectuals are supported by public funds. Conceiving of the relationship between the public and intellectuals as one of money for research in exchange for specific benefits from research and/or the duty to publicize renders moot questions about the influence of intellectual work, so central for Innis. In the view of the "popularization of science," the intellectual or scientist is expected to carry out activities within the domain of intellectual work without regard for the direct benefits of these activities to the public or society at large, but believing that such benefits will follow eventually. He or she receives public support for doing so. In return for this support, however, the intellectual has an additional duty: to inform the public about this work, if not in the specific sense, then about intellectual work or science in general, using a liberal sprinkling of examples. The two activities, intellectual work and popularization, are seen to be separate endeavours and part of an exchange. One is not supposed to overwhelm or pollute the other.

The ideal embodied in "the popularization of science" is as follows. The working scientist is pictured in her lab: she turns to the camera. A few sentences will do to explain why her work is important – i.e., why the money is well spent. The prestige accrues to science; it trickles down to her in the form of continued support for research such as her own (not necessarily her own research) on, for example, the moulting habits of butterflies. The wise old literary critic strokes his beard and ruminates on the importance of literature for the human experience. The young professor meets with her dean to be told that, while the offer from the CBC to do a series on Harold Adams Innis is impressive, she best not neglect her academic publications. The bargain represented in the implied contracts is summed up by the phrase "the popularization of science." It is one that leaves intellectual work intact, distinctly separated from public life, merely imposing a duty on the practitioner (but only on practitioners who have already established themselves as scientists or intellectuals) to relay the flavour of intellectual activity to an appreciative but ill-informed public in return for further support.

In fact, "the popularization of science" is based on two false dichotomies. The first is that one can clearly demarcate the domain of the intellectuals from that of public life, such that it is appropriate to speak of a transfer of information/knowledge from one domain to the other. The second is that the content of work in the first domain – science and other intellectual work – is necessarily complex but requires no translation among initiates, by contrast with the content of public life, which, however rich and varied, is straightforward and is accessible to all participants. If this second dichotomy is accepted, any popularization of science requires simplification, translation, and transformation of science to render it intelligible to those outside the domain of intellectual work who require the simpler version.

The first dichotomy is easiest to grasp and is intuitively attractive. There is no question that those expert in, for example, the intricacies of cell membranes, or Virginia Woolf's use of metaphor, or economic modelling, or semiotics, or ethnic identity each speak something akin to a different language within their own disciplinary debates, different again from what they would speak if they were called on to address yet other audiences including non-academic ones.[14] No one should expect otherwise, because intricate, both specialized vocabularies and complex theoretical accounts are fundamental to intellectual work (quite independent of any authority accruing to the expert in the process). Yet in fact only a small portion of intellectual work takes place within the rarefied circles of those fully cognizant of the technical specialization involved, or of a particular, narrowly construed research problem, or of a particular theoretical formulation. The cell biologists or semioticians speaking among themselves are the exception, not the rule.

A significant proportion of intellectual work is always carried out on the middle ground, somewhere between disciplines or communities rather than within them. Any conference held at a university, which is open to the public, is a good example of this middle ground. There are many other examples: scientists serving on expert committees; the research component of inquiries and commissions; any interdisciplinary research project, especially one involving non-university partners; writings in *Borderlines*, *Canadian Forum*, *Queen's Quarterly*, *Studies in Political Economy*, the op-ed pages of the *Globe and Mail*, even *Science*; publication of articles in a variety of non-specialized journals even within a single discipline (for example, an article on ethnic identity in a sociological journal that also deals with corporate crime, deconstructivist debates, feminism, and so on); book reviews; engagement in university departmental life; and peer review of articles outside one's own narrow specialization. In other words, there is much less distinction among intellectuals than disciplinary specialization implies. Intellectuals spend the greater portion of their time speaking to audiences that are inadequately conversant with the technical language they use. Also, they spend more time speaking to the public, through book reviews, conferences, and the like, than is presumed in "the popularization of science."

The implicit dichotomy between intellectual work and public domain is thus false, but not because no distinctions exist. A large proportion (more or less in different disciplines and interdisciplinary fields of study) of intellectual work and a significant part of public discourse (which includes reading the science pages of the *Globe and Mail*, *Canadian Forum*, and so on) are neither distinctly intellectual nor clearly public in orientation. The boundary between the domains is highly arbitrary; it is drawn differently, depending on one's criteria and purposes. Much of the same work can fall on either side of the line: it can be intellectual or public, depending on the circumstances. To speak then about "the popularization of science" as involving the movement of ideas between two separate domains makes little sense, except for the extreme case – the cell biologist or semiotician speaking to the mass media, which rarely occurs in practice.

The second dichotomy – the complexity of intellectual issues as compared with public ones – is similarly problematic. The problems here lie with conceptions of both domains. On the public side, in light of advances in theory and research since Innis's time, it is easy to put to rest any notion that public discourse is straightforward, that public debate is characterized by simple formulations of otherwise-complex ideas. Equally important, but less well understood, is the situation within the scientific domain, where translation, simplification, and transformation (supposedly characterizing only the public domain) are commonplace and very important (Hilgarten 1990). Even within a single specialization within a relatively cohesive discipline, for example, scientists always simplify their data, concepts, and formulations, presenting them in the form of tables and graphs. Further, all scientific work involves collective transformations and simplification because any specific conclusion (based on research) must first be integrated into the disciplinary debate, then mulled over by others with somewhat different points of view , and then subjected to review within a broader circle yet again, all before it can be accepted as worthy of further citation.

Beyond this, most research conclusions move far beyond the confines of disciplinary specialization and, in doing so, are yet further simplified, translated and transformed, so that they can be taken up by others who do not share the original expertise. In other words, simplification, translation, and transformation of intellectual work are not a foreign experience to intellectuals. No less often than when they engage in public discourse are intellectuals required to speak to others, who do not share their expertise, specialization, or concerns.

To be sure, the lay public often fails to comprehend the complex (occasionally impenetrable) formulations offered by intellectuals. Ironically, because his own work is so dense and inaccessible, Innis was among the first to cast blame for what has now become a widespread phenomenon. Yet any attempt to distinguish clearly between intellectual work and public debate and to speak about the movement of intellectual work into the public realm as a matter of rendering complicated ideas simple enough for the public to grasp is faulty. So much intellectual work takes place on the middle ground between intellectual work and the public, and neither simplification nor complexity is the prerogative of either realm.

Innis would have rejected outright, we suspect, the implicit contract in the "popularization of science": the notion that the intellectual's duty was simply to explain his or her work to others, including members of the public, particularly in return for public support. Notwithstanding his commitment to the craft of historical research and to the life of the university, Innis would not have been very comfortable with a simple dichotomy between the public and intellectuals. He had no doubt that university training engendered expertise, but his preoccupation was not with translating his, or anyone else's, ideas into more easily accessible prose.

On the contrary, his concern was with the university as a teaching institution and with the intellectual as a teacher. Research was not divorced from teaching, despite the high standards of scholarly research which he valued. Both were required to sustain the dialogue that formed the core of the intellectual enterprise, as most directly represented in teaching. Innis believed that intellectuals contributed to the democratic debate by engaging in teaching and the vibrant intellectual life that it stimulated (the "making of men").

It is in this context that Innis's references to classical ideals should be understood. In the classical ideal, it is the bringing together of people – intellectuals and others – into a single venue, combined with the medium of the spoken word and the dynamics of interaction, that sustains the contribution of the intellectual. The public role of the intellectual, best exemplified in teaching, is to contribute to the civilizing urge, which, Innis believed, brought creativity into balance with stability to effect the public good.

Mandated Science

What Innis seemed to fear most, partly because he had very mixed feelings about the subject, is that intellectuals would be drawn into the policy process on the basis of their expertise and used as advisers, members of expert committees, and the like. Scientists and other intellectuals are regularly called on to provide advice or participate in policy making and regulation today.

Before examining Innis's concerns, we should review some current analyses of the issues involved. Liora Salter's *Mandated Science* makes a distinction between academic science and scientific work produced or interpreted for the purposes of policy making.[15] It argues that intellectual work is shaped in quite specific ways by virtue of its intended audiences in domains other than science itself. First, mandated science is seldom investigative. Most often, it consists of evaluations of the work of others and is thus seldom creative. Second, while those in the scientific domain concentrate on particular problems or theoretical issues of interest to themselves, mandated scientists are expected to step back from these problems, to encompass and evaluate a broad range of literature, much of it outside their particular interests or expertise. For example, the expert epidemiologist evaluating a pesticide considers not only epidemiological research, but also toxicological and pharmacological studies, and occasionally even research from molecular biology and genetics. Thirdly, this same expert is regularly called on to deal with economic and social science data and often offers – unsolicited to be sure – a viewpoint on the influence of the media on controversies about pesticides. The assumption in mandated science is that scientists or intellectuals can span any number of disciplines or specializations easily, that the methods appropriate in one context are readily adaptable to others, that debates within particular disciplines are of little relevance, and that data or concepts from one field can be assimilated with others relatively easily. Not surprisingly, one almost never finds academically oriented researchers in the natural sciences engaging in mandated science.

Everyone involved – policy makers and their scholarly advisers alike – tends not to acknowledge any distinction between mandated science and science. "We need good science for policy making" is a common refrain. It is simply assumed that those familiar with the demands of both mandated science and science will find a way to bridge the gap.

So tenuous is this assumption, however, that it gives rise to the third characteristic of mandated science: it offers up a very idealistic picture of intellectual work. Within a laboratory, for example, scientists have no difficulty acknowledging the role that personal values play in the choice of research topic; the constraints imposed by problems of funding research; the limitations, complexity and uncertainties attendant on choices of particular methods, and the alternative formulations of problems current in the literature. Speaking to other scientists behind the closed doors of the laboratory, such scientists do not often claim that science is highly predictive, objective, or value free. Yet in the context of mandated science, these claims are made regularly and explicitly, and science is portrayed in the most glowing – and ideological – terms.

The ideal picture of science made available through mandated science is the one readily associated by non-scientists with science. This portrayal then provides *all* scientists with justification for their mantle of authority, and it permits policy makers to protect themselves from criticism ("the scientists say ... "). Its origins lie in something more than scientists' need for legitimation and authority and more than the philosophical underpinnings of modern industrial societies. The ideal picture of science also arises from contradictions within mandated science – *within* the public role of the intellectual, in other words.

The fourth characteristic of mandated science is the predictability of its debates. Any student of public controversies can write a reasonable script for the debate about science in any controversy not yet studied. Whatever is serendipitous or unpredictable about intellectual work is rendered routine and certain; issues are viewed in terms of dichotomies; the divisions among protagonists fall along predictable lines; evidence is marshaled for each side; and the familiar templates of public discourse – "right," "left," "conservative," "liberal," "feminist," and so on – are applied, even when it is not obvious how the issues fit into categories. The debates assume an ideological tenor. It appears to matter little whether the issue is pornography, pay equity, pesticides, or hazardous waste: once the debate is under way, it seems to have a life of its own and a propensity to resemble others.

The fifth characteristic of mandated science arises from the interpenetration of scientific and public issues with legal ones. This is most evident when scientists advise policy makers about a potentially dangerous chemical, because there are vested economic interests involved that are overseen and protected by legal counsel. It is also true in inquiries or environmental assessments – for example, where the avoidance of future possible legal liability for negligence is a consideration. Both "law talk" – about "guilty" chemicals, evidence, the burden of proof, participant rights, and so on – and procedural wrangling are common in inquiries and assessments even when lawyers are absent or when the inquiries take great pains to distinguish themselves from courts of law. It is less evident but equally true that legal issues are attendant on the policy advice offered by social scientists and humanists on pay equity, incomes policy, and similar issues, because even the most informally conducted policy inquiries are asked to deal with "rights" and to make recommendations that result in law. In this case, both the 'law talk" and the legal nature of the proposed outcomes have the effect of instituting a legal discourse, sometimes even to the exclusion of either a scientific or a public one.

Innis was constantly concerned with the problems of mandated science, but he worried mainly that intellectuals would be distracted or co-opted by their work in the policy process. To our knowledge, Innis commented relatively little on, for example, the fact that the relationship between intellectuals and policy makers might not be satisfactory from a policy point of view, that it might result in highly predictable and unproductive debates imbued with a legal discourse. Cooptation and distraction, issues identified by Innis, appear to be the least of the problems even for intellectuals in such relationships. When an idealized picture of science is combined with a view that scientists are invariably corrupted by their engagement in policy making, it undermines the capacity of intellectuals to carry out any public role at all, even in the sense that Innis envisioned this public role. It subverts the very notion that there can be a public role for intellectuals, as intellectuals – a role that has integrity or is directly relevant to social values and democratic debate.

In other words, Innis's and the contemporary critiques are complementary. Innis pointed out obvious dangers and the potential for cooptation in rewriting the intellectual enterprise to be concerned only with short term policy. His critique has been extended, so that these dangers are now understood in their full dimensions. The real danger for intellectuals drawn into the policy process is that intellectual work will be rendered impotent: it will be measured against an idealistic and unrealistic picture of science; it will become infused with "law talk"; it will be mainly evaluative, not creative in orientation; and it will become predictable and seemingly normless. Intellectuals, instead of expanding the horizons of public debate and contributing by virtue of their expertise and teaching to this expansion, will end up supporting new monopolies of knowledge. Their work outside the universities will become as unidimensional and lacking in imagination as Innis feared would happen within a rigid disciplinary specialization within the universities.

Innis did not argue for a retreat of the intellectuals from giving advice on public policy. Despite the dangers involved, he reasoned, expertise is needed and all too often not sought by those creating public policies. For Innis, the "relevance" of intellectuals is not bound up with policy advice or benefits of specific research, however desirable or useful they might be. Their relevance and accountability lie rather in whatever else they do to stimulate the imagination and creativity, to support the oral tradition, to offer perspective, to question bias and monopolies of knowledge, to foster tolerance, and to engender the "civilizing urge." Mandated science is problematic because it does none of these things, but instead institutes new monopolies of knowledge. However useful and necessary it is, mandated science does not constitute the public role of the intellectual. In sum, policy advice (mandated science), "the popularization of science," and accountability in the modern sense are not what Innis understood by the public role of the intellectual.

CONCLUDING REMARKS

Innis's formulation of the public role of the intellectual has figured little in contemporary debates. Many commentators of a conservative bent want to see intellectuals reined in and held to account to the public funders for the money spent on their work and for the products of their endeavours. For those on the left, the issue has now become one of sharing governance so that the university's various public constituents (members of staff, students, the surrounding community, and the community at large) can shape and benefit from the work taking place there. Feminist critics seek to render authoritative and influential the knowledge of those who are not intellectual, but who can usefully help to shape public priorities and policy. "Popularizers" of science want to make science and intellectual work accessible, to inform and educate the public. For mandated scientists, the challenge is to overcome the problems associated with transposing intellectual work from the laboratory or university into the public domain. In every case, regardless of the prescription or values involved, the analysis presumes a clear demarcation between science or intellectual work and the public domain.

Neither Innis, we suspect, nor we would dismiss any of the concerns raised today or the important contributions made to the understanding of both intellectual and public domains. What Innis offers, and we propose taking up again, is an alternative perspective that plays down the demarcation between intellectual and public life. The public role of the intellectual lies in the contributions made by the exercise of intellectual work. This is best represented through teaching and dialogue but is equally evident when scholarship itself promotes sympathetic imagination and expands the horizons of the public domain. Intellectuals can be helpful, but not because they are accorded authority and prestige. They are useful, but not because they have something to "give back" to the public. They are valuable because they are members of the public domain; they have a crucial role to play within it as intellectuals.

Innis believed that the future of civilization hung in the balance. Given the profoundly anti-intellectual tenor of public debate today, and the rise of new fanaticism and fundamentalism of every stripe, he may well be right.

NOTES

1 Throughout his career Innis was concerned with objectivity and bias, but
he addressed them directly in the early 1930s, when he turned to the
potential of the emerging social sciences to alleviate pressing social problems. Many in the small community of Canadian scholars, including
Innis, were called on by government to help to create social policy. The
country was deep in the second wave of the Great Depression, and war
loomed in Europe. Innis had been deeply affected by his experience as a
soldier in the First World War and in much of his interwar writing concerns himself with how what he does, and what other scholars do, might
restore some balance and moderation in a world seemingly bent on
destroying itself.

In 1935, E.R. Urwick published an article entitled "The Role of Intelligence in the Social Process." Social processes, he argued, involved free,
willed beings, and there could be no scientific laws in situations where
values were a variable. Furthermore, if the subject matter could not be
treated scientifically, the researcher was also human and could not divest
him or herself of values. Innis responded in "The Role of Intelligence:
Some Further Notes" (1935) and in a more elaborated way in many of
his writings thereafter. Innis's solution was to reconcile free will and
science by pointing to the ingrained, unreflective behaviour of human
beings, which is in large part predictable, and by studying this behaviour.
According to Creighton (1957), Innis saw Frank Underhill's call for social
sciences to drop "the pretence of scientific objectivity" and become
involved in the League for Social Reconstruction as just another version
of Urwick's argument (91).

For a more complete discussion, see Urwick 1935; Innis 1935, 283; Pal
1977; Creighton 1957, 1981; and Westfall 1981.
2 Innis, cited in Pal 1977, 33.
3 Innis discusses this problem at several points. See, for example, 1951a,
33–4, 134.
4 Innis commented that even though many people recognize that providing
grants to subjects that demonstrate their usefulness to government and
industry will destroy the unity and balance of the university curriculum,
and thereby pose a danger to the public, potential recipients will not refuse
the funding and will focus their work in such a way as to get it. He does
not expect that the emerging social sciences, though they should be more
cognizant of the danger, will refuse such funding. As he says, "I am afraid
that just as with other subjects if the federal government should provide
grants the social sciences will be on hand with the most beautifully developed projects for research that federal money can buy" (1951a, 85–6).

5 On the "mechanizing" and "rigidifying" influence of print, see Innis, "Adult Education in the Universities," which was included as Appendix II in *The Bias of Communication* (1951a, 203–14). It consisted of revised extracts from the *Report of the Manitoba Royal Commission on Adult Education* (Winnipeg, 1947), 141–8.

6 For a sense of what Innis meant by "the philosophical approach," see Innis 1977, 5, an updated and slightly edited version of an address given during the Second World War. See also Innis 1946, 64; 1951a, 208–10.

7 The question of balance occupied Innis from the early 1930s. His consciousness of the bias of print and radio, and the resulting preoccupation with territorial expansion, science, and the immediate utility of intellectual work, led him to advocate the retention of the oral tradition in universities. That tradition offers a balance to the bias of print and radio and creates an institutional environment in which the long-term well-being of society and the larger questions of human existence can be addressed. See Dahl 1989.

8 Innis (1946) discussed rigidity most extensively. Watson, in his article on the influence of classics on Innis's thought, provides an interesting discussion of this point (1977).

9 For training the character of the student rather than drowning him or her in information, see, for example, Innis 1956a, 389; 1951a, 84.

10 The National Roundtable, in March 1995, was the culmination of a series of conferences held in 1994–5, held under the auspices of the federal Department of Industry and designed to review Canada's science and technology policy.

11 The material in this section is taken from a report prepared in conjunction with the Canadian Association of University Teachers Commission on University Governance. It represents the views of one of the authors of this chapter, who was a commissioner.

12 The seminar series was sponsored by the Gerstein Program for Support of Advanced Research at York University under the auspices of the Department of Political Science. Meetings took place in 1993 and 1994. The series was designed to produce a book-length manuscript, but it became clear that little consensus emerged on the issues and on democratic administration.

13 For discussion of some issues raised here, see Whitley 1985; Charlton 1990 and various regular "briefings" in the same publication re scientists' duty to the public; Ames 1978; Birke, 1990; Chubin 1993; Hayes 1992; Hopkin 1993; Lewenstein 1992; Martin 1991; Nelkin 1977, 1979, 1987; Prewitt 1988; Sagan 1989.

14 Material for this section is from Salter and Hearn 1996.

15 Material for this section is from Salter 1988.

7 Harold Innis and the Canadian Social Science Research Council: An Experiment in Boundary Work

DONALD FISHER

As a result of the death of Harold Innis, the Foundation will soon need an overall review of other recent changes among Canadian social scientists ... They concern leadership of the C.S.S.R.C., continuity on some of its policy committees, and the role that the community of scholars can play in the learned societies without overcentralizing at Toronto. With his prestige, the advice of Innis was sought without his initiative, because he was thought of as "Innis of Canada"; his colleagues, however unselfish in aim, will be thought of as "men of Toronto".

Anne Bezanson, Rockefeller Foundation, Division of Social Sciences, November 1952[1]

The boundary analysed in this paper was established in 1941 with the creation of the Canadian Social Science Research Council (CSSRC).[2] This self-defined boundary separated the new "corps of social scientists" from the humanist tradition in which they had been housed (Ferguson and Owram 1980–81, 4). The council was the first national organization claiming to represent all the social sciences. Through a process of demarcation, the social sciences were separated from the humanities, the natural sciences, and, professional fields of study. The narrative begins in the early 1930s but focuses primarily on the period between 1938 and 1945. Throughout this period, Harold Innis was the dominant figure. As a result of his involvement, academic social science was separated from the state and placed firmly in the hands of university researchers.

The process of demarcation will be characterized as boundary work (Gieryn 1983; Fisher 1993). The reference is to the work that people do directly and through institutions to create, maintain, and break down boundaries between knowledge units. An assumption is that power penetrates knowledge systems in part through boundary work. This perspective seeks to understand and explain how power is inscribed into and attached to some ideas rather than others. Boundary work incorporates the process whereby legitimacy and cognitive authority are attached to ideas.

Our main objective is to provide a socio-historical account of Innis's role as the key boundary worker in the creation and organization of the CSSRC.[3] The issues in this struggle over territory were autonomy, independence, representation, coordination, and, academic/scientific respectability. The council that emerged was a mainly Anglophone body of researchers. The council was private, independent of government, non-administrative, and, within these terms representative of regions and universities. Its boundary was created around six disciplines – political science, economics (political economy), sociology, psychology, geography, and history. The council had representatives from four sponsoring organizations – the Canadian Historical Association (CHA), the Canadian Political Science Association (CPSA), the Canadian Psychological Association (CPA), and the Canadian Committee of the International Geographical Union (IGU). It shunned government support, while it sought and obtained foundation money from the United States. It denied agricultural economics, anthropology, demography, education, law, and statistics full membership because they were variously too practical, too professional, not scientific enough, or simply too closely tied to government policymaking. Social work was completely excluded on the same grounds. The council maintained a national focus, even though it was modelled after the United States Social Science Research Council (US-SSRC) and had been heavily influenced by input from U.S. foundations.

This chapter is divided into five sections. First, I describe and analyse Innis the social scientist and intellectual. This section draws on and overlaps with the contributions in this volume by Noble (chapter 1), Stamps (chapter 2), and Salter and Dahl (chapter 6). Innis's views on freedom, liberty, balance and stability, and the central place of universities and university researchers in furthering these values underpin his behaviour. The next sections examine critical episodes of the early 1940s in the formation of the CSSRC. The conclusion summarizes the previous discussion and makes brief reference to Innis's continuing influence on the development of the social sciences in Canada.

INNIS AND SOCIAL SCIENCE RESEARCH[4]

Innis believed that academic social scientists could best fulfill their function as "public intellectuals" by undertaking basic, fundamental research. The "spirit of free inquiry" that became so associated with his name was to be maintained at all costs. Only the flexible, open-minded, reflective researcher taking a "philosophical approach" had the potential of producing knowledge that in the long term could contribute to the collective good. Applied or policy research done at the behest of the state or private interests was antithetical to university traditions and by definition created only short-term, space-biased information. Innis believed that academic social scientists, rather than contributing to monopolies of power, should refuse to be drawn into such work.

Similarly, Innis favoured interdisciplinary research and pointed to the negative impact of specialization. Discipline bias and a narrow reliance on scientific practice led to monopolies of knowledge. He favoured time-based, holistic aproaches to scholarship. His definition of the ideal university placed history and the humanities at the centre. By resisting monopolies of both power and knowledge, academic social scientists could counterbalance and counteract the centralizing tendency in Canadian political life and ameliorate the "modern crisis" facing Western democracies.

For Innis, the freedoms inherent in academic culture were central to the long-term balance and stability of Canadian society. As one of the last bastions of the oral tradition, the university was the most important guardian of freedom. The tradition of autonomy creates a space of non-interference and the potential for producing "objective" knowledge and for making critical judgments. For Innis, freedom was the crucial and defining characteristic of a functioning democracy. Any threat therefore to university autonomy and the oral tradition meant more than regress from an ideal. A shift by academic social scientists towards the orientation of space and power, whether this be sponsored externally by the state or internally by university administrators, was an attack on the very fabric of democracy. For these reasons, Innis was totally opposed to academics' engaging directly in the policy-making process. The resulting concern with goals and practicality inevitably diminished the value of the public role of the academic. The job of academic social scientists was to confront bias and monopolies of power (the state) and knowledge (specialization) by doing basic research on the social problems facing Canadian society. These strongly held views Innis translated into institutional form as he took the leading role in the creation and organization of the new council.

AUTONOMY AND REPRESENTATION

The Canadian Research Council in the Social Sciences was formally established in September 1940 in order "to promote research in the Social Sciences in Canada." The council hoped that its broadly representative character would "allow it to further cooperation of scholars in the numerous branches of the social sciences."[5] The organizational phase of the CSSRC begins in 1938 and concludes with its adoption of the above title and a constitution, and the publication of the first annual report in 1942.

From the start this organization was seen as a means to coordinate people and disciplines around Canadian research problems. The founders hoped that this research would produce knowledge to help solve social problems and increase the sense of a Canadian national identity. Economic and cultural penetration by the United States was a central concern. The founders hoped that by expanding the social sciences in Canada they would decrease the flow of social science graduate students to the United States.

While the council was launched in the spring of 1938, earlier suggestions contributed to the movement. In 1931, Burton Hurd (Demography, McMaster University) had at the revived CPSA meetings in Toronto called for a Canadian Council modelled on the US-SSRC.[6] During the 1930s, U.S. foundations were funding Canadian projects such as the "Frontier Series"[7] through the US-SSRC. More directly, these bodies were supporting the Canadian–American Conferences and the McGill Social Science Research Council projects (Shore 1982; Irving 1986; Fisher 1985).The US-SSRC and its relationship with philanthropy were a source of ideas for Canadian social scientists and eventually became a model for the Canadian institution. The Rockefeller Foundation (RF) and the Carnegie Corporation (CC) were the major backers of the US-SSRC. Innis and Edwin Bott (Psychology, University of Toronto) were actively involved in the US-SSRC. They became members of its powerful Program and Policy Committee, established strong personal relationships with the foundation's officers, and, were perceived as "the" social science representatives of Canada (Fisher 1993).

The idea that Canada should start taking care of its own social science affairs was promoted first in the relationship between the RF and McGill University and then specifically by James T. Shotwell (History, Columbia University). In 1932, Shotwell encouraged Innis to get the universities of Toronto, Queen's, and McGill together in something equivalent to the US-SSRC. For Shotwell it was time that Canadians coordinated their own research instead of having their nation's problems "coming in at the odd corners of American research programs."[8] Later as part of the negotiations with the CC, Innis argued that the Canadian Council would eventually serve the same function in Canada as the US-SSRC did in the United States. He described how the Council might act as a "sifting agency" for the foundations.[9]

The immediate impetus for change came from R.H. Coats (Dominion Statistician, Dominion Bureau of Statistics)[10] who wrote to Innis as the pre-eminent social scientist in the English-speaking universities to ask if he would "stir up" interest in the social sciences about creating a national organization. Rather than taking the lead himself, Innis approached his old friend R.G. Trotter (History, Queen's University), vice-president of the CHA, and asked him to make contact with the organizations that Innis thought should be represented. Innis regarded this line of action as being strategically advantageous because history was still the most prestigious and senior social science discipline. As he made clear to Trotter, in his view the historians should take the lead, and then the other organizations, including the CPSA would fall into line.[11]

In these early years, a continuing theme was the issue of autonomy from other organizations such the Canadian Institute of International Relations (CIIA), the Royal Society of Canada, the National Research Council (NRC), and the Canadian Association for Adult Education (CAAE). The struggle over the territory called the "social sciences" was pushed to the forefront and became intense as a result of the new council's organizing efforts. Of the existing institutions, the CIIA was perceived by its members to have a prior claim to the title of "the" national social science research agency. With the support of the RF, the institute had embarked during the 1930s on a massive program of research and publication which extended far beyond international affairs.[12] The CIIA was the only national institution that attempted to coordinate and stimulate research that cut across the discipline boundaries in the social sciences. Given these involvements, the institute naturally regarded the committee as the newcomer.

Initial contacts between the two bodies were cordial and cooperative. N.A.M. MacKenzie (law, Dalhousie University) chaired the CIIA's research committee and became its representative to the council.[13] The potential for problems began to emerge in the summer of 1939. Innis was getting somewhat anxious about the breadth of the CIIA's research plans and asked MacKenzie to arrange for a discussion between his institute's research committee and the council.[14] In addition to MacKenzie, Trotter and Colonel G.L.P. Grant-Suttie (chair, IGU) were also active members of the CIIA.

The discussions took on a different tone with the outbreak of war. On behalf of the institute, National Secretary J.R. Baldwin suggested a new research program centred on making a lasting peace and postwar reconstruction. While Innis was agreeable to the institute's taking the initiative, he made it clear that the draft plan should be taken to the council. In addition to the research, Baldwin suggested a program of public education in international affairs. To further this aim Baldwin approached E.H. Corbett (director, CAAE). The end result was the decision by Baldwin, Innis, and Corbett to form a "united front" in order to carry out the "essential task" of research coordination and public education. Trotter wrote back to Baldwin endorsing the plan on behalf of the "New Social Science Research Council".[15]

In what the council regarded as another attempt to control the territory, the CIIA proposed joint research on the war effort. While Innis and Trotter had expressed their concerns about territorial expansionism,[16] this resistance now took on institutional form. The CPSA objected to the CIIA's plans to extend its research program "to include the effects of war on all phases of the Canadian Economy." After recognizing the institute's willingness to "cooperate" rather than "compete", and the Association's desire not to get involved in disputes about the "demarcation of fields of interest," the CPSA made a clear boundary statement concerning the CIIA. As they put it: "the Association is anxious to prevent any organization, including itself, from exerting undue influence on the direction of research in the social sciences in Canada." Further, it believed that "a healthier development results from leaving research to be undertaken under the direction of individuals in the Graduate Schools of Canada" which, it they noted, was the model adopted by the US-SSRC.[17]

The Council offered to cooperate with the CIIA without a formal partnership. While externally it justified the proposal to cooperate on the grounds that it was mediating between the CPSA and the CIIA, J.E. Robbins (chief, Education Branch, Dominion Bureau of Statistics, and secretary/treasurer), Innis, and Trotter were equally concerned about their council's being subsumed by the CIIA. Any attempt to make the proposed "Council" a "ward" rather than a "full partner" would, they felt, make its position both "difficult" and "unsatisfactory". For these men, the council ought to be the "senior partner" in any deal affecting the social sciences. The key was to avoid entanglement with other institutions and move forward at full speed to get their council firmly launched.[18]

By the end of 1942, Trotter was able to report to the CC that "the organization is now firmly on its feet and ready to move steadily forward".[19] After rejecting five other titles, and after taking into account the objections of the NRC, the council had finally opted for the name "Canadian Social Science Research Council".[20] F.C. Cronkite

(Law, University of Saskatchewan) had taken on the task of moving the committee towards legal status. The nagging "demarcation" issue of choosing an appropriate name had been a constant, and Cronkite anticipated a question of this sort being raised by the dominion secretary of State.[21] As early as December 1939, H.M. Tory (president, Royal Society of Canada) had suggested the title "institute" rather than "Council" in order to avoid confusion with the NRC.[22] After formation of the "Canadian Research Council in the Social Sciences" was announced in September 1940, the NRC registered a protest.[23] According to C.J.Mackenzie (acting president, NRC), the main objective was to avoid the confusion and embarrassment that would undoubtedly occur if the words "Research Council" were included in the title. He argued that the NRC was known in common usage as "the Research Council" and that the words "National Research Council" had become associated with government institutions in a number of countries doing scientific research.

The Secretary of State's Office did not seem inclined to reject the request but questioned the new body's inclusion of "research" in the title on the grounds that it would mislead the public into thinking that the new council was an affiliate of government in the same way as the NRC. Members wanted to avoid confusion with either the NRC or the US-SSRC but disagreed about the need to change. Innis thought that the council had worked hard to produce the present title and therefore ought to proceed.[24] R.A. MacKay (Political Science, Dalhousie University) accepted the removal of the word "research" from the title,[25] and while Trotter regretted the necessity of altering the title, he did look at different ways to order the words.[26]

Cronkite continued to redraft the constitution and at one point seemed willing to drop the word "research" entirely from the title.[27] Cronkite was unable to attend the second meeting of the council in February 1941, so the discussion about name proceeded without him. Just as the natural scientists were worried about their territory, so the social scientists feared dropping the word "research," because their council might then be confused with "organizations in the social service or welfare field." The c,ouncil decided to reshuffle the words to feature "social science" and adopted the name "Canadian Social Science Research Council." This name became part of the constitution and despite continuing pressure from the NRC,[28] remained unaltered until 1958.

In this process of demarcation, a number of disciplines and fields were excluded. For example, law, anthropology, and demography, which at one point were going to be members at large, had been dropped. Innis was adamant about representation.[29] From the beginning, Trotter and Innis had pushed for the inclusion of individuals from national organizations such as the CHA and the CPSA that had "a scientific interest in social and economic problems."[30] Innis insisted law not be listed and be represented by N.A.M. MacKenzie or Cronkite. Education, social work, and agricultural economics, and their respective professional associations, were excluded from full membership because they were regarded as being, in varying degrees, too practical, too professional, or too closely tied to government policy making.

In 1939, the council gave Trotter and Innis the responsibility of creating a permanent body. This meant tackling the sensitive issues of funding and "representation." Contact with U.S. foundations and the US-SSRC began early. These approaches were somewhat predictable, given the personal contacts but also acted as a response to suggestions of some CIIA members who wanted to seek unofficial support from government.[31] The understanding reached with both the CC and the RF depended both on Innis's standing in New York and the trust between Robbins and the Carnegie officers because of his involvement in the Canadian part of their dominion program. At the urging of the foundations, the new committee consulted with W.C. Mitchell, the eminent U.S. economist, and then with Robert T. Crane (executive director, US-SSRC). Even before the first formal meeting, the new council had agreed to act as the agent for a study of "Differential Birthrates in Canada" conducted by Dr Enid Charles because of a work-permit problem.[32] Subsequent grants from the CC and the RF to the council marked the beginning of long-term relationships.

On the issue of representation, the case of education is particularly interesting. Innis had proposed Trotter and Robbins as representatives of special-interest "constituent associations".[33] In Robbins's case, even though he was the de facto representative of the Canadian Education Association (CEA),[34] Innis meant "adult education." For Innis, representation and fund-raising were tied together. In reference to Corbett's association (CAAE) Innis noted that "they have access to the Carnegie purse in a big way and that a general coordination would be very useful from the financial as well as from other points of view."[35] This suggestion received no support, and Robbins opted for exclusion of adult education. He believed that it was unsound procedure to give membership to the association in return for financial gain and implied that such a move might damage the committee's case with the New York foundations. For Robbins, who was a founding member of the CAAE, the association did not fit the membership criteria.

While an approach from social workers had been rejected in 1938,[36] the case of agricultural economics was somewhat different. From the earliest days, D.F. Booth (dominion Department of Agriculture) made a strong case for its participation. He attended the first informal meeting and through Robbins provided an extended account of research under way and described the Canadian Agricultural Economics Society (CAES) as the central Canadian independent research body in this field.[37] Booth's position within government, his suggestion that the council approach Ottawa about setting up a system of dominion fellowships, and surveys of the field reinforced the impression that this field of research was tied to government policy making. The links to government were a problem for Innis and C.A. Dawson (Sociology, McGill University), while Robbins, we can infer, viewed them positively. Innis insisted agricultural economics should be represented by Booth as an associate precisely because this field was tied to the activities of government at both the dominion and provincial levels.[38]

Yet just as some disciplines and fields were denied full membership or excluded, at the insistence of Innis geography was brought in. The first draft of the constitution excluded the IGU. Robbins labelled this body as being of a "different order" to the others and raised the question whether or not the Canadian Geographical Association (CGA) ought to be a constituent body. While the matter is not discussed in the document, Robbins makes it clear elsewhere that Innis saw the CGA as far too "popular" in its outlook and not scholarly enough to be considered. The choice of the IGU had to do more with Innis' insistence on having geography represented than with the scholarly credentials of Grant-Suttie or the IGU. This attitude was probably an extension of Innis's attachment to interdisciplinarity. For Innis, geography was included in his integrated approach to political economy.[39] Innis insisted on the one-representative-member rule and was instrumental in getting geography back inside the "scholarly social sciences." As Trotter commented, Innis thought that the IGU was more of a "research organization" than the Geographical Society and that "it was wiser to extend the list of members at large rather than to include in the list of sponsoring bodies any but very definite professional organizations."[40]

Innis suggested social psychology as a "branch of study" that ought to be represented, particularly since Bott had left word that a Canadian Psychology Association (CPA) was almost certainly going to be created that summer. Yet Innis was against Bott's becoming the representative, on the grounds that the council was already overloaded with Toronto people.[41] During the 1938 meetings of the American Association for the Advancement of Science (AAAS) held in Ottawa, the CPA was founded with Bott as president and G.A. Humphrey (Philosophy, Queen's University) as secretary. This action was in direct response to the "bait" offered by the possibility of naming a representative to the new council.[42] The inducement was offered by Robbins, who was anxious to see the psychologists included. Yet it is clear that Innis was rather suspicious of psychologists. According to Robbins, he placed psychology in "a different stable"[43] from the other social sciences. As noted above, the CPA became one of the sponsoring organizations, and Bott, the first representative member.

A central issue for the founders was the extent to which "practical" or "applied" researchers and their professional organizations should be allowed to participate in the affairs of the new council.[44] From the beginning, the weight of opinion was clearly on the side of "pure," "scholarly social science." References to "welfare" and "social problems," which appeared in an early draft of the constitution, were deleted. In arguing for the inclusion of national organizations in their council, the founders wanted "only scholarly organizations specifically concerned with social sciences" – ones that had a "scientific interest in social and economic problems."[45] Their aim was the creation of "a purely *academic* body."[46]

At the first formal meeting of the Council, Dawson, chair of the Committee to Define Attitudes toward Requests from Social Welfare Organizations, read into the minutes the following statement: "the social sciences in general fall into two groups, broadly, the academic and the applied. The latter includes such bodies as teachers, ministers, welfare or social workers, lawyers, doctors and many others dealing with various aspects of human activity. These groups already have their own professional societies whereas the purely academic social scientists have had little organization, particularly in the field of research. It was in part to meet this deficiency that our organization was formed."[47] The council had formally drawn a distinction between "pure" and "applied" research and between "science" and "non-science".

INDEPENDENCE FROM GOVERNMENT AND ADMINISTRATORS

The debate among social scientists about the appropriate model for the relationship between the new committee and government in light of the war became intense as various suggestions surfaced. Four different initiatives emerged during the early fall of 1939. The first was an offer by Vincent Bladen (Economics, University of Toronto) to utilize the CPSA in order to help coordinate government efforts.[48] The second was the McGill plan to establish a social science division of the NRC in order to deal with war problems and the needs for special training.[49] The third was a plan put forward by the NRC to put the skills of social psychologists in the CPA to work on personnel selection and maintaining industrial production.[50] Finally, Tory (president of the League of Nations Society of Canada) wrote to Innis suggesting a social science section of the Royal Society of Canada be created.[51] This flurry of activity and the general uncertainty no doubt contributed to Trotter's thinking that the work of organizing a new council might be put on hold until after the war. Innis was certain that the time was ripe "to push forward" and to "bring coordination among the various bodies interested." Robbins was equally adamant, and, far from seeing the war as an impediment to organizing, he saw it as a positive factor.[52]

During these early years the council developed a set of policies, both informal and formal, that gave the institution its particular character. The most divisive issue was relations with government. As Robbins noted, interference, particularly "government interference," was the central problem facing the new council. Innis and a majority of members believed that the council should not in any way be dependent on government support.[53] Two series of events brought this issue to a climax within the council. First was the action of the CPA leadership. Bott and Humphrey were advocates for the participation of social scientists in the war effort. Their meetings with the NRC in October 1939 marked the beginning of direct and heavy involvement by psychologists in the Department of Militia and Defence on the classification of military personnel and in the area of propaganda and censorship. The CPA's position was opposed by the council.[54]

Second, there were invitations in 1940 and 1941 to participate in the dominion government's plans for rehabilitation and recontruction. For Innis, here lay a direct threat of government interference in the work of the council. He was passionately opposed to social scientists' taking any role that attached them to government as part of a monopoly of power. The first test came in September 1940, when Robert England and Walter Woods, representing the Cabinet Committee on Demobilization and Re-establishment (later called the Rehabilitation Committee), met with the Council.[55] This committee had been established three months after the outbreak of war to consider the problems of returning veterans. It wanted the council's help to undertake a research program.

Trotter saw the opportunity to serve "national needs" as a "field of opportunity," while the rest of the council spoke in favour of an "independent" stance. Cronkite warned against the danger of becoming "the tool of any political party or group" if money were accepted from government and noted that support from wealthy individuals or foundations might have "strings attached." Innis "urged the need for independence from government finance for the social scientist, and insisted that the origins of the Council in the minds of the public should not be associated with the war effort." Dawson summarized the consensus by stating that social scientists should not hesitate when asked to help "get the information necessary for emergency administration, but at the same time must attempt to retain the long range view."[56] Certainly, Coats, Cronkite, and Booth were in favour of research that could be used to advise government. The council rejected the offer from the Rehabilitation Committee.

The approach in May 1941 by Cyril James (principal, McGill University), chair of the National Committee on Reconstruction (James Committee) was a more serious threat. The council had already established the committee on the Impact of War.[57] As distinct from the CIIA's proposal and the emerging proposal from James, this committee emphasized research rather than policy making and complete independence from government. James believed it was appropriate for social scientists to work in partnership with the state to solve problems facing Canadian society.[58] The final report of the "Impact of War" committee stated that it would be impossible to mount a large comprehensive project as envisaged by Innis[59] because too many social scientists were already engaged in such research.[60]

In a preliminary discussion on the upcoming interview with James and Principal Wallace (Queen's University), Innis made it clear he would resign if the council decided to, in his words, "collaborate" with the Reconstruction Committee.[61] Innis was unable to attend the meeting with James and Wallace. The next morning the council listened to the proposals and after extensive discussions decided to pass the following resolutions which were transmitted to James the same day: "(1) That this Council co-operate with the Committee on Reconstruction to the greatest possible extent that is consistent with the basis on which it is established (2) That the Council accept the invitation to send a delegation to Ottawa to confer with the Committee, and that the Executive with such additional members as may seem advisable should comprise the delegation; the meeting to take place as early a date as can be arranged."[62] Innis made it clear that he and the CPSA had been betrayed and he resigned.[63]

The decision of the Council was relayed to Innis by T.F. McIlwraith (Anthropology, University of Toronto).[64] McIlwraith explained the resolution and pointed out that the decision was unanimous. Even so, against McIlwraith's urging to wait until he saw the minutes, Innis stated that the decision to have further conversations with the Reconstruction Committee was a call for his resignation. Innis sent copies of his resignation letter to Trotter, McIlwraith, and C.A. Ashley (secretary-treasurer, CPSA). In a covering letter to Ashley, Innis explained his decision. First, as the member sponsored by the CPSA, Innis was, in his own words, "impelled to oppose any proposals for direct subventions by private enterprise or by government." Second, this view had been upheld earlier when a proposal favouring co-operation with the Rehabilitation committee was rejected. Third, Innis went over the specific events leading up to his resignation. He recalled his statement on Sunday evening that any "collaboration" with the committee on Reconstruction would "involve my resignation, not only as it conflicted with strong personal views, but also as it conflicted with the position of the Canadian Political Science Association, as I had interpreted it."[65]

Trotter, Cronkite, and McIlwraith were disturbed by what they regarded as Innis's unnecessary and inappropriate action. The group met with the James Committee in June.[66] The council was asked by the committee to consider consulting on and/or taking on responsibility for two projects – namely, a demographic study on population resettlement and a study of the situation following the 1914–18 war. In response, the council's delegation refused to take on either study and instead suggested that the Committee set up two groups of experts to work under its "direct auspices." For the demographic study it suggested that Coats, Booth, Hurd, and possibly Enid Charles might be best. W.A. Macintosh (Economic Advisory Committee, Ottawa) was proposed as the chair for the First World War study. While the tone of the letter was polite, there can be little doubt that the council had come firmly down on the side of "pure" rather than "applied" research. It recognized that it was being asked to undertake contract research whose results would be "confidential and entirely at the disposal of your Committee and of the Government". While James took issue with the council's distancing itself from government[67] the decision was final. In July, Leonard Marsh (economist, McGill University) was appointed research director for the Reconstruction Committee.[68] The council saw this appointment as a clear signal that the James Committee had "really undertaken to have its research done more directly under its own auspices"[69]

In this crucial phase Innis's definition of independence and autonomy, and therefore of the appropriate context for scientific research, won the day. Yet it is not clear whether his resignation actually made that much difference. The majority of the council was terribly sceptical about getting involved directly in government research and demonstrated this in its negotiation on rehabilitation. More than likely the threat of losing Innis was the catalyst that confirmed its resolve. Innis was eventually persuaded to withdraw his resignation.

Meanwhile the debate about the appropriate role for social scientists received a public airing in the *Canadian Historical Review*. In March 1941, the journal presented an article by A.R.M. Lower (History, United College, University of Manitoba), "The Social Sciences in the Post-War World", where he argued that social scientists could not remain aloof but rather should be active in solving society's problems (Lower 1941). This piece was discussed at the annual meeting of the CHA, and in June the review published a symposium on the topic. McIlwraith supported Lower and argued that social scientists, as members of the body politic, must consider how best they could play their part. Innis was adamantly opposed to any such consideration. Increased involvement with government would, he was convinced, lead to the "withdrawal of social scientists from research work of a fundamental character," which in turn would lower the standards of intellectual work. For Innis, "the individual becomes accustomed to governmental requirements and the academic profession becomes a standing surplus reserve labour pool to meet the varying demands of governments."[70] Social scientists would therefore reach the stage where they were dependent on governments and could no longer claim to be scholars.

Honour was satisfied on both sides. While no commitments were made to Innis, the line between 'pure' and 'applied' research was firmly drawn, so henceforth it was unlikely that the dominion government would approach the council. In this way, Innis's strongly held views and those of the majority of council with regard to relations with governments held sway. McIlwraith's (1941) report for the council, reinforced the idea that "pure" research was superior to "applied" or "purposive" projects, because the latter were "inevitably chosen according to governmental needs."[71] Yet while the Council refused to become involved, many social scientists took positions in government, and members of the council performed contract research for the government during the war. This "firm compromise" became the council's official position at the November meeting.[72]

The awkwardness of the council's acting as an agent for the CC in regard to the Charles study on birth rates reached a climax in 1942, when the Canadian government decided to undertake the research. For Innis, the available material was unsatisfactory, and he believed that "it would be a grave mistake to put ourselves in the position of assistants to the government." He recommended returning the money to the CC unless it could be transferred to another project. The remaining funds were transferred and used to support a grant-in-aid for C.B. Sissons (History, Victoria College) for his work on Egerton Ryerson.[73]

Innis opposed not only institutional involvement with government but also the participation of administrators in the council's affairs. Innis and Trotter were quick to reduce the number of civil servants to four associate, non-voting members early in the organizational phase. In turn, this view received support from both Mitchell and Crane, and therefore, by extension, from the New York foundations. As Robbins commented later, this limitation "made the university academics feel secure in their purity. Governments and their servants were suspected of something less than purity in their research interests, as were the university Presidents. They were supposed to be administrators first, with axes to grind, researchers second."[74] The position of Coats and Robbins was always somewhat ambiguous, though the former retired as dominion statistician in 1942 and joined the faculty at the University of Toronto. Robbins, the anomaly in face of this rule, was made a special case because of his skills, his foundation contacts, and his personality.

Innis's image of the council was that of a body of university researchers whose views were not distorted by an administrative stance. He wanted no taint of practical, applied or purposive intent and extended his criticism of the administrative stance to university administrators. Innis hoped that the council "would gradually raise the prestige of the social sciences and increase the possibilities for research." Perhaps in an attempt at self-irony he went on to say "if we could stimulate self-esteem and self-confidence to the point that University Presidents and heads of departments ceased to clutter up the scene, we should have done much."[75] So it became an "unwritten rule" of the council that when a member became a full-time government employee, a university president, or a dean, then he or she was expected to resign.[76]

N.A.M. MacKenzie withdrew from council affairs when he accepted the position of president of the University of New Brunswick in the summer of 1940.[77] Bott was replaced in October 1940 when he took up a position with the Department of National Defence – a drastic change, given Bott's central role in creating the council.

Yet there is some evidence which suggests personal antagonism between Innis and Bott[78] and the psychologists had been under suspicion from the beginning. The purer social scientists such as Innis were shocked by the psychologists' apparent willingness to accept money from any source.[79] H.A. Angus (Economics, University of British Columbia) resigned in July 1941 when he became special assistant to the secretary of state for external affairs.[80] Further, the "rule" probably accounts for some of the antagonism between Innis and Dean Cronkite. Mackintosh, on loan from Queen's University to the dominion Department of Finance, was viewed with great suspicion. Not only had Leonard Marsh been ignored by the early organizers, but his acceptance of the position as research director with the James Committee was regarded by Innis and Dawson with distaste. It confirmed their worst fears about the quality of Marsh's work.[81]

COORDINATION AND INTERDISCIPLINARITY

The founders hoped that the existence of the council would contribute in a general way to coordination and liaison among disciplines. In line with this objective, the first meetings of the organizing committee were arranged to coincide with the overlapping annual meetings (the "learneds") of the Royal Society of Canada, the CPSA, and the CHA, intended as a measure of national coordination. In addition, the founders regarded their council as a means for coordinating the social sciences to work on Canadian social problems. Innis favoured inter-disciplinary work under the general umbrella of political economy. He was opposed to specialization, believing that it would lead to strife and dogmatism and away from understanding.[82] The council could thus provide a counterbalance to the negative impact of specialization (monopoly of knowledge). Knowledge of social problems could in the long term help to preserve democracy in Canada.

CONCLUSION

The CSSRC had become a mainly anglophone but representative body of researchers that was private, independent of government, and non-administrative. Innis's influence had been decisive. Not only did he have the confidence of the foundations, but he was also the only scholar who had a place in just about all the discipline associations and the interested organizations. He was president of the CPSA (1937–38), a member of CHA Council (1937–40), and a fellow of the Royal Society of Canada, and he was recognized as both a geographer and someone who was active in international relations. He was the trusted and acknowledged "dean of the corps" both at home and abroad. As John Marshall (director, Division of Humanities, RF) observed, Innis was without doubt the "leading figure" in Canadian social science.[83]

The council had established a nationalistic focus and was regarded by its members as the first national organization to represent all the social sciences. It was a typically Canadian mix – a private institution rather than a public body, which shunned government support while seeking and obtaining U.S. foundation money. Its members believed that this reliance on non-governmental support meant that these disciplines and their research on social problems would be more scholarly, more scientific, more "pure," and hence more legitimate. Yet the national focus was preserved because representation was sought not only by discipline but also by region, by university, and, in a token sense, from Quebec and francophones. The institution was modelled on the US-SSRC both structurally and operationally.

The council was made in Innis's image. He was the key "boundary worker" throughout the organizational phase. The weight of his reputation and the dominance of his personality meant that many on the council simply went along with him.[84] Rather than taking part in government research, which in his view was nothing less than a "retreat to barbarism,"[85] the council would exercise its appropriate cultural function as the sponsor of independent scholarship. In effect, academic social science had been separated from the state and placed firmly in the hands of university researchers.

As Innis himself put it, the council "became accustomed to certain rules such as the exclusion of administrators, deans, presidents and the like from membership, a primary concern with scholarship as a prerequisite to membership, a tradition that the Council must avoid government entanglements, that it must concentrate on assisting smaller institutions outside the central provinces and that the work of the scholars, worthy of support requires time, meaning years." The general principle was that everything should be done to support the individual researcher, in the form of scholarships and fellowships, grants-in-aid, research professorships, book bursaries and sabbatical leaves. These "rules of conduct" dominated the affairs of council for the next fifteen years.[86]

For the rest of his life Innis had direct control. He sat continuously as a member of the council from its creation through to the end of 1949. He first represented the CPSA and then in 1945 was named to a four-year term by the IGU.

Innis's influence on the council continued after his death. His "ghost" was present for the rest of the 1950s through the actions of such protégés as S.D. Clark (Sociology, University of Toronto) and George E. Britnell (Economics, University of Saskatchewan). At the November Council meeting in 1954, during a discussion of the role of the Council if a "Canada Council" were formed, Roger Myers (Psychology, University of Toronto) reported in scathing terms how members still deferred to Innis' viewpoint.

"Right from the start of this discussion the cold dead hand of Harold Innis rested heavily on the Council table. Lower in grim tones reminded the Council that Innis had always been afraid of government domination. There followed a chorus of others who shuddered at the thought of even accepting any filthy money from the Government through the Canada Council (not that anybody had been offered anything yet)."[87] In 1956, Britnell, in a discussion of the Ford Foundation's grant to the economists at Queen's University, made it clear that the approach was "a long way from the Innis tradition."[88]

For Innis, the ideal social science was scholarly, pure, and academic. Liberty and democracy were best preserved when university researchers were given the freedom to conduct basic research without interference from government or university administrators. Innis's "quest for certainty" was imprinted on the CSSRC. Through this organization he became the dominant influence on the development of the social sciences in English-speaking Canada through to the creation in 1957 of the Canada Council, which marked the beginning of a new relationship between the state and these disciplines.

NOTES

Material from archival collections has been quoted with permission.

1 Rockefeller Archive Center (RAC), Rockefeller Foundation, Record Group 1.1, 427 Canada, Box R954, File 427S, University of Toronto-Innis, 1952–54, Anne Bezanson (Officer, Rockefeller Foundation) to J.H. Willits (Director, Division of the Social Sciences, Rockefeller Foundation), 18 November, 1952.
2 Department of Educational Studies, University of British Columbia. I wish to acknowledge the financial assistance of the Social Sciences and Humanities Research Council of Canada as well as the research assistance of Bill Maciejko, Leita Richardson, Theresa Richardson, and Paul Ridding.
3 While the biography of John Robbins, the CSSRC's secretary/treasurer (McLeish 1978), and the Timlin-Faucher Report (Timlin and Faucher 1968) both briefly describe the events leading up to creation of the council, the only full account is in Fisher's (1991) general history of the cssrc, which does not provide a detailed account of Innis's role in Council affairs. See also CSSRC 1940–41, 1950.
4 In addition to the chapters by Stamps (2), Noble (1), and Salter and Dahl (6), refer to Innis 1946, 1952a.
5 CSSRC 1940/41, 1942. Also see Social Science Federation of Canada (henceforth SSFC), Volume 20, File, J.E. Robbins, 1938–1940, "Press Release," September 1940.
6 John Robbins referred to a speech at these meetings as the earliest suggestion for a social science council. Interview (by author), Ottawa, John Robbins, December 1986. I have not been able to locate any record of this announcement in the proceedings of the CPSA.

7 This project was an investigation of the "pioneer areas" Canada. This research, which led to an eight-volume series, was published as *Frontiers of Settlement* (Dawson 1934, 1936; Dawson and Younge 1940). For accounts see Hiller 1982; Shore 1982; and Helmes-Hayes 1985.

8 University of Toronto Archives (henceforth UTA), Harold Adams Innis Papers, Box 14, Folder 14, Shotwell to Innis, 27 July 1932. James T. Shotwell directed the interdisciplinary studies on Canadian–American relations supported by Carnegie Philanthropy. He was director, Division of Economic History, Carnegie Endowment for International Peace.

9 Carnegie Corporation Archives (CCA), File – Canadian Social Science Research Council 1938–1945, Interview: John M. Russell (assistant to president, Carnegie Corporation) to Innis, 23 June 1939.

10 Interview: Robbins, December 1986.

11 Queen's University Archives (henceforth QUA), R.G. Trotter papers, Additions, Box 3, Folder 1, Innis to Trotter, 12 April 1938. In this letter Innis refers back to the letter from Coats asking him to "stir up" interest.

12 RAC, Rockefeller Foundation, Record Group 1.1, 427 Canada, Box 30, File 427S, Canadian Institute of International Affairs, 1936–1938; and File 427S, Canadian Institute of International Affairs.

13 SSFC, Volume 20, File – J.E. Robbins 1938–1940, Mackenzie to Robbins, 21 November 1938. Mackenzie was a founding member of the CIIA and remained active in it through the 1930s and the war years. See Waite 1987.

14 CCA, File – Canadian Social Science Research Council 1938–1945, "Note on Meeting of Innis, Mackenzie, Trotter and Robbins at Canton, June 21 re problems of Social Science Research Committee," attached to letter Robbins to Dollard, 22 June 1939.

15 SSFC, Volume 20, File – J.E. Robbins 1938–1940, Baldwin to Trotter, 20 September 1939; and Trotter to Baldwin, 21 September 1939.

16 UTA, Innis Papers, Box 12, Folder 12 – Committee on Social Science Research in Canada, 1939–1940, Trotter to Innis, 18 October 1939. In this letter Trotter concludes that the Institute was laying claim to all social science research.

17 Ibid., "Memorandum on the Research Project of the Canadian Institute of International Affairs," 4 November 1939.

18 CCA, File – Canadian Social Science Research Council 1938–1945, Robbins to Dollard, 21 November 1939, and Robbins to Dollard 9 November 1939; and Robbins to Trotter, 10 November 1939.

19 CCA, File, Canadian Social Science Research Council, 1938–1945, Trotter to Robert M. Lester (Secretary, Carnegie Corporation), 15 December 1941.

20 The rejected names, in chronological order, were the Social Science

Research Committee, the Committee on Research in the Social Sciences, the Committee on Social Science Research in Canada, the Canadian Council for Research in the Social Sciences, and the Canadian Research Council in the Social Sciences.

21 SSFC, Volume 22, File – R.G. Trotter 1940–1951, reference to Dean Cronkite raising the issue in the letter, Trotter to Robbins, 30 September 1940.

22 SSFC, Volume 20, File – J.E. Robbins 1938–1940, Robbins to Trotter, 4 December 1939; and Trotter to Robbins, 6 December 1939.

23 SSFC, Volume 26, File – National Research Council, 1948–1950, S.J. Cook (officer-in-charge, Research Plans and Publication Section) to Robbins, 23 September 1940.

24 University of Saskatchewan Archives (henceforth USA), Cronkite Papers, Box 27, F. Organization, 3(a) Correspondence; (5)a 1940 CSSRC, C.J. Mackenzie (acting president, NRC) to Cronkite, 19 November 1940; Alex A. Cattanach (Department of Secretary of State, Company's Branch) to Cronkite, 1 October 1940; and Innis to Cronkite, 12 October 1940.

25 SSFC, Volume 18, File – R.A. Mackay 1940–1958, Mackay to Robbins, 10 October 1940.

26 SSFC, Volume 22, File – R.G. Trotter 1940–1951, Trotter to Robbins, 30 September 1940.

27 SSFC, Volume 12, File – Cronkite F.C. 1940–1945, Cronkite to Robbins, 30 November 1940 with attached draft Constitution; and Cronkite to Robbins, 23 January 1941.

28 USA, Cronkite Papers, Box 27, F. Organization, 3(a) Correspondence; (5)a 1941–42 CSSRC, Robbins to Cronkite, 12 February 1941; and, C.J. Mackenzie to Cronkite, 12 April 1941. Also SSFC, Volume 12, File – Cronkite F.C. 1940–1945, Cronkite to Robbins, 25 April 1941.

29 SSFC, Volume 14, File – H.A. Innis, 1939–1940, Innis to Robbins, 10 May 1940.

30 Social Science Federation of Canada Office (henceforth SSFCO), Minutes of SSRC 1940–1944. Appendix 1, Minutes of Meeting to discuss ways of improving ongoing social and economic research, Ottawa, 22 May 1938.

31 SSFC, Volume 20, File – J.E. Robbins 1938–1940, Baldwin to Trotter, 20 September 1939.

32 CCA, File, Canadian Social Science Research Council, 1938–1945, Charles Dollard (Carnegie Corporation officer) to Robbins, 6 September 1940.

33 SSFC, Volume 14, File – H.A. Innis, 1940–1953, Robbins to Innis, 18 October 1939.

34 CCA, File – Canadian Social Science Research Council 1938–1945, Robbins to Dollard, 8 November 1938; and, SSFC, File – J. E. Robbins

1938–1940, J.G. Althouse (Secretary/Treasurer, Canadian Education Association) to Robbins, 30 January 1939.

35 SSFC, Innis to Robbins, 6 October 1939.

36 QUA, Trotter papers, Additions, Box 3, Folder 1, H.M. Cassidy, "Some Essentials in Canadian Social Welfare," attached to a letter, Robbins to Trotter, 24 October 1938; and SSFC, Volume 20, File – J.E. Robbins 1938–1940, Bott to Robbins, 21 October 1938.

37 SSFC, Volume 20, File – J.E. Robbins 1938–1940, Booth to Robbins, 26 January 1939.

38 SSFC, Volume 14, File – H.A. Innis, 1939–1940, Innis to Robbins, 10 May 1940.

39 SSFC, Volume 20, File, J.E. Robbins 1938–1940, Trotter to Robbins, 4 March 1940, and, Robbins to Trotter, 1 December 1939; Attachment: "Point for Discussion re Constitution of Research Body"; also John E. Robbins Papers (henceforth JERP), Volume 2, File, Canadian Social Science Research Council 1938–1973, J.E. Robbins, "Reminiscences, C.S.S.R.C. (later SSRCC) to 1951"; and Interview: Robbins, Ottawa, December 1986.

40 UTA, Innis Papers, Box 12, Folder 12 – Committee on Social Science Research in Canada, 1939–1940, Trotter to Innis, 15 December 1939. Also see SSFC, Volume 20, File – J.E. Robbins 1938–1940, Robbins to Trotter, 1 March 1940; and Trotter to Robbins, 4 March 1940.

41 QUA, Trotter papers, Additions, Box 3, Folder 1, Innis to Trotter, 21 April 1938.

42 Ibid., Robbins to Trotter, 4 July 1938; JERP, Volume 2, File – Canadian Social Science Research Council 1938–1973 Reminiscences, "C.S.S.R.C. – (later SSRCC) to 1951."; and Interview: Robbins, December 1986.

43 Interview: Robbins, December 1986.

44 Other organizations whose names were mentioned as possible members were the Canadian Welfare Council and the National Committee for Mental Hygiene. SSFC, Volume 20, File – J.E. Robbins 1938–1940, Robbins to Trotter, 8 September 1938.

45 SSFCO, Appendix 1, Minutes of Meeting to discuss ways of improving ongoing social and economic research, Ottawa, 22 May 1938. Minutes of SSRC 1940–1944; and SSFC, Volume 20, File, J.E. Robbins 1938–1940, Trotter to Robbins, 28 February 1940, with attached draft constitution.

46 SSFCO, Minutes, 22 May 1940, Appendix 3, "Summary of Individual Views." Minutes of SSRC 1940–1944. Underlined in the original.

47 SSFCO, Minutes of the CSSRC 1940–1944, 17 September 1940, p. 6.

48 SSFC, Volume 20, File – J.E. Robbins 1938–1940, Bladen to Coats, 21 September 1939.

49 Ibid., Robbins to Trotter, 23 September 1939. This was a revival of a plan first put forward in the mid-1930s by H.M. Tory, (President of the NRC from 1930 to 1935). See JERP, File – Canadian Social Science

Research Council 1938–1973, Reminiscences, "C.S.S.R.C. – (later SSRCC) to 1951."

50 SSFC, Volume 20, File – J.E. Robbins 1938–1940, Robbins to Trotter, 3 October 1939.

51 UTA, Innis Papers, Box 12, Folder 12 – Committee on Social Science Research in Canada, 1939–1940, Tory to Innis, 24 October 1939.

52 SSFC, Volume 14, File – H.A. Innis, 1940–1953, Robbins to Innis, 21 September 1939, and Robbins to Innis, 18 October 1939; Innis to Robbins (n.d., after 21 September 1939 and before 6 October 1939); and Robbins to Innis, 18 October 1939.

53 SSFC, Volume 22, File – R.G. Trotter 1940–1951, Robbins to Trotter, 21 August 1940. For an account of Innis's opposition to social scientists becoming involved in government research and the importance of independent scholarship, see Creighton 1957; Berger 1970, Chap. 4.

54 SSFC, Volume 20, File – J.E. Robbins 1938–1940, Bott to Robbins, 12 October 1939; Robbins to Trotter, 3 October 1939; and Dawson to Robbins, 11 October 1939.

55 QUA, Trotter Papers, Series A, Box 1, Folder 20, Correspondence 1941, July – December, see reference to meeting in letter Robbins to Trotter, 8 September 1941.

56 SSFCO, Minutes of SSRC 1940–1944. Minutes, 22 May 1940, Appendix 3, "Summary of Individual Views."

57 SSFCO, Minutes of SSRC 1940–1944, Minutes of Second Meeting, 8–9 February 1941.

58 When James was installed as principal in January 1940, he used his inaugural address to commit McGill to a program of integrated research and studies that would help solve society's problems (Shore 1982, pp. 11–12). Similarly, in late 1940, in conversation with C.J. Mackenzie, James made clear his intention "to get some machinery which (will) provide the effective types of cooperation in economics, financial and political affairs" that already existed with the NRC in the scientific and industrial field. USA, Cronkite Papers, Box 27, F. Organization, 3(a) Correspondence, (5) a 1940, CSSRC, C.J. Mackenzie to Cronkite, 19 November 1940.

59 Innis had proposed earlier that the council might undertake surveys on the impact of war in different parts of the country. SSFC, Volume 22, File – R.G. Trotter 1940–1951, Trotter to Executive Committee, 23 October 1940. Attached "Memorandum on Proposed Studies of the Impact of the War on Canada to be submitted to the Canadian Research Council in the Social Sciences" by Harold Innis, 18 October 1940.

60 Canadian Political Science Association (henceforth CPSAP), MG 28 1 86, Volume 13, File – Canadian Social Science Research Council 1940–1964, Innis to C.A. Ashley (Secretary/Treasurer CPSA), 23 May 1940. Reference to the letter, Trotter to Willits (RF), 27 May 1941.

61 CPSAP, Volume 13, File – Canadian Social Science Research Council 1940–1964, Innis to Ashley, 28 May 1941.

62 SSFC, Volume 22, File – R.G. Trotter 1940–1951, Trotter to James, 26 May 1941.

63 SSFC, Volume 14, File – H.A. Innis, 1940–1953, Innis to Robbins, 27 May 1941.

64 SSFC, Volume 18, File – T.F. McIlwraith 1940–1960, McIlwraith to Robbins, 28 May 1941; also Volume 22, File – R.G. Trotter, 1940–1951, Trotter to Executive, 30 May 1941.

65 CPSAP, Volume 13, File – Canadian Social Science Research Council 1940–1964, Innis to Ashley, 28 May 1941.

66 SSFCO, Minutes of SSRC 1940–1944, Minutes of Executive Committee, 14 June 1941.

67 SSFC, Volume 22, File – R.G. Trotter 1940–1951, Trotter to James, 17 June 1941; and James to Trotter, 21 June 1941.

68 Since 1930 Marsh had the director of research of the Rockefeller-funded Social Research Council at McGill. See Shore 1982, Chaps. 6 and 7; Irving 1986; and, Fisher 1985.

69 USA, Cronkite Papers, Box 27, F. Organization, 3(a) Correspondence, 5 (a) 1941–1942, CSSRC, Trotter to Cronkite, 10 September 1941; also SSFC, Volume 25, File – Canadian Government Departments and Agencies 1942–1952, "Committee on Reconstruction" Précis of Main Program, September 1941.

70 CHA Symposium; footnote 2, p. 119.

71 SSFCO, Minutes of the SSRC 1940–1944, Thomas F. McIlwraith, "Current Research in the Social Sciences in Canada," p. 4, attached to Minutes of Second Meeting, 8–9 February 1941.

72 Ibid., Minutes of First Annual Meeting, 7–8 November 1941.

73 SSFC, Volume 14, File–H.A. Innis, 1940–1953, Innis to Robbins, 25 June 1942; and Memo to Members of the Executive Committee, 12 August 1942.

74 Interview: Robbins, Ottawa, December 1986.

75 QUA, R.G. Trotter Papers, Box 1, Series A, Folder 20, Correspondence 1941 July-December, Innis to Trotter, 11 July 1941. The irony is that Innis was the head of the Department of Political Economy, University of Toronto, from 1937 to 1952. See Drummond 1983.

76 Interview: Robbins, Ottawa December 1986. Also JERP, Volume 2, File, Canadian Social Science Research Council, 1938–1973: Reminiscences, John E. Robbins, "C.S.S.R.C. (later SSRCC) to 1951", p.7. Robbins specifically refers as cases where this rule was observed to N.A.M. Mackenzie, who became president of the University of New Brunswick, and Henry Angus, R.A. MacKay, and Bott, who all took positions with government.

77 UBCA, Mackenzie Papers, Box 22, File 2, Trotter to Mackenzie, 21 September 1940. Trotter extends an invitation to Mackenzie to continue as a member of council.

78 SSFC, Volume 14, file – G. Humphrey, 1940–1944, Robbins to Bott, (n.d.). There is evidence that Bott and Innis did not get on very well, see Interview: Robbins, December 1986.

79 Interview: Robbins, December 1986. This is a reference to Humphrey who said he would accept money from anyone – including the communist party – to do research.

80 QUA, Trotter Papers, Series A, Box 1, Folder 20, Correspondence 1941 July – December, Trotter to Angus, 11 July 1941; also SSFC, Volume 22, File – R.G. Trotter 1940–1951, Trotter to Robbins, July 10, 1941.

81 Interview: Robbins, December 1986.

82 UTA, Innis Papers, Box 11, Folder 15-E.J. Urwick to H.A. Innis, 1936–1944, Urwick to Innis, 24 April 1944. Urwick refers back to comments made by Innis.

83 RAC, RF, 1.1, 427 Canada, Box 25, File 427R, Canadian Humanities Research Council Visit, 1944, John Marshall (Director, Division of Humanities, RF) Interviews: 21, 22 March 1944, Toronto.

84 Interview: Robbins, December 1986.

85 CHA 1940/41: 85.

86 SSFC, Volume 20, File, J.E. Robbins, 1950–1965, Harold A. Innis, "To Honour John Robbins," speech read at the 1951 retirement dinner for John Robbins, p. 5; and Volume 23, File – Sponsoring Bodies, 1942–1951, IGU November 1945.

87 Canadian Psychological Association Papers, MG 28 I 161, Volume 4, File, Committee on Research Financing, 1954–1956, Myers (former secretary/treasurer, CPA) to Julian Blackburn (Psychology, Queen's University, and president, CPA), 24 November 1954.

88 SSFC, Volume 9, File – Professor G.E. Britnell, 1948–1961, Britnell to Robbins, 18 May 1956.

8 Monopoles du savoir ou critique culturelle journalistique? Innis et Victor Barbeau discutent la presse, le nationalisme, et les pratiques intellectuelles

MICHÈLE MARTIN AND
WILLIAM J. BUXTON

Les travaux de Victor Barbeau et Harold Adams Innis ont atteint, chacun a leur manière, un statut quasi iconique dans les milieux francophones et anglophones respectivement. En même temps, les travaux de Innis ont été très peu influents au Québec et l'oeuvre de Barbeau est probablement encore moins connu au Canada anglais. Cet article essaie de juxtaposer quelques-unes de leurs idées sur la culture, le nationalisme, la presse, et le journalisme dans le but d'encourager une réflexion sur les différences et convergences des traditions intellectuelles canadiennes-françaises et canadiennes-anglaises.

De prime abord, il semble exister très peu de points commun entre les deux penseurs, d'autant plus qu'ils ont travaillé à différents registres. Chez Innis, on trouve l'académicien quintessentiel qui renonce à s'engager dans des activités pratiques, préférant les recherches académiques documentées. Barbeau, par contre, tout en s'étont consacrée l'enseignement universitaire,[1] trente ans de sa vie à enseigner à l'École des Hautes Études commerciales (HEC) à Montréal, l'homme a d'abord taillé sa réputation dans le domaine du journalisme polémique, pionnier de la critique culturelle journalistique, surtout avec ses écrits dans *La Presse* de Montréal. S'il n'existait, dans ces deux formes d'activités, que des divergences de valeurs et de présuppositions, il n'y aurait aucun intérêt à comparer les deux penseurs. Mais, chez Barbeau comme chez Innis, on est frappé par un même diagnostique sur le malaise de la civilisation moderne, même si le premier examine le Québec et le second le Canada anglais. Qui plus est, leurs points de vue se rapprochent à plusieurs égards. Se situant au coeur de la société où ils vivent, les deux épousent des perspectives profondément marginales quant à la pensée dominante.

Comme le fait remarquer John Watson, le point de vue d'Innis se révèle celui d'un "homme marginal." Élevé dans un milieu très modeste de l'Ontario rurale, il adoptera, sa vie durant, la perspective de l'étranger, même après avoir connu la réussite et une influence certaine dans le milieu académique (Watson, 1981). Barbeau, d'autre part, malgré son appartenance à l'élite canadienne-française, demeure marginal face au puissant clergé et à l'élite anglo-canadienne. De plus, les deux hommes se greffent très peu au centre du pouvoir pan-canadien. Ils partagent aussi un sens profond d'aliénation de l'empire britannique en déclin, d'une part, et une inquiétude face à l'expansion de l'empire américain d'autre part. En ce sens, les deux se préoccupent de la menace de l'impérialisme américain face à la vie culturelle de leurs communautés respectives. Chez Innis, cette préoccupation se manifeste dans sa crainte pour la survie de la culture canadienne face à l'invasion américaine. Chez Barbeau, l'invasion américaine se révèle comme une menace face à la langue et à la culture canadienne française.

Jusqu'à un certain point, nous pourrions attribuer ces parallèles aux similarités dans les trajets de vie respectifs de ces deux hommes. Barbeau et Innis sont tous deux nés en 1894, se sont engagés dans les forces armées durant la première guerre et ont été blessés en action. La connaissance d'Innis des horreurs de la guerre l'a transformé en pacifiste pour la vie, se méfiant du nationalisme et des monopoles du savoir qui pourraient le stimuler (Watson, 1981; Gwynn, 1992). Pendant leur vie, ces deux Canadiens ont été témoins de la croissance et de la centralisation des agences fédérales et nationales. Leurs orientations face aux grandes institutions de la vie canadienne sont remarquablement similaires: volontaires et individualistes, ils se retrouvent souvent en conflit avec des agences officielles. Par exemple, Barbeau et Innis ont démissionné de la Société royale du Canada, après moins de deux ans pour protester contre des pratiques qu'ils ne pouvaient tolérer!

Tandis que ni l'un ni l'autre n'est politiquement radical, les deux adhèrent aux courants libéraux, quoique avec des variantes, ce qui, compte tenu de l'importance qu'ils attachent à la liberté individuelle, les rendent critiques face aux institutions établies. Pourtant, ni Innis ni Barbeau ne peut être qualifié d'homme du peuple. Tous deux ont des penchants nettement élitistes, croyant que l'agence pour le changement social progressif se trouve chez les gens éduqués et friands de culture classique.

Malgré ces orientations similaires, les deux penseurs ont abordé la critique sociale de façon différente. On peut remarquer un contraste marqué entre les préoccupations intellectuelles d'Innis quant à la compilation massive de documents et l'engagement pratique de Barbeau en journalisme. Dans cette étude, nous essayons d'expliquer comment ces deux intellectuels ont pu en venir à des pratiques si différentes malgré la similarité de certaines de leurs valeurs. Nous porterons une attention toute particulière à leur divergence de vues sur les monopoles du savoir, le nationalisme et la culture en analysant leurs écrits associés à la presse, au journalisme et au rôle des intellectuels dans la société.

Nous affirmons que leur divergence n'est pas le simple produit de leur différences individuelles. Elle prend plutôt racine dans les enseignements religieux inculqués à chacun par leurs Églises respectives et dans la notion de travail intellectuel associée à chacune de leurs communautés. Les diverses facettes du point de vue de Barbeau fourniront le fil conducteur de notre étude, les opinions d'Innis sur une série de questions connexes nous serviront de point de comparaison et de critique. À travers ce processus, nous espérons pouvoir éclairer quelque peu les contextes différents entourant le travail intellectuel dans les milieux canadiens-français et canadiens-anglais.

CRITIQUE CULTURELLE, IDENTITÉ CULTURELLE, CULTURE DOMINANTE

Victor Barbeau se défend d'être un intellectuel. Se définissant plutôt comme un praticien voulant améliorer la culture des siens. Il orientera toute sa carrière en ce sens, publiant, en plus de ses chroniques journalistiques, des ouvrages en économie politique, et en culture pour permettre à la majorité d'accéder à ses ouvrages et il choisit de distribuer plusieurs de ses publications gratuitement dans les institutions scolaires. Sa carrière, Barbeau la commence néanmoins comme journaliste, polémiste, un style qui ne le quittera pas de toute sa vie.

Victor Barbeau[2] a publié, dans le quotidien *La Presse* entre 1918–20 et 1931–33,[3] des chroniques quotidiennes constituant la principale source de données de cette étude. À la fin des années 20, ce journal distribue quotidiennement environ 160 000 copies sur semaine et près de 200 000 le samedi. Le contexte de l'analyse fourni par ces données repose sur une construction, au quotidien, d'une culture dominante, établie à partir de l'énonciation du légitime et du non légitime, les droits du premier et les torts du second; du savoir et du non-savoir; du faire et du laisser-faire, ces dualités représentent les deux côtés d'une même médaille s'interinfluençant. Autrement dit, l'étude examine la relation entre culture d'élite et culture populaire établie par Victor Barbeau à cette époque, en terme de "démocratisation" d'un savoir qui, jusque là, avait peu intéressé la presse.

Selon Barbeau, la presse représente un média approprié pour

éduquer les masses à la culture d'élite, en leur indiquant la forme correcte de penser et d'agir. Pour lui, l'accessibilité des masses à la Vraie culture représente un processus de démocratisation culturelle. Innis, par contre, voit la presse comme un média dont la mécanisation et la commercialisation ont entravé son utilisation comme moyen d'améliorer la culture des masses. Tournés essentiellement vers l'immédiat, les quotidiens sont obsédés par le divertissement et le sensationnalisme, allant d'un sujet à l'autre sans continuité ni profondeur. Ainsi, Innis suggère que, sous les pressions du marché pour augmenter la distribution, le "journalisme nouveau" a mis l'accent sur l'incitation et les slogans au dépens de la réflexion. Ce genre de journalisme refléterait, d'après lui, la mécanisation de la production des journaux et la "marchandisation" des nouvelles. En ce sens, le journalisme critique pratiqué par Barbeau deviendrait impraticable. On constate que le cadre étroit d'analyse d'Innis ne lui permet pas de voir la possibilité de pratiquer une certaine forme de journalisme critique à l'intérieur d'une presse commerciale.

Notre analyse inscrit un bémol dans la conception d'Innis sur la presse qu'il considérait biaisée dans le temps et l'espace et de plus en plus contrôlée en termes de discours publics, encourageant le pouvoir au détriment du savoir (voir Salter et Dahl, chapitre 6). Nous considérons plutôt que la presse est un moyen de communication, parmi d'autres, et qu'elle peut être utilisée par des intellectuels et lue par des individus dont les idées et les prises de position sont influencées par leurs milieux socio-économique et culturel. Dans ce contexte, notre étude doit tenir compte des préjugés, des idéologies, des conditions politiques et économiques selon lesquels la relation entre la presse et le public s'est organisée en une culture dominante devant représenter la culture "nationale" des Canadiens français. Elle semble aller à contre-courant de la monopolisation du savoir selon les termes d'Innis, puisque la démocratisation d'un savoir culturel devrait être partie prenante de la formation d'une identité culturelle, d'une culture nationale. Mais une culture nationale "imaginée" à partir d'interventions médiatiques est-elle pour autant démocratique?

D'après une étude de Corrigan et Sayer (1985) sur la formation de l'État, la formation d'une culture dominante dite nationale consiste en un projet visant à donner une expression unitaire et unifiante des expériences historiques de groupes multiples et différents, appartenant à une société systématiquement inégale, et structurée selon les classes, les sexes, les groupes ethniques, l'âge, la religion, l'occupation, et la localité. Le projet de formation de toute culture nationale serait loin d'être démocratique, tendant plutôt à effacer la reconnaissance et l'expression des différences, d'abord en représentant les membres d'une communauté "imaginée," pour reprendre l'expression d'Anderson (1993), comme une "nation" ayant une culture à laquelle ils doivent s'identifier avec loyauté. En même temps, ce projet assignerait à chacun des groupes une individualité spécifique définie selon les différentes particularités de leurs pratiques sociales, politiques, culturelles, toutes formes de représentation différentes de la culture dominante n'ayant pas de légitimité. Bref, la formation d'une culture nationale implique des aspects limitatifs, des exclusions. Il est donc légitime de se demander comment ces limitations sont reproduites par les intellectuels s'adonnant à la critique culturelle journalistique.

Victor Barbeau se défend bien d'être nationaliste, bien qu'il tienne toutefois à préserver ce qu'il appelle le "national," c'est-à-dire l'identité canadienne-française du Québec. Il suggère cependant une approche d'ouverture universelle plutôt que le repli sur soi prôné par certains groupes identifiés comme des régionalistes. Il répète que l'éducation culturelle du peuple canadien-français devrait être fondée sur une culture d'élite universelle, et propose des moyens économiques, politiques et sociaux qui rendraient ce savoir accessible à tous, et amélioreraient l'image de la culture canadienne-française, sans toutefois perturber l'ordre social établi.

Cette prise de position de Barbeau sur la culture d'élite coincide largement avec celle d'Innis, qui, lui, la conçoit en termes de tradition des humanités devant se regrouper au coeur de l'enseignement des universités des sociétés occidentales. Barbeau et Innis s'entendent sur le fait qu'un intellectuel a le devoir de promouvoir l'éducation publique. Cependant, alors que le premier voit cette participation aussi bien sur le plan médiatique qu'universitaire, Innis demeure sceptique quant au rôle des médias de masse face à cette question, comme le démontrent ses commentaires sur l'éducation aux adultes, que Barbeau par ailleurs encourage. Pour ce dernier, tous les moyens sont bons pour éduquer le peuple canadien-français.

Donc, contrairement à Innis qui limite le rôle de l'intellectuel à l'enseignement et à la recherche, Barbeau voudrait l'associer à la vie quotidienne des gens afin de faire leur éducation. *La Presse*, reconnue à cette époque comme un journal libéral prenant le parti des ouvriers (26 novembre 1918), constitue donc un lieu privilégié pour ses interventions qui nous font découvrir, au fil des jours, les invasions, luttes et résistances, impliquées dans la formation d'une culture canadienne-frànçaise. Ses chroniques sont particulièrement intéressantes du fait qu'elles nous font entrer dans le quotidien de ses lecteurs et lectrices, recréant les informations que des milliers de gens pouvaient lire chaque jour.

D'une certaine façon, l'engagement public de Barbeau correspond à ce qu'Innis appelait les "nouveaux monopoles du savoir." Dans une société dominée par l'Église et la bourgeoisie anglophone, la presse constitue une sphère permettant le développement de nouvelles formes culturelles. Que penser de la position d'Innis affirmant que les nouvelles formes de résistance ne peuvent surgir que des départements d'humanités des universités – en marge des centres de pouvoir et des médias biaisés dans le temps? Barbeau, pour sa part, veut profiter de la distribution massive de certains journaux pour provoquer des changements culturels.

Pour comprendre la nature et l'importance des interventions de Victor Barbeau, nous verrons d'abord la relation qu'il établit entre "culture," "savoir" et "pouvoir," puis le rôle qu'il attribue aux classes bourgeoises, dans lesquelles il inclut les critiques culturels, quant à l'éducation des masses.

CULTURE, SAVOIR, POUVOIR

Selon Victor Barbeau, le savoir, la connaissance, sont indubitablement liés au contrôle, à la survie, à l'expansion de la culture canadienne-française. Innis soutenait relativement le même point de vue sauf que, pour lui, le pouvoir et le contrôle ne pouvaient s'exercer que par le dialogue. Barbeau, d'autre part, voyait le journalisme comme un moyen d'obtenir une telle forme de transformation culturelle, en plus, évidemment, d'autres moyens comme la publication de revues culturelles accessibles à tous et l'enseignement à tous les niveaux.

Barbeau l'intellectuel n'adhère pas à l'idéologie nationaliste, qu'il considère limitative, mais est un ardent promoteur du français et espère que les oeuvres canadiennes-françaises pourront, un jour, contribuer au rayonnement de cette culture dans le monde. Néanmoins, selon lui, pour augmenter leur pouvoir culturel dans le monde, il faut accroître le savoir des Canadiens français. Pour ce faire, il suggère la démocratisation du savoir culturel, mais au moyen d'une culture nationale unifiée "vers le haut," acquise en éduquant les groupes "ignorants" ou "incultivés," pour utiliser ses expressions, à développer des goûts identiques à ceux de l'élite, les seuls reconnus comme légitimes par la société bourgeoise.[4] En même temps, il s'oppose à l'idée d'une société égalitaire et sans classe: dans la culture canadienne-française idéale de Victor Barbeau, des classes sociales différentes, et même opposées, seraient le foyer de goûts identiques. Pourtant, même à l'intérieur d'une culture hégémonique, formée par une dialectique entre culture bourgeoise et culture populaire, la première restant toutefois dominante, on retrouve différents goûts et sens esthétiques qui s'affrontent, s'opposent.

En effet, dans *La distinction*, Pierre Bourdieu (1979) établit un lien direct entre différence de classes et différence de goûts. Ce n'est donc pas par hasard que les styles de vie de classes qui s'opposent produisent des goûts si divergents que les uns deviennent "intolérables" à ceux qui s'imaginent détenir le "goût légitime," c'est-à-dire ceux dont le style de vie et les préférences culturelles ont été socialement reconnus comme "légitimes," rendant les autres "arbitraires" (59–60). Il y aurait ainsi une relation savoir/pouvoir imbriquée dans la formation d'une culture dominante, le savoir pouvant seul donner sa légitimité à cette culture. Mais ce savoir peut-il, et doit-il, être acquis au même titre par différentes classes? Le critique culturel, élu parmi les privilégiés à posséder ce savoir, devrait-il être un élément formateur, un médiateur guidant les masses vers une culture légitime? Culture dominante et critique culturel devraient-elles être irrémédiablement reliées et interagissantes?

Victor Barbeau, qui adhère, je dirais presque naturellement, au libéralisme-catholique,[5] est préoccupé par des problèmes culturels qu'il considère aigus au Québec à cette époque: la "paresse intellectuelle" des Canadiens français et l'envahissement de leur culture par la culture anglophone, surtout américaine, exacerbé par la popularité montante du cinéma, entre autres choses. La "plastique mouvante," comme il l'appelle ironiquement, est presque entièrement de fabrication américaine, les productions québécoises étant peu nombreuses et habituellement de mauvaise qualité, et les productions françaises se faisant rares au Québec à cette époque. Même dans les films muets, insiste le critique, la culture américaine transpire!

L'américanisation de la culture canadienne-française signifie également son industrialisation, ce qui n'a rien pour rassurer notre chroniqueur. Il blâme le gouvernement provincial de ne pas intervenir au niveau de cette invasion "sauvage," et de ne pas fournir les fonds nécessaires pour supporter la création canadienne-française. Ses écrits journalistiques expriment ses préoccupations au sujet de la dégradation de cette culture, du point de vue de la langue, mais aussi des activités culturelles, dégradation qu'il lie constamment aux conditions politico-économiques transformant la culture en une forme de marchandise.

Innis partage cette inquiétude en regard de la culture canadienne anglaise. Il croit aussi que les industries culturelles américaines mettent en péril la construction d'une identité canadienne. En même temps, il a peu d'espoir de voir le gouvernement fédéral se transformer en protecteur de la culture. Il pense plutôt que la principale préoccupation de ce gouvernement est de développer un monopole du savoir qui se rapprocherait dangereusement du facisme. En quelques occasions il fera référence au Québec, soulignant que le caractère distinct de cette province en termes de langage, culture et institutions religieuses la rend moins vulnérable à l'invasion de la culture américaine. Ce point de vue n'est évidemment pas partagé par Barbeau.

L'intérêt profond manifesté par Barbeau à l'égard du culturel s'associe à son souci constant de le lier au politique et à l'économique. Il appartient au critique culturel d'établir cette relation, croit-il. Si Barbeau se distingue d'Innis sur ce point,[6] il rejoint par contre l'approche socialiste qui affirme que la critique culturelle a des dimensions socio-politiques et économiques importantes dans une société. Elle est liée à une certaine forme d'éducation de masse et influencée par les groupes d'intellectuels dont font partie, du moins le croient-ils soutient Gramsci, les journalistes couvrant les événements culturels. Gramsci (1957) – lui aussi un contemporain de Barbeau, né en 1891, issu du même milieu socio-économique et religieux et ayant pratiqué le journalisme pendant plusieurs années – raconte que l'éducation culturelle populaire est essentielle, car elle permet à la masse d'acquérir un sens critique qui pourrait l'amener à s'émanciper de l'élite de la communauté et se former une identité propre (304).

Louis Chevalier (1984) croit également que l'éducation culturelle populaire est essentielle aux masses en permettant l'émergence "d'intellectuels organiques," pour utiliser l'expression de Gramsci, ayant acquis un savoir profondément enraciné dans des points de vue de classe. Ces intellectuels fournissent aux classes dominées des outils d'émancipation – un langage, des mots, des expressions – qui leur permettent d'exprimer clairement leurs frustrations, leurs attentes, leurs demandes. Ces points de rassemblement culturels non seulement permettent aux masses d'acquérir une pensée critique envers l'ordre social établi, mais également de développer de nouvelles solidarités (658–60). Chevalier, comme Gramsci, laisse cependant plus d'initiative aux classes populaires que Barbeau, qui croit qu'elles devraient être éduquées en tous points.

Il est généralement reconnu que les intellectuels jouent un rôle important dans divers domaines de la vie sociale. Ceux-ci possèdent le savoir nécessaire pour façonner leur propre conception critique du monde, conception influencée, cependant, par leur classe d'origine. De plus, issus principalement des classes petites-bourgeoises, ils font le lien entre classes dominantes et classes dominées. Le problème, affirme Gramsci, c'est que les intellectuels sont généralement les "commis du groupe dominant," c'est-à-dire qu'ils exercent des fonctions subalternes visant à obtenir un "accord spontané" des masses à la vie sociale organisée par les groupes dominants, alors qu'ils devraient plutôt se préoccuper d'aider les masses à développer une pensée plus critique.

De prime abord, les chroniques de Barbeau semblent se préoccuper principalement d'aider les Canadiens français à se façonner un esprit critique, du moins sur le plan de la culture. La question fondamentale, toutefois, est de savoir s'il veut éduquer les masses sur le plan culturel pour les aider à préparer leur émancipation des élites, ou à se soumettre aux goûts culturels et aux valeurs morales dominantes, et ainsi être plus facilement dominées?

Les écrits journalistiques de Barbeau dans *La Presse* montrent qu'il voit l'éducation des masses comme un projet de dépendance, leur permettant d'absorber la culture d'élite, la Culture, qui leur apportera les valeurs morales et les normes sociales assurant leur soumission à l'ordre social établi. Les expériences pratiques du journaliste – il fréquente les lieux culturels, se mêle aux publics – l'amènent à affirmer que les Canadiens-français perdent peu à peu leur identité culturelle permettant, par paresse intellectuelle, l'industrialisation de leur culture. En ce sens, il se rapproche des préoccupations d'Innis au sujet de la survie de la culture canadienne. Néanmoins, son modèle d'éducation ne remet pas en question les causes réelles de cette "inculture." Pas plus qu'Innis ne propose-t-il des "remèdes" pour aider les classes dominées a s'émanciper de leur position de dépendance économique, politique et culturelle.

Les idées de Victor Barbeau sont conformes aux principes soutenant certains courants libéraux qui existent au Québec de l'époque (Dion 1987; Couture 1991; Linteau 1992; Bouchard 1993), et qui supportent les mouvements démocratiques encourageant la pluralité de l'information menant à l'éducation des masses, la libre diffusion des idées et le développement de l'esprit critique, en autant que ceux-ci demeurent dans les limites de l'ordre social et des rapports de classe établis. Malgré l'existence de courants libéraux, plusieurs éléments de l'idéologie ultramontaine sont toujours très actifs dans la société canadienne-française analysée par le chroniqueur, particulièrement quand il s'agit de censurer des activités culturelles. Barbeau est donc continuellement déchiré entre sa volonté de se soumettre aux principes de la presse religieuse – usant de paternalisme pour "protéger" les paroissien(ne)s des dangers des "mauvaises lectures" et à les "catéchiser" plutôt qu'à les informer – et son désir d'adhérer à une presse libérale, vue comme "une tribune d'enseignement destinée à informer le citoyen de ses droits"[7] (Rajotte 1991, 154).

D'une certaine façon, Innis fait face au même dilemme. Bien que ses travaux démontrent qu'il établit une nette séparation entre l'Église et l'État, Innis croit que l'État canadien, dû à son monopole du savoir et à ses tendances autoritaires, s'apparente à l'Église gallicane de la Nouvelle-France (Dorland, chapitre 3). Ainsi, Innis, comme Barbeau, se demande jusqu'à quel point il devrait encourager l'État à simpliquer des questions de politiques publiques.

Quant à Barbeau, sa lutte contre l'assimilation anglophone et l'impérialisme culturel américain se fait au nom de la fortification de la culture française au Québec et non de l'isolement culturel, économique et politique. Il aspire donc à un monopole du savoir qui permettrait la démocratisation au lieu du contrôle de la culture. Innis aurait sans doute trouver l'idée utopique, lui qui croyait que les monopoles du savoir menaient indubitablement au pouvoir et contrôle d'un groupe sur un autre.

Barbeau n'a qu'un but, utiliser un média de masse comme *La Presse* pour gagner les divers publics canadiens-français à la cause de cette culture. Pour lui, l'identité culturelle ne peut passer que par la culture d'élite, la seule capable d'élever le niveau intellectuel de la masse. Ce n'est qu'avec une identité culturelle forte que les Canadiens français recouvrerons leur pouvoir économique et politique. Comment éduquer les masses pour renforcer leur identité culturelle et améliorer l'image de leur culture nationale?

POUR "DÉGROSSIR" LA MASSE

Pour éduquer les masses, il faut d'abord comprendre le pourquoi de la grande popularité des oeuvres de mauvaises qualités. Le roman non artistique est populaire parce qu'il est financièrement et intellectuellement abordable, affirme Barbeau. Malheureusement, il est de mauvaise qualité littéraire, ce qui n'empêche pas les gens de toutes les classes de lire ces produits. En effet, autant les classes ouvrières que les petits-bourgeois ou les bourgeois semblent fascinés par ces romans. Alors que Barbeau explique cet état de chose par le manque de goût des individus, certains chercheurs, comme Gramsci par exemple, croient que cet attrait relève d'une réaction au "caractère trop aventureux de la vie quotidienne, c'est-à-dire [au] caractère trop précaire de l'existence, joint à la conviction qu'il n'y a aucun moyen individuel d'endiguer cette précarité de l'existence: aussi les gens aspirent-ils à l'aventure 'belle' et intéressante" (1977, 663) pour oublier les "laides" et "révoltantes" conditions de vie de tous les jours.[8] Un socialiste comme Gramsci situe le débat à un niveau social de culture de classe. Pour ce dernier, il ne peut y avoir amélioration au niveau culturel sans gain au niveau socio-économique.

Barbeau, par contre, limite son analyse à une question de goût. Pour lui, le lien entre niveaux culturels, sexes et classes n'est pas fondé sur des conditions socio-économiques, mais plutôt sur des aptitudes intellectuelles et esthétiques, associant intelligence et esthétique aux classes bourgeoises; rusticité et vulgarité aux classes populaires. Le chroniqueur place le débat sur un plan individualiste de culture personnelle.

Dans ces conditions, l'amélioration du niveau culturel des masses doit se faire par l'éducation à la culture, une éducation sans lien direct avec l'amélioration de leurs conditions socio-économiques de vie. Les moyens qu'il suggère pour arriver à cette fin seront donc tournés vers les réalisations personnelles.

Le point de départ de l'éducation à la culture se situe dans la famille où les parents devraient enseigner aux enfants le "savoir-vivre," le fondement de toute esthétique. L'enfant issue de famille modeste, "livré à la seule science des trottoirs," sans surveillance, a besoin d'être "civilisé." Barbeau refuse, cependant, l'utilisation de méthodes négatives et répressives comme solution à des problèmes sociaux: "Au contraire de ce qui se passe dans l'ordre physique où l'on cherche d'abord à éduquer afin de prévenir, dans l'ordre moral on commande, on interdit ... je reste cependant sceptique quant à son efficacité générale" (*La Presse*, 14 novembre 1932).

Néanmoins, le manque d'éducation et de culture chez les enfants dépasse le cercle familial, c'est un problème social que l'école pourrait contribuer à remédier. L'école est l'endroit crucial pour transmettre, à tous les enfants, une base d'éducation à la culture générale, surtout pour les familles ouvrières qui ne possèdent pas le savoir-vivre bourgeois. La première étape de l'apprentissage à ce savoir consiste à apprendre aux jeunes à parler un français correct. L'éducation à la culture passe d'abord par l'enseignement de la langue, soutient Barbeau. Quant à l'éducation morale, qui pourrait éloigner les publics de pièces de théâtre vulgaires et souvent malhonnêtes, elle ne devrait pas se limiter aux interventions de l'Église dans les journaux, interventions dénonçant certains types de pièces et certains théâtres qui se spécialisent dans les productions "légères" et "immorales." Ce rôle devrait s'étendre aux bourgeois qui possèdent le savoir et qui ont le devoir de le transmettre publiquement et de forcer les directeurs de théâtre à changer leur répertoire. Selon le journaliste, les gens choisiront "instinctivement" de la bonne culture si on leur en offre, et si elle est à la portée de leur budget. Personne, semble-t-il, ne peut résister à la Culture, légitime et reconnaissable entre toutes. Il faut contrer "l'effet industriel" sur la culture.

Voici un sujet qui tient au coeur de Barbeau. Pour lutter contre la culture industrialisée, il propose un budget gouvernemental pour la culture, budget qui permettrait d'accorder des subventions aux institutions culturelles, aux théâtres, aux éditeurs et aux artistes, permettant ainsi de baisser les prix des représentations ou des livres de qualité, de faire vivre les producteurs et les créateurs et de rendre des produits artistiques accessibles à tous. Encore une fois, on constate un écart entre la pensée de Barbeau et celle d'Innis. Ce dernier craint que la participation financière de l'État ne renforce la monopolisation du savoir.[9] Il est par contre en faveur d'interventions privées venant des organisations comme "Carnegie Corporation of New York" et "Rocke-feller Foundation," qu'il semble trouver plus démocratiques, en ce sens qu'elles permettraient de créer des monopoles du savoir différents de ceux de l'État. D'après lui, des fondations américaines de ce genre peuvent aider à créer des agences indépendantes et autonomes comme le Conseil de Recherche en Sciences Sociales du Canada qui permettraient de produire un savoir indépendant des intérêts pratiques.

Barbeau, par contre, réprouve fortement ce genre d'interventions, les considérant comme des intrusions, surtout quand elles viennent d'individus de culture et de religion différentes.[10] En fait, il pense que les Américains utilisent ce genre de fondations comme moyen d'étendre leur monopole et, contrairement à Innis, ne peut croire qu'ils sont désintéressés et de bonne foi.

Dans une chronique sur Andrew Carnegie, la position de Barbeau sur l'intervention de l'Américain ne fait pas de doute. Il fustige ce philanthrope qui a offert de l'argent aux administrateurs de Montréal pour leur permettre d'ouvrir des bibliothèques publiques et de rendre accessible à tous une importante collection de livres. L'offre de Carnegie est toutefois fermement déclinée par l'administration municipale, sous les pressions de l'Église qui a cru que des bibliothèques ouvertes grâce à l'argent d'un anglophone protestant contiendraient des livres dont les contenus seraient contraires aux doctrines de l'Église! Le journaliste approuve le refus de la municipalité.

Victor Barbeau se voit ici confronter à un paradoxe créé par son allégeance idéologique. Comme libéral, il supporte l'idée d'accès populaire à la littérature, incluant celle offrant des points de vue critiques à l'égard des doctrines de l'Église. Plusieurs de ses chroniques en témoignent. Comme catholique, il se voit obliger de refuser au peuple "ignorant" l'accès à un type de littérature qu'il pourrait interpréter incorrectement. "Andrew Carnegie, le père des bibliothèques universelles ... en conviant la masse à tous les livres ... a peut-être fait plus de mal que de bien." À cause de lui, les bibliothèques ne sont plus fréquentées pour s'instruire, mais pour lire des romans. Pour un petit groupe de gens qui vont à la bibliothèque pour s'instruire, des milliers d'autres ne les fréquentent que pour "la satisfaction d'instincts dont la réalisation mine petit à petit l'édifice social" (*La Presse*, 14 août 1919).

Barbeau est conscient de la contradiction soutenant sa position qu'il tente s'expliquer en affirmant que les livres n'affectent pas tous les individus de la même façon. Ses propos paternalistes et condescendants nous révèlent son opinion sur les Canadiens français: un peuple infantile dont le manque de maturité culturelle et de sens critique, surtout chez les classes populaires, empêchent d'identifier le "légitime" et le "non-légitime." Comment leur permettre d'acquérir plus de maturité, sinon par la lecture accrue?

Par une éducation encadrée, contrôlée par les intellectuels canadiens-français catholiques qui effectuent le tri pour la masse. On gardera ainsi cette masse dans une ignorance qui permettra sa domination plus facilement. Il semble bien que Barbeau veuille tenir les classes populaires éloignées, non pas de toute culture, mais de toute culture non légitime, risquant de perturber les valeurs dominantes, un moyen encore plus sûr de préserver l'ordre social. Prévenir les luttes de classes fait partie du programme d'éducation de Victor Barbeau qui n'hésite pas à affirmer que les classes "inférieures" ont leur utilité dans notre société, à la condition d'être dominées par les classes "supérieures" qui pourront les guider dans les différentes sphères de leur vie (1939b, 61).

CONCLUSION

L'éducation des masses au moyen de la critique culturelle journalistique n'est donc pas aussi démocratique qu'elle ne paraît de prime abord. Les choix, les goûts des publics dépendent de l'économique: on produira ce qui attire les gens et ce qui rapporte des profits, avant de penser à l'amélioration de la "race" ou de la "masse." Ils procèdent également du politique: non subventionnés, les théâtres sont obligés de vivre de leurs publics qui, semblent croire les producteurs, préfèrent les pièces faciles. Mais, à l'époque des écrits de Barbeau, le politique au Québec est intimement lié aux religieux. Dans la société à caractère ultramontain de cette époque, le rôle du critique est délicat en même temps qu'important, en ce sens qu'il peut aider les gens à acquérir une conscience critique. En fait, il peut tout aussi bien éclairer les publics, et ainsi les aider à s'émanciper, que leur donner des informations qui les gardera dépendants des classes dominantes.

Les critiques de Barbeau, avec leurs constantes et leurs contradictions, ont sans doute contribué, directement ou indirectement, au développement d'une identité canadienne-française au Québec. Mais dans quel sens? Son projet d'une identité culturelle nationale exclut plusieurs groupes sociaux, les forçant à adhérer à la culture que lui considère comme légitime. Les classes populaires, en particulier, doivent se soumettre aux exigences de la culture d'élite.

Il ne fait aucun doute que Barbeau veut populariser le savoir culturel, le rendre accessible aux masses afin d'élever le niveau de culture de la société canadienne-française. Les anglophones sont de plus en plus intéressés aux arts et à la culture, et les francophones perdent du terrain dans ces domaines. Si on veut rester "les plus fins, ... il faut au préalable que nous cessions de considérer le savoir comme un privilège de classe, qu'au lieu de nous contenter de vingt dyspeptiques parcheminés, nous ayons une armée de jeunes au yeux ouverts, aux oreilles propres et aux curiosités inassouvies" (*La Presse*, 25 février 1932).

Si certains écrits de Barbeau semblent sortir de la plume d'un socialiste, le contexte de ses interventions les replace toutefois dans sa position idéologique: éduquer les jeunes des différentes classes pour anéantir la "vulgarité" et la "grossièreté" qui les affublent et leur donner la fierté de leur culture "nationale," de leur identité culturelle. Mais, considérant que la culture nationale est unitaire et unifiante, peut-on parler de "culture nationale" dans une société de classes, d'ethnies, de races et de sexes différents? Si oui, qui exclut-elle?

Les critiques culturels contemporains font face à des contradictions toutes aussi importantes. Par exemple, les complaisants, personnes voulant plaire surtout aux groupes qui détiennent le capital, seraient-ils en fait, comme l'affirme Gramsci, "des commis du groupe dominant"? Ne doivent-ils pas se commettre avec des positions de soumission aux producteurs, promoteurs et distributeurs qui leur offrent ces produits culturels, s'ils veulent préserver leur ouverture auprès de ces groupes? Innis aurait-il été prévoyant en mettant les intellectuels en garde contre les interventions publiques?

L'analyse détaillée de la relation entre une forme de communication et la société dans laquelle elle se développe permet toutefois de nuancer la position d'Innis. Les interventions des critiques culturels sont démocratiques dans le sens qu'elles permettent la diffusion d'un savoir culturel parmi les masses, mais, en même temps, elles sont monopolistes en ce sens qu'elles ne couvrent et n'approuvent que la diffusion de la Culture, celle dont les classes dominantes possèdent la connaissance. Ainsi, Innis n'a pas tort lorsqu'il affirme que les médias sont biaisés. Cependant, cette étude montre que le biais n'est pas dû à la technologie comme telle, mais plutôt à ceux qui en font usage sous des contraintes socio-économiques et culturelles précises.

Les convergences et divergences dans la pensée de Barbeau et d'Innis prennent racine dans leurs visions différentes des monopoles du savoir. Bien qu'ils partagent une sérieuse préoccupation au sujet de l'américanisation de la culture, ils y répondent de façon très différente. Pour Innis, la mentalité américaine du marché menace de détruire une culture orale canadienne-anglaise. Barbeau, par contre, s'inquiète plutôt de la qualité de la culture canadienne-française et des moyens de la préserver.

Barbeau prend la défense de la presse écrite comme véhicule d'un changement culturel positif. Guidé par son catholicisme libéral, il croit qu'un monopole du savoir existant peut se faire miner par un autre en progression, tout en utilisant le même média. Innis, par contre, considère la presse comme un média biaisé dans l'espace. Il affirme que la capacité de la presse à cultiver une large audience, grâce à un processus de dissémination mécanisé, a créé des communautés dispersées dans l'espace. Selon lui, la résistance viendrait donc non pas de ce média – trop intimement lié aux relations de dominance existant dans la société – mais plutôt de la tradition orale des études classiques. Contrairement à l'imprimé qui ne permet qu'une transmission à sens unique des idées dans l'espace, l'étude des humanités encourage le dialogue en face à face, la pensée critique et le maintien de la conscience collective fondée sur une conscience de l'histoire et de la temporalité, soutient-il.

Nous croyons que les opinions divergentes de ces deux intellectuels sur les monopoles du savoir pourraient s'enraciner dans leurs éducations religieuses différentes. Innis, le baptiste, voyait les monopoles du savoir comme des formes de contrôle anti-démocratique; Barbeau, le catholique libéral, les croit nécessaires pour contrer les idées hérétiques.

Pour comprendre pourquoi les idées d'Innis et de Barbeau divergent à ce point sur le rôle des idées et de la culture dans la vie publique, il faut finalement examiner les différences entre la définition et l'organisation de l'activité intellectuelle au Canada anglais et au Québec. Au Canada anglais, les Églises ayant été reléguées à un rôle mineur dans la vie du pays, l'organisation de la vie publique revenait à l'État et au marché. Pour la plupart, les intellectuels se trouvent marginalisés dans les universités, elles-mêmes chargées d'instruire les élites et de leur transmettre la tradition, largement européenne de la culture classique. D'après Innis, une telle vocation pour les intellectuels, bien que marginale, représente néanmoins une forme de résistance dans le sens que l'étude des humanités se fonde sur le dialogue, le débat et la pensée critique. Ses plaidoyers pour la préservation de cette tradition deviennent de plus en plus fervents à mesure que l'État et le marché empiètent sur les universités afin de les rendre plus pertinentes. Il n'est donc pas étonnant que l'opinion d'Innis sur le rôle des intellectuels ait été beaucoup plus modeste que celle de Barbeau.

Au Québec, la présence et le pouvoir de l'Église permettent l'intellectuel conformiste d'occuper une place beaucoup plus importante et visible. Étant donné que l'Église continue à jouer un rôle dominant dans la définition des valeurs, on y voit un prototype de vie intellectuelle institutionnalisée. De plus, les universités francophones du Québec sous contrôle religieux, réprouvant les points de vue dissidents et/ou non confessionnels, se trouvent étroitement surveillés. Les médias deviennent ainsi des véhicules disponibles pour définir et transmettre les valeurs traditionnelles, avec quelques dissonances à la manière Barbeau.

NOTES

1   Il a enseigné, dans diverses universités, mais principalement aux HEC.

2   Il emprunte le pseudonyme de Turc dans ses chroniques de *La Presse*.

3   Il a également publié dans d'autres quotidiens qui ne sont pas considérés ici.

4   Barbeau croit que les "bourgeois" (il entend par ce terme les gens instru- its et éduqués, utilisant l'expression "parvenus" pour les riches sans édu- cation) possèdent le monopole du savoir. Il exprime clairement cette idée dans plusieurs de ses chroniques, mais plus particulièrement dans un texte intitulé "La bourgeoisie et la culture" (1939, 57–90). L'étude de Salter et Dahl (4–6) laisse croire qu'Innis était sensiblement du même avis, puisqu'il affirmait que la culture occidentale ne pouvait être sauvée que par l'intermédiaire des intellectuels dans les universités.

5   Lui même lui donne ce nom, d'autres l'appelleront le libéralisme- conservateur, ou le néolibéralisme. Nous avons préféré garder le qualifi- catif attribué par Barbeau.

6   Innis croyait que les médias contribuaient à la dégradation et non à la préservation de la culturel occidentale. Voir le chapitre 6, de Salter et Dahl, sur ce sujet.

7   En fait, à mesure qu'il avance en âge, le courant conservateur prend le dessus sur le libéralisme de sa pensée. Pour plus d'information sur ce sujet, voir Michèle Martin, 1997.

8   Il peut aussi y avoir un certain snobisme à lire surtout les romans d'aven- ture ou les romans policiers (1977, 304). Barbeau lui-même avoue en lire de temps à autre, non seulement pour faire son travail de critique, mais parce que, dit-il, il aime les sentiments extrêmes que leur lecture eveille.

9   Par contre, Barbeau, comme Innis, croyait que les intellectuels devaient garder leur indépendance en refusant de participer à des commissions et des comités organisés par l'État. Toutefois, contrairement à Innis qui a cédé sur ce point, Barbeau a toujours refusé les invitations des gouverne- ments en place à cet effet.

10 Il aurait aimé, par contre, que des philanthropes canadiens-français et catholiques s'impliquent dans ce genre d'initiatives culturelles.

PART TWO

Gaps and Silences

9 From Silence to Communication? What Innisians Might Learn by Analysing Gender Relations

JANE JENSON

The contact of Europeans with the Indians was essential to the development of the fur trade.   – Harold Innis 1956b, 9

[P]rivate information is practically the source of every large fortune.
    – Oscar Wilde, *An Ideal Husband*, quoted by Harold Innis 1946, 89

[M]any ... look to the titles of his works, and ... conclude, mistakenly, that they are studies in communication and the effects of different media of communication. Innis' real interest lay in the underlying political and cultural issues, and the studies in communication were to a considerable degree a device for getting at more important questions. At heart Innis was a moralist whose hatred of oppressive social institutions led him to examine the manner of their subversion from many angles.   – William Christian 1980, xi

This chapter could be very short.[1] Harold Innis was stonily silent about matters of women and gender relations. Like most of his generation, he never wondered about women's place in political economy. Nor did his life-long assault on oppressive social institutions extend to examining the ways in which the inequalities of gender power shape and reinforce markets, trade, development, or communication. Whereas *The Fur Trade in Canada* (1956b, 4–5) devotes full attention to the beavers' mating habits (monogamous), family structure (multi-generational cohabitation), and rearing of the young (weaned at two weeks; independent of mother at a year), this classic work is virtually silent on the same issues for the Europeans and Indians whose contact was essential to the development of the fur trade.

So why bother dealing with such a non-subject as Innis and gender? The answer is that the exploration of the non-event, the non-encounter of Harold Innis with the social relations of gender, is of little importance if the focus is Innis himself. He was a man of his time, and his silence was the silence of that time.[2] None the less, there is the "other Innis," the books that are the foundation of much of Canadian political economy and communication studies. My analysis is addressed then to his intellectual heirs, who cannot be so easily excused from asking questions about family and sexuality, about the gender division of labour, and about gender power. A reconsideration of Innis's approach permits us to chart its limits as well as allowing us to identify any spaces within it for thinking about the analysis of gender relations.

With these goals in mind, this chapter does several things. The first is simply to demonstrate the silence and assess the modifications to the picture of Canadian history which follow from an incorporation of attention to gender relations into the stories that Innis told and that many of his – male – heirs continue to recount. The second level, following directly from the first, involves addressing the theoretical sources of these silences and the reasons why it has been difficult for students of women's history or feminist political economy to appropriate his categories without substantial revision.[3] The third level is to propose that there might be space for finally filling this silence with the sounds of profitable and real communication. There is a program for the future, once we take seriously Oscar Wilde's contention that private – and even intimate – communication also contributes to the accumulation of wealth.

THE RADICAL PARTICULARITIES OF TIME AND SPACE

This is not the place to recount Innis's theory and method in detail. Instead, I simply set out his basic postulates, in order to proceed to the analysis mapped out above. In doing so, moreover, I ignore the standard division between "the early" and "the late" Innis, assuming instead that there is – at least in terms of basic postulates – more continuity than rupture.[4]

Any appreciation of Innis must begin, of course, with his thesis that forms of social organization follow from forms of communication. The latter are structured by technology, trade, production, and so on. Thus his greatest contribution to political economy remains the staples thesis – the notion that changing demand for Canada's resources in Europe "left their distinctive stamp on the Canadian social formation"

(Watkins 1989, 17). The country's development derived from the encounter of external demand and internal conditions, mediated by available technologies.

The impact of the staple was not unidirectional. While Innis always described the structuring effects of staples development and trade *on* the Canadian economy, society, and polity, later work began to stress the consequences *for* the purchasers of the staple. For example, pulp and paper production provoked a decline of culture and the rise of unstable and uninformed public opinion, shaped by unrestrained advertising. In the first instance, Canada increased its resemblance to Switzerland, "a country without art ... of more than one language, a federation, and dependent on the tourist trade" (Innis 1952a, 1).[5] But more than that, Canadian politics, by distorting the price system to foster the new staple, contributed to the same pattern of decline in its neighbours. "Pulp and paper production supported by provincial governments facilitated the rapid growth of advertising in the United States, and contributed to the problems of industrialism and the destruction of a stable public opinion" (Innis 1946, ix–x).

Innis recounted similar patterning effects of technology and trade in his studies of communications in ancient civilizations. Clay tablets and the birch-bark canoe occupy comparable positions in the theoretical argument, as do the valleys of the Tigris-Euphrates and the St Lawrence. Ideas, beliefs, and ideologies as well as political, economic, and cultural institutions follow from resources and the techniques of communication that they simultaneously demand and make possible.[6]

In this theoretical position we see Innis's method. He was interested first and foremost in macro-historical analysis (Melody 1981, 8; Carey 1981, 78ff.). This meant that he sought "to account for particular big structures and large processes and to chart their alternate forms" (Tilly 1984, 61). In other words, his focus was on variations across time and space, on why each development experience had followed its specific patterns in particular historical cases.[7] He rejected the epistemological stance of much communications theory in the early postwar years, which was modelled on the natural sciences and sought universal generalizations, often by deploying social psychological approaches. Instead, he insisted "that all scholarship must be grounded in the analysis of the radical particularities of time and place, history and geography" (Carey 1981, 79).[8]

For Innis, institutions of trade, religion, and politics varied across time and place, and the only way to seize these variations was via historical analysis, indeed *genuinely historical* analysis.[9] At times he worked at the boundary between the world-systemic and the macro-historical levels. Influenced by Thorstein Veblen, who, in launching his own criticism of the universalizing pretensions of marginal utility theory, had argued forcefully for historical analysis of institutions, Innis focused on the survival capacity of big institutions such as cultures and empires (Christian 1980, xi).[10]

None the less, Innis was also something of a culturalist. He located some of his work at the border between the macro- and the micro-historical levels, that space in which individuals and groups encounter the big structures and large processes of history (Tilly 1984, 61).[11] The notion of encounter of civilizations and the structuring effects for everyday life of the artifacts and social relations of contact pervades his work. For example, his presentation of the history of the dairy industry made a classic Innis-style statement: "Migration of technique from the United States was followed by migration of institutions." The latter included farmers' organizations such as the Grange and unions such as the Patrons of Industry and the Knights of Labor (Innis 1937, xvi). *The Fur Trade in Canada* (1956b) is replete with descriptions of how the "cultural traits" of indigenous peoples were altered by their engagement in the fur trade. From the wearing of woollen clothing to the use of firearms and the consumption of alcohol, Innis recounts the reshaping of Aboriginal peoples' life conditions by the fur trade and the specific practices of traders.[12]

What are the implications of choosing the method of historical analysis and these two levels of analysis? The first is that analyses will be concrete, taking real times, places, and people as their referents, rather than abstract categories (Tilly 1984, 14). Such studies will also be historical, both limiting their scope in time and demonstrating that historical time – and the sequences according to which it unrolls – matter. This method was always Innis's strongest suit.

A second implication, following directly from the choice of level of analysis (as Charles Tilly passionately – and appropriately – argues) is that the macro-history must get the micro-history "right" (1984, 74). Historians must correctly trace the encounters of individuals and groups with the big structures and large processes of history. In such studies, "the structures at issue are ... *relationships* among persons and groups, the processes are transformations of the human interactions constituting these relationships" (64, emphasis added).

For many students of history, a third implication of these choices has been the need to make space for human agency in any account of both macro- and micro-history. One goal of macro-history is clearly to uncover structures that open or close possibilities for development and change, whether they are understood by historical actors or not. Yet students of history are also aware that attempts at social transformation as well as the power relations involved in protecting existing prac-

181 From Silence to Communication?

tices are a crucial part of any well-told story (Dennis Smith 1991, 1). Structuralist analyses are insufficient (Abrams 1982). Similarly wanting are analyses that cast actors simply in the role of "victims" of power relations, rather than as actors in complicated relationships, albeit often unequal ones, who are "making history."

On these last two dimensions (namely, micro-history and agency), Innis's work has sometimes fallen short. While giving nuanced attention to the ways in which big structures and large processes varied in space and time, he often presented the actions of groups and individuals more as determined by their structural locations than as the result of their strategic actions. We might ask, for example, whether the best way to understand the emergence of institutions representing farmers and workers in nineteenth-century Ontario is to see them as a direct and unmediated consequence of the transfer of a particular technique. If the relationship between production technique and forms of organization were as straightforward as Innis suggests, then variations in institutional strength and political success should be much less than we know them to be. Moreover, whereas Innis provides a detailed account of the actions of corporate bodies, such as the directors of the Hudson's Bay Company and powerful individuals who organized the fur trade, he presents the Indian traders in a much less nuanced way. Indeed, they are often victims of decisions taken elsewhere, their constantly changing circumstances being the consequences of contact. The strategic qualities of their response to the unequal power relations of the fur trade are invisible.

It is hardly surprising therefore that studies of women's history or the history of gender relations have rarely adopted Innis's approach wholeheartedly. The research program of such studies has precluded such a playing down of the micro-history of relationships and of human agency. For example, Pat Connelly and Pat Armstrong describe the recent trajectory of feminist political economy: "[It points] to the need for an analysis that looks at the historically and regionally specific conditions in and out of the households that encourage people to join together around particular issues and on the basis of different shared relations at different times ... The central questions are concerned, then, with the various configurations of gender, class and race which form the basis for action under specific regional or national political, economic and cultural conditions" (1992, x). While such an approach obviously shares Innis's commitment to studies sensitive to time and place, historians of women and feminist political economists also insist on analysing the lived conditions and strategic calculations that move individuals and groups to action.

Historians of women and feminist political economists, if they had

had the opportunity to address Innis, would have said that even though they admire his analysis of big structures and large processes, he did not get the micro-history right. Fortunately, they now have the opportunity to speak directly to his heirs, who continue the Innis tradition of political economy.

GETTING THE HISTORY RIGHT: WHO WAS THERE?

Macro-history of the sort practised by Innis provides detailed analysis of complex interactions of processes and institutions. His focus was widely cast in order, for example, to capture the interconnected and historical constitution of markets (Melody 1981, 9). Despite this conceptualization of history, neo-Innisians continue to ignore institutions and relations central to the functioning of those markets as well as the impact of markets on social institutions. In particular, they have paid too little attention to the ordinary family as a location for production and capital accumulation.[13] As a result, feminist political economists and historians of women have had to correct the picture of Canadian economic development by analysing the family structures associated with a staple economy. In addition, they have explored the tensions between the structures of an economy dominated by staple production and the ongoing efforts of families, particularly in the nineteenth century, to form independent economic units in agriculture (Cohen 1988, 37).

The goal of such a strategy of analysis by women's historians and political economists can be most easily characterized as one pointing out that "we were there" (Higonnet et al. 1987, introduction). Marjorie Cohen's work (1988) is probably the best example of this strategy. By examining nineteenth-century development in Ontario, an economy still shaped by staple exports, she uncovers the blindness to women's economic activity in most previous analyses of staples. She demonstrates that production depended not only on market conditions of demand and technology, but also on the subsistence activities of women. These latter guaranteed daily and intergenerational reproduction of the labour force. Thus only history that takes into account non-marketized production, and makes visible the role of women who have tended to predominate in that sector of production, will get the story straight and understand the real nature of capital accumulation.[14]

A similar corrective to the gender blindness of analyses of staple production comes from the historians and sociologists working on production of and trade in fish. They document the gender division of labour in fishing families and the centrality of women's labour to production.[15] Those working in fishing live not as individuals but within families, with all of the complicated gender and intergenerational patterns of work and commodity production thereby implied.

This insistence on the family as an economic unit and on women's reproductive as well as productive labour involves more than simply rendering justice to all the women who have participated in the making of history. By documenting and underlining the role of an institution too long ignored and the presence of heretofore invisible social actors, such studies also raise questions about the staples story itself. If we add the family as an institution of production, accumulation, and reproduction to the macro-history, a rereading of the developmental literature follows. Thus Bonnie J. Fox, drawing on the work of Cohen among others, reconsiders the story of capital accumulation in Canada. When one does so, the developmental question shifts. Once we imagine history as a history of family production for subsistence and for the market rather than one of trade, even trade in agricultural staples, we begin to ask, "What happened to agriculture?" Why was it not the generator of surplus for manufacturing in Canada that it was in other countries (Fox 1989, 156ff.)?[16]

Scepticism about the staples story can also follow from more in-depth analysis of the technology and social practices of staples production. Heather Menzies's study of cheese-making in Ontario, and particularly women's contribution to technological innovation, challenges a number of assumptions. One is the official history, which represents that the cheese industry – second only to timber in export volume in Canada in the late 1880s – began only in 1864, when an expatriate American established the first commercial factory with imported technology (Menzies 1994, 11, 26).[17] Menzies describes technological improvements and large-scale production that antedate 1864 (29–32). Moreover, if the technology of cheese-making is not exclusively imported, Innis's bald statement about institutions migrating in the wake of technique must be nuanced. As well, Menzies questions Cohen's assertion that women participated in cheese-making only in its "subsistence" phase and that large-scale production was the domain of men. Her research in Oxford County documents female cheese-makers of repute who both produced for the market and made important contributions to technological innovation (29–34).

Menzies's tripartite critique, as well as other studies by the women's historians and political economists cited above, became possible only when analysts decided to end the invisibility of women in so many historical studies. Innumerable investigations in women's history and political economy have demonstrated the biases involved in assuming no gender differences in development experiences. Therefore they explicitly ask how women encountered the structures and processes of the staples economy, looking for their structuring effects for women's lived experience as well as women and men's response to these effects. In doing so, such studies have provided novel twists and a goodly amount of new detail in the story about the ways in which production and trade in staples left their distinctive stamp on the social formation.

However, even if this strategy for representing who was there at the making of Canada marks an improvement, it does not fundamentally reject the staples thesis. By putting women into Canadian history one makes the story more complex and more exact, but not totally different from what Innis might have said if he had ever thought to ask where the women were.

GETTING THE HISTORY RIGHT: HOW DID IT WORK?

Feminist political economy has done more, however, than insist on the presence and contribution of women to staple and non-staple production. It has also identified and analysed a crucial social relation – that of gender. Feminists who insist on considering structures of patriarchy or on highlighting the unequal power relations of gender are participating in the more general criticism of many neo-Innisians – that their approach to political economy ignores social relations of power, especially those of class (Clement and Williams 1989, 9–10; Cohen 1989, 29–30; Mahon 1993, 3–6). They fail to understand the contribution of private communications, whether part of the intimacies of sexual and family relations or simply those between individuals.

In making such criticisms of the silences and gaps in the stories, feminist political economists and historians of women have also had to tussle with their erstwhile allies, who have tended to focus too much on a single social relation – that of class. For feminist political economy, getting the history right also means uncovering and assessing the intersections of the social relations of unequal gender and class power.

The structure of this intellectual struggle has had far reaching consequences for the way it has unrolled and the focus it has adopted. "As Marxist feminists have reiterated over and over, mostly to nodding heads with deaf ears, there are problems with Marx's original analysis of class" (Connelly and Armstrong 1992, 25), and they have had to work hard to put their concerns onto the agenda. Feminist political economists of all tendencies have sought to develop and use an integrated, comprehensive theory of gendered social relations. The articulation of social reproduction and production, of waged and unwaged labour, and of class and sex has been the testing ground for these debates.[18] As a result, even when the object of analysis is social relations in a traditional staple industry (the fishing and dairy industries have often provided the empirical grounding for this work), the developmental issues of the Innisian approach and its questions have been sidelined in favour of working out the complexities of the social relations.

This displacement is a shame, however, because attention to gender relations can shed new light on the developmental story. Reading *The Fur Trade* (1956b), one finds that a sense of "mystery" remains. While stressing that traders needed to develop good relations with Indian communities, Innis does not explain how the ties between strangers actually were made. For example, in describing the dependence of the Hudson's Bay Company (HBC) on the "native population," Innis emphasizes difficulties of provisioning, which are overcome by Indians' hunting for the Company. He then describes sickness and high mortality rates and says simply: "The borrowing of Indian cultural traits was important to the elimination of these particular difficulties and to the success of the Company" (1956a, 134).

Reading this with the sceptical eyes of someone who has lived through the second wave of feminism, one can only ask about who cooked them the geese, moose, and other strange fare, who taught them about local medicines, and who made them warm clothes, shoes and snowshoes. But more than that, how did these strangers in a strange land manage their needs for intimacy and their fears as they were forced to travel far afield in search of trade? There are hints of answers in *The Fur Trade*, but always oblique, under the heading "personnel policy" (1956b 135, 163, 277). However, detailed studies are now available, and the mystery is solved. The fur trade begins to take on the rich detail of micro-history and reveals more human agency.

Jennifer Brown's (1980) study of fur trade families provides an intriguing example of ways in which gender relations intersected with economic forces in the fur trade and set limits on development (Fox 1989, 159). The HBC understood that agricultural production competed with the fur trade, in terms of land use and labour supply. Therefore it virtually banned European women from the west and refused to allow retired employees with Aboriginal wives and children to remain in fur country, except in the Red River Settlement. Yet even in that community, the arrival of women of European origin marked a real change in the role of the staple. As Sylvia van Kirk's history tells us, "like the missionary, she symbolized the coming of a settled, agrarian order" (van Kirk 1980, 5). Patterns of settlement were, in other words, a consequence of concrete decisions taken by the HBC about the sexuality and family strategies of its white employees. At the same time, shifts in the gender and ethnic composition of the population set up new pressures on the trade itself. Therefore there may be some real benefits for feminist political economists as well as for Innisians in returning with new eyes to the story of development and its communications.

GETTING HISTORY RIGHT: WHO WAS COMMUNICATING WITH WHOM?

Recent studies by women historians have revealed in great detail the distinctive stamp that the fur trade gave to the western Canadian social formation, and in doing so they have uncovered another part of the story of the organization of the trade, the forces to which it responded, and the kinds of communication that it involved. As Sylvia van Kirk asserts:

Like most of the staple industries which characterized the economic development of pre-Confederation Canada, the fur trade generated a distinctive regional way of life; this was reflected in patterns of work, family life, modes of transport, and items of food and clothing. One important difference between the fur trade and other staple industries was that it was the only one which was based on a commodity exchange between two divergent groups of people. The growth of a mutual dependency between Indian and European trader at the economic level could not help but engender a significant cultural exchange as well. As a result, a unique society emerged which derived from both Indian and European customs and technology. (1980, 2–3)

Yet even as she refers to the staple industries and their structuring effects, van Kirk moves away from a strict Innisian approach in two major ways. The first is that she explicitly addresses the issue of "active agency," associating herself with others writing on the role of Aboriginal traders as well as Europeans in strategizing to construct a fur trade within which they both could live (van Kirk 1980, 7–8; Brown 1980).[19] Thus, even if the trade fundamentally altered the lives of Aboriginal peoples in what was to become Canada, it was neither completely imposed on them by Europeans nor the inevitable result of demand, supply, and technology.

The second move away from Innis is as dramatic. Both Jennifer Brown and Sylvia van Kirk demonstrate that the very success of the fur trade as well as its modes of operation were the consequence of particular forms of communication between European males and Aboriginal women, both Indian and mixed blood.

By 1821, when the companies merged, practically all officers of the Hudson's Bay and North West Companies, and many lower-ranked employees as well, were allied with women born in the Indian country. Such alliances were by then, in fact, normal adjuncts of fur trade social life, and their general acceptance is reflected in the widespread use of a standard descriptive phrase – marriage "according to the custom of the country" – in records of the early to mid-1800s ... The growth of these customary unions and the multiplication of their progeny over a period of many decades gave a distinctive social character to the fur trade and provided a basis for its development as an ongoing and to some extent self-perpetuating semi-autonomous community. (Brown 1980, 51–2)

Thus, in Innis's terms, gender relations formed through sexual alliance and family activity were a medium of communication. This was a form of communication in which individuals and social groups made their history by acting out and creating one of the most fundamental bonds of human society, the "many tender ties" – and not-so-tender ties – of family life.[20] Without this communication, the fur trade in Canada would not have been what it was.[21]

As the European traders arrived in the west, they encountered Aboriginal peoples interested in trading. But, even more significant for our story, they encountered Aboriginal women who were able to be liaisons between the two groups. Raised in a society in which the public-private split was attenuated if non-existent, these women were both *interlocuteurs valables* for their communities and skilled in the work necessary to sustain a fur trader.[22] Women acted as translators and as go-betweens as well as symbols of ties forged between Aboriginal communities and particular traders and companies. As George Simpson instructed his employees: "Connubial alliances are the best security we can have of the goodwill of the Natives, I have therefore recommended the Gentlemen to form connections with the principal Families immediately on their arrival" (quoted in Brown 1980, 73).

While the HBC at first tried to prohibit sexual liaisons between its male employees and Aboriginal women, it soon had to give up the ban. Not only did the men refuse to conform, but the company soon discovered the real advantages of the presence of women in the trade. They travelled with the traders, serving as translators. But in addition they worked, providing fresh food and making snowshoes and other items absolutely essential to the fur trade. Indeed, without the snowshoes, the traders were fort-bound. Moreover, the women also, in effect, worked *for* the HBC, preparing furs (Brown 1980, 64–6). All these activities reflected the traditional gender division of labour in the Aboriginal communities, and it was labour without which the trade would have had difficulties flourishing. Yet it was also "labour" provided in the context of an intimate sexual and very often family relationship, responding to the norms of fur society-in-becoming, that being a mixture of Aboriginal and European habits and values.

Whatever the pattern, however, women were active in constituting them. Women were often willing to develop relationships with European traders because they had, as much as Aboriginal men, an interest in the trade goods provided. The exchange, in other words, was one of goods to be sure, but one that was in effect as much between European traders and Aboriginal women (kettles, cloth, knives, and so on) as between the two groups of men. Therefore, in western Canada as elsewhere, van Kirk describes "native women playing an active, even leading, role in promoting the economic change brought about by European technology" (1980, 6).

The activities of Aboriginal women were also crucial to the creation of the "fur trade society," which was a closely knit and familial society and within which the fur trade was actually conducted. It was they who had privileged access to European men, who in turn had need for their survival skills and their capacity to move between the two worlds. If not perhaps completely accepted in European settlements, Aboriginal wives and "girls" of European traders were valued links between those traders and communities with which they were trading. Without this inter-married and linked society, the patterns of the fur trade would have been very different.

These forms of communication were, of course, not uniform across the trade. Significant variations depended on communications among communities and the strategies – both economic and personal – of the men and women. Jennifer Brown documents differences in the practices of various North West Company traders, both anglophone and francophone, as well as the Aboriginal peoples with whom they had contact (1980, chaps. 3–4). The "use" made of the women, as communicators and as symbols of communication also varied. Whereas HBC men tended to stay longer "on assignment," because of the employment practices set down in London, and because they came into contact with particular Aboriginal peoples, their relationships tended to mimic those of Europe in terms of longevity and feelings of responsibility. North West traders, who moved more frequently between Canadian and fur trade society and who were in contact with Aboriginal peoples who themselves practised trade in women, had less stable and sometimes much more exploitative practices. The North West traders, drawn from French-Canadian and Scottish communities, were more likely to have strong and intact family ties in Canadian society. Their relatives continued to exercise power over their financial and other family dealings, making it more difficult for them to grant the same importance to their relationships in fur trade society that HBC employees did. HBC employees, in contrast, were often orphans whose stint in the Canadian north began when they were no more than fourteen years old.

Practices also shifted over time, as the needs of the trade changed, as the European and Aboriginal came better to comprehend each others' ways, and as the traders' situation altered. As fur trade society took form, frequently the daughters of other traders became marriage partners (Brown 1980, 72; van Kirk 1980).[23] Therefore the meaning of gender relations, the practices of sexuality, and family forms varied a great deal, depending on by whom, when, and where they were being constituted.

It is possible to imagine, as part of a counter-factual analytical strategy, even greater differences. What if Aboriginal communities had withheld and forbade sexual liaison and marriage *à la façon du pays*? We might then have seen, for example, fur traders confronting real and severe limits on their capacities to move away from the forts and trading posts or to winter in the interior of the fur country. Survival would also have been more of an issue as loneliness and isolation were more prevalent. Or what if, for example, the Europeans had maintained the racist assumptions of their societies of origin and had therefore insisted on the presence of European women? We might then have seen an even more conflictual encounter of European and Aboriginal societies, unmediated by the community liaison effected by Aboriginal women's back-and-forth movement. Such conflict might very well have restricted the capacity of companies to meet the demand coming from Europe, which Innisians identify as such a crucial causal variable. In addition, the earlier arrival of European women might have hastened the expansion of agricultural challenges to the fur trade.

In other words, even these simplistic counter-factual propositions strongly suggest that the actions of women and the forms of gender relations in Aboriginal society before contact and in fur trade society during the trading years structured the outcomes.

Examination of other cases of European–Native contact reveals a great deal of variability in how two social groups experience their encounter with the large processes of history – the spread of such phenomena as capitalism, colonialism, and trade. The Canadian fur trade may very well have taken the shape it did because of the uniqueness of the gender relations that took form in a situation in which communication took place among mutually dependent, if unequally powerful, groups, rather than between colonizers and colonized.[24] The status of the actors in the trading relationship opened spaces for certain kinds of gender and family relationships that were not possible at other points of contact.

The important Canadian trait distinction is that marriage *à la façon du pays* emerged as European and Aboriginal men regularized the contact. As the traders came better to understand Aboriginal practices such as wife-lending and marriage vows, they demonstrated a capacity for adaptation, both in exhibiting greater loyalty to their families and in sometimes following some Aboriginal peoples' practices of taking multiple wives. Thus, though Jennifer Brown attributes some of the willingness to undertake marriages *à la façon du pays* as an effort to mimic British marriage styles, she also documents cases of traders being perfectly willing to maintain two households (one in Britain; one in Canada) and to take multiple partners (1980, 62ff.). Such marriages often involved a formal commitment to the father of the woman and through him to the community. That the traders accepted their liaisons as a form of marriage is evident by the steps that HBC officials took to execute the wills of their former employees, who frequently made provisions for their wives and children in the fur country.

Elsewhere sexual contact has often been illicit (thereby creating a pariah group), sometimes very limited (and therefore largely irrelevant to the social and economic practices), or sometimes absolutely central to the whole national experience.[25] In his study of miscegenation, Fernando Henriques demonstrates that marriage was extremely rare – because prohibited – in encounters between Anglo-Saxons and African and Asians in the context of colonialism. Sylvia van Kirk also describes the power of colonialism. As the Canadian west began to be colonized, gender relations between European and Aboriginal communities and within the trade changed dramatically. Racism intensified with the arrival of European women as potential marriage partners and the imposition of European legal and religious systems. In the early periods, however, despite the HBC's effort to model the regulations for its employees in Rupert's Land on the rules for the British military, and to impose "military monasticism," the Company did not succeed in preventing its employees from organizing – and regularizing – their sexual liaisons.[26] It eventually had to accept these practices, even establishing the Red River Settlement to cope with the resulting "problem."

Similar reasoning can be applied to the other staple industries. One asks first what form gender relations took and then about their contribution to or interference with the industry itself. Such questioning and the judicious use of comparative analysis are likely to reveal a great deal about staple-based societies.

Such a correction is equally crucial for anyone interested in the continuing legacy of Innis for understanding communications. As we know, Innis used a broad definition of a medium of communication, never confining himself to a limited list of media when examining the so-called bias of space versus the bias of time. Thus transportation routes (rivers, oceans, canals, and so on) were media reflecting a bias of space, while long-standing institutions (churches, priesthoods, political forms) were media displaying a bias of time (Patterson 1990, 3–4). Moreover, the medium shaped the message, limiting or facilitating certain types and styles of communication.

It is hardly necessary to mention the extent to which Innis's discussion of the fur trade depends on his appreciation of the technology of communications as well as the media available. Yet, as later students of the fur trade have shown, there was an additional – and crucial – pattern of communication not captured by exclusive attention to technology or transportation routes as media. Later studies demonstrate that forms of social organization and the successful pursuit of the fur trade follow in part as well from the media and patterns of communication formed by women and men in sexual and family relationships. Therefore it is high time to modify our stories to include this form of "private communication."

NOTES

1 It would have been even shorter without the helpful comments of Ted Magder, Heather Menzies, Liora Salter, and Mel Watkins, who made suggestions and forced me to clarify my writing. Great Innis scholars all, they bear no responsibility for any errors or perversities that remain.

2 Innis mentioned women or sexuality rarely. His "Idea File" makes a few obscure references to women. For example, he writes that the rise of abstract philosophy was "at the expense of the place of women and largely limited to men" (2/12), and "Troubadours (1071–1294) and ladies of Middle Ages developed concept of romantic love" (Innis 1980, 7–8). *The Strategy of Culture* recounts an interesting interaction between women's status as consumers and the rise of advertising. It also describes the role of the *Ladies' Home Journal* in promoting "truth in advertising" for medical preparations as well as the restraining effects of puritanism on such magazines (Innis 1952b, 8–11). I argue below that "the family" received more direct attention in Innis's work, especially with respect to capital accumulation.

3 Feminist political economists and historians of women have paid attention to Innis. They tend to cite his classic studies. Moreover, they often set off to analyse a developmental problem familiar to Innis or the neo-Innisians of Canadian political economy. However, they also quickly diverge from this scheme, finding it wanting for various reasons. See, for

example, Connelly and MacDonald 1983; Cohen 1988; and van Kirk 1980.

4 Here I am obviously much influenced by the position of Patterson (1990) and several of the chapters in Melody, Salter, and Heyer, eds. (1981).

5 The comparison to Switzerland is elaborated several times and used inter alia to account for the rise of brokerage political parties. One characteristic of multilingual societies such as Canada and Switzerland, according to Innis, is the need for compromise. In Canada the result has been that "the political party is apparently no longer able to provide necessary compromise without the sacrifice of principles. The absence of consistency in the attitude of any English Canadian party or public leader points to the fundamental corruption of political life. Even the French Canadian has been exposed to the same influence though consistency has been more evident and moral fibre more conspicuous" (Innis, 1946, xii). This is an early formulation of what would become a favourite argument of other functionalist interpretations of Canadian politics – that the country's cultural diversity compelled parties to resist taking principled positions (Jenson 1995).

6 See, for example, the story of Babylonia, which begins with the clay deposits of the Tigris and Euphrates valleys and concludes with the observation that "political and economic forces were subordinated" to priests and institutionalized religion (Innis 1972, 52 and chap. 3). Anticipating the structure of this argument, *The Fur Trade in Canada* (Innis, 1956b) begins with a chapter on "The Beaver" and ends with the decline of the major institution of that trade – the Hudson's Bay Company.

7 This analytical stance with regard to time and space is not to be confused with Innis's theoretical propositions about the temporal and spatial biases of communication.

8 Carey associates this epistemological position with Innis' nationalism. "To avoid intellectual colonization he felt Canada must, in scholarship as in other matters, turn to an analysis of the radical particularities of Canadian experience and reach out from them to the experience of others" (Carey 1981, 79). This analytical strategy was followed by the neo-Innisian nationalists, who also resisted American intellectual paradigms and generalizations, which position led them directly to dependency theory (Brym and Fox, eds., 1989, 44–5) It also accounts in large part for their differences with the so-called internationalists, who sought to map Canada's particularities as one of a set of like countries (Brym and Fox, eds., 1989, 51–6) and with Marxists, who tried to push Canadian political economy towards general Marxist categories of class analysis as an explanation for the same particularities (Panitch 1981).

9 In this, Innis should be included among other historical sociologists, such

as those discussed by Charles Tilly, who also defines "genuinely historical" studies (1984, 79).

10 For a more detailed summary of the commonalities between Innis and
Veblen's worldview, at least as presented by Innis, see Clement and
Williams (1989, 8).

11 For Tilly, the distinction between the two levels is that micro-history
takes as its primary object the ways in which individuals and groups
experience history and understand that experience.

12 For one example, see Innis quoting at length and approvingly Capt. John
Franklin's assessment of the destructive effects of trading practices, devel-
oped so as to compete, which were themselves undermining the trade
(Innis 1956b, 273–4).

13 He did pay attention to the family as an institution shaping capital accumulation among big capitalists. First, the *Idea File* (Innis 1980, 11–12)
reveals his belief that publishing was an industry in which family was
important (sections 2/13 and 2/44). Second, in *The Fur Trade* he
describes, without commentary, the responsibility of traders' wives for
organizing the sending of canoes and men to their husbands at their posts
in the interior (for example, 1956b, 91). Third, discussing the links
among the printing press, the decline of religion, and the "collapse of
Western civilisation which begins with the present century" (1946, 94),
Innis details the ways in which sects have fostered capital accumulation
via intermarriage, a strategy in danger in the twentieth century because
"the decline of the Church in Europe reflected the impact of birth control
on the confessional" (92).

14 The other principal theme of Cohen's work, and the reason she maintains
a focus on staples, is to correct the tendency of sociologists and historians
to assume that the history of Canadian women replicated that of women
in other industrialized countries (1988, chap. 2). Labour-supply characteristics of production of staples for export – a shortage of workers for
industrial production – meant that industrialization brought women into
the paid labour force more quickly in Ontario than elsewhere. As a
result, the gender division of labour in Ontario was different than that
traditionally observed in Europe, at least in Britain. The public–private
split was less marked in Ontario, where more women gained access to
the labour force as agricultural producers or waged workers (Cohen
1988, 156–7).

15 See, for example, Connelly and Macdonald 1983, as well as the other references in Fox 1989, 156–63.

16 Marjorie Cohen finds a partial answer in the competition for labour
between staple production and farming: "[T]he logic of staple development forestalled the economic integration necessary for the growth of
independent agrarian units, at least for substantial periods of time"

(1988, 37). This statement offers another indigenous reason for Canada's continuing dependence on foreign inflows of capital, in patterns of capital accumulation, rather than in external patterns of demand by the metropole. Nevertheless, posing the question as Fox does can lead to a complete rejection of the staples thesis and neo-Innisian positions, as it did for Gordon Laxer (1989).

17 Innis is in agreement with this official history, referring to "the spread of the cheese-making industry from New York" (1937, xvi). The chapter in *The Dairy Industry in Canada* by J.A. Ruddick et al. describes in somewhat more detail the importation of technology and the trade in cheese (Innis 1937a, 5).

18 For overviews of feminist political economy, see Maroney and Luxton 1987 and Bakker 1989. For two useful collections, see Hamilton and Barrett 1986 and Connelly and Armstrong 1992.

19 Innis was not insensitive to the local struggles of hinterlands to both accept and reject the dominance of the metropole (Carey 1981, 83). Yet overall, he believed, the power of technological determinants tended to make such struggles futile, producing the same model of development everywhere.

20 Van Kirk 1980 is especially valuable for its analysis of two processes. She looks at the ways in which traditional assumptions about gender relations made by European men limited the lives of their wives and – especially – their daughters. She also exposes the rising rates of racism and rejection of Aboriginal women that followed the late arrival of European women in the West and the winding down of the fur trade. In other words, she well demonstrates that the family ties were not all so tender. See Brown, too, on the efforts of European men to transplant their sexual practices, particularly imposition of sexual demands and abuse of women's autonomy, and the reaction of Aboriginal women and men to such unacceptable practices (1980, 61ff).

21 As Valaskakis (1981, 209 and passim) documents, Innis may have come to his interest in communication from thinking about the impact of new media "dropped into" existing systems organized according to other principles and cultural forms. He did not, however, consider the medium or the cultural forms on which I am concentrating here.

22 For a discussion of another situation, in which men played many of these roles, and were the agents of change, see Valaskakis (1981, 211–12).

23 Innis dealt with this phenomenon in all its complexities, under the heading of cost control, citing efforts to limit personnel expenses. In 1806 the Proprietors of the North West Company found that "the number of women and Children in the country was a heavy burthen on the concern ... [I]t was therefore resolved that every practicable means should be used throughout the country to reduce by degrees the number

of women maintained by the Company." As a consequence, no one was to take "under any pretence, whatsoever," an Aboriginal woman "to live with him after the fashion of the North West, that is to say, to live with him within the Company Houses or Fort and to be maintained at the expence of the Company ... It is however understood that taking the daughter of a white man after the fashion of the country shall be considered no violation of this resolve" (quoted in 1956b, 277).

24 The trader was sometimes a broker or middleman between his employer and his suppliers. At other times the relationship was a complicated one of patron–client (Brown 1980, xviii).

25 In Colombia, for example, the "hierarchy of races" established as a result of miscegenation was the central metaphor in the nineteenth century discourse of development, organizing political practice and economic forms (de Ferro 1994).

26 In the British army this monasticism required celibacy rather than chastity (Brown 1980, 11–12). Liaisons and the resulting children were defined as products of "licentiousness" rather than as "family." For the story of the HBC management's evolving position on this matter, and the ways in which it was pushed and prodded by the joint pressures of its employment needs and employees' practices far from the sight of their London masters, see Brown 1980, chap. 1.

10 Innis and Quebec:
The Paradigm That Would Not Be

DANIEL SALÉE

To many Canadian intellectuals and social critics,[1] Harold Innis still stands today as an incontrovertible reference point, as somewhat of a historical figure, larger than life. Curiously – and disappointingly, some might add – the resonance of his work in Quebec is virtually non-existent. One has to look quite far in the deepest recesses of Quebec scholarship to find the trace of Innis's influence. Except for economic historian Albert Faucher, whose own work borrows directly from Innis's emphasis on technological and geographical factors (Faucher 1970; 1973; Faucher and Lamontagne 1953), and Alain-G. Gagnon and MaryBeth Montcalm's analysis of Quebec's economic peripheralization (Gagnon and Montcalm 1984; 1990), which faintly echoes Faucher's geographical contextualization of Quebec's economic development – and thus, only indirectly, Innis's vision – interest in Innis's political economy among Quebec historians and social scientists has always remained rather superficial. Indeed, as Innis scholar Robin Neill has noted, "verification of the proposition that the staple theory explained what happened in Quebec ... is simply not possible on the basis of the literature produced in Quebec" (Neill 1991, 171).

During his own lifetime, Innis seems to have elicited little attention from his Quebec contemporaries. Laval University's Albert Faucher, who did his graduate work under Innis's supervision in the early 1940s, was, by his own admission, devoted to his master's views (Faucher 1953; 1989). However, he never really succeeded in establishing a thriving, typically Innisian school of thought in Quebec, despite being one of the province's pre-eminent economists and economic historians from the 1950s through the 1970s. Similarly, the Marxian revival of Innis by English-Canadian, left-nationalist political economists in the 1960s and 1970s had little appeal to Quebec nationalist and radical intellectuals. Though neo-Innisian political economy articulated the anti-imperialist and anti-dependence themes with which they were familiar, there is virtually no evidence that it might have left some kind of imprint on their own analyses.[2]

When one considers the formidable intellectual influence Innis has had and continues to have in English Canada,[3] his inability to penetrate Quebec's historiography and social sciences in any significant way seems all the more dramatic, and somewhat enigmatic. Beyond the all-too-facile "two solitudes" type of explanation that one may be tempted to offer, there are more fundamental reasons for the failure of Innis's model of economic history to take root in Quebec. These are related to Innis's theoretical bent, the different perception Quebec intellectuals seem always to have had of their social role, and the paramountcy of Quebec's national question in any attempt at constructing a theoretical space to account for Quebec's social and economic particularities. This paper examines these reasons in an effort to elucidate the vow of silence that Innis and Quebec's intellectuals seem to have observed towards each other.

INNIS AS A THEORIST

The paucity of scholarly interest in Innis on the part of Quebec intellectuals is not unconnected to the fact that Innis said very little about Quebec that could have elicited any response from them. This may seem a rather bold statement about an author whose main historiographical contribution, *The Fur Trade in Canada* (1930), dealt extensively with central aspects of New France's and post-Conquest Quebec's economic history. Unlike almost all of English-Canadian historiography produced until his time, Innis's writings did not articulate any position likely to hurt the sensitivity of Quebec intellectuals. His friend and colleague Donald Creighton, in contrast, disturbed and irked many Quebec nationalist historians with his unabashedly pro-English intimation that French Canadians were mentally and culturally ill-equipped to make up for their social and economic lag. Time and again, they have taken issue with such a view.[4] One would be hard pressed to find in Innis echoes of Creighton's idiosyncratic interpretation, which explains in part why his work remained mostly unnoticed by Quebec historians and social scientists.

Innis was not unknown to his Quebec contemporaries. Albert Faucher, of course, was a personal friend, and Jean-Charles Bonenfant, in his review of Innis's last work, *Changing Concepts of Time* (1952a), celebrated Innis's creative interpretive bent and deplored the untimely death of a man "who was on his way to become English Canada's most original thinker" (1953, 208). In *La nation "canadienne" et l'agriculture (1760–1850)*, Maurice Séguin (1970) never refers to Innis's historical writings,[5] but the book's general interpretive bent leads one to believe that Séguin had some intellectual sympathy for the Laurentian thesis and the idea of the hinterland–metropolis dynamic developed by Innis and his colleagues. That about sums up the extent of Quebec interest in Innis's work. Innis never really seemed to strike a chord among the Quebec historians of his time.

Part of the problem may stem from the fact that references to Quebec in Innis's work might as well have been about North Africa or Southeast Asia. Innis's *oeuvre* in its entirety, with the range of his historiographical and analytical corpus, from *A History of the Canadian Pacific Railway* to *Changing Concepts of Time*, represents a conceptual and theoretical enterprise rather than a purely historiographical one. His early works of economic history are mostly studies of a single topic and based on the accumulation of an inordinate number of historical facts and data. Those works, it would seem, give credence to the critics who might find Innis's work undertheorized and lacking in conceptual guidance. Yet Innis was concerned not so much with constituting a body of historiographical evidence as with verifying his own pre-established ideas and notions about economic change.

In a belated, but vigorous review of *The Fur Trade in Canada*, W.J. Eccles has clearly shown that Innis took rather unorthodox liberties with historical method. Eccles reproachfully noted Innis's propensity to begin "with answers, not with questions," contrary to the 'proper' method of historical research. Innis, Eccles argued, used historical evidence to his convenience, "approach[ing] the subject with certain *a priori* premises and conclusions already formed, [choosing] to disregard any evidence that pointed to different conclusions" (Eccles 1979, 441). Carl Berger echoed these sentiments when he wrote that Innis presented a "dehumanized" version of history (Berger 1976, 98), concerned almost exclusively with the interplay among geographical elements, technological developments, and economic forces.

One may dispute Innis's craftsmanship as a historian, but his historiographical endeavours were predicated on his personal concern to explain, even produce economic theory. He was at least as motivated, if not more, by a desire to make sense of the general mechanisms of socioeconomic change and the principles of social interaction as he was interested in unveiling the particularities and peculiarities of Canada's past. Beyond the flaws of his historical method, Innis contributed, perhaps more than any other Canadian scholar of his time, "to the discussion of important philosophical questions dealing with the human condition and survival" (Zerker 1983, 390). He was just as much a social theorist and something of a philosopher as he was a historian. In this sense, Canada figured in his work as little more than the site of his own life experience. Canada was the country in which he lived; it was only natural that he drew from it the material with which to expound his view of the world and his attempts at fashioning some logic to it.

For all his attachment to his country and his well-known anti-imperialist bias, Innis's choice of Canada as the prime focus of his narratives was not necessarily founded on a political crusade. Reviewing a series of articles that Innis wrote between 1937 and 1944 on the political changes of Canada, Britain, and the United States, Robin Neill noted: "Each of the articles covered the same factual data in the political evolution of the British Empire, but each stressed a different point of view, insight or dimension of the Innisian scheme of social sciences. It was as though he had selected the institutional evolution of the North Atlantic community as a laboratory for testing his own ideas" (Neill 1967, 236).

Canada was primarily an object of scholarly study to Innis. The fruit of his scholarship did a great deal to expand Canadians' awareness of the source and basis of their nationhood, but Canada, seen in the broader spectrum of his whole work, appears more appropriately as the matrix from which Innis would later develop his more abstract theorizing and formulations about change, the organization of society, and the general direction of humanity (Havelock 1982, 27 et seq.; Patterson 1990). To acknowledge this fact is not to diminish the centrality of Canada in Innis's thought process, but the documentary evidence of his research paled beside what was truly a theoretical pursuit, almost from the beginning. Inevitably, such pursuit was probably unnoticed by those who saw the study of Canada's past as a necessary prerequisite for political action in their own contemporary setting. Innis simply operated in a different intellectual sphere. Indeed, he had little patience for those whose academic endeavours served political, bureaucratic, or activist purposes. As Carl Berger has indicated, "Innis believed that the social scientist should make a deliberate effort to sharpen his awareness of the bias of the times in which he worked and appraise his own limitations. He would thereby attain, if not an ideal position of detached objectivity, at least a sense of perspective and perhaps a more penetrating insight into the determining forces in social development" (Berger 1976, 105; Creighton 1957, 81–94).

INNIS'S QUEBEC CONTEMPORARIES

At the time when Innis was reaching the pinnacle of his academic and intellectual career in the 1940s, firmly establishing himself as

"Canada's senior academic statesman," as Donald Creighton once described him, the Quebec intellectuals and academics with whom he could have been exchanging ideas were of a quite different cloth.

Innis came out of a young but fairly solid tradition of "secular" social science. The already long-standing existence of departments of political economy at Queen's University and at the University of Toronto, where Innis spent all his professional life, bore witness to the fact that English-Canadian intellectuals had, by the early years of the twentieth century, broken free from the deeply moral and religious philosophy that impregnated the dominant interpretations of the world until then (Ferguson 1993).

In contrast, higher education in Quebec was still pervaded with an irrevocably clerical social program, not simply in the institutional structures but also in the very modes of intellectual action. The creation of the École des sciences sociales, économiques et politiques at the University of Montreal in 1920, and of the École des sciences sociales at Laval University in 1938, did little to secularize social thought. These new institutions were intended "to propagate the social doctrine of the church and, in so doing, to combat religious indifference, socialism, communism, and anti-clerical liberalism" (Brooks and Gagnon 1988, 30; Fournier 1986, 118–20).

Between 1920 and 1950, members of the clergy and religious congregations, as well as academics and intellectuals with close links to the clergy, were responsible for the bulk of intellectual production on social, historical, and political issues. Theirs was essentially a compendium of normative political essays, doctrinal reflections, and primitive data gathering, inspired by a strongly Catholic and nationalistic perspective (in the sense of the ethnocultural preservation of the French-Canadian "race") (Fournier 1986, 117). One is hard-pressed to find in this literature any concern for the theoretical and conceptual questions that so preoccupied Innis. In the late 1940s, the first crop of graduates from Laval's École des sciences sociales returned from the United States and English Canada with postgraduate degrees to fill new academic positions. It was only then that a more positivistic and theoretically inclined outlook on social questions began to emerge in Quebec's sociographical and historiographical discourse (Fournier 1986, 117; Brooks and Gagnon 1988, 33–4).

Between 1920 and 1950, Quebec was "entering" modernity. Men such as Édouard Montpetit, Esdras Minville, and Father Georges-Henri Lévesque, who were as influential in Quebec as Innis was in English Canada, were consumed by a genuine desire to modernize Quebec and give Quebecers the tools of their emancipation. Though their immediate field of action was the academic milieu, their concerns extended far beyond it. They closely overlapped with their sociopolitical environment to the point of being indistinguishable from it. Though they may have shared Innis's views on the importance of social scientists' having a good grasp of the realities that surround them, their goals did not extend to understanding the inner workings of society and history. In a sense, the imperatives and urgency of the necessary socioeconomic changes precluded any such reflection. It seemed more important to bring to light the facts that could nourish the right kind of sociopolitical and pedagogical action than to ponder the inner meaning of those facts and the general sociohistorical process of which they are a part.

Esdras Minville is an interesting illustration of the meeting of the minds that could have occurred between Innis and Quebec intellectuals. An economist, Quebec government adviser, and one of Quebec's premier and most prolific academics, Minville taught at Montreal's École des Hautes Études commerciales (HEC) of which he was head in the 1930s and 1940s. He was also one of the founders and editor of the influential *Actualité économique*. A staunch Quebec nationalist, he was extremely concerned about the subordination of the Quebec economy to U.S. and English-Canadian capital (Neill 1991, 154; Angers 1969). In this regard, he shared much of Innis's own worries over the negative impact of American economic imperialism on the Canadian economy and culture.

Yet Minville had little use for Innis's scholarship. Its underlying theoretical and conceptual preoccupations were foreign to him. As disciple and colleague, François-Albert Angers has noted, Minville was not interested in theorization or conceptualization: "Ce n'est pas de la théorie économique, ou de la modelisation, ou de la vérification de modèles qui l'intéressent; mais bien l'avenir d'une collectivité donnée, 'la province de Québec, foyer principal de la nationalité canadienne-française'" (Angers 1969, 471). Minville's intellectual and scholarly efforts were comprised mainly of descriptive studies of Quebec's economic environment. The point of these studies was to take stock of the economic problems of the province, so as to elaborate eventually a corrective *modus operandi*. Minville aimed essentially to build among his fellow Quebecers an awareness of the actual economic woes of the province. His was also an active vision, motivated by a search for the tools that would enable Quebecers to gain control of their destiny. Indeed, Minville stands as the direct precursor of the economic nationalists who would steer Quebec into its Quiet Revolution.

Though Minville and Innis were inspired by a strong sense of their respective nationhoods, they differed considerably in their intellectual relationship to nationalism. Innis's nationalism was undoubtedly rooted in personal experience – at war notably (Berger 1976, 87) – but it was not necessarily the motivating force behind his intellectual endeavours. His own realization of Canada's perennial economic dependence, which resulted from his historical studies, may have further consolidated his nationalistic convictions, but his analyses were not tailored to fostering that nationalism. Innis's nationalism is not linked *a priori* to the preconceived image of a culturally or linguistically homogeneous national group. He was much more concerned with freeing Canada from British and American economic influence than with promoting a particular vision of the nation. In fact, his strong, critical position (Innis 1940b) against the centralist bias of the Rowell-Sirois Report (Canada 1940) points to a rather flexible and pluralistic sense of both the Canadian state structure and nationality. In contrast, Minville's nationalism was closely tied to his self-identification with, indeed his belonging to a particular ethnocultural group. He cited his commitment to promoting the French-Canadian nationality to justify most of his work.

In any event, Innis and Minville would have hardly agreed on the proper methods to promote their nationalism. Like most members of the clerical elite, Minville was suspicious of Anglo-Saxon capitalism and believed that the only way to circumvent the pernicious effects of modern industrial society was for Quebec to foster, through state intervention, the emergence of an entrepreneurial class. Such a class would develop agriculture and small industries without falling prey to the individualism of capitalism (Angers 1969, 475; Neill 1991, 154). Minville's nationalist vision hinged on the socio-corporatist and agriculturist ethos of his day.

Innis's nationalism was, in contrast, profoundly liberal. While he may have been critical of some of the social and economic practices to which capitalism lent itself, particularly within the context of empires, he did not question the fundamental assumptions of capitalism as a mode of socioeconomic organization (McNally 1981). Wary as he was of planning and bureaucratic power (Berger 1976, 103–5; Neill 1991, 134), he would have certainly disapproved of the statist and centralist bent that Minville's reforms implied.

Clearly, Innis had very little in common with the Quebec intellectuals and academics of his generation. The scholarly traditions out of which each emerged, the imperatives of their milieux, and the characteristic objectives of their respective intellectual endeavours were so divergent that they would have had little to say to each other. The generation of economists that would follow Minville and Montpetit would find Innis even less relevant. The increasing institutionalization of the economics profession, the attractiveness of Keynesianism, the growing mathematization of economics, and the utterly a-historical character of their studies made Innis's preoccupations look passé (Neill 1972, 115–16; Paquet 1989). In Quebec, as in the rest of Canada, Innis would appear to economists only as the symbol of an outdated way of doing economics.

Among historians, Albert Faucher would carry Innis's torch practically alone. He would be joined by Fernand Ouellet, whose work has an obvious affiliation with the interpretation that Innis, but also Creighton and Lower, made of Canadian history. Ouellet, however, unlike Faucher, never directly acknowledged any kind of intellectual debt to Innis; his work owes more to the general heuristic approach of which Innis was a major exponent than to the man himself.[6] At any rate, in the 1960s and 1970s, the overwhelmingly nationalistic orientation of historical writing and sociological analysis in Quebec (Salée 1983) left Faucher and Ouellet largely isolated, their work implicitly dismissed for their pro-Canadian, federalist penchant. The methodological revolution that would lead after 1970 to the sectoralization of Quebec historiography (i.e., diversification into labour history, business history, women's history, and history of mentalités) virtually ended the search for broad interpretive and analytical frameworks like Innis's. The resonance of his work fell on deaf ears among that generation of Quebec historians.

QUEBEC AND THE "NEW POLITICAL ECONOMY"

Though enthusiasm for Innis waned in the decade or so after his death, interest was revived in the late 1960s and early 1970s, first by left-leaning economists and economic historians such as Mel Watkins, Abe Rotstein, Kari Levitt, and Tom Naylor, and then by sociologists, political scientists, and historians who shared similar, critical perspectives on Canadian economics and society. Extrapolating Innis's teachings about Canada's perennial economic dependence, all were generally united by radical, Marxist-oriented, nationalist, anti-imperialist, and anti-American sentiments. Their work, however, soon went beyond dependence-related issues to include fresh analyses of the state, labour history, class struggles, industrial strategy, nationalism, regionalism, and gender relations. Together, they came to be identified as the "new Canadian political economy" tradition. They constitute, as Pat Marchak has pointed out, "an academic community sharing a history, a paradigm, a social network, and a general perspective on both its subject matter and the engagement of academics in Canadian political life" (Marchak 1985, 673; quoted in Clement and Williams 1989, 14).

Unlike their predecessors, who were by and large oblivious to the

204 Gaps and Silences

Canadian political economy tradition, Quebec social scientists today are perfectly aware of this critical, intellectual revival. Many have of late associated themselves with this academic community, publishing in the same journals, appearing in the same anthologies or readers, and occasionally joining forces on political issues. Yet they are not adhering to the Innis-style interpretive framework or finding Innis's vision applicable. Despite the resurgence of his thought in recent English-Canadian critical, social discourse, Innis has remained virtually absent from Quebec's intellectual space. He has not been any more relevant to later social scientists – even to those sharing the premises of the new Canadian political economy – than he was forty or fifty years ago.

At the time when Mel Watkins was reintroducing Innis to the Canadian theoretical sphere (Watkins 1963) and analysing foreign ownership in Canadian industry,[7] his Quebec counterparts were formulating analyses with similar concerns but from a different point of view. The nationalist critique of American imperialism implicit in Innis's work was the bedrock on which many young English-Canadian scholars and intellectuals in the 1960s and early 1970s founded their anti-americanism and their consequent attack on Canada's perceived economic dependence. In Quebec, maverick intellectuals of essentially the same generation were looking rather to Frantz Fanon's *Les damnés de la terre* (1961) and Albert Memmi's *Le portrait du colonisé* (1966), to Jean-Paul Sartre and the Paris left intelligentsia, and to the anti-colonial struggles then raging in North Africa (Milot 1992, 79 et seq).

Beyond the shared radicalism of their politics, Quebec and English-Canadian intellectuals positioned themselves vis-à-vis imperialism and the national question in qualitatively different ways. The left-Innisians were extremely sensitive to Canada's "silent surrender" – to the want of an "internally rooted sense of national self" (Rotstein 1976, 109; quoted in Drache 1978, 43). Such a sensitivity was glaring in their early works, as they denounced the dependent character of the Canadian economy. Alarmed at Canada's brittle economic sovereignty and at the weak autonomous capacity of the Canadian state, they sought to produce a body of factual knowledge that would raise the collective consciousness of Canadians. To Mel Watkins, the programmatic and intellectual ambitions of the new political economy lay in the increased "analytical attention [which] should be devoted to the process by which the Canadian state successively suppressed re-emerging domestic capital within the staple sector itself, and within the manufacturing sector, in the interest of foreign capital" (Watkins 1977, 89). The early contributions of the new political economy thus, constituted a political exhortation for Canada to break free from U.S. economic sway.

Quebec's young radical intellectuals and academics found much with

205 Innis and Quebec

which to agree in such an objective, but that was not going far enough. They explained Quebec's experience in the light of its political, economic, and cultural oppression in the post-Conquest (English)-Canadian state. Their reading of Quebec's situation through authors such as Fanon and Memmi clearly indicated that they equated Quebec's plight with that of Third World colonies and developing nations. While the neo-Innisians and the Quebec radical nationalists of the 1960s pursued similar goals, they were in reality treading diverging paths: neo-Innisians were longing for the autonomization and political reinforcement of the Canadian state; Quebec radical nationalists were hoping to emancipate themselves from it. The latter couched their conception of the national question in poetic, almost tragic terms. As the intellectual revival of Innis was geared primarily towards the construction of Canada's economic independence, it could have little resonance in their worldview. In fact, it had no relevance to them.

By the early 1970s, most Quebec left intellectuals and academics had moved into French Marxist structuralism (Milot 1992, 94 et seq), distancing themselves further from the neo-Innisians. In the ensuing decade, their discussions and debates followed European controversies within Marxism and were totally absorbed by epistemological questions, Marxist exegesis, and the proper way of analysing the particularities of the class configuration of Quebec society in relation to the national question (Legaré 1980).

Intellectual and theoretical commonality between Quebec left social scientists and their counterparts was still possible within the new political economy tradition. Though the new political economy may have been inspired by Innis, it was not exclusively Innisian. If it did not appeal to Quebec academics, other branches of the new political economy would. The second wave soon took its distance from dependency analyses and seriously questioned the strategy of dependency scholars, who promoted state-led Canadianization of capitalism. The writings of Leo Panitch (1977) and his collaborators in the collection *The Canadian State* pointed to the social and political difficulties of a class alliance of Canadian capitalists and subordinate classes against foreign interests. The ensuing proliferation of class analyses marked a shift in analytical focus from the structure of international economy to domestic social relations. This new emphasis was more familiar to Quebec Marxist scholars and eventually led to more frequent associations with their English-Canadian colleagues.

In the early 1980s, neo-Innisian political economists came under attack within the very tradition they had initiated. Their theory and method were discredited for inappropriately juxtaposing Marx and Innis within the same analytical framework (McNally 1981; Panitch

1981; Schmidt 1981). In defence of their position, they lamented their critics' tendency to adopt European theoretical frameworks that, in their view, were ill-equipped to account for Canada's particularities. Daniel Drache expressed concern that his colleagues' propensity to turn to "metropolitan" (European) Marxism, away from the left-Innisian, dependence-oriented – and thus quintessentially Canadian – perspectives could weaken not only the intellectual heterodoxy so vital for the renewal of Marxism in Canada but also the analyses of Canadian society and politics. "[H]ighly generalized Marxist theory," he wrote, "creates a narrow methodological imperative defining the principal orientation of the researcher. More than this, it runs the risk and indeed the very high risk of turning into a 'closed' discourse based on a deeply rooted preconception of what Canadian society is" (Drache 1983, 41).

It is thus hardly surprising that neo-Innisians failed to make any inroads within Quebec's academic left. Concerns over the propriety of applying Marxist frameworks borrowed from Europe were never an issue within the Quebec left, which readily endorsed the latest theoretical developments to arise out of European – in particular, French – controversies within Marxism. The project of wedding Innis and Marx never seemed to serve any particular purpose, or be of relevance to Quebec's social scientists. It was never even contemplated as an alternative. It has been, and has remained, an exclusively English-Canadian debate.

Today, when Quebec's left social scientists and English-Canadian representatives of the new political economy join in intellectual ventures, Innisian thinking has little influence. In recent years, France's *école de la régulation*[8] has served as the common ground. Innis will probably always remain a central, historical pillar of the Canadian intellectual legacy. However, his relevance for the analysis of contemporary economic issues has faded as the problems that he addressed subsided or simply changed. As Canada became irremediably integrated into the broader continental and international economy, questions of dependence and the characterization of Canada as a periphery no longer held the same intellectual sway. As a result, European–American discourses on the economy have unavoidably gained more appeal. In a sense, the replacement of Innis by other theoretical and metatheoretical frameworks is but a function of Canada's evolving circumstances. New questions bring new answers.

CONCLUSION

Harold Adams Innis is an intellectual and cultural icon in English

Canada, sitting in the limited pantheon of great Canadian intellectual figures on a par only with George Grant and Marshall McLuhan. No doubt his place is well deserved. In some ways, however, this all-too-often uncritical veneration is strange and somewhat disturbing. Is it the want of genuinely Canadian intellectual and theoretical models that brings some scholars, sometimes desperately, to raise one of their pioneers to intellectual sainthood? Or is it their desire to prop up what is often lamented as a weak sense of nationhood? Innis rightly remains an inspiring intellectual influence, but the exaltation of his contribution seems odd to many who stand outside the intellectual tradition that his thinking has begotten. In the line-up of great twentieth-century economists, historians, and social critics, he occupies a rather secondary position, quite far behind the likes of Schumpeter, Polanyi, Braudel, Althusser, Foucault, and Habermas.

Still, to those who have made it a career to uphold and promote Innis's vision, a nagging question remains: why have Quebec intellectuals not found or even sought in Innis conceptual guidance and interpretive inspiration? Why has Innis been so relevant to English-Canadian political economists and social scientists, but hardly to most Quebec intellectuals?

Beyond the sheer intellectual divide between Innis and Quebec social scientists, which this paper has attempted to clarify, lies a fundamental reality that is sometimes overlooked. Innis's scholarship and positions often left him standing at the margins of the intellectual mainstream of his own time; he was nevertheless socially defined by the culturally hegemonic, white, Anglo-Saxon, central Canadian context in which he evolved and lived. Admittedly, Innis did denounce u.s. imperialism, and his work did serve the same purpose to a later generation, but his experience was not that of a member of a political community virtually condemned to internal colonialism for most of its history – nor was it that of his epigones. However universal some of his themes, their appeal to Quebecers, as he formulated them and as they would be formulated by his followers, could be only limited. American imperialism has never been perceived as a problem in Quebec to the extent that it has in Canada: it is not what moves Quebec's sense of nationhood. That is why, for example, Quebecers have been more willing to support free trade initiatives in recent years.

Quebec's intellectuals have always had different concerns, largely at odds with those of the rest of Canada. They still do. Though their approach to political economy may have similar objectives to that of English Canadians, it has had by and large, and will in all likelihood continue to have, different theoretical underpinnings and resonance.

NOTES

1 I would like to thank Charles Acland and William Buxton for their comments on an earlier version of this article and Anne-Marie Field for her assistance in revising it.
2 Bourque (1970) refers in passing to the staple thesis without acknowledging Innis's contribution to its formulation (23–6). He is perhaps the only radical nationalist Quebec intellectual to mention the thesis in his work. Though Bourque saw some merit in the idea that staple production may account for economic development, he eventually dismissed it as incomplete and insufficient to explain the whole dynamic of social development.
3 To wit, Daniel Drache's edition of Innis's selected essays (Innis 1995) and Robert Cox's (1995) engaging, but surprising essay in which Innis's thought appears as the cornerstone of a reinterpretation of current, global socioeconomic transformations.
4 For an unequivocal expression of the exasperation of French-Canadian nationalist historians with English-Canadian historiography, see Brunet 1967. See also Rudin 1997: chap. 3.
5 However, Séguin uses abundantly the two volumes of *Select Documents in Canadian Economic History* (Innis, ed., 1929; Innis and Lower, eds., 1933). See Séguin 1970 – the belated publication of Séguin's 1947 doctoral dissertation.
6 Ouellet (1966) quotes Innis approvingly. His references to Donald Creighton are more numerous, however. Ouellet partook of the general Laurentian thesis, though he cannot be said to be an Innisian as clearly as Faucher.
7 The so-called Watkins Report, resulting from the 1968 federal task force on foreign ownership (Canada 1968). See also Watkins 1970.
8 The best and most obvious example is Boismenu and Drache 1990.

11 Innis in Quebec: Conjectures and Conjunctures

ALAIN-G. GAGNON AND
SARAH FORTIN

INTRODUCTION[1]

The Innisian approach has attracted little attention among social scientists in Quebec. Contrary to the situation in English Canada, where it is considered one of the dominant themes of Canadian economic historiography, the work of Harold Innis has been spread only recently and rather modestly across Québécois academic circles. Indeed, it was only in the 1950s, when Albert Faucher returned from Toronto to teach at the Université Laval, that economic history began to be studied more systematically and that political economy became a legitimate analytical framework in Quebec.

The centenary of Innis's birth seems a most propitious time to examine the reasons for this lapse. The scope and richness of Innis's work would alone serve to justify such an exercise, but it also provides us with an invaluable opportunity to analyse the development of the social sciences in a state as fragmented as that of Canada.

We intend to discuss the circumstances of and reasons for the silence surrounding Innis's work in Quebec, particularly the role of intellectual traditions and the institutionalization of the social sciences and their networks. We submit that the uniqueness of the Québécois social sciences and the rather late establishment of such networks explain the limited welcome of Innis in Quebec.[2]

THE ROLE OF INTELLECTUAL TRADITIONS

The development of Canadian political economy owes a great deal to

Innis. In Quebec, however, his approach has attracted far fewer devotees. *Settlement and the Mining Frontier* (1936b), *The Cod Fisheries: The History of an International Economy* (1940), and *The Fur Trade in Canada* (1930) have had little influence on Quebec's social scientists.

Social scientists in Quebec were, however, not completely unaware of his work. The writings of Stanley Ryerson (1968) on the unequal relations between Quebec and the rest of Canada are enlightening on this subject. The Department of Political Economy of McGill University was in general more receptive to Innis's work than other institutions of higher learning in Quebec. While himself hardly an Innisian, James Mallory (1954) introduced McGill students to Innis's work. More directly in the Innis tradition was John McCallum's doctoral dissertation, defended in 1977 and published as *Unequal Beginnings* (1980). McCallum was one of the first Innis-inspired students registered in a Quebec university. These political economy–inspired analyses strongly suggest that Quebec offers a congenial ground for the advancement of Innis's ideas.

A few francophone scholars have expressed disappointment at the general lack of interest in Innis among their colleagues. Jean Blain, for example, deplored the fact that French-Canadian historiography showed disdain for an Innis-style approach that "invited researchers to examine closely deeply-entrenched colonial realities, thereby providing, as early as 1930, the point of departure for a promising social and economic history to which the Labroussian detour provides only partial and problematic access" (27–9). He explains this detour: "Apart from the handicap of its Anglo-Saxon origin (much could be said about the stubborn separateness of the two national historiographic currents in Canada), the staple model was disadvantaged in Quebec by its materialism, an optic that was an anathema by those working hard to perpetrate and encourage explanations rooted in voluntarism and 'race'" (27).[3]

From the early 1950s, Michel Brunet criticized French-Canadian misconceptions of the Canadian reality: "French Canadians are capable of expounding at length on the domestic policy of France, but ... are unaware of the MacMillan Report, the Inquiry into Federal–Provincial Relations [Canada 1940], and the Marsh Report [Canada 1943]." He urged them to show interest in English-Canadian periodicals, especially the *Canadian Journal of Economics and Political Science*: "It is simply a matter of growing up and realising that in certain areas France has nothing to teach us. We urgently need to come to this awareness, particularly in the political and economic sciences" (Brunet 1953, 301).[4]

The weak relations between (and even at times segregation of) francophone and anglophone historians has often been explained along lines suggested by Jean Blain, who described two distinct historiographical traditions. Jean Lamarre elaborated on this idea: "Generally speaking, these two traditions are opposed at a philosophical level. ... [T]his opposition relates to the fact that neither agrees with the other's sense of the fundamental problem to be resolved. For French-Canadian historiography, the problem is to interpret the destiny of French Canada inside a broader society that the Conquest ensured would remain British. Anglophone historiography, for its part, has been especially concerned with defining a foundation for English-Canadian identity that could distinguish English-Canadian society from that of the United States" (1993, 30).

With respect to the lack of interest in the staples theory in Quebec, we would be hard-pressed to deny the importance and the role of distinct intellectual traditions. In economics, the tradition inaugurated by Errol Bouchette (1977) and developed by Esdras Minville, director of Montreal's École des Hautes Études commerciales (HEC) from 1938 to 1962, dominated the discipline until the end of the 1940s. This nationalist and *milieuiste* interpretation of economic phenomena led to numerous publications in the "Études sur notre milieu" series, most notably in agriculture, forestry, fishery, mining, manufacturing, commerce, and transportation.[5] While staples theory also examined these categories, the *milieuiste* approach sought to make an inventory of natural resources in order to develop them more effectively.

French-Canadian historians focused on the political dimension as well as the national question and aimed at explaining the impact of the Conquest on French-Canadian society. As Jean Blain observes ironically, such an orientation was far from compatible with the propositions of a Harold Innis. Innis was hardly interested in family, *ruralité*, and peasant society and seemed unaware of the truncated class structure that characterized Quebec society until the end of the 1960s. Moreover, his analysis did not take into account the development of a heterogeneous Canada, founded on two distinct sociological bases.

Politically speaking, the traditional Quebec elite, including the Catholic leadership, was very suspicious of the interventionist model at the time of Innis's writing. The Tremblay Report (Quebec 1956) on constitutional matters represented a clear example of this elite's rejection of a Canadian cultural model said to be rooted in materialism, federal intervention, and American-style capitalism (Coleman 1984, 64–87; Trudeau 1956).

Insisting too heavily on distinct intellectual traditions may, however, lead to an underemphasis of the divisions within Québécois intellectual life. In history, for example, the interpretive framework of Lionel

Groulx clashed with that of Thomas Chapais and Abbé Maheux.[6] Their debate began years earlier, in the context of the polemic between Henri Bourassa and Jules-Paul Tardivel, and was reproduced afterward in the debates between the Montreal historical school and the Laval school, which included Fernand Ouellet.[7]

Gilles Paquet and Jean-Pierre Wallot argue that, despite the work of such precursors as Innis, Arthur Lower, and Donald Creighton, interest in economic history in English Canada, like that in Quebec, remained within a traditional framework until the postwar era. Only "[a] minority," they insist, "engaged in modern economic history and the new economic history" (1969, 278).[8]

It is not our task to assess Paquet and Wallot's judgment of the state of English-Canadian historiography.[9] Nevertheless, their decision to study the evolution of Canadian historiography in abstraction from the cultural and linguistic cleavage that characterizes the Canadian social sciences has led to serious distortions. Paquet and Wallot suggest that the institutionalization and modernization of scientific activity in Canada have advanced in a homogeneous fashion, when in fact it has come about in two different waves: first in English Canada and then in Quebec. It strikes us as significant that the precursors to Canadian economic history were English Canadians.

INSTITUTIONALIZATION OF THE SOCIAL SCIENCES IN QUEBEC[10]

Contrary to what Paquet and Wallot would have us believe, the institutionalization and modernization of the social sciences in Canada did not proceed at the same pace and in the same way across the country. Economic history and the professionalization of history began in English Canada in the 1920s, whereas in French Canada the same developments emerged only decades later.[11] In economics, the participation of English-Canadian economists in the (Rowell-Sirois) Commission of Inquiry into Dominion–Provincial Relations (Canada 1940) confirmed their ascension to scientific status, whereas Québécois economists had to wait until the 1950s for their rite of passage.

Exploring this disjuncture, we would suggest, is the key to understanding the relatively late and (modest) diffusion of Innis's ideas in Quebec. English Canada preceded Quebec in establishing economic history, thereby favouring the cultivation of intimate ties with Innis's political economy approach.

In Quebec, the increased attention accorded to Innis coincided with profound changes in Québécois social sciences that marked the culmination of institutionalization. This crucial phase, as Marcel Fournier has noted, marked the development of a new conceptual relationship to reality (tradition versus science, doctrine versus empiricism, exegesis versus experimentation) and a new type of intellectual activity (1986, 7–40).

This process of institutionalization, begun in the 1920s with the establishment of the École des Sciences sociales, économiques, et politiques de Montréal in 1920 and the Association canadienne-française pour l'avancement des sciences (ACFAS) in 1923, came to fruition after the Second World War, in the wake of the expansion of Laval (1943) and Montréal (1950) universities. In the case of the HEC, institutionalization progressed at an even slower pace, as Pierre Harvey (1994) underlines.

The development of the social sciences in Quebec can be appreciated by comparing its status within ACFAS before and after the 1950s.[12] Between 1923 and 1947, only three of its presidents came from the social sciences. In 1947, when the annual congress treated the situation of French Canadians in scientific careers, the person in charge of the social sciences failed to present a final report because of the lack of content. The various disciplines within the social sciences attained independent, sectional representation within ACFAS only relatively late: sociology in 1955, economics and geography in 1956, history in 1957, and political science in 1962.[13] Nevertheless, in its role as a mechanism for mobilization and exchange of ideas, ACFAS has served as a catalyst; numerous professional associations were formed in the course of its annual congresses.[14]

The difficulties that McGill's interdisciplinary Social Science Research Committee had in recruiting francophone students illustrates the state of the social sciences in the 1930s. The first efforts at establishing interdisciplinary research networks, like that of the Canadian Pioneer Problems Committee, took place without a significant contribution from French Canadians (Shore 1987, 172–6, 253–60). The precariousness of the social sciences in Quebec lasted until the 1960s.

There was, moreover, little to encourage an early discovery of Innis's work. When those in the Quebec social sciences looked outward for guidance,[15] they turned almost exclusively towards Europe, particularly France. The professorial corps was often of European origin, or at the very least European-educated. Many French-Canadian recipients of scholarships in the social sciences studied in Europe,[16] and visiting academics came for the most part from the Old World. The Institut scientifique franco-canadien, created in 1927, aimed initially at bringing professors from France to Laval and Montréal.

This orientation has led some scholars to study the history of the social sciences in Quebec to 1950 not only in the context of institutionalization but also in terms of "nationalization." Broadly speaking, the maturation of the social sciences was characterized by initiatives that served to favour the emergence of a specifically Québécois social scientific field. Notable examples include the Académie canadienne-française (1944), the Institut Canadien des affaires publiques (1953), and the periodical *Recherches sociographiques* (1960).[17]

The reason for such a strategy, in place of integration within the existing English-Canadian network, is open to question. One should recall the marginal position of francophones within "Canadian" institutions, such as the Royal Society of Canada, and their difficulty in obtaining scholarships for further training. For example, French Canadians obtained only 3 per cent and 5½ per cent of all scholarships offered by the National Research Council of Canada in the 1920s and the 1930s, respectively (Gingras 1994, 73). Overall, French-Canadian presence within the Royal Society was weak. Yves Lamarche reports that there has always been an autonomous French humanities section of around forty members, but that there was hardly any communication between the French and English sections, thus diminishing its usefulness for intellectual exchange. The society also suffered from a lack of prestige in the eyes of eminent French-Canadian researchers, while many others refused to participate for ideological reasons (Lamarche 1975, 145–53).

Still, one can hardly conclude that it was the exclusion of Quebec social scientists from federal bodies that forced them to create their own national bodies. Obviously their minority status encouraged such a move, but a typically French-Canadian "fundamental problem," both in history and in political economy, was also a factor, as discussed above.

According to Marcel Fournier and Louis Maheu (1975), French Canadians created their own institutions and other instruments of communication and exchange so as to avoid direct competition with English Canadians for positions in universities and the (English-dominated) federal civil service. Their objective was thus not so much to create a field more independent from the English-Canadian one than to modify the ethnic division of work and ensure access to higher positions for French Canadians (Owram 1986).

In fact, even though both the Quebec government and ACFAS contributed to this effort by establishing their own funding programs, Ottawa continued to be a major financial backer. The rather conservative politics of the Duplessis era may have had a lot to do with this. As Fournier and Maheu observe, the harmony between intellectuals and politicians was not perfect, despite a shared nationalist discourse.

"As soon as the government neglected to fight the big corporations, favored agriculturism, refused modernisation and rationalisation, it has alienated a growing number of intellectuals" (1975, 99).

"Nationalization" was apparently flexible enough to allow decisions more conducive to the professionalization of the social sciences. For instance, a certain number of Québécois during the 1940s and 1950s maintained their desire to be integrated into the pan-Canadian scientific establishment. Fournier and Maheu note the increased publication rate of articles by francophones in the *Canadian Journal of Economics and Political Science*, along with more intensive participation in the Canadian Association of Economics and Political Science (101). Also of importance more recently is the increasing enrolment of francophone students in American and English-Canadian universities.[18] Perhaps more revealing was the recommendation of ACFAS, despite its rather harmonious relations with Duplessis's Union Nationale government, to accept the federal subsidies for postsecondary education in Quebec (Gingras 1994, 170–5).

Québécois social sciences benefited as much from federal as from provincial commissions of inquiry that succeeded one another in the 1950s and 1960s. Calls for the expertise of specialists in the social sciences – including economics, political science, sociology, and geography – came from bodies as diverse as the (Massey-Lévesque) Royal Commission on the Advancement of the Arts, Letters, and Sciences (1949–51), the Tremblay Commission, on constitutional problems (1953–56), the Gordon Commission, on economic matters (1955–57), the (Laurendeau-Dunton) Royal Commission on Bilingualism and Biculturalism (1963–69), the (Gendron) provincial commission on language policy, and even the Bureau d'aménagement de l'Est du Québec (1963–66), designing models of development for Quebec's outlying regions.

Still, the government of Quebec – through its financing of new university programs, its establishment of a network of Quebec universities, commissions of inquiry, and research institutions, and its other public-sector initiatives – became progressively more involved in the 1960s. All these programs aimed to foster the training of research personnel and the learning of French as an economic asset.

The 1960s represents the culmination of institutionalization, after which period it becomes more difficult to talk of the social sciences as a whole. The multiplication and diversification of training centres, research institutes, and teaching institutions, along with the fragmentation of researchers along well-defined disciplinary lines, seem to compel an analysis by discipline and by institution.

Keeping this broad historical context in mind is essential if one wishes to grasp why interest in Innis's staples theory has been rather weak in Quebec. In the first historical phase, until 1950, the diffusion of Innis's work was handicapped by the underdeveloped state of the social sciences in Quebec. In the following period, the "great leap forward" – involving the rapid diversification of the social sciences and the growth of the provincial state – discouraged widespread interest in Innis. It was no longer possible to speak of one and only one developmental trend in the social sciences in Quebec.

INNIS IN QUEBEC: LAVAL

It was not until the 1950s that Maurice Lamontagne (1944–54) and Albert Faucher (1945–82) joined forces to introduce a political economy approach in the Department of Economics at Laval. They attempted to impress on their students and readers the idea that economic history ought to be studied in a systematic manner and that the moral dimension of economic matters – which had been central in their department – ought to be left aside (Thibault 1988, 139–40).[19] It is surely not a coincidence that in 1947, five years before his death, Innis was awarded an honorary doctorate at Laval, where his work was highly praised as a vital contribution to the development of Canadian and Québécois historiography.[20]

The influence of political economy was soon evident in a speech of Lamontagne's before a group of researchers at Dalhousie University (Lamontagne 1948). Having obtained his master's degree from the University of Toronto in 1945, Albert Faucher echoed Innis's themes and ideas throughout his career.[21] Two studies confirmed Innis's influence at Laval: Faucher and Lamontagne's "History of Industrial Development" (1953) and Lamontagne's Le fédéralisme canadien (1954). The work of Fernand Ouellet, notably his Histoire économique et sociale du Québec (1966), is also worth citing.

Contrary to the view defended by Daniel Salée in chapter 10, we do not believe that Faucher, Lamontagne, and Ouellet were marginalized in Quebec simply because they were "federalists." On the contrary, their work in economic history encouraged many researchers to question the established ideas of the discipline. Even certain well-known "nationalist" social scientists called upon them to strive for a wider audience by making their work more accessible (Dumont 1962).

To understand why Innis's thought found a modest foothold at Laval, rather than elsewhere in Quebec, the concept of the network is key. At the instigation of Father Georges-Henri Lévesque, the École des Sciences sociales became more connected with English-Canadian and American institutions, and he encouraged Laval students to further their education in English Canada and in the United States. Lévesque was also an active participant in the Massey-Lévesque Commission, and he was the one who invited the eminent American sociologist Everett Hughes to spend the academic year 1942–43 at Laval.[22] This visit had a lasting influence on the institutions.

Hughes used his stay in Quebec City to establish a program of sociological research focusing on Quebec, especially on the family as a functional unit, on family businesses, and on the parish (Hughes 1943). The publication in 1943 of his *French Canada in Transition*, available in French after 1945 as *Rencontre de deux mondes: la crise de l'industrialisation du Canada français* (1972), marked a watershed in Québécois sociology.[23] Jean-Charles Falardeau, who studied under Hughes at the University of Chicago in the 1940s, picked up where his mentor left off and initiated his students into the ways of the Chicago School. Religious and moral preoccupations took up less and less space in an analysis of the problems confronting Quebec as a modernizing society.

The intimate ties between the Chicago School and researchers at Laval should cause no surprise. Members of the former drew on the teachings of a particular European tradition: the French school of Le Play, a theorist of "human geography," social ecology, and demography known for his positivism and his analyses of working-class life. Hughes, for example, studied at the University of Chicago under Robert Park, who was influenced by Le Play's approach (Shore 1987, 270). Le Play's ideas thus profoundly influenced Hughes's work and hence the development of the social sciences in Chicago (Clark 1975). His influence at Laval, however, was not just indirect; the founder of Quebec sociology, Léon Gérin, had studied in Paris under him in 1885 and 1886 (Trépanier 1987; Nock 1974).

Thus "[f]rom 1943 on, a group of young professors ... had become more interested in developing a positive social science than in propagating a social philosophy," in contrast to the Université de Montréal, and had, along with Hughes, adopted the approach of the Chicago school (Fournier 1986, 127). These initial contacts with social science predisposed researchers at Laval towards a favourable reception of Innis's ideas. Significantly, Innis himself had completed his studies in Chicago, and, as Marlene Shore (1987) points out, his work clearly converges with many of the preoccupations of the Chicago School: "[T]he similarities in his work and that of MacKenzie, Dawson, and Park are so strong that they are impossible to deny. While Innis never studied directly with Park, he was influenced by the Chicago Economics Department, particularly Duncan's lectures on marketing. Duncan's ideas on marketing – that the physical characteristics of a community influence its marketing structure and in turn the cultural community built in relations to it – all stemmed from Park's ecological theories and penetrated into Innis' books" (272).

It is perhaps premature to trace the influence of Innis's ideas at Laval directly to the existence of a network linking Innis to the Faculté des sciences sociales via Chicago and its LePlayian roots. It would be easier to underline the role of such Laval professors as Lévesque, Falardeau, and Faucher.

The path taken by Laval's social scientists was generally not popular in Quebec, where the influence of the Chicago school was often looked on askance. Professors at Montréal, for example, criticized the Laval's adoption of positivist methods of social inquiry as a dangerous Americanization (Garigue 1958). Moreover, while the analyses of Faucher, Lamontagne, and Ouellet undeniably helped shape economic history and political economy in Quebec, other theoretical perspectives were available.

In Montreal, researchers at the HEC followed Esdras Minville. The Service de documentation économique which he founded became known in 1959 as the Institut d'Économie appliquée, following the visit of François Perroux of the Institut d'Économie appliquée de Paris. Minville wished to turn the HEC into a school of administration, on the model of the Graduate School of Business Administration, where research would promote the economic interests of the collectivity, but his goal was never brought to fruition. From its very beginning, a struggle over HEC's vocation pitted Minville's supporters against those who wanted more specialized, technical training in business management, accounting, and the actuarial sciences. At the end of the 1940s, the school offered four areas of specialization, including economics.[24]

A certain rivalry characterized relations between the economists of the HEC and Laval, as crystallized in the writings of François-Albert Angers, director of the Institut d'Économie appliquée, who severely criticized Laval's methods.[25] As Gilles Paquet points out, HEC had a heritage to respect, associated with an inductive, empiricist method propagated within an interventionist and nationalist tradition (1985, 365–97).

During this same era, a new type of pure economics, heavily weighted in favour of geometric and mathematical models, was introduced into the Department of Economics at Montréal with the arrival of the Belgian Roger Dehem, following the transformation of the older Faculté des sciences sociales into a full-fledged university faculty (1945).[26]

In history, the école historique de Montréal (the Montreal school) emerged, with the work of Michel Brunet (1958), Guy Frégault, and Maurice Séguin attracting adherents from a large number of Québécois historians. Unlike Innis, who always conceived of Quebec as part of the Canadian whole, these authors sought to describe Quebec as a self-contained society. The historiography practised by the Montreal school "placed politics and the nation at the centre of historical intelligibility" (Lamarre 1993, 21). These historians thus offered an alternative to the theses and the approach of Faucher and Ouellet.

The Montreal historians were just as interested as their colleagues at Laval in introducing more scientific methods and in allowing economic factors to play a role in the interpretation of history. Their interests, however, were integrated into a nationalist rubric: "Montreal School theorists converge around a hypothesis concerning the global fate of the collectivity with which they identify and which they develop together, whereas [the Quebec School] rallies around a similar conception of the historian's vocation" (Lamarre 1993, 22–3).

In the light of the pluralism of Quebec intellectual life, it is clear that Innis's ideas, while finding fertile soil at Laval, faced formidable obstacles elsewhere, in institutions where alternative practices, methods, and traditions were well-established. It is also possible that, during this postwar era when Quebec was redefining itself as a modern nation, the socioeconomic conjuncture rendered Innis's preoccupations less relevant. Notwithstanding the work of Laurier Turgeon (1981, 1986), Gilles Paquet and Jean-Pierre Wallot (1969), Maurice Saint-Germain (1973), and Alain-G. Gagnon and MaryBeth Montcalm (1990), all of whom remind us that Innis has not been completely ignored, Innis has had only a marginal influence on a field of research characterized by growing fragmentation of interest and approach since the 1950s.[27] The pace of this fragmentation accelerated during the 1960s and 1970s, with the establishment of the network of Universités du Québec, especially of the Université du Québec à Montréal (UQAM), where the Marxist approach, in combination with a preoccupation with the national question, has dominated until the 1980s.

CONCLUSION

In the course of this chapter, we have hypothesised that the networks put in place during the first half of the twentieth century discouraged fruitful exchange between English and French Canadians. We have noted the existence of parallel and differentiated networks, reflected in differing schools of thought (such as the Montréal versus Laval), the changing social value of various disciplines, and the types of training acquired by researchers in certain universities rather than others. There can be no doubt that the network has explanatory power; our study, while only preliminary, has demonstrated its usefulness in explaining the development and orientation of particular institutions, departments, and even disciplines.[28]

While the concept of network has been underused in the study of the social sciences, it has been applied more often in the study of new social movements (Brooks and Gagnon 1994a).[29] Admittedly, the aims and focus of such study are quite different from that which examines the social sciences, but its exploration of collective identity and of identity formation leads us to believe that this method would be helpful in the study of social science communities.

The development of the social sciences in Canada has been the subject of many scholarly books and articles. Almost all these works have looked either at distinct French and English social scientific communities or at just one of the two. English-Canadian scholars have tended to treat the Québécois reality dismissively or to assimilate it to the larger pan-Canadian context.[30] French-Canadian academics have studied the Québécois context in isolation from the Canadian whole, as a means of drawing attention to its specificity, tending to underestimate cleavages within Quebec's social sciences. Both approaches reveal a natural reflex to erect two, fully autonomous national communities.

In the course of this investigation of the trajectory of the Innisian idea, we have confirmed that Canadian social science is indeed composed of two distinct communities, each with its respective language, set of traditions, and concerns. Yet our results suggest that scholars should re-examine the assumed homogeneity of Quebec's intellectual life before 1960 in the light of the abovementioned conflict between Montreal and Quebec City, and they should study the French and English scientific communities in a parallel or comparative fashion. Further research on networks would help us understand the ties that bind the two communities together in the Canadian scientific world.

Moreover, our examination of institutionalization in the social sciences suggests the influence not simply of "internal" dynamics; the wider social, political, and economic fields all played a role. This social, economic, and political context has defined their *raison d'être* (as part of a national project) as well as the strategy of their principal agents (nationalization). A proper analysis of social science networks must take this 'external' dimension into account. Once again, we are obliged to transcend the strictly Québécois domain and take the English-Canadian field into account, particularly its earlier institutionalization and the resulting impact on its Québécois counterpart.

Quebec's less-than-enthusiastic welcome of Innis's work can be explained by a complex combination of these elements. Rapid postwar transformations impelled researchers to seek out the indigenous analytical tools that seemed most propitious for an investigation of the evolution of Quebec and its transformation into both a modern society and a national community. What is more, the institutionalization and modernization of the social sciences occurred rather late, and traditional political and clerical elites saw them as potential arenas of opposition to the established order. The small number of social scientists hardly facilitated a rapid development of the disciplines, and the speedy economic changes after 1945 obsessed the few available specialists for a long period. Given the linguistic cleavage, the disjuncture between the French and English social scientific communities impeded the exchange of ideas and favoured the establishment of parallel, autonomous networks.

NOTES

1 This paper was translated by Fredrick Appel, Department of Political Science, McGill University. We would like to thank Professors François-Albert Angers and Fernand Ouellet, as well as Michel Sarra-Bournet, for the interviews that they so kindly accorded us in the course of our research.

2 According to the *Social Science Citation Index*, Innis's work was not cited by francophone researchers between 1966 and 1970 (forty citations sampled) and cited only twelve times between 1971 and 1975 (forty-eight citations sampled).

3 See also Fernand Ouellet (1985), for whom "French-Canadian historiography distanced itself from the anglophone historiographic tradition, and the staple theory that supported it, because of the national question in Quebec" (23).

4 In the same piece, Brunet's positive assessment of Innis's work is noteworthy: "It is interesting to follow closely the intellectual démarche of a conscientious and original scholar who attempts to explain the world in which we live. His explanations are representative not of arbitrary preconceptions, but rather of the conclusions of patient and disinterested research."

5 On Minville, see Harvey 1976. On the role of the HEC in the development of the social sciences in Quebec, see Marcel Fournier 1986, 43–73.

6 This controversy belongs to political and national history and concerned relations between the "two founding peoples." See Lamarre 1993, 66–76.

7 Fernand Dumont has frequently taken issue with the claim that Laval

represented the viewpoint of one particular school: "Considerable ideological differences are the order of the day in the Faculty of Social Sciences ... In their courses, professors speak rarely of nationalism, of [Léon]
Gérin and of M. [Philippe] Garigne, but more appropriately of demography, social stratification, the culture of the Sioux, or Durkheim" (cited in
Gagnon 1988, 112).

8 Paquet and Wallot explain this "cultural delay" by invoking the difficulty
   "until very recently" of propagating new work in a field with a "strong
   anti-formalist bias within journals of history and a bias against quantita-
   tive methods in economics periodicals." They also criticize the
   researchers: "Their disorganisation ... ensured that the level of discussion
   remained rather diffuse and engendered ideological polemics. In other
   words, they mobilised historians into schools rather than incited them
   towards experimentation and objective research" (1969, 280–1).

9 Their opinion is shared by Fernand Ouellet (1985, 13).

10 The term "institutionalization" is here defined as "the process of acquisition of material and human resources, and of the independence necessary
   for self-regulated intellectual activity, which is translated into the establishment of a departmental structure within a faculty of social sciences,
   the development of a specialised programme of studies and the hiring of
   a tenured corps of professional specialists" (Brooks and Gagnon 1994b,
   47).

11 Lamarre 1993, 32–53.

12 For other data (number of graduates, professorial corps, university training, and so on) rereading the changes in higher education in Quebec in
   the 1950s and 1960s, see Lévesque et al. 1984; Fournier 1986; and
   Maheu et al. 1984.

13 On the history of ACFAS, see Gingras 1994, 114–18, 166–8. Gingras
   remarks that the minority position of the social sciences was not unique
   to Québec, for a similar situation existed within the British Association
   for the Advancement of Science. The relationship between social science
   and "pure" science is reversed in the Royal Society of Canada, where
   French-Canadian scientists are practically absent (Lamarche 1975).

14 The Association of Canadian Economists was established in 1960; the
   Association canadienne des sociologues et anthropologues de langue
   française in 1961; and the Canadian Political Science Association, in
   1963 (Gingras 1994, 117).

15 Here, once again, the situation of the natural sciences differs from that of
   the social sciences. The Québécois natural science milieu cut its umbilical
   cord to Europe earlier than its social science counterpart under the influence of Marie-Victorin, who "was not fond of the francophile tendencies
   of some of his colleagues and [who] insisted that in most scientific disci-

plines, the model to emulate was that found in the United States, rather than in France" (Gingras 1994, 63, 67).

16 An analysis of the chosen destinations of recipients of ACFAS scholarships in the social sciences reveals that "professors of social science tend to be oriented towards France." Also of note, and another sign of Québécois francophilism, are the "European scholarships" offered by the provincial government beginning in the 1920s to encourage studies in Paris. Amendments allowing for study visits to the United States were passed only in 1937 (Gingras 1994, 69–70).

17 See the detailed chronology in Fournier 1986, 160–73.

18 Cornell University (Marc-Adélard Tremblay, Gérald Fortin), Harvard University (Guy Rocher, Maurice Tremblay, Maurice Lamontagne, Arthur Tremblay), and the University of Chicago (Jean-Charles Falardeau) are the most highly regarded institutions in Quebec.

19 On the development of this field in Quebec, see Angers 1961; Fortin 1984; Ouellet 1985; Paquet 1985; and Sales and Dumais 1985.

20 See the testimony of Faucher (1953), following the death of his mentor.

21 Albert Faucher and Maurice Lamontagne were probably the first "Innisian" Franco-québécois social scientists.

22 The extracurricular activities of Father Lévesque, whether sitting on the Massey Commission or supporting the Asbestos strike, earned him the scorn of the Duplessis government, which drastically reduced the subsidy of his faculty one year (from $37,500 to $25,000) and eliminated it completely the next (Fournier 1986, 140).

Lévesque's visit coincided with the transformation of the École des sciences sociales into a Social Science Faculty. According to Albert Faucher, this represented "une adaptation aux impératifs nord-américains ... c'était la lune de miel des néophytes keynésiens, avance sur Montréal, on le reconnaissait, mais dans la voie de l'américanisation et l'anglicisation" (cited in Fournier 1986, 152, note 33).

23 As far as we know, there is no such translation of any of Innis's works.

24 For a more detailed account see Rumilly 1967.

25 This methodological question often came to the surface in an interview that we had with Angers while preparing this essay. See also his comments in Lévesque et al. 1984, 117–29.

26 Gilles Paquet deems this intellectual current a more deductive, abstractly theoretical method disengaged from practical matters of concern to the ambient community and less enamoured of intervention (1985, 365–97).

27 To remind us that even such a small opening is not without its value, note that it is through the work of Gilles Paquet and Jean-Pierre Wallot (1969) that Paul Claval, a French scholar "maître de conférence" at the

Université de Paris-Sorbonne, discovered the staple theory and the work of Harold Innis (Claval 1974, 394, note 1).

28 Mullins 1975 and Harp and Curtis 1971 offer a starting-point for such an undertaking.

29 Research of this sort has been done within feminist studies. See, for example, Phillips 1991 and Lamont 1984.

30 For example, compare Rush, Christensen, and Malcomson 1981 with Harp and Curtis 1971.

12 Too Long in Exile: Innis and Maritime Political Economy

JAMES BICKERTON

Harold Innis's *The Cod Fisheries* (1940) was an immense historical study, spanning several countries and centuries, and marked the end of the second stage of Innis's scholarly work. (It came a decade after the publication of *The Fur Trade* (1930), a product of the first stage of his career.) During the 1930s Innis spent a great deal of time and energy researching the history and economic problems of Atlantic Canada, especially Nova Scotia. His work on the region was rewarded not only by the recognition accorded to him by his fellow academics, but by that very Canadian tribute sometimes paid to esteemed social scientists by politicians: an invitation to sit on a royal commission – the Jones Commission (Nova Scotia 1934). It would not be the last time Innis would be consulted by the Nova Scotia government.

But a half-century later, Innis's historical analyses and judgments about the region's twentieth-century economic malaise did not solicit the same attention or high regard from the Maritimes' historians and political economists. On the contrary, they credited Innis with founding (or at least mentoring) a "new orthodoxy" that attributed the Maritimes' decline to certain blameless economic and technological forces; this approach, they thought, had lent intellectual substance and solace to the creation by others of an unflattering regional stereotype of the Maritimes' conservatism and sloth.

Which of these impressions of Innis is correct? This chapter argues that Innis has been the victim of a "bum rap." His virtual absence as a point of departure or reference for post-1970 regional scholars is regrettable if understandable, given the "new problematic" driving

Maritime political economy for the last quarter-century. The staples tradition was portrayed as antithetical to this new problematic, or at the very least irrelevant. Consequently Innis's work and that of other staple theorists was ignored, undervalued, or else explicitly rejected for its narrow, resource-industry focus and its technological and geographical determinism.

There are two problems, however, with this expulsion of Innis from Maritime political economy: a rather disturbing tendency for Innis's work to have been either misread or misrepresented by his critics and a too-ready acceptance of the new problematic *tout court*, including its rejection of the staples tradition, even though the new problematic was itself rather narrow in focus and contestable and unsettled in some of its key propositions. Innis deserves to be brought back from exile, and the long silence on his significant intellectual contribution to a political economy of the Maritimes ended.

THE MARITIME CRITIQUE OF THE STAPLES TRADITION

Bruce Archibald's essay on "Atlantic Regional Underdevelopment and Socialism" (1971) appeared in LaPierre et al., *Essays on the Left* (1971). That same year, historian T.W. Acheson defended his PhD thesis at the University of Toronto, to be followed by a seminal article in *Acadiensis* entitled "The National Policy and the Industrialization of the Maritimes, 1880–1910" (1972). This marked the beginning of a sustained blooming of regional scholarship on the Maritimes – particularly on its social and cultural history and its political economy. While both essays presented radical reinterpretations of the economic history of the Maritimes within Confederation, they chose starting-points based on different interpretations of "what happened" to the Maritimes.

Archibald, a sociologist, made use of Andre Gunder Frank's satellite–metropolis model. Atlantic Canada was a satellite producer of primary products for the benefit and profit of a succession of external metropoles. Diversification into manufacturing was restricted and discouraged. As a result, the region failed to break out of its "Golden Age" concentration on fisheries, timber exports, shipbuilding, and trade, leaving it vulnerable to changes in the international trading regime on which its economy was based. When such a change occurred after 1873, outmigration increased rapidly, leaving a stagnant economy and population behind (Archibald 1971, 108). This neo-Marxist version of the "staples trap" idea would later be reformulated in the work of sociologist Henry Veltmeyer.

Much more influential, however, was Acheson's work on the supposed period of the Maritimes' decline after 1875, as well as that of colleague E.R. Forbes. In a 1981 article in the socialist journal *Studies in Political Economy*, James Sacouman credited Acheson and Forbes as correcting the scholarly neglect of the Maritimes and the wrongful regional stereotyping typical of pre-1970 historiography. By demonstrating that the Maritimes had industrialized rapidly in response to the tariff protection afforded by the National Policy, the new regional historians had punctured the myth of inevitable and inexorable decline dictated by the passing of the "Age of Sail." With the establishment in 1971 of a journal of regional history at the University of New Brunswick (*Acadiensis*), the reconstruction of Maritime history around a new problematic began. Several questions needed answers. How was this successful transition accomplished? How and why was it reversed in the post-1918 period? What accounted for the deindustrialization of the Maritimes?

Acheson and Forbes blamed this economic collapse on regionally insensitive national policies and predatory central Canadian interests. In effect, the Maritimes were "done in" by an economic system controlled at its centre by monopolistic corporations bent on the elimination of regional competitors and by a political system that could not or would not defend the Maritimes' vital interests. (See Acheson, "The Maritimes and Empire Canada" [1977], and Forbes, "Misguided Symmetry" [1977]). This analysis placed the new school of thought directly at variance with the widely accepted view that technological change was the chief culprit and with more pejorative explanations that suggested cultural conservatism (an inability or unwillingness to adapt to change) as the main problem.[1]

If uncovering the hidden history of the post-Confederation Maritimes became the scholarly obsession of the new regionalists, then discrediting the orthodox interpretation of the region's decline and exposing negative cultural stereotyping of Maritimers as baseless in fact and self-serving in purpose was its political twin. In both these efforts regional historians were joined by neo-Marxist sociologists and political economists, and the attack widened and intensified. Notable in this regard was Brym and Sacouman's *Underdevelopment and Social Movements in Atlantic Canada* (1979) – a more radical critique of the capitalist system and the Canadian state than that offered by the Acheson–Forbes school, but sharing its problematic and supportive of its rejection of technology and resource-based explanations. Both schools saw the staples tradition as the main theoretical pillar of this maligned orthodoxy. By implication and association, they cast Innis in a distinctly negative light:

While historians were being studiously ignorant, Innis' staples approach provided the geographical and technological base for confirming the Maritime stereotype of conservatism. The regional staples that were investigated by Innis, especially fish and lumber, were found to be spatially diffuse and technologically backward in production, creating conditions that supported conservative values. In the late 1960s when social scientists did look at the Maritimes, they waxed psychological, consistently falling back on the unexamined Maritime stereotype: lack of entrepreneurial drive ... social-cultural backwardness ... political conservatism ... the inherently tradition-bound Maritimer. (Sacouman 1981, 136)

Acheson more directly tied Innis to the construction of the orthodox interpretation. It was Innis's mind at work through his student S.A. Saunders (1984), whose *The Economic History of the Maritime Provinces* first appeared in 1939. It was "the most rigorous and comprehensive examination of the regional economy ever undertaken ... The assumption which underlay this first systematic treatment of the Maritime economy and the perceptions revealed in it became a new orthodoxy which challenged prevailing interpretations" (Saunders 1984, 9). "Following in the footsteps of Innis and Fay's earlier work, Saunders wrote the script for the explanations that dominate state policy, professional economics, and pre-1971 regional historiography. Conventional thinking is still based on the viewpoint on Confederation, the causes of Maritime decline, and the possibilities of Maritime development which Saunders articulated in 1939" (Clow 1986, 148).

The "prevailing interpretations" were those of the regionalists associated with the Maritime Rights movement of the 1920s, who had blamed the Canadian state for the problems of the Maritimes. This regionalist interpretation did not sit well with Saunders's "strong Canadian patriotism ... the idea of a single common Canadianism untrammelled by region, race or class" (Saunders 1984, 6). Innis provided Saunders with an intellectual basis for challenging the regionalists, whose arguments Saunders regarded as "unscientific and potentially dangerous myths."

Saunders's own findings regarding the course of the region's history within Confederation were dramatically different:

Neither Confederation nor the National Policy adversely affected Maritime economic development, he declared; world economic forces had turned against the region after 1875 creating the need to shift from an ocean to an inland market ... The consolidation of industry in Central Canada reflected both the natural evolution of industry and the market and transportation advantages possessed by the Laurentian heartland ... Natural law, expressed in a rigorous and uncompromising determinism, became for Saunders the explanation for most economic change which occurred in the Maritimes in the sixty years following Confederation. The fate of the region in Canada had been predetermined by nature and geography ... These inevitabilities produced the growing backwardness of the regional economy relative to the rest of Canada and the consequent decline of regional living standards (9-10).

There was little in the new orthodoxy spawned by Saunders with which the regional historians and political economists in the 1970s and 1980s could agree, and much that they found repulsive. And according to Acheson, the founder of the new Maritime history, it was really Innis who was to blame. Saunders was merely "a disciple of Harold Innis by conviction" whose work "reflected the views of his mentor ... Like Innis, Saunders was convinced that the Canadian state not only had virtue in itself but was the expression of a natural economic order" (9): "Toronto afforded [Saunders] the opportunity to study with Harold Innis who was then engaged in constructing the economic justification for a Canadian state ... Innis became his supervisor and suggested the Maritime economy as an appropriate research subject ... [a subject that] had received little scholarly treatment before Saunders. His work reflected the views of his mentor: in two brief studies on the Maritimes, published in 1930 and 1931, Innis had recognized the regional crisis but attributed it to geography and the mismanagement of natural resources" (6).

This view of Innis, Saunders, and the staples tradition was adopted wholeheartedly by others working on the Maritimes from a political economy perspective. Both James Sacouman (1981) and Michael Clow (1984) published articles on Maritime political economy that adopted the view that "traditional liberal orthodoxy" about the Maritimes, "with its focus on staples and a failure to industrialize," was exploded by the work of Acheson and Forbes (Clow 1984, 119). What was perhaps most irksome about the staples tradition for these political economists was its tendency to limit the explanatory factors of regional economic history to resource endowments and the market orientations of the primary sector. As noted by Clow,

Manufacturing was discounted as an important part of the economy of the region by assumptions rooted in this [the staples tradition] theoretical toolbox, and with it the social organization of the economy, the role of the state and Canadian financial institutions, and the whole shift from merchant to monopoly capitalism in Canada. The theme that the Maritimes was a marginal region doomed by remoteness (from Montreal and Toronto), backwardness and resource exhaustion – which Saunders sealed into conventional wisdom – was implicit in the theoretical rigor mortis of staple theory's approach to the region's economic history. (Clow 1985, 147–8).

Clow's outright dismissal of the staples tradition represents the high-water mark of criticism of the staples approach within Maritime political economy. In retrospect, it was also the culmination of fifteen years of scholarly reproach to Innis and the staples tradition. As is often the case when one dominant theory or school of thought gives way to another, nothing is learned, no insights are gleaned from the predecessor, and babies do get pitched out with the bathwater.

A REASSESSMENT OF INNIS AND HIS MARITIME CRITICS

Acheson appears to have formulated his view of Innis on a rather slim basis: two brief essays published c. 1930 – a paper presented to the Canadian Historical Association (Innis 1931) and an essay on the Maritimes written with C.R. Fay and published in the *Cambridge History of the British Empire* (Fay and Innis 1930). Though Acheson noted the piece's glaring omission of any reference to the growth and decline of secondary manufacturing in the Maritimes, the description offered of the region is generally positive, and the analysis of Maritimers' "struggle against adversity when the pull of the land increased" (Fay and Innis 1930, 670) is at the very least accurate. Fay and Innis (1930) see the regional populace as "remarkably adaptable," with "individual enterprise ... the keynote of their economic life" (658). The authors note that the Nova Scotian government did not sit idly by when its wooden shipbuilding industry went into decline but responded by stimulating the development of the province's coal resources and steel industry. The province used its ownership of the resource to facilitate amalgamation of the collieries so as to attract new capital resources and modern mining equipment. Nor was the mixed blessing of industrial development controlled by external capital lost on Fay and Innis. "Industrialism was late in its arrival, but once launched it developed rapidly by aid of a technique perfected elsewhere. Community life, which depends on control of natural resources, was weakened. In the exploitation of coal and iron outside capital met none of the resistance which fishing and lumbering with their natural diversity were able to offer. The resistance came, not from industries as such, but from the workers to whom they gave employment" (664–5).

This pattern of development, so typical of heavy industry in the twentieth century, the authors contrasted with the region's nineteenth century economy: a "magnificent achievement, an integration of capital and labour, of lumbering, fishing and agriculture, on which rested a progressive community life. The linchpin [of shipbuilding] was broken [by the competition of cheap iron and steel] and industrialism continued its inroads upon the people of the Maritime provinces" (663). As thumbnail sketches go, this rendering is not bad.

This same concentration on natural resources and heavy industry is evident in Saunders's (1939) *Economic History*, soliciting the same negative reaction from Acheson and others working within the new problematic. A number of points need to be made about this focus. First, staples industries remained a vital component of the regional economy throughout the period of industrialization and deindustrialization; they were in no way unimportant or marginal to the course of economic and industrial development in the region. Second, both Newfoundland and Prince Edward Island failed to experience the industrialization that marked the economies of Nova Scotia and New Brunswick, making the former provinces almost exclusively cases of staples-based development. Third, the attention given to the coal and steel industry in Fay and Innis and in Saunders reflects both its size and significance in the interwar period (employing one in five Nova Scotians) and the widely held perception that it was the crux of industrialization and essential to national economic success in the industrial age – the economic "muscle" of countries was usually measured in terms of its production. Because it was almost exclusively a Nova Scotian industry, however, industrial-age developments in New Brunswick – specifically the rise and decline of its secondary manufacturing – received short shrift from scholars. In the 1970s, New Brunswick–based historians took the lead in reformulating the key questions of Maritime history while launching the attack on the staples tradition.

Even granting Innis's critics their due, in terms of oversights and all-too-obvious empirical and analytical gaps, their characterization of Innis and the staples tradition as somehow anti-Maritimes in either its stated or implied propositions seems unfounded. The reference in Fay and Innis to the Maritimes' "magnificent achievement" is revealing here. Innis, it appears, was a true Scotiaphile. He expressed strong admiration for the province, its people, and their accomplishments. In *The Cod Fisheries* (1940a), he praises the province's political, economic, and diplomatic feats, as well as its considerable cultural contributions (497–9). Even its failures were wondrous for the grand nature of the goals attempted; thus, like France before it, Nova Scotia failed to establish an integrated trade among the St Lawrence, the Maritimes, and the West Indies (Innis 1956a, 363).

We should see this fascination with Nova Scotia's historical role and exploits in the context of Innis's larger and life-long preoccupation: the conditions for the creation of a stable society based on a dynamic harmony between technology and culture (Kroker 1984, 82–3). Unlike the practitioners of the new Maritime political economy, he harboured no longing or affection for the changes wrought by modern industrialism. For Innis, Nova Scotia during the era of commercialism came close to this ideal of a culture and technology in balance and harmony. He wrote despairingly about industrialism "making inroads upon the people of the Maritimes," as though it were an unwelcome incursion.

Another point of difference between Innis and later Maritime political economists is his view of Confederation. He saw it as not an inevitable development, or political annexation, or even political defeat, but merely part of the province's search for a "new instrument" in its resistance to New England competition. In this struggle, the province "took refuge behind an organization more efficient for the checking of encroachments on British fishing grounds" (Innis 1940a, 364). This new defensive measure followed realignment of the British colonial system, cooperation with other provinces, and reciprocity and would be followed by the Treaty of Washington (1870). Innis believed that Confederation was for Nova Scotia "a device for opening American markets, whereas the St. Lawrence region thought of it as a basis of protection against American goods" (Innis 1956a, 397).

Innis also had a high opinion of Nova Scotia's political and economic elite, which aggressively and effectively pursued the province's interests. "Nova Scotia assumed a position in the forefront of the struggle for control over legislation dealing with the fishery partly as a result of her ancestral and New England tradition of assertiveness which was in turn based on the fishery, and partly as the result of the inherent peculiarities of her own fishery ... The intensely competitive character of the industry was a driving force which demanded revisions that would place Nova Scotia on a position of equality, if not superiority, in the legislation of the mother country" (Innis 1940a, 373).

"The imperialistic outlook of the statesmen of Nova Scotia when dealing with the fishery and world trade was destroyed by the breakdown of the commercial system in Britain, but revived when given the larger scope of Confederation" (374).[2] "Nova Scotia ... enlisted the support of Canada against the encroachment of the United States. The price of this enlistment was Canadian tariffs and the high price system of the St. Lawrence. Construction of the Intercolonial and its extension to Sydney, tariffs and subventions on coal and iron, upward revisions of federal subsidies, and the Maritime Freight Rates Act constitute evidence of higgling" (Innis 1956a, 367). Indeed, Innis even attributed

Canada's decentralized federalism to the designs and demands of Nova Scotia.[3]

Despite such high regard, Innis was not a complete romantic, nor oblivious to the historical inequalities of provincial society.[4] He abhorred in particular the poverty of the fishermen and the unprofitability of their enterprise, which kept them "literally in a state of bondage ... destitute of the means of improvement ... doomed to perpetual servitude" (Innis 1940a, 287). The way out of this cycle of poverty would involve "a long period of expensive readjustment and restoration" (508), requiring "a major revolution in the fishing industry, involving a shift in dependence on low-standard-of-living countries [such as the West Indies] to dependence on high-standard-of-living areas in North America," something that could be accomplished "only with tremendous effort" (443). He also argued that the wages and standards of living of fishermen and woodsworkers in the Maritimes would rise to levels more closely approximating national averages only when more effective producer organizations were formed to rectify the power imbalances within their industries (Bickerton 1990, 83).

Innis's stated hopes for the future of fishery and forestry workers in the Maritimes were one aspect of a broader concern for the quality of the overall relationship between centre and periphery in Canada. He was not blind to the serious problems created for the Maritimes by Confederation and the National Policy. Thus he contrasted the centralized and rigid economic and political structures created by the vested interests associated with the continent (fur, wheat) with "the elasticity and flexibility of the political and economic structure which has been an important contribution of the fishing industry" (Innis 1956a, 42). He recognized that "the tendency toward centralization in continental Canada ... and decentralization in the Maritimes" (39) foreshadowed long-term difficulty rooted in the imposition of a foreign and inappropriate political and economic structure.

It is therefore difficult to comprehend the characterization of Innis by his Maritime critics as a committed centralist professing (as his "disciple" Saunders evidently did) "the idea of a single, common Canadianism untrammelled by region, race or class." Innis warned against "social scientists carrying fuel to Ottawa to make the flames of nationalism burn more brightly" (Innis 1946, xii). And far from being a centralist, he was convinced of centralism's ill effects on the Maritimes and of the need to protect and enhance provincial autonomy in the face of centralizing tendencies in the 1930s and 1940s. For example, with regard to the fishery, he favoured provincial control as part of the solution to its many problems, and his opposition to trawler technology was linked to this question. "So long as the fisheries are involved in a conflict of jurisdictions in which the Dominion determines policies and the province is compelled to face the result of those policies in unemployment, resistance to trawlers is justified" (Innis 1940a, 435).

This position – that the province should be given control over the fisheries – was one of the recommendations of Nova Scotia's Jones Commission of 1934, on which Innis sat and which was set up to investigate "the effect of the fiscal and trade policies of the Dominion of Canada upon the economic life of ... Nova Scotia ... and any other matter affecting the economic welfare of Nova Scotia, or its relation to the Dominion of Canada" (Creighton 1957, 88). Innis issued his own "Complementary Report" (see Nova Scotia 1934), which placed greater emphasis than the main report on the injurious effects on Nova Scotia of "the national policy in the broad sense rather than in the narrow fiscal sense" (Creighton 1957, 89).

Fundamentally, Innis saw the compromises associated with Confederation to be at the expense of the Maritime region, which sacrificed its decentralized pattern of development, with low tariffs and inexpensive water transportation, for the centralized, high-tariff, high-cost transportation of continental development (Nova Scotia 1934, 151–2). The province was also politically and socially divided, and therefore weakened, by Confederation. National policies reorganized interests within the province by introducing new cleavages, transforming the province's political economy, with implications for the assertion and protection of provincial interests within Confederation.

Confederation tended to accentuate diversity rather than unity in its emphasis on the development of coal and iron regions and in its burden on regions engaged in the fisheries, agriculture and lumbering. The Eastern portion of Nova Scotia with access to the St. Lawrence tended to benefit from Confederation and the Western portion with access to the United States tended to suffer from a narrowing of markets with higher tariffs from the United States and higher tariffs and freight rates from Canada. The decline in the rate of expansion and the depression tend to accentuate the diversity of interests between the coal-producing eastern portion and the exporting western portion of the province. (155)

But just as Innis thought that Confederation contributed to the disunity of Nova Scotia, so he believed a strong developmental policy would help establish provincial unity (225). His long-term solution involved revisions to the national policy that devolved powers and responsibilities to the provincial government.[5]

[A] revision of the national policy ... must be essentially intensive and regional in character and must depend on a strong provincial civil service. Direction from Ottawa has become increasingly difficult and from our observation increasingly dangerous ... The trend to centralization in railways, banking, finance, and industry tends to become less efficient in relation to outlying areas and must be offset by a definite reversal in terms of developmental policy. Increasing centralization must be offset by increasing devolution if the more distant regions are to guard effectively their interests ... Compensation is not enough. (221, 226)

Innis's preference for political and economic decentralization was thus not limited simply to fisheries jurisdiction. With reference to the "tragedy" of the replacement of commercialism by capitalism for the Maritimes and Newfoundland, Innis emphasized the need to give these provinces greater control over their industries and economic development. "Readjustment and restoration" of the region's economy could not take place "without policies which foster the revival of initiative under responsible governments" (1956a, 508). Only enhanced provincial autonomy would provide Maritimers with the flexibility to adapt to and accomplish change. The "patchwork solutions and plans of the central bureaucracy" were no substitute. Indeed, the provinces would require their own "elaborate machinery to protect themselves against the exploitation of haphazard federal policies" (371).

Innis adopted these positions at a time when most English-Canadian intellectuals had become convinced centralists. But Innis had grave doubts about the supposed benefits of this centralization. He thought that the dominion government had been carried away with its enthusiasm for Keynes, the Bank of Canada, and bureaucratic and wartime interests and necessities. Dominion reliance on fiscal and monetary policy to produce high and stable levels of employment would result only in a drain of population and revenues to the St Lawrence basin. His advice to the Nova Scotia government at the end of the Second World War was to resist handing over control of any further revenues to Ottawa until there was much more evidence that the dominion government would work through the complications of specific regional problems and implement special measures to overcome the handicaps imposed by the tariff and other national measures.

Innis was not content, however, with merely preventing further centralization. He wanted an activist state at the provincial level and suggested that the province build up its own machinery of government as a barrier against encroachment by Ottawa. Innis's concern was rooted in fears for the quality of democracy experienced by Maritimers. He thought that the growth of provincial dependence on funds doled out from Ottawa would so erode the responsiveness and effectiveness of the provincial civil service as to threaten the very foundations of responsible government in the region.[6]

CONCLUSION

None of the foregoing seems to support the critique of Innis's work offered by Maritime political economists. Their critique consisted primarily of perfunctory and seemingly obligatory swipes at the geographical and technological determinism of the staples tradition. Where they made direct reference to a published work, it was often that of an author clearly outside the tradition (such as Pepin or Rawlyk[7]) who used the staples analysis for their own purposes; other, more pertinent examples of staples-based analyses were conveniently overlooked.[8] Where the complaint concerned the lack of scholarly attention to the Maritimes in Canadian historiography, as effectively argued by E.R. Forbes (1981), it clearly did not apply to Innis, whose work Forbes did not include in his review.[9]

In fact, the Maritime critique of the staples tradition turns on Saunders, who offered a less nuanced, more determinist vision of the region's political economy than did Innis himself. Still, Saunders's linking of the region's economic decline to its failure to husband its forest and ocean resources properly, and his prescription for economic renewal through "careful planning and development of selected industries which could compete in both Canada and world markets" (Saunders 1984, 10), seems quite pertinent; indeed, it was perhaps quite prescient. Perhaps the critics did not like the fact that Saunders's application of the staples approach (unlike Innis's) was shaded by his preferences for a "single, common Canadianism" under a strong central government. But even on this score, the judgment rendered on Saunders seems unduly harsh, given that in the 1930s most intellectuals (as well as the liberal and socialist left) considered support for centralization a progressive stance and the only viable solution to the country's serious economic and social problems. (Tellingly, Innis was not among those swayed to this point of view.)

Maritime political economy pilloried or ignored the staples tradition because earlier staples theorists had played down or failed to note adequately the rise and fall of secondary manufacturing in the Maritimes and had not given proper weight to the region's industrialization/deindustrialization dynamic. For this rather glaring oversight, they condemned the whole staples tradition and expelled it from "right-thinking" intellectual discourse on the new Maritimes problematic.[10]

The long exile of the Innis staples tradition from Maritime political economy is both unfortunate and ironic, given the many reasons for the new regionalists to embrace Innis: his critique of the effects of the National Policy on the region; his scorn for Canada's rigid, centralized, monopolistic economic system; his recognition of the need to rebalance relations in the primary sector in order to give producers more power through effective organization; his concerns about and desire to control the harmful effects of modern fishing technology; and his call for a reassertion of community control over the region's natural resources and other powers relevant to devising an integrated and appropriate development strategy for the region.

Now that the industrial age is passing, and mass production, assembly-line manufacturing of the sort once coveted by the Maritimes is associated with the old economy or with Third World countries, and now that tariffs and national protection and even an integrated national economy are increasingly features of a bygone era, is the "new Maritime problematic" any more salient than the staples tradition? Can the new problematic's narrow preoccupation with the historical deindustrialization of the Maritimes and with centre–periphery relations within Canada illuminate the situation today? Can it suggest a way forward in the dawning era of global integration and the information economy?

As noted by Leo Panitch, Innis's most important bequest to political economy is his insight that metropole–periphery (and even periphery– periphery) relations are not one-way, static relations of dependence (Panitch 1981). Instead, they are reciprocal, with developments in one region directly related to reactive developments in another. New England's independence hurried political development in Nova Scotia, which had a concomitant effect on Newfoundland. The United States's resort to tariff and other protections for a key regional industry (the New England fishery) helped push Nova Scotia into Confederation, leaving Newfoundland isolated and politically weak. Nova Scotia failed in its attempt to create an integrated triangular trade with the St Lawrence and West Indies, in part because the growth of Newfoundland's population attracted too much of the province's trade. Radio crossed boundaries that stopped the press, giving rise to a defensive nationalism, which precipitated a reactive regionalism.

These are the offsetting and reciprocal tendencies, the dialectical and contradictory effects, the dynamic interplay of internal and external factors, that so animate Innis's political economy. It is this "rich repository" that the staples tradition has to offer. Maritime political economy would benefit from its restoration.

NOTES

1 For instance, George Rawlyk referred to "the widespread parochialism and inbreeding of the population" as a feature of the Maritimes that buttressed distrust and dislike of "Upper Canadians"; he also referred to Nova Scotia's "old business elite ... who had invested a great deal in the old system and naturally resisted the necessary major readjustment in their thinking and policies" (Rawlyk 1969, 101, 108).

2 Innis even excluded the Maritimes from his denunciation of Canadian party politicians as stupid and inept, citing Sir Wilfrid Laurier's argument that perhaps the Maritimes continued to send individuals of talent to Ottawa, in contrast to other regions, "because of the small character of business there" (Innis 1956a, 404).

3 "Sir John A. Macdonald attempted to avoid the difficulties of the American constitution ... by emphasizing federal power but the position of Nova Scotia limited federal power in the constitution and in its later development" (Innis 1956a, 234).

4 Innis noted, for example, the extermination, impoverishment, and internal exile of the Atlantic region's Native population, characterized by Innis as an incidental result of the region's outward or sea-bound orientation, in sharp contrast with the fur trade's dependence on friendly relations with Indians (Innis 1956a, 39). This aspect of Maritime history is only now receiving significant attention, with the growing political and cultural assertiveness of the surviving Native population.

5 Besides his general recommendation regarding devolution of economic powers, Innis suggested a number of specific dominion measures such as a truly regionalized transportation policy, closer dominion–provincial cooperation on trade policy, government support for efficient marketing organizations for small producers, greater protection from monopolistic practices through tougher anti-combines legislation, and a federal trade commission to ensure fair trade internally (including laws against 'dumping' of central Canadian goods on Maritime markets).

6 H.A. Innis to A.L. Macdonald, 17 Jan. and 13 Feb. 1946, Angus L. Macdonald Papers, Nova Scotia Public Archives, Halifax.

7 Sacouman notes the work of these two authors on the Maritimes as contributing to the negative stereotyping of Maritimers. But neither was a staples theorist, and both made only the vaguest references to the findings or propositions of the staples tradition (Sacouman 1981, 147).

8 One example is the work of J.M.S. Careless, who published "Aspects of Metropolitanism in Atlantic Canada" in 1969. This study was clearly in the staples tradition that emphasized not regional decline but the adaptation of Maritime businesses to late-nineteenth-century shifts in transportation, technology, and markets. Careless noted that between 1874

and 1914 the region's major cities shifted economic activities to a new, more viable (if more proscribed) basis. The region met the enormous challenge posed by political, economic, and technological change through elaboration of a new role within Canada, development of new industries, and adoption of new technologies. While Careless thought that techno-logical change helped force adjustments on Maritime cities, he concluded that business and government decisions facilitated adaptation.

9   Perhaps Forbes was interested in the work of historians per se, or perhaps he was simply unfamiliar with Innis's work. Certainly, unlike most Canadian historians of the first half of this century, Innis rejected Turner's frontier thesis. As he noted, the Maritimes had a frontier: the submerged continental shelf, which provided all the physical challenges and potential riches that the interior did for the westward-bound (Innis 1956a, 39).

10 The same cannot be said of Newfoundland political economy, and in par-ticular the relatively brief career of David Alexander, whose work stands as a corrective to the critique of Innis and the staples approach. Perhaps because Newfoundland did not join Confederation until well after the demise of the National Policy and never experienced industrialization and deindustrialization, interpretations of its past have not generated the same contentious debate over the staples approach. Dealing with a more classically staples economy, Newfoundland's political economists have worried less about the staples tradition. Instead they incorporated, devel-oped, complemented or reinterpreted its analyses and concerns in the light of new data and events and alternative theoretical models. No new central question or historical conundrum emerged that required displace-ment of an earlier preoccupation with the region's staples-based economy. Instead, political economists have continued to work on the history, per-mutations, and current dynamics of staples-based development/underde-velopment in Newfoundland. In addition to Alexander 1983, see, for example, House 1986; Ommer 1991; and Cadigan 1995.

PART THREE

Innis and Cultural Theory

13 Histories of Place and Power: Innis in Canadian Cultural Studies

CHARLES R. ACLAND

Without a doubt, there has been a minor industry of Innis interpretation; Daniel Drache has even coined the term "Innisology" to refer to it (1982, 35).[1] The intellectual mapping of Innis has involved charting his impact on an array of disciplines, including communications, economics, history, and Canadian studies. Generally, there are enormous stakes in the process of situating ideas; in so doing, one constructs a theoretical context, however provisional, in which the work then speaks to other works and sets of questions. For Innis, various disciplinary contexts grant his writings a series of incarnations, and in turn allow disciplinary frameworks to emerge as well. In this respect, the rereading of Innis has helped us to think about Canadian communications theory and Canadian economic history.

Arguably, one of the most vital qualities of Innis is this disciplinary and theoretical mobility. While I concur with those who suggest that Innis's work is best seen as a continuous oeuvre, this is not because his thought had a singular direction or program. Instead, it is precisely the shifts, the interdisciplinary encounters, and the ongoing stakes on his influence that mark Innis's contributions. So it is not without coincidence that Innis is now being taken as a central figure in Canadian cultural studies. As an area of investigation, cultural studies is multidisciplinary as well as anti-disciplinary. Significantly, its questions and contributions are quite distinct from those of the many disciplines that seek to claim it as their own. Cultural studies, despite its name, must not to be mistaken for anthropology, comparative literature, modern languages, literary criticism, communication studies, art history, or sociology, though it has an effect on, and draws from, all those disciplines. Instead, it is a theoretical axis for a variety of writings traditionally engaged in a neo-Marxist critique of the place of culture in the social formation.

Cultural studies has been continuously reconstituting itself, its history, and its relevance. As Lawrence Grossberg writes, "Cultural studies is always remaking itself as it responds to a world that is always being remade" (1993, 1). In part, this process has involved asking national and local questions with an eye to a certain international intellectual discourse. Recent discussions of nationhood, identity, and space push the complex issue of what a "national" cultural studies tradition might look like ever more into prominence. Ien Ang and Jon Stratton (1996a) have gone so far as to propose the emergence of a "critical transnationalism" that highlights the complexity of globalizing forces. In their discussion of Australia's formation as both an Asian and a European nation, they suggest that binaries demarcating nation-states are no longer analytically useful unless we interrogate the notion of unity implied by the term "nation." Instead, the very idea of a national "tradition," and its historical emergence in the light of a multitude of global forces, form a site at which to evince the related characteristics and powers involved.[2]

The ample reference to Innis's status as a spark to a Canadian cultural studies tradition is complicated. Though he is already being situated in that position, what is appreciably distinct about this from his role in communications, history, or economics? How do we deal with an emergent multidisciplinary frame through a single thinker's influence? What does Innis add, if anything, to cultural studies and its political analysis of culture?

Of the many reasons to ask these questions, two stand out. First, cultural studies in Canada has become an active, if ambiguously designated, intellectual project.[3] Or perhaps I should say, a site of scholarly discussion on culture now exists against the many attempts – by publishers, international journals, university programmes, and so on – to deny its particularity to Canada. And even in the briefest mention, Innis appears as an unknowing forefigure. John Hartley writes that in the "ancestralization" of cultural studies "Harold Innes [sic] and Marshall McLuhan would figure in any Canadian genealogy" (1992, 17). Alison Beale (1993) notes, "Innis is often held responsible for influencing the reigning generation of nationalist, communication and cultural studies scholars and bureaucrats, through a combined legacy of 'dependency' political economy and – depending on one's point of view – the anti-populist, or nationalist, Massey cultural ethos" (75). Andrew Wernick (1993) has seen Canadian cultural studies as an incomplete project that has not as yet assimilated "a powerful tradition of cultural thought indigenous to Canada itself," including McLuhan, George Grant, and

Innis (300). He suggests that what the current "incoherence" of Canadian cultural studies "points to, more positively, is a task of theoretical bridging that might not only yield substantive insight about Canada but would also, at the international level, enrich cultural studies itself" (300). This echoes a special issue of *Continuum* about Innis's place in North American cultural studies and beyond (Angus and Shoemaker 1993). Through the work of James Carey, Innis sits comfortably in the history of American cultural studies (noted in Hardt 1992, 196). Additionally, a number of essays in this volume demonstrate an increased engagement with Innis and his place in the formation of Canadian cultural studies, including those of Jody Berland (chapter 15), Andrew Wernick (chapter 14), and Kevin Dowler (chapter 18).

Second, British cultural studies as a specific body of texts and approaches to media studies entered this country through communications departments and rapidly found a comfortable home there. Consequently, a substantial debate about its specific relevance to North America unfolded, often with connections to a more immediate legacy. As Will Straw (1993) notes of communications in the early 1980s, the field seemed to be "the most appropriate context for an articulation of British cultural studies with the legacies of the Chicago School of Sociology and the McLuhan–Innis tradition of Canadian research" (96). Further, cultural studies "came to function less and less as a project for the redefinition of communications studies as a discipline. Increasingly, it designated a subculture which was highly visible within the discipline but involved in a variety of ways with communities outside it" (97).

It is in these circumstances that national distinctions became prominent concerns: if cultural studies is to provide a meaningful critique of the Canadian situation, what then do we need to know about this context? One avenue into this question is to remember that it is in communications departments that cultural studies bumps up against Innis; in a way, the critique of technology, media, and culture became a meeting place for communications and cultural theorists, with Innis as required reading for both. This is of special importance to Canadians, who, in Arthur Kroker's (1984) terms, have a particular "technologically mediated relation" to one another. I suggest instead that, as much as technology, *a set of ideas about technology* mediates our understanding of Canada. This is exactly where Innis's relation to cultural studies can begin to be understood.

CULTURE AND CONTEXT FOR INNIS

What role did culture play for Innis? On the one hand, we have his admission of having read few novels and of his lack of interest in all things cultural (see Creighton 1957). As Creighton recounts, Innis's understanding of literature was so slim that he absurdly "attributed the vividness and accuracy of *Sunshine Sketches of a Little Town* to the fact that Leacock was an economist!" (1981, 16). As for his marriage, Innis's lack of interest appears to have reproduced an extremely conventional gender split, in which his wife, Mary Quayle Innis, as a published poet and arts patron, was the keeper of their cultural life.

On the other hand, there is the more significant evidence of his involvement with agencies to secure funding for cultural and intellectual enterprise in Canada, in which he had an extraordinary and lasting effect. Innis was extremely active in the creation and promotion of publishing venues for intellectual discussion (Watson 1981, 312). Less convincing, but worth noting, is the attempt to retrieve his elliptical writing as a modernist literary tactic.[4]

The question of culture certainly became more prominent as Innis's work continued. One need only examine the explicit shift from the discussion of pulp and paper to newspapers (Innis 1942) to see his growing interest in the role of culture. His "On the Economic Significance of Culture" (1944), in a clear move towards an epistemological critique, presents a strong argument for "an economic history of knowledge or an economic history of economic history" (80). This he does by linking observations about the newspaper industry to the effects of printing technologies on the development of national markets and the changing role of the Church. Significantly, as Innis begins to write specifically about knowledge and its technological structures, he also comments on what he sees as "the background of the collapse of Western civilization" (91). The central characteristic of this collapse is a mechanization of art and knowledge, which creates an "obsession with the immediate" (92). In effect, the demise reported here is one of balance in ethical and intellectual practice. Consequently, Innis's cultural essays, which express a damning appraisal of the modern, appear alongside his call for the counterweight of time and the role of the intellectual (see "A Plea for the University Tradition" in Innis 1946).

For Innis, culture was not especially a site of enjoyment or diversion; it was where the poverty or exultation of values could be assessed. His concerns about changes in the modern world, its disregard for historical continuity, and the horrors of world wars arose from what he saw as an increasingly depraved culture, overrun with commercialism and an unbalanced emphasis on speed and breadth of dissemination. On the effects of industrialized cultural forms, he wrote: "Modern civilization, characterized by an enormous increase in output of mechanized knowledge with the newspaper, the book, the radio and the cinema, has produced a state of numbness, pleasure, and self-complacency perhaps only equalled by laughing-gas. In the words of Oscar

Wilde, we have sold our birthright for a mess of facts. The demands of the machine are insatiable. The danger of shaking men out of the soporific results of mechanized knowledge is similar to that of attempting to arouse a drunken man or one who has taken an overdose of sleeping tablets" (1956a, 383).

As John Watson puts it, communication and media initially appear in Innis's work "as a grim motor force for cultural collapse" (1981, 297). Towards the end of his life, Innis expressed a sense of loss for the potential of democracy, which seemed destined to be misplaced or to self-destruct. McCarthyism and the Korean War fuelled this despair and led him to suggest that the culture, as at the end of all previous empires, was committing suicide (Innis 1951b, 209).

Innis's understanding of the place of culture in the modern world was commensurate with developments in Canada at the time. The two decades after the First World War saw the ferment of a number of ideas about nationhood and culture. In particular, a growing awareness developed that culture was needed not only to enrich Canadian life but to ensure its continued sovereignty. This awareness initiated the rise of cultural nationalism, whose proponents promoted their particular vision of national cultural life.[5] The individuals involved organized a number of interconnected cultural organizations that, among other things, lobbied the federal government for funding support. They included the Canadian Association for Adult Education, the Canadian Institute of International Affairs, the Canadian Library Association, the Canadian Citizenship Council, the Canadian Radio League, and the National Film Society.[6] As voluntary societies, they consisted of members who largely represented upper-class Anglo-Canadian society of the day. Their activities involved radio, film, magazines, concerts, libraries, conferences, and lectures. In direct response to mass entertainment, they focused on local community activities. Instead of commercial enterprise, they set out to organize a new national cultural infrastructure at places not occupied by commercial mass media (for example, community halls, church basements, public radio, and small publishing ventures). And, because Canada had few funding sources, American philanthropic foundations provided much of their initial revenue.

The discourses of culture and nation that emerged and circulated through this structure of national cultural authorities are crucial. A popular discussion about the nature of citizenship in the context of new mass communications provided many of the ideas about how culture should operate. Training and education came to the fore, with Matthew Arnold's (1983) earlier choice between culture and anarchy seemingly ever more relevant. Paul Litt (1992) demonstrates how this agreement about the role of culture in nationhood was grounded in a liberal humanist ideal. In this vision, culture was to educate, not to entertain; good culture instilled proper values and created responsible citizens. Concern arose from the dual observation that leisure time was increasing and that it was spent engaged in pursuits of popular entertainment. In this view, leisure time was not only wasted, but also a potential breeding ground for unhealthy ideas and practices. Thus it ought to be policed and made educational.

This apparatus of ideas about national culture and cultural strategies inspired specific quarters of Canadian society. Perhaps the crowning achievement of the voluntary societies was the Royal Commission on National Development in Arts, Science and Letters (Canada 1951). At this point, this emergent cultural apparatus and its association with the voluntary societies became even more central. The Massey Commission could not but reproduce those ideas, which was largely the interests of a particular class. As a moment of cultural and discursive settlement, the commission echoes the same need for an ideal national culture, poised against an imported popular culture. This apparatus of national culture represented a disjuncture between an imagined ideal national subject and the actual cultural life of the nation, one that in many ways continues to form our common sense in scholarly and popular discussion about Canadian culture.

Innis's extensive and effective dealings with American philanthropic foundations suggest a certain fit with those other cultural nationalists. His later support for federal cultural funding equally demonstrates his alignment with those lobbying efforts. And, as one would expect, similar discourses of nation and culture appear in Innis's work.

Innis's (1952b) *Strategy of Culture* continues his interest in publishing and remains a work that, though initially serving as a self-described footnote to the Massey Commission, could be appended to the North America Free Trade Agreement. The essay is a final political and intellectual position paper, laying out Innis's views on the role of culture in modern life. Here, he clearly falls into line with the cultural nationalists, even railing (1952b, 3) against the omission of culture from the series "The Relations of Canada and the United States" for which he was an editor and contributor.

His strategy argues that culture, as a vehicle of national life, is where the effects of new monopolies of knowledge can be observed. American publishing is understood as an industry that distributes particular notions about freedom of speech and freedom of the press as much as it does newspapers and books. A structured cultural relation, involving publishing markets, founding ideologies, and industrial conditions such as postal regulations and tariffs, has developed between Canada and the United States, and not to the former's advantage.

The nationalist turn in this argument links up with dependency theory: "Vast monopolies of communication have shown their power in securing a removal of tariffs on imports of pulp and paper from Canada though their full influence has been checked by provincial governments especially through control over pulpwood cut on Crown lands. The finished product in the form of advertisements and reading material is imported into Canada with a lack of restraint from the federal government which reflects American influence in an adherence to the principle of freedom of the press and its encouragement of monopoly" (Innis 1952b, 15).

The international flow of staples and commodities connects with a flow of ideologies in an example of media imperialism. This becomes an argument about national sovereignty and aesthetics. "Canadian publications supported by the advertising of products of American branch plants and forced to compete with American publications imitate them in format, style and content. Canadian writers must adapt themselves to American standards. Our poets and painters are reduced to the status of sandwich men" (Innis 1952b, 16). As represented in this way, concern with national specificity is concurrent with fear of commercialization, almost as though market forces alone were initiating an unbalanced new monopoly of knowledge.

Liora Salter sees Innis's monopolies of knowledge as having been formed in the separation of production and reception, which "robbed the public of legitimacy in the interpretation of its own experience" (1981, 205–6). Salter discusses this issue in the context of debates about the public and the media. But *Strategy and Culture* (1952b) equally demonstrates the extent to which Innis inherited some of the dominant views of the mass media of his day – namely, the early, propagandistic model of mass communications, where the new media stifle democratic potential and deny "true" experience. Here, as with the cultural nationalists before him, his vision of culture links further back to the radical conservatism of Matthew Arnold, with whom he shares a sense not of reform but of despair.

One of his few mentions of motion pictures is a quotation from George Jean Nathan, who called them "the drama of a machine age designed for the consumption of robots" (Innis 1952b, 14). Innis worries about "a continuous, systematic, ruthless destruction of elements of permanence essential to cultural activity. The emphasis on change is the only permanent characteristic" (15). Innis concentrates on new, spatially biased technologies because they encourage and accelerate an unchecked and ultimately fatal rate of change. Yet his call for the "balance" of time remains an Arnoldian image of the importance of sacred bastions, where the best of Culture can safely reside outside the daily life and contaminating influence of "robots."

His key rhetorical claim is that new international monopolies of knowledge reassert a spatially biased empire that tears away the potentials of a Canadian nation and confirms its peripheral position. The American monopolies "threaten Canadian national life. The cultural life of English-speaking Canadians subjected to constant hammering from American commercialism is increasingly separated from the cultural life of French-speaking Canadians" (Innis 1952b, 18). In the end, "[w]e are fighting for our lives" (19). This view lends support to Jody Berland's observation that the question of culture in Canada "was instantly conservative and defensive" (1993, 59). Moreover, this conservative critique, understood as an embattled response necessary for national survival, was equally a modernist pessimism vis-à-vis mass culture and mass society.

And yet Innis's ambivalence towards nationalism sets him apart from other cultural nationalists of his day. Indeed, William Christian opines, "It would be much fairer to say that he was opposed to nationalism as a programme or an ideology, and even more strongly opposed to the exclusivist and intolerant spirit which that doctrine usually incorporated" (1977b, 70–1). To be sure, Innis's (1952b) observation that "[c]ontinentalism assisted in the achievement of autonomy and has consequently become more dangerous" (20) is not to suggest that the unit of the nation is any less dangerous. Instead, it is an assessment of the contemporary moment and of potential future directions.

Innis was critical of a brand of cultural nationalists who, in a cynical manner, used the alibi of nationalism to produce a monopolistic publishing industry, hence creating an increasingly homogeneous literary culture. He condemned this as "[t]he incipient fascism of Canadian intellectuals ... evident in nationalism, isolationism, and the boosting of Canadian literature in the interests of Canadian publishers" (1956a, 267). Here, the economics of cultural nationalism needs to be inverted, for, as Innis suggests, "the publication of a wide variety of books increases the cost of education to the publishers, the state, and the purchaser of books, but it tends to break down broad stereotypes" (268).

Innis's awareness of the political slipperiness of nationalism informed many of his assessments of the relationship between culture and economics. For instance, one of his most famous statements – that "Canada moved from colony to nation to colony" – comments on more than Canada's shifting colonial status. Innis is also showing how nationalism is malleable enough to fit a variety of programs, hence should be regarded with suspicion. As he puts it, "Canadian nationalism was systematically encouraged and exploited by American capital" (405).

None the less, through his historical writings, Innis presents "a case for Canada," which, when he begins to discuss culture more explicitly, becomes a critique of lost cultural potential rather than an argument for national partisanship. Innis saw the position of the nationalist as strategic. When he writes, "we are fighting for our lives," he is referring as much to ways of thinking other than those promoted by monopolies of communications as to Canadian sovereignty. This ambivalence may seem ironic for a scholar who has been so instrumental in Canadian thought. However, he offers something most valuable to cultural studies: recognition of the contingent nature of nations and the potential of a provisional nationalism.

In brief, Innis's understanding of culture borrowed much from the thinking of the day. Yet there are threads to suggest that he looked beyond its limitations, in particular towards a scepticism about nationalism that none the less led him to support the public culture proposed in the Massey Report. In the same way that McLuhan can be seen as a connecting figure between F.R. Leavis and the study of popular culture, Innis similarly acts as the historical bridge between an Arnoldian vision of culture and an epistemological critique of power and empires.

INNIS AND POLITICS IN COMMUNICATIONS

Perhaps the most resounding argument for Innis's place in a North American cultural studies tradition comes from James Carey, whose ongoing critique of American empiricism has assured a place for the "cultural approach" (Carey 1975) in communication studies. In Carey's purview, Innis is the essential example of "the road not taken" by early American communication scholars.

Carey comments: "Innis provided in communication studies, at a moment when no one else in the United States was doing so, a model of scholarly investigation that was historical, empirical, interpretive, and critical" (1981, 79). His "work was critical in the contemporary sense in that he was not proposing some natural value free study, but a standpoint from which to critique society and theories of it in light of humane and civilized values" (80). This certainly aligns Innis with other "roads not taken" in communication studies in the 1940s, including the Frankfurt School.[7]

In its similar commitment to social critique, cultural studies arguably attempted a Marxist interpretation of culture appropriate to the contemporary world, which resulted in its dismissal by more traditional, economic Marxism. A similar conflict has raged around Innis, though on very different grounds. When reading Innis as part of Canadian cultural studies, it is instructive to re-examine his possible contribution to Marxist analysis. Innis owed a large debt to critical economic thought, and, most directly, Thorstein Veblen. Like Veblen's, his is a critical economics for a New World price system and resource exploitation. But claims about the political underpinnings of staple theory have a more quarrelsome ring. Mel Watkins (1981) concludes that there are (at least) two versions of staple theory – one liberal and one Marxist (66). While no one disagrees with the former, the latter is more contentious.

When David McNally (1981) questions the usefulness of Innis to Marxist analysis, he postulates a certain intellectual affinity among Innis, Adam Smith, and Thorstein Veblen. From the latter, Innis received a form of technological determinism, not a radical critique of class in the United States, and from both a liberal political economic critique. McNally's seeks to demonstrate that despite the appeal of dependency theory for Marxists, it is another argument for a natural liberal economic balance. For McNally, staple theory, with its emphasis on single products, is "*commodity fetishism* writ large" (46). He thereby refutes a number of essays that posit the possible convergence of Innis's and Marxian thought (Watkins 1973; Drache 1977, 1978; and Parker 1977).

McNally argues that "[b]y ascribing the creative role in the historical process to the primary commodity itself, Innis' staple theory systematically ignored the role of social relations of production in shaping and reproducing society" (1981, 47). Consequently, Innis cannot account for the formation of classes through the mode of production. In the "Marxist" Innis, according to McNally, staples become capital, which further abstracts and alienates labour from its own historical experience (48).

There are two main problems with McNally's position. First, staples do not act like capital in Innis; they are a raw element around which capital grows. Methods of extraction, processing, transportation, and eventually communication – in other words, modes of production that ignite further capital investment – develop in the context of a particular expertise, geographic determinants, and markets. Innis elucidates this dynamic in his discussion of the determining forces of unused capacities, overhead costs and the price system (see 1956a, 141–55 and 252–72).

Along with the industrial investments come a variety of community and cultural developments. An example occurs in Innis's analysis of the cod fisheries, in which the same staple led to different forms of resource exploitation and settlement by the French and English because of divergent knowledge and markets (Innis 1940). As Robin Neill notes, *The Cod Fisheries* "is not about cod, but is rather an analysis of the shifting structure of a politico-economic system in relation to technical changes affecting primarily the dominant means of transportation. From there it was a short step to Innis' later work on empire and communications" (1972, 48).

Second, McNally's critique is essentially of staple theory; to dismiss Innis's critical potential, he must effectively ignore the rest of Innis's oeuvre. For it is in the communications writings that Innis is most explicit about how the technological structure is a key force in social relations. For Innis, monopolies of knowledge are written onto a core–periphery relationship, which led Drache (1977, 1978) to suggest that this finding, as it connects to structured underdevelopment, contributes to a Marxist reading of Canadian social and economic history.

Innis did not stop at an analysis of commodity production; instead, he built a theory of the structuring of society around the economic and cultural things it does – modes of production and communication. Sut Jhally (1993) sees a connection here to cultural studies. Moreover, he suggests that cultural studies, through the concepts of articulation and discourse, "has mostly focused around issues of meaning and content, and has not addressed, in any useful way, issues connected with communication technology, aside from the important issues of ownership and control" (163). Though this claim ignores much research in this area, he sifts through Innis's determinism for a technological "framework of possibilities and parameters – the limits and boundaries within which social power (as well as modes of cognition) operate" (165).

At this juncture, Jhally indicates Innis's similarities with Raymond Williams's (1974) work on television and technology. Communication technologies act as a landscape that frames monopolies of knowledge and the exercising of spatial and temporal biases. Jhally (1993) concludes with Richard Johnson's definition of the cultural studies project as "to abstract, describe and reconstitute in concrete studies the social forms through which human beings 'live', become conscious, sustain themselves subjectively" (45). Jhally argues that Innis provides a route into the concrete study of social forms through the matrix of monopolies of knowledge, technological bias, and the structuring of social power.

Angus (1993) also explores Innis's potential contributions to critical and post-colonial theory. Taking the essence of Innis as a critique of modernity, Angus suggests that "Innis' humanism both makes possible, and forecloses, a post-colonial, cultural and communication theory" (19). Writing from the periphery, Innis sees into the operations of empire; his humanism facilitates an ethical investigation of how the centres of empires exercise their power. But this also connects him to a Eurocentric history, whose ideological assumptions post-colonial theory seeks to expose. As Angus indicates, the "twilight of humanism" marks the limits of Innis's contemporary contribution; it is for this reason that he appears conservative, hoping to hold onto a unity that may not be worth keeping. Angus suggests that Innis's counterpoising of orality and time harbours a non-Eurocentric critique; its emphasis on the local and the proximate "requires a turn against the universalising and homogenising dynamics of civilization and thought" (38). Arguably, this view neglects the way in which Innis's humanism leads the privilege of the local back to a unity of community values, and headlong into European thought, not to mention European romance about orality.

Hanno Hardt (1992) expressed concern about the centrality of Innis in American cultural studies. He writes that the Innisian "approach ignores the fact that a cultural history of communication must also be a political history. This is particularly relevant when individuals face shrinking private and public spheres and increasing bureaucratic and technological control of everyday life" (202). However, I think it is quite clear that Innis's historical analyses were always a form of political and cultural critique. This is especially true of his concern about cooperation between academics and government; he warns of the hazards of participation in the burgeoning "bureaucratic and technological control of everyday life."[8] For Innis, the technological landscape – indeed, its administration – is fundamental to the structuring of power in social and cultural life.

CULTURE AND UNEVEN DEVELOPMENT

Carey (1981, 75) suggests that Innis had certain continuities with the Chicago School but says that too much is often made of this fact, especially since his entire time at the University of Chicago seems to have provided precious little contact with Robert Park and George Herbert Mead. However, Innis posed questions that were commensurate with American thinkers of the day, particularly about the nature of technologically established links between individuals and national life (cf. Dewey 1927 and Lippman 1922).

While concern about the new electronic nation was mounting, Innis proposed that nations emerge in particular historical conditions and that structural determinants shape that broadcast nation. As Carey (1981) comments, "[L]ong distance communication cultivated new structures in which thought occurred – national classes and professions – new things thought about – speed, space, movement, mobility – and new things to think with – increasingly abstract, analytic, and manipulative symbols" (84).[9]

If, as Carey has suggested (1981, 80), Innis was among the first to theorize international media imperialism – his relation to dependency paradigms – he was then also the first to link this to knowledge and ideas in addition to the economics of the culture industries. This conclusion bears similarities to Antonio Gramsci, whose thinking also emerged in the context of an increasingly American cultural environment and a seemingly decreasing or at least changing indigenous national cultural space.

Though contemporaries, Gramsci and Innis were separated by distance, culture, and ideology. But their points of convergence and divergence reveal their different roles in cultural studies. Reg Whitaker (1992), while warning that Gramsci and Innis offer a "*curious* parallel" at best, contends that "in both cases there is the same interest and concern with the non-coercive elements of ideological social control, which exists in somewhat problematic relationship to forms of coercive social control" (126). Innis confronted a history of empire, which led him to couple the economic with monopolies of knowledge. Gramsci saw the struggle of competing systems of knowledge and its provisional settlement in what he described as hegemony. The two share an interest in geography, technology, knowledge, and power, but their political and historical contexts brought them to differing conclusions.

In "Americanism and Fordism," Gramsci remarked on the new worker needed for the new labour processes (1971, 286). The Fordist scheme required, and promoted, social and cultural reorientation. More than economic determinism, these shifts were the result of a "historical bloc" of political, ideological, and moral designs. Gramsci described this as a process of "becoming American," the consequence of a historical conjuncture around, and not originating from, the mode of production. His question of the industrialization of culture is analogous to that of Innis, whose similar (contingent) determinism equally involved the relation between technological change and the circulation of knowledge. The mode of communication, and the manner of its incorporation in social practice, shapes Innis's idea of Americanness. As he noted, one does not simply gain a new way of doing things with the adoption of a different technique; one also potentially gains a new way of thinking.

Both Gramsci and Innis understood that "new ways of doing things" lead to conditions of uneven development. In "The Southern Question," Gramsci (1957) shows how intellectual work is organized differently, and hierarchically, across regions and cultures. For Gramsci, the "problem" of northern Italy encountering the south, often seen as an encounter between the developed and the underdeveloped, is instead one of competing ways of thinking and living. The north is more closely associated with the centre of governmental and industrial power and hence exercises a position of dominance over the periphery. This hegemony indicates that the issue of Southern Italian development is in fact a question of a structure of social power reconstituting its tenure.

Innis's role in the formation of the metropolitan paradigm demonstrates similar attention to uneven development. His analysis of how metropolitan centres exert their economic, cultural, and administrative influence over regions is seen as one of his lasting contributions (Careless 1954). Innis's work can be read as an investigation of the power structures of core–periphery relations and their organization along the material vectors of distance and time. We could, for example, extend Innis's history of the cod fisheries to today's crisis of Canada's east coast industry. The conflict involves not only environmental emergency and modes of extraction, but a particular tension between the centre's knowledge and the periphery's. Central are ideas about the environment, industrial techniques, national and international relations, and the place of the fishery in local and national life. The federal government has imposed and administered outright bans on particular modes of extraction, extending these in 1994 to include the previously innocuous method of "jigging." The result has been the further unravelling of communities, whose earlier development Innis chronicled, in the face of a shift in control towards the knowledge of the distant federal government. "Uneven development" refers to economic disparity between regions and factions of society, but it is maintained by institutionally sanctioned knowledges.

As Neill has pointed out, the usefulness of staple theory lies in our ability to wrest it from a determinism that teleologically links economics and politics. Geography, methods of extraction and transportation, and untapped resources do not in and of themselves explain social structure, as though every cod holds the seeds of its own commodity and labour market. Instead, Neill (1981) writes, "in reality the causation runs the other way. Reliance on staple exports has been the result of political circumstances" (152). Such circumstances include the thinking, or common sense of the day; thus the "political" encompasses not only public office but even the ideas about social reality that circulate through everyday life. What is the thinking that justifies ongoing structures of core–periphery relations? How are these multiple margins articulated to dominant ideas about the Canadian nation as either necessary or inevitable? How are the apparent contradictions of social division explained away? In this respect, *the epistemological dimensions of uneven development becomes a key conceptual link between Innis and cultural studies.*

The one thing that Gramsci can deal with that was outside Innis's thought was the notion of people struggling in the world they inhabit. McNally (1981) points out that "the making of history by human beings, albeit in conditions not of their own choosing, plays no role in his work" (47). Unlike Gramsci, for Innis the notion of the popular or of folk culture does not enter his world, except marginally. The closest he gets is in his discussion of religion, which returns him to variations on a plea for time. This "absence of the people" means that he cannot deal with popular culture except in the most facile of terms (mechanized entertainment for robots, numbed by laughing gas).

As stated above, this position connects him with a long Canadian tradition of cultural criticism characterized by elitism (cf. Berland 1992). Within an Innisian critique of the epistemological dimensions of uneven development, a persistent problem for cultural studies in Canada has been how to put people into the equation. The challenge for Canadian critique is to produce more "history from below" and more work on the notion of a Canadian popular – a concept long understood only as absent or as an American proxy.

INNIS IN THE NEW CENTURY

Canadian thought participates in an international intellectual discourse that encourages the continued absence of a national discourse, except in hushed tones and in semi-secret locations. In a self-imagined global world, the idea of utopian, borderless societies effectively masks growing divisions and exclusivities; one is told that cultural particularity is the somewhat archaic dream of multiculturalists; and the various programs for mere representation ultimately cloud the actual relational structures of racism. Within this context there exists a struggle to assert the language of context and place, to fight for the possibility of speaking from *here* in the overlapping realms of intellectual and cultural life. This is why Innis becomes ever more important. This is not an argument for ethnocentrism or for the assertion of a single national identity. On the contrary, Innis's scepticism about nationalism is crucial to his place as a Canadian thinker. The post-national environment, initially mistaken for the passing of the nation, involves its reconstitution and reassertion. One therefore needs a critical discourse of nation that does not speak of general qualities or boosterism but of the aesthetic, philosophical, and economic life of the country.

Innis was not the geographical determinist that he is sometimes taken to have been. He understood that there were specificities on which history, economics, and culture were written, to the benefit of some and to the detriment of others. Rereading Innis through critical theory is more than an effort to find the Marxian grain lodged in the non-Marxist scholar; it is an acknowledgment that there is something indispensable about his observations about the structure of Canadian economy and life. Innis's history of the flow of power and resources is a touchstone for any critical discussion of core–periphery relations, as told with an eye to this colony and its imperial history.

What does Innis set up for Canadian cultural studies? First, Innis offers a perspective on the relationship among media, monopolies of knowledge, and the structuring of power. He provides a useful way to understand empire and, in particular, the multiple peripheries that make up Canada through transportation and communication technologies. Second, Innis emphasizes the transformation of resources into economic and cultural commodities.

As Innis's thinking developed, this becomes a history of the neo-colonialism of – and, I would add, within – Canadian cultural life, as is evident in his observation that Canadians export pulp and paper and import books. One can see the same dynamics in the production and circulation of culture within Canada, hence a form of self-colonization. This link between the economic and the cultural, not solely in terms of commodification but the mode of circulation of ideas, led to his analysis of how a contemporary empire is able to define its outermost reaches.

Beyond staple theory, this view introduces the administration of borders and of exchange that structures the circulation of culture.[10] With every seizure of gay and lesbian books and magazines by Canada Customs, with every decision pertaining to culture that is turned over to Industry Canada, and with every budget cut to artist-run centres, the materiality of the production, movement, and regulation of cultural products becomes a site of struggle among competing social factions. Further, the multiple locations of core–periphery struggles become apparent, revealing the "margins" as a multidimensional and unstable relation of force. To talk of core–periphery struggles, after Innis, is to recognize that this is not a fixed template in which the effectivities of power can be explained; instead, core–peripheries are diffused and provisional and form the myriad borders that inflect everyday life.

Participation in, and development of, an international dialogue is crucial; but much is lost in the notion that old superpower relations are levelling off, as though a new democracy of post-nations exists. There has been a reinstitutionalization of how borders operate, who polices whom, and how. The movement of people and capital may be increasing, but it is directed, steered, and regulated. Estimates place the number of refugees at 23 million world-wide; if we do not limit the definition to international movement, and add the internal displacement of people, the number grows to 49 million (Darnton 1994, A1). As long as there are areas in which some may enter and others may not, there is a need for a critical discussion and understanding of how nations work in and through discourse, how the administration of "aid" operates, and how the abstract concept of the border becomes a material force in the well-being of peoples. In this respect, Innis's discussion of core–periphery arrangements assists a critique of race; the writing of power relations in a spatial dimension is a decisive place to understand the enactment of ethnic and racial discourses and divisions.[11]

Innis – the thinker and his work – has existed in the intellectual ante-room he described so well; he was engaged in a marginal discourse that sought to understand the construction of the core–periphery relation in a neocolonialist world. Innis has become a sign over which there is a struggle for meaning. And while the contest shifts his place from the centre of one tradition or political framework to the next, this mobility seems to set up his status ever more surely. In this interdisciplinary turf war, the sign value of Innis is as a Canadian intellectual engaged in the question of what it means to write from *here*.

This notion of "writing from here" – not necessarily about "here" – may be Innis's central connection to cultural studies. Cultural studies is a project of radical contextualization – an understanding of the complex forces that form the social, whether at the level of nation, psyche, ethnicity, sexuality, or gender. Stuart Hall (1985) proposes "no necessary correspondences" as the axiom of the progressive anti-essentialist. This approach defines cultural studies by its flexibility, its suspension of assumptions before the analysis or investigation of the context, its methodological appropriateness to various situations, and its consideration of just how far one critique can go. As a shuttle between the humanities and the social sciences, cultural studies always works best when it provides epistemological critiques of specific traditions and their methods. Cultural studies in its multiple incarnations remains a project that investigates the theoretical problem of how one makes political decisions in a post-Enlightenment universe, within the boundary of specific cultural locations.

Innis hardly had his feet firmly in the post-Enlightenment. But he demonstrated ample awareness of a shift in the first half of this century from, as we would have it, an industrial to a post-industrial order, from the dominance of print to broadcast, with coinciding shifts in monopolies of knowledge. In the context of decolonization, Innis saw new conditions of colonization, new regimes of thought, new forms of empire. Today, the pundits of the new alignment of nations promote the regulation of world economies, flexible accumulation, and global capitalism as the path to development and peace. In response, we would be well advised to return to Innis's analyses and scepticism.

NOTES

1   The author acknowledges the valuable counsel received from the people who commented on this chapter at various stages, including William Buxton, Barri Cohen, Kevin Dowler, Beth Seaton, and Will Straw.

2   Kuan-Hsing Chen (1996) offers a critique of the "internationalization" of cultural studies as presented by Ang and Stratton (1996a). He is especially concerned that their approach can not fully account for material relations of power between core and peripheral regions. See Ang and Stratton 1996b for their response.

3   By "cultural studies in Canada" I designate not a unified set of questions in a single, nationalist rhetoric, but Canada as a complex historical, political, economic, and geographical context in which a particular strand of cultural studies is emerging. Clearly, this is not emphasized to the exclusion of the multiple locations in Canada to which cultural studies speaks with a different specificity; perhaps most notably the counter-discourse of Quebec nationalism and its cultural dimensions. For some of the reasons for Innis's limited influence in Quebecois thought, see in this volume Daniel Salée (chapter 10) and Alain-G. Gagnon and Sarah Fortin (chapter 11).

4   This claim is made by McLuhan (1964a; 1953, 389) and more recently Graeme Patterson (1990). It seems a forced attempt to lend order to Innis's sometimes-chaotic rhetorical style, which was often a product of reading and writing rapidly, working from small quotations on index cards – in short, a streamlined style for efficiency rather than effect.

5   This history has been described by Ron Faris 1975; Mary Vipond 1980; and Maria Tippett 1990.

6   For a more complete version of how this tension affected the development of film in Canada, see Acland 1994.

7   Judith Stamps (1995) explores the connected critiques of the modern offered by Innis, McLuhan, and the Frankfurt School.

8   Ferguson and Owram (1980) have commented on Innis's skepticism about the rush to government policy and advisory positions by social scientists. They say that he was critical "because of the weakening effect it had on universities" (9). In Innis's view, the institutional alliances created a too powerful, and overly bureaucratic, monopoly of knowledge.

9   This epistemological level of Innis's thought prompts Paul Heyer (1981) to point out certain affinities between Innis and Foucault.

10   Though not Innisian in approach, Allor and Gagnon (1994) offer an exemplary attempt to chart the administration of cultural citizenship in Quebec.

11   Valaskakis (1981) begins to develop Innis in exactly this manner.

14 No Future:
Innis, Time Sense, and
Postmodernity

ANDREW WERNICK

The fashionable mind is the time-denying mind – that is the paradox.

> – Wyndham Lewis

Here we are now – entertain us.

> – Kurt Cobain

We would be remiss in a reflection on Innis's thinking about time on the occasion of his centenary not to note the ambiguity of such an occasion. With Innis looking over our shoulders, we are prompted to recognize that all the commemorative activity is not only (in aspiration) an active moment within a living intellectual tradition, but also a complex of commerce, status competition, and advertising at the interface of academe and the publishing industry. Its link to the decimalized solar calendar – an emblem at once for nature, for tradition, for social time, and for machine rationality – allows the first definition of the situation to provide an alibi for the second. The very attempt to revalorize Innis, which I support, promotes the section of the English-Canadian intelligentsia that seeks to achieve it.

This is not to impugn the validity of a respectful retrieval, only to emphasize its difficulties. Innis would be the first to caution us against any expectation that his project, or any project, can be straightforwardly passed on. A concatenation of tendencies intrinsic to our form of civilization, including the fashion dynamics that have come to surround the making and fading of authorial names, impedes cultural transmission. Even in the hold-out, oral culture of universities, whose growing industrialism he lamented, discontinuity reigns. In the past decade, for example, a revived preoccupation with the transformed temporality of advanced capitalist civilization has been discernible in the much-studied writings of Baudrillard (1990), Harvey (1990), Jameson (1984), Meyerowitz (1985), and others. Linked, however, to a preoccupation with the thematics of "postmodernity," it often proceeds blithely as though the shattering of the temporal continuum by economic, technological, political, cultural, philosophical, and military forces had not been a matter of profound culturological debate for more than a century and a half. Any problem in transmitting Innis's heritage is tied to a larger cultural problem, which that heritage might help bring into focus.

In the remarks that follow I want to develop the claim that can be made for Innis along these lines by foregrounding, from within his later writings, his problematization of time and Western culture. I do so particularly with an eye to the criticisms made by McLuhan in his preface to the 1964 reprint of *The Bias of Communication* (1982). How Innis would have replied we cannot know, and it would be presumptuous to speak for him. None the less, and even thirty years later, there are good reasons for seeking to clarify Innis's meaning in the particular context of McLuhan's objections.

First, given the wider reception of McLuhan, and the resulting misunderstanding of Innis as a mere precursor, establishing the differences between them continues to be exegetically useful. In addition, McLuhan's objections to Innis's appraisal of contemporary (i.e. mid-century) Western civilization present a substantive challenge. At issue here are the validity and implications of Innis's judgment that post-print developments have only intensified the existing bias of industrial capitalism for space against time.

McLuhan's counter-theses about the electric age's "implosion" and "reversal" invite us to two tasks. We must revisit Innis's comments about the continuity between the popular press and the then-new media of radio, film, and TV. And we ought to ponder whether the effects of "the publishing industry" on the organization of social time and space can be considered paradigmatic, as Innis seemed to believe, for the still-later world of multimedia and virtuality. To the extent that they can, an updated Innisian analysis would significantly weaken the currently fashionable case for arguing the ruptural specificity of post-modernity, as a type of formation, or for postmodernism considered as a "cultural dominant" (Jameson 1984). Of course the reverse is also true. If McLuhan and the postmoderns are correct about the cultural change wrought by the electronic media, high-intensity consumer capitalism, and the cyber-economy, then Innis's preoccupation with "continuity" itself becomes suspect. At worst it could be dismissed as futile – nostalgia for values that have become unreal by becoming, in their very attachment to historicity, obsolete.

THE DETERMINATIONS IN PLAY

A first step in clearing away the misunderstandings that surround Innis's problematization of time, media, and culture is to resist reading it as a technologism. Yet in his prefatory essay this is just what McLuhan does. Thus he praises Innis above all for his insight that "the dominant technology of a culture ... was the cause and shaping force of the entire structure" (McLuhan, 1964a, xii). Of course, as a pioneer in such study Innis could cover only part of the ground, and he was "quite capable of inaccurate observation." Hence McLuhan argued, the need for some corrective assistance.

But the critique is also conceptual. In effect, McLuhan makes two charges: first that Innis was inconsistent about the sensory dimension of media, and second, that Innis tended to conflate the character and effects of electric technology with those of the mechanical. These errors led in turn to Innis's "mistake in regarding radio and electric technology as a further extension of the patterns of mechanical technology." While the visual power of print is indeed spatially centralizing, "the auditory power extended electrically" abolishes "time and space alike" (McLuhan 1964a, xiii). As a result, Innis had failed to appreciate the salutary, not to say salvific, implications of the wider shift (from the mechanical/visual to the electric/multi-sensory) which the rise of broadcasting heralds. "Visual technologies, whether based on paper or papyrus, foster fragmentation and specialism, armies, and empires. Electric technology favors not the fragmentary but the integral, not the mechanical but the organic" (xv). Innisian pessimism, then, is misplaced. Contemporary turbulence marks only the contradictions of transition on the way to a new dispensation beyond the linearity and violence of print.

Whatever the merits of his own story, McLuhan proceeds as though Innis's analysis of the modern "bias against time" concerned solely the cultural and political effects of visuality and "light and transportable" media. In fact, Innis's account weaves together three determining strands, only one of which concerns media technology, and then not as an autonomous or unmediated force.

To be noted first is the disciplinary basis from which Innis always spoke. "A Plea for Time" (in Innis 1964a) – given originally as part of the sesquicentennial lectures at the University of New Brunswick in Fredericton in 1950 – begins by pleading "the bias of my special interest" as an "economic historian" (61). This is not just highlighting Innis's later attention to such matters as the link among department stores, newspapers, forests, and Canadian–American relations, or the significance of circulation wars and press monopolies for arguments about free speech. I also emphasize that here, as throughout all his writings, Innis shares with such forebears as Smith, Veblen, and Marx the civilizational perception that what distinguishes our epoch – not just economically, but also socially and culturally – is the totalizing advance of the market.

For Innis, studying the amplified booms and busts of a staples economy had already thrown into relief the spatial and temporal disruptions associated with market-driven economic development and the consequent difficulty of establishing durable forms of collective life. But discontinuity was not just a matter of upheaval; it was ongoing. In consumption, as in production, market demand is always geared to the short term. The needs it registers are those of the present, in line with Keynes's dictum (which Innis liked to quote) that "in the long run we are all dead." Innis drew too on Veblen's turn-of-the-century observations (Veblen 1899) about dawning consumerism, accelerated status competition, and the growing impact of fashion, particularly its incessant focus – whether in looks or books – on the constantly destabilized horizon of up-to-dateness.

In tracing the rise of the printing industry, Innis showed how the commercialization of communications intensified all these trends. The rise of entertainment values pervasively spread the emphasis of consumer goods on novelty and immediate appeal. Through the news industry the media commercially colonized time itself. As well, the commercialization of media coincided with the rise of mass production and the need for mass marketing. Hence the economic and functional subsumption of newspapers, magazines, and so on by advertising, with further presentist consequences for the culture. The more the market has expanded its spatial reach, the more pronounced has been its "bias against time." This devaluation was evident for Innis in the dominance of economic theory by marginalist neoclassicism (1979, 252–72). Even the countervailing vogue in the 1930s and 1940s for state economic planning typically drew the line at five-year periods, prompting Innis to remark (following Polanyi) that "laisser-faire was planned, planning is not" (1964a, 86).

A second level of Innis's argument concerns industrialism. Here, to be sure, a technological question is broached. "Industrialism implies technology and the cutting of time into precise fragments suited to the needs of the engineer and the accountant" (1982, 140). Under its aegis, social and lived time has become homogenous, linear, and clock-divided, in line with the need to coordinate the increasingly intricate and far-flung division of technical labour implied by the application of machines to production. The clock, and the gearing of the rhythms of life to it, is at once a model and a most powerful cultural result.

Innis did not imagine of course that a universal temporal grid was the unique product of the industrial revolution. His history of the modern mapping of time goes back to the discovery of lunar, solar, and sidereal cycles in the ancient empires of the Middle East. He also traces from Babylon through Rome and medieval Europe the increasingly refined effort to fix the periodicities of ceremonies and festivals through calendar reform. Industrialization, however, reflecting the unprecedented rise of secular economic activity, gave a massive impetus to this development.

It is only the third strand in Innis's argument that concerns media directly. At its core is an appraisal of media forms – defined in terms of what materially bears the message – in relation to their lightness and durability, and thus their aptness for communication through space or time. The portability of media influences the extent, and the durability of media the longevity, of empires, institutions, and cultures. The speeded-up production and dissemination of printed paper by road and rail had vastly improved communication through space but not through time. A second wave of inventions – photography, film, telegraphy, radio, "and beyond" – had amplified the effect. As a result, Western culture was beset by a communications bias that chronically favoured synchronous over diachronic linkage, so that an omnipresent present overwhelmed the past and precluded contact with the future.

Here, no doubt, Innis was putting in play a technological determination in the stricter sense. Even in abstraction from other shaping forces, other mediations, however, the argument is not as simple as it seems. The first complication is introduced by Innis's reference to the sensory dimension and – what troubled McLuhan – the apparent inconsistency it led to in Innis's (few) remarks about radio. With radio, we are told, we "exchanged an eye for an ear," which has led to "a new attention to time." However, the actual (and centralizing) use of radio as commercial device or political mouthpiece has shifted but not broken the mould. "The bias of communication in paper and the printing industry was destined to be offset by the bias of [the] radio. Democracy which in the words of Guizot sacrificed the past and the future to the present was destined to be offset by planning and bureaucracy" (1964a, 60).

The second complication is that the media transformation initiated by the rise of the print industry has not only given modern communications a positive bias for space over time. It has also led to the externalization of collective memory (through libraries and the production/storage of information) and to the substitution of mediatised for face-to-face communication. In so doing, mass media have thereby undermined "oral culture" as a possible counter to their own effects.

When we fill out the model in this way, the reason for its tragic pathos begins to be clear. Innis's account reveals a vicious circle in which the atemporal bias of technologized media is fatally exacerbated by the resulting annihilation of their potentially transcendent negative pole: orality. Judith Stamps (1995) has shown the affinities between Canadian communications theory and the Frankfurt School, suggesting in particular that Innis's later work exhibits a conceptual strategy somewhat akin to Adorno's negative dialectics.

For McLuhan, "what Innis had missed" was that electric media globally extend the interactive communication of which oral culture consists. This disagreement, however, coexists with a different conception of the defining attributes of oral culture itself. For Innis, but not for McLuhan, these clearly include a shared sense of continuity in time. In any case, all three determining elements – market dynamics, industrialism, and media – combine for Innis, who does not assess their causal priority in generating the modern "obsession with present-mindedness." The market drives industrialism via a compete-or-die compulsion to efficiency. The conversion of writing into advertising depends on the mass production of messages to satisfy the distribution needs of consumer-goods industries. Nor is technology itself formed independently of the political-economic setting. Radio's lightness as a medium is exacerbated by commercial emphasis on the fragmentary and topical, and to the extent that public radio had to compete for attention it was itself bound to assimilate entertainment values and the star system and be commercial in its way. If we were to draw Innis forward, we could make the same kind of points about the techno-economic moulding of TV as miniaturized, ad-based home entertainment, and the relation of this function to time-pastiche in the age of the image; or about computers, data banks, "social auditing," and accounting control.

Thus McLuhan's criticisms about Innis's failure to see the novel significance of electronic media for advanced capitalism's cultural bias address only part of his argument. In McLuhan's account, the second of Innis's determining moments – industrial technology – is assimilated to the third, media, and deemed surpassed. The market is likewise either treated as an aspect of visuality and print, or ignored altogether.

But there is an even bigger problem. McLuhan's saving moment is not in the least, as it would have to be for Innis, a recuperation of time. It is the "abolition of space and time" in trends towards the formation of a global village. The speed up and synesthesia of electric technology would reverse the print-age fragmentation of individual and society by fostering new forms of integral subjectivity and community. In this figure of oneness and healing, which perversely embraces the media beast, it is easy to catch a sense of McLuhan's excitement. What it offers, however, is a solution not to Innis's problem but to his own, a fact hidden by their equally approving, but differently intended, uses of the term "oral culture."

For McLuhan, orality evokes community in space, integrated through the immediacies of association and talk; for Innis, a tradition-ality in which the lived moment is continually related to what has gone before and might come later. His leading idea, indeed, is not commu-nity at all. Communication through time is neither interactive, nor does it permit the co-presence of those it joins. For Innis the model for orality is "Greek," with Golden Age echoes of vitality, excellence, and *phronesis*. For McLuhan, it is tied, via the idea of communion, to a Christian (and implicitly millenarian) eschatology. What was "oral" in the "footnote" was not "oral" in the text; and what McLuhan saw as the basis for a saving *peripateia* was for Innis just an intensification of the same.

This semantic disagreement registered, moreover, not only a differ-ent appraisal of electric media, but an ideological difference that deeply affected their thinking about time. Where McLuhan (for all his proto-postmodern enthusiasm for the pagan maelstrom) is teleological, Innis sees civilizational rhythms as cyclical, before which (however prophetic his alarm) his stance is ironic, stoical, and resigned.

THE GREEK CONNECTION: ORALITY, PAIDEIA AND PRAXIS

While the Athens–Jerusalem tension has long been pivotal to Western thought, there is a more proximate provenance of the Greek element in Innis's case. It derived from the neo-Hellenic revival that gripped a wing of the European intelligentsia around the turn of the eighteenth century, particularly in Germany, where it was promoted by the *gym-nasium* system as well as by von Humboldt's academic reforms. The initial impulse was constructive. The virtues of a humanist education such as the classical Greeks were held to have perfected – particularly in the Athenian *polis* before the Peloponnesian Wars – were promoted as an ideal for emerging industrial civilization.

Increasingly, though, the counterposition of *Kultur* to *Civilisation* became the basis for the latter's critique – a critique that pitted Renais-sance values against those of the Reformation and was positioned ambiguously between romantic *Naturphilosophie* and populist or socialist egalitarianism. Arnold's *Culture and Anarchy* (1983) and Newman's *Idea of the University* (1996) rendered similar themes into English, and Innis encountered them directly in the mood of academic revival that wafted through interwar North American universities, including his own at Toronto, during the period of Whiteside and Sidney Smith.

Altogether, Innis's bias was entirely explicit, as was his relativizing recognition that such a bias was ethnocentric. The power of Greek civilization "has been such that it becomes impossible for modern Europeans who have participated in the heritage to approach it from an objective point of view" (1964a, 52). The nature and import of his ideological attachment have nevertheless been remarkably hard to grasp. One supposes that this is in part because of its historical strangeness, which stems from Innis's now impossibly distant status as the last major echo of academic neo-Hellenism in Canada, if not in North America. But also, and unusually for an Anglo North American, he linked this complex not to the literary and fine arts but to the social sciences, which, as McLuhan (1964a) observes, Innis imbibed, together with other European influences, at Chicago (xiv–xiv).

The far-reaching importance of Innis's "Greek" element for his thinking about time and Western culture becomes clear when we disentangle its principal theses, which can be arranged in two series. The first is an argument about civilizational balance: the strength and survival value of a civilisation depend on its capacity to combine effective political coordination with cultural durability, which depends largely on the bias of its media. The happiest results – the obverse of the present – flow from a strong mix of space-binding and time-binding media (for example, papyrus and parchment, talk and writing), whose biases cancel one another out.

The second line of argument concerns cultural reflexivity. In effect, for Innis, our situation is irretrievably worse, for the space-biased forces of economy and techne have, by weakening oral culture, not only diminished a potential counterbias, but our civilization's very capacity to comprehend its own chronic and debilitating imbalance. The booming postwar university – popularity-chasing, over-specialized, seduced by research money, and oriented to exams, vocationalism, and the production of information – incarnated the issue in an institution that was historically charged with responsibility for grappling with just such matters. An excess of data, specialism, and relevance complemented a deficit of self-knowledge. "All of us here together seem to be what is wrong with Western civilisation," noted Innis to a room full of university presidents in 1950 (1964a, 191).

I mentioned above the ironic fatalism with which Innis regards the necessities driving the civilizational spectacle. But what needs to be drawn out is the reliance of Innis's *whole* argument on an appeal to what are explicitly labelled "Greek principles." Throughout, his analysis remains faithful to the two Delphic maxims he was wont to cite: know yourself, and nothing in excess. What he urges and bemoans the lack of is self-knowledge in the face of excess, it being understood that such self-knowledge itself entailed a balanced appreciation of time and space.

Honouring these maxims pervaded Innis's work. Concern for self-knowledge underlies his stress on perspectival reflexivity. It appears too in the *memento mori* proffered in such concluding lines as "Each civilization has its own methods of suicide" (1964a, 141). As for the virtues of balance, the content and the very form of his writing, by upholding the ideals of orality, counter the present imbalance against time. Thus he eschews a complex metalanguage, strives for plain speech, coins aphorisms, and is for ever telling stories. Against the grain of the medium, his printed words aim to be oral in their communicative effect. In every respect, then, Innis aligns himself with what he takes to be Apollonian virtues. He takes heed of the oracle, and by living its sayings he means to prove and prolong their longevity precisely as that.

Against that background we can perhaps elucidate what Innis called "oral culture" itself. But here there is a puzzle. For how, we may ask, can oral culture be presented both as a time-binding corrective to the space bias of print and electronic media and as the meta-place where the interests of space and time are themselves judiciously weighed? A provisional answer lies in Innis's multidimensional meaning of the term "oral culture." For Innis, as for Havelock's Plato (Havelock 1963), the milieu formed by direct speech and its appurtenances is the medium not only for face-to-face communication but also for the cultivation of memory, indeed for cultivation as such. It is the place, that is, of education, of *paideia*, of the formation of character and intelligence, and thus the link between memory and tradition, on the one side, and reflection and praxis, on the other.

In taking this view, Innis diagnoses current ills not just by taking his lead from his understanding of fifth-century Greece but also, and more specifically, by extending Plato's critique of writing for its inducing of forgetfulness into a critique of print and other modern media.[1] Innis's commentary on Plato's critique of writing in the *Phaedrus* is presented in the third of the Reith Lectures, published as *Empire and Communications* (1950, 68–70). Indeed, doubly. For, on the one hand, the original sin of Thoth's invention has been vastly multiplied by the effects of commerce and industry, developed to excess. On the other hand, what is at stake is not simply memory, with all the weight that Plato placed on it, but (in the good, hybrid sense) "oral culture" as a whole. "The oral dialectic is overwhelmingly significant where the subject-matter is human action and feeling, and it is important in the discovery of new truth but of very little value in disseminating it" (Innis 1964a, 191).

We can see here the force of the distinction that Innis draws (1964a, 4) between the custom-bound oral culture of primitive peoples examined by anthropologists and that of the Greek *polis*. While both were marked by a strong tradition, the latter's cultural hallmarks were "vitality" and "flexibility." The same distinction, however, should put us on theoretical guard. For oral culture in the "Greek" sense was actually orality twinned with phonetic writing and thus given, as Innis puts it, "fresh powers of resistance." Innis is not talking about oral culture in an originary, or pristine sense. His ideal-critical reference is rather to orality as supplemented – albeit to an optimal degree – by writing.

It need hardly be said that Innis's references to orality frequently elide the distinction between its meaning as direct speech (plus internalized memory) and, more generally, as face-to-face communication; as also between the pure case, hybrid cases, and the case of an oral culture (labelled "Greek"), whose orality is optimally supplemented by various kinds of writing and external information storage. It is no surprise either that the slippery concept of the latter, so crucial to Innis' problematization, never receives anything like a rigorous theoretical treatment.

Nevertheless, the implicit refinement that Innis's heterogeneous supplemented notion of oral culture introduces into the schema of the *Phaedrus* is profoundly consequential; for it enables him to pursue a phono-philic cultural critique while abjuring both a primitivist (or transparent) cultural ideal and a foundationalist epistemology. (Derrida's strictures [1976] against the continuing "phonocentrism" of Western communications theory, in continuity with the whole history of Western metaphysics, do not in any simple way apply to Innis.)

In Innis's "Greek" attachment to oral culture, a final comment is needed concerning the central role it ascribes to education. A sentence or two from his submission to Manitoba's Royal Commission on Adult Education in 1947 indicates the general flavour. "We have assumed that government in democratic countries is based on the will of the governed, that people can make up their minds, and that every encouragement should be given to enable them to do so ... We should, then, be concerned like the Greeks with making men not overwhelming them by facts disseminated with paper and ink, film, radio and television. Education is the basis of the state and its ultimate aim and essence is the training of character" (Innis 1964a, 202).

Education qua *paideia* is not the learning of facts but a process of moral and intellectual formation that facilitates independent thought. It is crucial to long-term social interests not just because of the intrinsic value of an enriched culture but because education in the full sense synthesizes the passive moment of retention/transmission with the active one of creativity, thinking, and praxis. "The danger that knowledge of the past may be neglected to the point that it ceases to serve the present and the future – perhaps an undue obsession with the immediate, support my concern about the disappearance of an interest in time" (61).

Putting aside the hostility and incomprehension that such views brought then – and we know how reactionary they seem now – I would note only the plurality of time issues they evince. One concerns the need, in education itself, for a time–space mental balance. For Innis this issue runs deeper than curricular reform. Both *paideia* and, still more, the cultivation of the minds needed to sustain it involved total immersion. Even for the ablest, serious study requires suspension of mundane distractions. "Once the university, and in particular the arts faculty, becomes thoroughly seized of the vital significance of its role in Western society and staff and students realize the necessity of constant emphasis on training to produce the open mind, the whole educational system will begin to show signs of vitality ... Society must regard the university as a community of scholars concerned with its vital problems" (210). In this special sense *schole* means leisure and requires it, raising a further issue about *free time*.

Finally, as Innis notes, "the traditions of universities in the Western world have centred around the direct oral method of instruction" (209), but swelling numbers and mechanization have tended to substitute print (and audio-visual) representations for direct contact between teacher and student. Add this to what he further remarks about the significance of orality for "uncovering truths," and we can see that Innis's stress on *paideia* also, and paradoxically, emphasizes the vital importance of the here and now. To be sure, he sympathises with those who defend free time in the name of the purely useless; but he does so less to pronounce in favour of the *vita contemplativa* than to protect thinking from encroachment from the pressures of the short term. "The universities must concern themselves with the living rather than with the dead" (195).

McLuhan's remark about Innis's erroneous use of Wyndham Lewis' line about fashionable minds being time-denying omits its conclusion –

"That is the paradox" on which Innis builds. From this we may suspect that the full range of what Innis is pleading for in his "A Plea for Time" (Innis 1964a) passes McLuhan by. He misses Innis's interest in the relation between time-sense, education, knowledge, and the possibilities of a self-corrective praxis. He emphasizes only Innis's "deep concern with the values of tradition and [temporal] continuity" (McLuhan 1964a, xiii), not the flag that Innis also raises on behalf of the living moment and its address to the future. What links these pleas is indeed, for Innis, the paradox observed by Lewis: that the modernist obsession with the present accepts its severing from larger rhythms and is not in fact care for time at all.

TIME MODES

But time in what sense? What is Innis's "plea for time" pleading for? The essay's title appears self-explanatory. It is a plea for attention to the temporal dimension of social life, in the face of a civilizational bias that, both in practice and in theory, results in time's denial or neglect. Time versus no-time. Yet the closing lines of that essay (in Innis 1964a) stress not only "attempting a balance between the demands of time and space" if "conditions favourable to an interest in cultural activity" are to be developed, but also "freeing ourselves from time" (90). Current enmity to Greek antiquity, we are told, stems precisely from the "the fact that its mind was ahistorical and without perspective." Conversely, if good time is escape from time, the negative pole of Innis's diagram is not occupied simply by the absence of temporality. What it represents is a dominance that has come to be exercised over the organization, conception, and experience of time by a *particular* temporal mode: – an overarching chronotype that Innis calls "linear time."

Innis's argument is thus for one mode of time as against the dominance of another. However, the terms of that argument are confused because the time pleaded for is not recognizable as a time mode at all through the optic of the one that prevails. To complicate matters further, in Innis's account, the dominance of linear time-consciousness provides a critical reference point for two sets of reflections – the one substantive and concerned with the possibilities for "cultural activity," the other methodological and concerned with the exigencies of reflecting on the culture- bound categories with which we think. These are tangled together in the text, but they point in somewhat different directions, so they must be considered separately.

The body of "A Plea for Time" (twenty-five of its thirty pages) consists of a historical account of linear time and its rise to power, indexed to Innis's wider reconstruction of Euro-Asiatic civilization. In the register of critique, that narrative figure itself becomes a ground for hinting at the suppressed alternatives. Innis gives us only quotes and facts, refusing to show us directly the thinking of his thoughts, leaving the reader to fill in the blanks.

With the licence granted by that procedure, I would like to suggest that, at least as a cultural argument, Innis's essay is an attempt to synthesize the seemingly divergent insights gleaned from the two works cited at its beginning and end: Nietzsche's *The Use and Abuse of History* (1956) and Wyndham Lewis's *Time and Western Man* (1957). The guiding thread, as we move from one to the other, is the Greek idea of poetic rupture, with Lewis taken as a corrective to Nietzsche with respect to the historical circumstances in which the obstacles to such a time mode were posed. In his biography, Creighton reports (1957, 141) that Innis was invited to give a talk at the Collège de France in 1951: "The Concept of Monopoly and Civilization," read at a meeting chaired by Professor Lucien Febvre on 6 July of that year. Creighton does not indicate its theme, but the question of time was preoccupying the college at that juncture. Braudel also gave an invited lecture on the complexity of historical time, and it was at the turn of the fifties too that Foucault was engaged there on his dissertation about the history of madness. All of which is to suggest that the French were much quicker than Innis's Canadian and British admirers to appreciate his significance in the modern and postmodern discussion about time.

Nietzsche's starting point in the work cited is that the will for great deeds depends on an actor, thinker, or artist being able to inhabit a certain "atmosphere" of timelessness. The problem is that humans live in time, and free creation entails a break from our normal mode: a willed break from becoming, and the positive strength to forget. At this level the human time problem is generic and perennial. But for Nietzsche it was exacerbated in contemporary European culture, especially German, by a veritable excess of time consciousness. Contemporary pride in historiography as a cultural achievement masked the perils of an excessive engrossment with the past that could be paralysing when rendered deterministic or providential, as in the pernicious extreme of Hegelian historicism. Hence, against the burden of such doubled self-consciousness about time, the "untimeliness" of Nietzsche's meditation, as well as the superhuman effort it called for if the creative forces of life were to evince the needed will to forget.

Such forgetting, of course, was not the same as having nothing to unremember. History, in the three forms that Nietzsche identified, had had its uses: the antiquarian could teach us piety, the monumental could bring us into an encounter with greatness, and the critical could enhance our powers of judgment. It was just that if the historicity of the present could not be set aside, no space could be cleared within which monuments could be built, not even those founded – as they must be if they were to perdure – in the most advanced motives and needs of the here and now.

For Wyndham Lewis the same problem had manifested itself in reverse. In the 1910s and 1920s (if we leave aside the cataclysm of war) the culturally requisite "unhistorical" atmosphere was lacking not because of a prevailing historicism, but because there was too little sense of temporal continuity, and far too much dominance of consciousness by the here and now. Championing, against Spengler, the "plastic" (visual-tactile) over the "musical" arts, Lewis (1957, 285–99) linked up the Spenglerian figure of Faustian Man, Bergsonian time philosophy, stream-of-consciousness literature, urban–industrial speed up, and the sensationalist and fragmentary character of popular entertainment and the press. The obsession with time masked the fact that no one had any, and the radical discontinuity experienced between one moment and the next made it impossible to develop a monumentalizing perspective that could rise, and create, above the pressures and fashions of the moment.

Innis's ability to blend and balance these two positions comes not only from his sharing their common preoccupation with Greek notions of *poiesis*, but also from his elaboration of the "concept of linear time," the history of which provides the context for both. Thus Innis traces the rise of modern historiography (and so Nietzsche's problem) to several factors – the improvement of astronomical calculations in Renaissance science; the rise of secular activity, leading to the church's losing its monopoly over time; printing; and the inception of history writing as continuous chronology. In turn, the concept of time as a unidirectional line extending to infinity in both directions, and measurable in terms of stellar regularities, was deemed to have been fixed in Newtonian physics, whence it developed as a frame for reconstructing the human story backward: first as self-documented, next so as to include its preliterate phases, and finally, via evolutionary biology, geology, and speculative cosmology, so as to merge with natural history in the largest sense.

But that same development – of time as chronology – also subverted its own historicizing effects. For if the rise of linear time underwrites modern historiography, it is also, for Innis, associated with industrialism, the market, and with the need for a measurable time grid to coordinate the activities of society as it took on, as if mimetically, the character of an intricately interacting machine. All this coincided, too, with the replacement of church and state by the business corporation and the newspaper in their control over time. Thus the linearization of time produces not only Nietzsche's problem – too much history – but also, in a subsequent moment, Lewis's. The problem of too little history emerges when "the devices of industrialism and commerce" have torn time into sensate fragments, and when, under conditions of chronic present-mindedness, "knowledge of the past may be neglected to the point that it ceases to serve the present and the future" (Innis 1964a, 61).

While Innis presents the rise of linear time neither as autonomous nor as a sole cause of these cultural problems, its critique provides a backdrop for his appropriation not only of Nietzsche and Lewis, but also of Plato's critique of writing as the externalization of memory. From this angle, the rise of information industries, and the over-whelming of intelligence by facts, could be regarded as materially underpinning (but at different media moments) both Nietzsche's concern about *Gelehrheit* having become decorative rather than useful, and Lewis's, about the baleful effect on aesthetic imagination of an overloaded and fragmentary presentness.

The weight that Innis placed on orality, however, and the fact that though he speaks of "culture" in the aesthetic-intellectual sense he has in mind praxis as well (including that of economic long-term plan-ning), suggest that the argument is not quite as coherent as this account would make it seem. Innis's concern for temporal continuity (and here McLuhan is right) exceeds that of Nietzsche or Lewis. While its pre-suppositions are never spelled out, such concern might be said to rest on a psychological assumption about the conditions for secure ego for-mation in the case of individuals able to take "the right steps at the right time." Co-mingled in Innis's account are concern for the condi-tions for monumentalizing *poiesis* – "continuity in form" – and a related but distinct concern for the conditions for what we might call wise praxis. The remainder is the excess of praxis over *poiesis*, with that difference masked by the moment of "vision," in which the eternal time of art slides into the *longue durée* of a politic addressed to civi-lizational matters.

Innis thus allows a kind of historicism to slip in through the back door. If the substantive argument in Innis's plea for time concerns the conditions for cultural activity, there is a methodological subtext con-cerning the new kind of historiography that would be required to facil-itate – as theory to practice – the historically informed strategic states-manship whose absence he bemoans. At this level of Innis' reflection, the problem posed by the dominance of linear time is cognitive rather than existential and raises issues about the writing of history itself.

Innis's thinking circles, in effect, around two points. The first involves critical reflexivity and is neo-Kantian. Repeating a question raised by an old philosophy teacher, Innis presents the essays in *Bias of Communication* (1951a) as an attempt to explain "why we attend to the things to which we attend." "Economic historians," Innis tells us in the opening lines of "A Plea for Time" (1964a), "and indeed all historians, assume a time factor and their assumptions reflect the attitude towards time of the period in which they write." We cannot escape that bias, but we can achieve a kind of objectivity by "appraising" it and its dangers with reference to that of others. Following the historicization of Kant's Copernican turn – for which Innis's most immediate source is Cassirer (1950) – Innis's project, then, problematizes the fundamental ordering categories of space and time; and it does so by attempting to discern their multiple, changing, and differential character as social constructs.

The epistemological stance to which this leads him is positioned between positivist objectivism and a dissolvent perspectivalism as was championed (in sober tone) by Urwick, Innis's predecessor as head of Political Economy at Toronto. Every (re)writing of history implies a time concept on the part of the writer, but this can be provisionalized, and rendered multiple, through a historical focus on the formation and deployment of this and other time concepts. Such a stance implies a perspectival mobility on the part of the historiographer, as on that of the historically aware actor. It would be free yet self-controlled, enabling them to dance through different historical and civilizational configurations while maintaining a certain ironical balance through the at-least-relational knowledge to which this mobility can lead.

Such qualified adhesion (in the *Positivismusstreit* of his day) to the claims of objectivity evidently involved a delicate balancing act. And it was made all the more delicate by the way in which Innis's work pointed towards the possibility of developing, in the teeth of the prevailing continuism, an encompassing (yet temporally reflexive) history of (human) time itself. For, in relating this story of stories, what sense of time was to underlie *it*?

The principle of bias countering bias suggested that the answer could not lie simply in singularly adopting some other time concept – for example, the monumental time of Burkhardt and Nietzsche. It could be conceived only in terms of an openness to the irreducible complexity of human times in the plural. In this view, we may add, Innis was by no means fixed in a binary opposition between linear and creative/ruptural/transhistorical time. Beyond these, his list of chronotypes extends to the varieties of "social time" taxonomized by social scientists (he specifically cites Sorokin and Merton), as well as to the cyclical time of seasons and river floods, the rhythms of collective memory and cultural duration, and – in his earlier writings – the "cyclonic" course of capitalist development. The list is certainly incomplete. Mortality disappears, as does biological reproduction, the succession of generations, and all that Kristeva (1986) calls "women's time." It is wide enough, none the less, not only to open up, against all essentialism and teleologism, and alongside contemporaries such as Braudel, old questions about historical ontology, but also to do so at the very limit of his initial question.

At this limit, a giddying intuition took shape. Historical time, conceived as the concatenation of a multiplicity of time modes, and within whose horizons the knowing subject is always inscribed, was evidently unimaginable in Newtonian terms. Time thought this way could not be wholly abstracted from the dimension of space. Its constituting rhythms and tempi were biologically marked and inextricably shaped by geography and climate. Whereas Wyndham Lewis abjured the early modernist fascination with the metaphorical possibilities of Einstein's "time space contiuum," Innis emphatically called for a paradigm shift in the human sciences parallel to the relativity upheaval in physics. In the preface to the *Bias of Communication* (1964a) he writes: "[I]t is assumed that history is not a seamless web but rather a web of which the warp and [the] woof are space and time woven in [a] very uneven fashion and producing distorted patterns" (xvii). McLuhan was preoccupied with a similar metatheoretical issue, and we may wonder, with him, why Innis did not go all the way.

Can we not detect in the emergent post-linear multiplicities of the twentieth-century media environment the outlines of a sensibility that might facilitate the required epistemic change? That Innis was not wholly impervious to such a move is suggested by an anecdote which has him admitting that his style derived from an attempt to write as if sending a telegram to Australia. From Innis's standpoint, nevertheless, what became McLuhan's move was barred even in its own terms. For the shift beyond linearity and print involved not only field awareness and the intuitive grasp of strange synchronicities but, above all, a new grasp of the diachronic, and one certainly freed from the evolutionism (media history as the unfolding prosthetic outering of Man) that marks McLuhan himself as still boxed in linearity.

THE CHALLENGE OF THE "POST"

In staging the elements of an Innisian reply to McLuhan's criticisms I have implicitly used the latter as a stalking horse for the "post." It might have been tempting to follow McLuhan in pointing to the inconsistency between Innis's path-breaking uses of symbolist (or "Einstein-ian") modes of expression and his stubborn clinging to the singularity of a point of view that rests – yet worse! – on the pre-print values of "temporal continuity and tradition." If we adopted Habermas's taxonomy (1983), this would be to cast Innis as a conservative anti-modernist, albeit one whose aesthetically modernist mode of expression points another way.

However, as I have tried to suggest, such a judgment would rest on a misreading. Leaving aside his stylistics (which can be otherwise explained), Innis exhibits no nostalgia for the past; and if he challenges modernization in the name of values drawn from ancient Greece, he does so with an eye not only to rectifying "neglect of the past" in its service to the present, but also to escape from "antiquarianism ... present-mindedness ... and ... bogeys of stagnation and maturity" (1964a, 62). Nietzsche's "moment" frees time from the fatal flow of becoming for creative acts of will. In just that vein for Innis, Minerva's line of flight (i.e., "the strategy of culture") is towards a recovery of timeless Apollonian vision. Without it, as he biblically notes, "the people perish" (91). Moreover, the oral culture that serves as his axiological reference point is neither romanticized nor made the basis for any epistemologically fixed point of view. In its Greek mode it is, to the contrary, always already a hybrid of direct and mediatized/disseminated speech, a non-original origin and self-deconstructing construct *avant la lettre* that precludes any easy lapse into a metaphysics of History or the Social.

As for the challenge to Innis's critique of "Western civilization" presented by subsequent developments in the "real," everything from economic globalization to the internet points not to a reversal but to an intensification of the anti-time bias he discerned. Rather than abandoning Innis to the antiquarians, then, we might do better to elaborate the concepts necessary to secure his line of engaged analysis in the context of contemporary theoretical discourse and then use that apparatus in a consideration of what might count for a "strategy of culture" today.

Any attempt to do that would have to take cognizance of the actual inconsistency I have tried to expose in his thinking between a practical and a poetic interest in repairing the industrial-capitalist ravages of time. These interests ambiguously intersect in Innis's preoccupation with the vanishing prospects for achieving "vision." In that regard, one salient theme that Innis largely neglects, but which the recovery of "Innis-sense" might help bring into focus, is what I would call the lost horizon of the future. Communication through time involves not only the ability to receive messages (binding or polysemic) from the past, but also the possibility that meaning (again, whether fixed, or as readerly signs) can be sent forward. Innis's gloomy peroration to his essay on "industrial values" points out: "The nationalism of the Jews left them without a country. The Catholic Church renounced the world and became the heir of the defunct Roman empire. Universal suffrage heralded the end of parliamentary government" (140). In a similar vein we can add that the century after Edison's invention of recording has seen the death of social memory and a decisive weakening of individual and collective power to pass thought on. The constant rebuilding of the built environment, the instability and turnover of "communities," and the top–down elision of institutional autonomies (including that of the university) by marketization, bureaucracy, and state regulation indicate the scope of what has occurred, in which context the five-year planning horizons to which Innis scathingly referred have come to seem idealistically long term.

In Innis's day, the foreclosing of the future in the social imaginary was still partially covered up by progress myths that cast a rosy glow even over the reconstructive prospects of a war-devastated Europe and Asia. For him, "pessimism from strength" still to some extent consisted (as it had for Nietzsche) in demythologization – in facing up to the unpalatable hollowness of a culture that was straying, despite its bad faith optimisms, both official and oppositional, "as in an infinite nothingness." In our own day, at least in this region, the projections of a better future have receded, first in the imagined horrors of nuclear or ecological apocalypse, and then in ideological disillusionment. History in the meaningful, teleological, Enlightenment sense has come to an end. For some – pre-war Frankfurt provides the model – this is because capital has evolved structural processes for obviating transformist possibilities. For others, it is the very fulfilment of Enlightenment goals that has brought history to a close – a figure than can be traced through Kojève's reading of Hegel (for whose formative impact see Descombes 1980) to the postmodern preoccupation with *post-histoire*.

Either way, this whole dissolvent movement has combined – and not only among mass unemployed urban youth – with a sober sense of human powerlessness to self-direct individual life, let alone to put history (in Weber's railway phrase) on to another track. Approaching the futurelessness of postmodernity from a socio- structural direction, Luhmann and others have pointed to the qualitative effects of the growing complexity of synchronization required by hyper complex systems. The "risk society," Armin Nassehi has written in a recent essay, lives in "absolute time" – in the cold vastness of cosmic periodicities that we have learned to measure with the precision of an atomic clock. With the victory of Chronos over other time concepts – including utopian time and Benjamin's "time of the now" – the foreshortened time horizon of the contemporary life-world is as disenchanted as the succession of style decades to which, in media retrospect, it is made to belong. "Meaning and time have become indifferent to one another" (Nassehi 1994, 65).

Such straws in the pop cultural wind as the most familiar tag-lines from the youth anthems of punk and grunge suggest that the collapse of a future horizon towards which communication or praxis might be aimed has become self-conscious, and not only among the intellectual mandarins of postmodernism. From John Lyden's "No future" to Kurt Cobain's "Entertain us" we might even see a dialectical development in which despair itself has lost its meaning in the dis-continuum of time. But by the same token, nihilism has become hip. Nirvana did entertain, as for that matter does Baudrillard, whose fees are rumoured to be not much less. Under the circumstances, a maintenance of Innis's would-be Apollonian stance would require critical scrutiny, and not only of the new obstacles that have arisen to thwart "forward communication," indeed any kind of world-shaping praxis. It would also require a strategy for releasing such an inquiry from the mythical closure of horizons that imitates but is not identical with the gathering dusk into which we are trying to peer.

NOTE

1   Innis commented on Plato's critique of writing in the *Phaedrus* in the third of the Reith Lectures, published as *Empire and Communications* (1950, 68–70).

15 Space at the Margins: Critical Theory and Colonial Space after Innis

JODY BERLAND

The 1994 centenary of the birth of one of Canada's most influential intellectuals, economic historian and communication theorist Harold Innis, has stimulated scholars from many regions and disciplines to enter into dialogue with his work and with one another. For those of us writing about culture, revisiting Innis has also been informed by the emergence of a major body of writing in critical cultural theory that focuses on the cultural and spatial strategies of European colonization and their ongoing effects in the trend subsequently termed "globalization." Among the significant works in this oeuvre, which began to appear in the late 1970s and continues today with no signs of diminishing, we might include, roughly in chronological order and with no claim to comprehensiveness: Edward Said's *Orientalism*, Neil Smith's *Uneven Development*, Doreen Massey's *Spatial Divisions of Labour*, Edward Soja's *Postmodern Geographies*, Timothy Mitchell's *Colonizing Egypt*, David Harvey's *The Condition of Postmodernity*, the English translation of Henri Lefebvre's *The Production of Space*, Michael Featherstone's *Global Cultures*, Rob Shield's *Places on the Margin*, Said's *Culture and Imperialism*, Anthony King's *Culture, Globalization and the World System*, Keith and Pile's *Place and the Politics of Identity*, Derek Gregory's *Geographical Imaginations*, and Lash and Urry's *Economies of Signs and Space*, as well as related work by Fredric Jameson, James Clifford, Arjun Appadurai, Meaghan Morris, Sharon Zukin, among others, and important articles published in *Antipode, Cartographica, Inscriptions, New Formations, Public Culture, Society and Space*, and other journals.

The books I have just mentioned, however, do not contain a single reference to Innis's publications, ideas, or influence. I find this rather startling and significant. I began to have suspicions that it was also bizarre when I heard a reputable scholar assert – at a recent conference in Buffalo, NY, on "Postcolonial Geographies and Changing Sites of Subjectivity" – that what was lacking in the literature was a materialist analysis of colonial space. "Excuse me," I said, "but Innis did introduce such an analysis, and scholars have been elaborating it for some half a century – how do you account for its absence in this discussion?" "Oh," said he in the casually helpful manner of a British academic teaching at a prestigious American university; "you have to understand about intellectual capital."

Happily I was able to go home and share this anecdote with a community that could recognize its ironic implications. As every reader of Innis knows, the differential production of "intellectual capital" is a necessary cornerstone of the very complex dynamic constituting modern and contemporary centre–margin relations. Innis's principal contribution to the history and theory of culture is his insistence on the central role of communication and transportation technologies in materially mediating economic, administrative, cultural, and intellectual life. Shaped by their commercial and geographical context, these technologies facilitate the ongoing production of centres and margins – that is, spatially differentiated hierarchies of political-economic power. Placing technology and space at the centre of his research enabled Innis and critical scholars influenced by him to establish a reflexively marginal approach to the strategic imbrications of technology, geography, culture, knowledge, and power that have shaped Western imperialism, and in particular ways in the twentieth century.

My above-mentioned search of book indexes suggests that Innis's approach might be somehow incompatible with the critical discourses on culture and politics now proliferating in international academe, which tend to concentrate on the construction of individual subjects/identities and to treat the material circulation of knowledge as a transparent frame for their thought. Further, we could surmise that white anglophone Canadian scholars (especially political economists of any description) do not offer sufficiently charismatic models for the struggle against European colonial practices of the past two centuries, at least as this struggle is currently defined by subaltern scholarship in the United States. Canadians are not perceived as "other" there because of the terms in which culture and identity are understood.

These "absences" of Innis in contemporary scholarship on post-colonial culture and globalization furnish a convenient pathway to an exploration of the notion of the "margin" as a geophysical, cultural, and political entity. Given the rapid globalization of communication and information, the omnipresent evocation of marginality as the cornerstone of postmodern experience, and the radical decentring claims made on behalf of Internet and other cyber-technologies, this has become an important critical task. Fredric Jameson includes a feeling of being on the periphery among his seven features of postmodernity; de Certeau claims that "marginality is becoming universal"; and modern liberalism is reconstituting itself by calling for "the incorporation of the 'marginal' into a de-politicising framework that co-opts it" (Shields 1991, 276–7).[1] In these accounts, marginality is both everywhere and nowhere. My purpose here is to consider what Innis contributed to the notion of the "margin," what research on the production and representation of space can teach us about this concept, and whether marginality remains a spatial relationship in the contemporary global order of things.

TRAINS AND BOATS AND PLANES

Innis's analysis of centre–margin relations in modern colonial history antedates his work on communications and to a large extent shapes its parameters. For Innis, as for any theorist of colonialism and imperialism, the notion of the margin implies a notion of a centre and of a necessary, dialectically productive relationship between the two. As James Carey explains Innis' challenge to the dominant model of American history: "Every frontier, in short, has a back tier" (Carey 1989, 151). American historians had identified the experience of conquering the new frontier as the foundation of "manifest destiny." "Big spatial ideas," wrote Ellen Churchill Semple in 1911, "born of ... ceaseless regular wandering, outgrow the land that bred them and bear their legitimate fruit in wide imperial conquests" (in Kern 1983, 226). This suggests that it was solely contact with the land, or even the land itself, that gave rise to the culture of conquest, a proposition that (as we see again when we turn to the "nature" of colonial territories) deserves a most sceptical response.

Innis's scepticism about the frontier hypothesis originated with his research on the fur trade, which led him to emphasize the development of the canoe, boat, and rail routes that transported European commerce to the new world. European settlers entered into the fur trade in order to obtain profitable export goods to trade with Europe for imported goods conducive to the continuation of their way of life in the new country. As Innis argues, "The importance of metropolitan centres in which luxury goods were in most demand was crucial to the development of colonial North America. In these centres goods were manufactured for the consumption of colonials and in these centres goods produced in the colonies were sold at the highest price" (Innis 1995, 4).[2]

Two crucial and thoroughly imbricated historical patterns emerged in Canada from this trade: the development of increasingly rapid transport routes across the Canadian Shield and eventually through to the Pacific coast, and the emergence of a mercantile policy organized around the export of natural resources, or "staples," for external markets. The combination of natural, technological, and administrative forces producing the fur and fish trades helped subordinate "agriculture, industry, transportation, trade, finance, and governmental activities ... to the production of the staple for a more highly specialized manufacturing community" (5). The manufacturing community, or "back tier," is located in Europe.

Innis showed that patterns of transportation and trade in Canada were shaped by the ongoing imposition of European administrative and commercial imperatives onto indigenous landscape and culture, first through trade routes that traced and swallowed up traditional hunting and travel routes, then in the administrative patterns of governance, industry and finance that created Canada as a colonial nation-state. The transformation from settlement to colony (and later to nation, and then – as Innis reminds us – back to colony) was facilitated by the strategic construction of transport and communication technologies along patterns that enabled European colonizers to conquer and appropriate the land, the natural resources, and the cultures of the "New World." In emphasizing the material practices through which Europe produced a new geography of colonial space, Innis anticipates the critical interventions of "post-colonial geography" by some fifty years. Like Lefebvre, Soja, and Jameson, Innis seeks to define a materially and ontologically based relationship between space and time that requires a fundamental reconceptualization of space itself. Space is neither an empty frontier nor a backdrop for history, but the very subject-matter of historical change. Like these theorists, Innis conceives topographical space as produced space and shows that the production of space and the production of social life are one process. Communication technologies are understood as practices that both respond to and mediate the social relations of a particular society, by setting the limits and boundaries within which both power and knowledge operate (Jhally 1993, 64). While natural resources play a role in the creation of geopolitical margins, colonial space is a product not of nature but of social practice.

Central to the production of imperial space for Innis is a dynamic inverse interdependence between time and space through which communication technologies shape the materialities of knowledge. The relationship between space and time is inversely interdependent in that communication technologies, developed in imperial civilizations seeking to perpetuate or expand their power, seek to create monopolies of knowledge by emphasizing either time or space at the relative expense of the other. Communications media shape societies drawn into the axis of imperial power through the various effects of "space bias" and "time bias," each of which grows in proportion to the diminishing of the other. The dominance of one over the other (i.e., the attempt to control the transmission of knowledge over space or over time) ensures the foundation but also the downfall of every historical empire.

In modern Western culture, space-biased modes of communication such as paper and telegraphs (and related technologies: ships, trains, satellites, computers) allow the acquisition, transmission, and control of information over an ever-expanding geographical space. Because they are light, easily reproduced and disseminated, and quickly replaced, they do not further the elite's monopolization or preservation of knowledge for perpetuity. Power is sought through development of the most "advanced," most up-to-date, farthest reaching, and most quickly disseminated information. Access to space becomes the precondition for all empowering knowledge, including knowledge of or continuity with the past. Distance and history – space and time – are themselves redefined through mediation by these technologies.

In analysing societies in terms of their balance of inverse dynamics of space and time, Innis's framework is arguably more subtle than that of many space theorists today who posit, as Doreen Massey has cogently argued, a variety of binary oppositions between space and time. With important exceptions, these theorists still tend to conceive space as stasis, as a passive entity that registers response to change and thus stands opposed to time, which is dynamic and active. It is no coincidence, she suggests, that both "space and the feminine are frequently defined in terms of dichotomies in which each of them is most commonly defined as not-A" (Massey 1994, 257). In this paradigm, space is a wheat field and time is a train shooting across it. For an alternative critical vantage point she turns to physics, from which she concludes that "definitions of both space and time in themselves must be constructed as the result of interrelations" (261). Massey refers here to the transformation of physics by Einstein and Minkowski, who concluded that "henceforth space by itself, and time by itself, are doomed to fade away into mere shadows, and only a kind of union of the two will preserve an independent reality." Einstein rejected "the evolution of a three-dimensional experience" in favour of a four-dimensional physical reality (Kern 1983, 206). Innis introduces a similar notion of space–time interaction into his history of communication, which (without adding direct insight to the relationship between space and gender) identifies material processes through which time and space achieve their specific configurations and inter-relations. The space of western Canada is both sought and produced by the building of the railway. The wheat cannot be understood apart from the train.

Like more recent theorists, Innis viewed colonial space as traversed space – not the empty landscape of a wilderness, or geometrical, abstractly quantifiable space, but space that has been mapped and shaped by specific imperial forms of knowledge and interest. Thus the fur trade routes, the Canadian Pacific Railway (CPR), the rise of American newspaper monopolies in interdependence with Canada's pulp and paper industry, and, later, cars, television, data processing, and satellite broadcasting all form part of the apparatus whereby space is transformed into colonial space. A central aspect of this production of colonial space is the capacity of technology to mediate ontologically between power and knowledge, as well as spatially between centre and periphery. Modern space-binding communications media facilitate not only the growth of empire, but also the shaping of cultures within its reach.

As several commentators have observed, Innis's emphasis on the particular space-binding imperatives of modern imperialism arose from his own experience as a mid-century Canadian: returning from a devastating war in which victorious Canadian soldiers had been humiliated as colonials, tracing the routes, strategies, and effects of the founding European empire while witnessing the rapid rise of the new empire to the south.[3] If European officers brutalized colonial soldiers on the basis of assumed cultural superiority, democracy seemed unlikely to fare any better under the new forms of monopoly accompanying what he called "the change from British imperialism to American imperialism" (Innis 1995, xiii). Steven Kern, tracing Europe's obsession with spatial expansion, notes: "By 1900 ... all nations assumed that growth was good, and none questioned the wisdom of trying to achieve it." National cultures across Europe shared the conviction that "big is good," along with the "implied political imperatives – to expand for greatness or fall into mediocrity" (Kern 1983, 235–6). For Innis, the postwar expansionism of American economic and political power both reiterated and departed from Europe's imperial traditions and the imperial strategies of Greece and Rome, from which Innis derived his model of communication and empire. The rapid "mechanization of knowledge," which was flinging recorded music, films, and television programs across the large terrain of North American culture had to be understood as the basis for a new mode of imperial expansion that both continued and departed from older patterns of imperialist history.

In "A Plea for Time," Innis argues that "the balance between time and space has been seriously disturbed with disastrous consequences to Western civilization. Lack of interest in problems of duration in Western civilization suggests that the bias of paper and printing has persisted in a concern with space. The state has been interested in the enlargement of territories and the imposition of cultural uniformity on its peoples" (1951a, 76). Like Spengler, whose *Decline of the West* he mentions in this essay, Innis is dismayed by modern culture's Faustian obsession with spatial expansion and conquest and its consequent vulnerability to an unstable body politic, in which "even moments seemed of overwhelming insignificance" (in Kern 1983, 139, 259).[4] Responding to the acceleration of space-biased communications precipitated during this period, Innis directs his critique to the political and cultural consequences of the accelerating mechanization of knowledge. He describes "the modern obsession with present-mindedness" (1951a, 76) as a necessary consequence of space-biased communication and as a crucial strategy of modern industrialism, affecting every region touched by its imperatives. This obsession is evident in every domain of knowledge production: in journalism, which creates newsworthiness increasingly separate from place, ethics, or community; in science, which accumulates knowledge by "continually liquidating its past"; in academe, which suffers from overspecialization and the bureaucratic fragmentation and transience of knowledge;[5] and (to extrapolate once again) in modernist aesthetics, with its will to release perception from memory.

Innis's later essays are haunted by anxiety about the growth of monopolistic, American-dominated mass media fuelled by marketing and sensationalism, the ideological ascendancy of economic rationality and technological change, Canada's distinct but disempowered scepticism about the marketplace as fountainhead of democracy, the increasing power of metropolitan centres, growing political instability, and social atomization. Innis shares with many interwar intellectuals a constellation of military experience, education, and disposition, which produced a strong, modernist pessimism vis-à-vis mass media and mass culture.

In his peculiarly Canadian resistance to these new developments,

Innis represents, as Charles Acland suggests (p. 251, above), a "historical bridge between an Arnoldian vision of culture and an epistemological critique of power and empires." This connection is as characteristic of postwar Canadian thought as the alliance of nationalism and liberal humanism culminating in the report of the Massey Commission (Canada 1951).[6] Innis constructs this bridge with his critique of new communication technologies as monopolies of knowledge and his countering evocation of oral culture, whose capacity for dialogue and creative thinking offers an antidote to the stifling of independent thought in the new regime. Oral culture becomes a mode of resistance from the "margins" against the expansionist monopolization of knowledge at the centre, with its now-dangerous lack of self-reflexivity, cultural flexibility, and dialogue.

SPATIAL STRATEGIES

For Innis, the struggle between continuous technological change and the residual practices and (dis)continuities of oral culture characterizes modern history. In this history, control of and access to information technology shape the parameters of communication, knowledge, and memory and thereby more generally determine the proximity to and nature of power itself. A "margin" is a space drawn into the axes of imperial economy, administration, and information that remains "behind" (to put it in temporal terms) or "outside" (in terms of industrial and political power). The capacities of communication technologies facilitate this simultaneous integration and extrusion of colonized territories. The margin is a spatial concept, but colonial space is the product, not the predecessor, of colonizing practices. In other words, colonial space is not simply acquired. In the course of being "mastered" it is *produced*: its usable topographies are shaped, in dialectical interaction with its own resources, to serve the requirements of empire.

We hear echoes of this idea in Lefebvre's insistence that "(social) space is a (social) product" (1991, 26). As Lefebvre puts it:

The state and each of its constituent institutions call for spaces – but spaces which they can then organize according to their specific requirements; so there is no sense in which space can be treated solely as an *a priori* condition of these institutions and the state which presides over them. Is space a social relationship? Certainly – but one which is inherent to property relationships (especially the ownership of the earth, of land) and also closely bound up with the forces of production (which impose a form on that earth or land); here we see the polyvalence of social space, its "reality" at once formal and material. Though a *product* to be used, to be consumed, it is also a *means of production*; networks of exchange and flows of raw materials and energy fashion space and are determined by it. Thus this means of production, produced as such, cannot be separated either from the productive forces, including technology and knowledge, or from the social division of labour which shapes it, or from the state and the superstructures of society. (85)

Innis's ideas complement Lefebvre's history of space, emphasizing structures and "biases" of communication, rather than land and labour, as productive forces mediating between imperial power and the social, political, and cognitive transformation of space. Media and information technologies and the entire material, spatial, and social organization of knowledge are part of (and central to) the "means of production" whereby natural space is produced as productive space, as part of the hierarchically organized social space of contemporary capitalism.

This process of making spaces useful is both positive and negative. It both makes (produces, enables) and *un*makes (dispossesses). Derek Gregory (1994) reminds us that a central concern of post-colonial scholarship is the emphasis on "the dispossession that the West visited upon colonial societies through a series of intrinsically *spatial strategies*." He invites us to interpret this claim with reference to de Certeau's notion of "strategy," which describes "the means through which a constellation of power is inscribed in its own – its 'proper-place.'" De Certeau defines "strategies" as "[a]ctions which, thanks to the establishment of a place of power (the property of a proper), elaborate theoretical places (systems and totalizing discourses) capable of articulating an ensemble of physical places in which forces are distributed. They combine these three types of place and seek to master each by means of the others. They thus privilege spatial relationships. At the very least they attempt to reduce temporal relations to spatial ones through the analytical attribution of a proper place to each particular element" (1984, 38; cited in Gregory 1979, 168). Gregory concludes from de Certeau's passage that strategies "mark the triumph of space over time (the production of a 'proper place') ... the mastery of places through sight ... and the power to 'transform the uncertainties of history into readable spaces'" (Gregory 1994, 168). Of course the securing of a "proper place" can never be complete; in modern capitalism, as David Harvey has shown in many writings, place must be constantly defined and redefined, built and rebuilt, claimed and reclaimed. The triumph of space over time is necessarily contingent and temporary. Secured space must be continuously reproduced, and its meanings reconsolidated through new strategies, new technologies of power, and new modes of negotiation and resistance.

Like other colonial historians, Innis understands colonial power as the right and capability to determine, in interaction with colonial space itself, the principle strategies (or technologies) for the mastery and development of social space. His essays on communication describe a range of intellectual and symbolic ramifications arising from conflicts between space and time, orality and visuality, community and hierarchy shaping centre–periphery relationships. Rather than emphasizing modes of representation, Innis contextualizes these dynamics (space–time, visuality–orality, hierarchy–community, centre–periphery) in relation to material developments in print, navigation, rail, and other modes of transport and communication. The organization of space and time effected by these developments – by means of "content-free" media such as the telegraph and the train, as much as the newspaper or the photograph – structures the material forms and limits of knowledge, as well as our relationships with place and with one another. Here Innis reveals the limits and inadequacies of analysing power in terms of representation.

Like de Certeau, Innis describes sight, or visual knowledge, as a privileged mode of communication. If visuality emerged as a preferred vehicle for authoritative or colonizing strategies of representation, this is because visual media promote specific, limited modes of perception and understanding and of economic and spatial organization, which shape the society and culture in which they circulate. "Communication based on the eye in terms of printing and photography had developed a monopoly which threatened to destroy Western civilization first in war and then in peace," he writes, in "A Plea for Time." "This monopoly emphasized individualism and in turn instability and created illusions in catchwords such as democracy, freedom of the press, and freedom of speech ... As modern developments in communication have made for greater realism they have made for greater possibilities of delusion" (1951a, 80–2).

Innis refers here to his theory that the doctrine of freedom of the press was a key instrument in the formation of press monopolies that relied on (and helped to maintain) Canada as the source of raw materials for American industry. He does not set out to analyse what is in the newspapers. Instead he analyses how the production of newspapers, as a mediation of the materials, technologies, and "systems and totalizing discourses" (to borrow de Certeau's words) surrounding them, participates in the production of centres, which produce and disseminate those "systems and totalizing discourses" and margins, which produce newsprint along with a certain scepticism about that knowledge. Newspapers, together with the transport technologies that produce and disseminate them, facilitated a centralization, or "geographic bundling," of newswriting. News from a variety of places is gathered and juxtaposed, yielding a process through which place is emphasized through the expansion of technological capabilities, but de-emphasized through the editorial process. This simultaneous centralization (of both content and distribution) works to reorient the sense of both place and time among readers.[7] Through newspapers, the centre seeks to maintain power over the margins: through productive relationships (wherein manufactured goods are exchanged for raw materials), through the dissemination and influence of a particular mode of knowledge, and through the monopolizing ideology of the freedom of the press.

Thus the production of American industry (i.e., the production of a centre) cannot be separated from the production of a staples-based economy in Canada (the margin), and the dialectical relationship that arose between them and produced them both is economic, technological, spatial, and cultural all at the same time. To this day we cannot escape its effects. In the cultural industries, we export musicians, actors, and writers (along with one or two select series) and import the schedules of entire TV networks. The process of spatial transformation exemplified here by the newspaper can be deciphered in all subsequent technologies.

TECHNOLOGIES OF THE MARGIN

"What *is* a margin?" I asked a friend recently. "You know what a margin is," she replied, "It's outside the body of the text. It's what holds the page together. Also," she added, "it's where you write your notes." By pointing to the metaphor's roots in the spatio-visual configuration of the printed word, this description raises useful questions for interrogating the heterogeneous nature of marginal space. How does it hold the page together? What text is it outside of, and how is it kept there? To what extent is the margin's shape determined by its text? Is the determination unilateral, or fragmented, dynamic, and contradictory? To what extent does the determination go the other way? Isn't a text also shaped by its margin? And does this occluded margin necessarily wish to be included in the central body from which it stands apart and observes?

As we have seen, Innis defines a margin as the external or dependent pole in a spatially administered dynamic hierarchy of politico-economic power mediated by technologies and modes of communication. His research describes the formation of monopolies that control the circulation of knowledge and information and the simultaneous emergence of territorial dependencies, which centralize and decentralize such knowledge and information. Marginal uses of technology can be innovative, critical, and destabilizing and can momentarily disrupt the control of information. However, their efficacy is limited by the complex nature of communication technology itself, which (and it is here that Innis differs most strongly from McLuhan) is not just a formal mechanism, but a set of relationships, shaped by economic, legal, and cultural constraints as well as by technological capacities in the pure sense. Through control of such constraints – copyright, ownership and distribution, economies of scale, technical standards, technical obsolescence, government regulations, research and citation, and so forth – the centre works to maintain power over communicative space.

Centre-margin relations are tied then to social, technical, and ontological imbalances of time and space, whose symptoms include an acceleration of speed in technological and cultural change, a constant displacement of oral culture and of collective memory, and an increasing instrumentalization of space as central to the practices of power. Historically, as Innis argues, the rise of print media facilitated the democratization of knowledge and the triumphs of humanistic culture. Yet the spread of space-biased communication technology has led to the accelerating marginalization of oral culture, rationalization of knowledge, and displacement of difference, reflexivity, and duration. The American empire's predilection for conquering space through media thus represents both a continuation of Western culture and a movement towards its destruction. The continuity with Western culture is expressed in its extension of the modernizing, visualizing, and rationalizing space bias of paper and print, but this bias exceeds the possibility of spatial or ontological balance, marginalizing or obliterating media appropriate to memory, tradition, spirituality, and dialogue – all aspects of oral culture that have been appropriated and transformed through the production of technological space.

Unlike other postwar intellectuals hostile to the degradation of (Western) humanistic culture, Innis characterizes this threat not in terms of symbols, meanings, or the degradation of values, but rather in terms of the material processes through which knowledge is disseminated, that work to shape the ratios of reason and emotion, technique and memory, power and location, space and time. This is a history not of ideologies, states, classes, or popular struggles, but of rivers, railways, and radios. Each of these represents a changed productive mediation between centralized imperial power and its proximate and distant subjects. Innis's approach is thus strongly materialist, but not Marxist; aside from its lack of interest in class it focuses, as Daniel Drache has observed, on relations of trade – and thus the production of space – rather than on production itself (1995, xx).

Still, there are striking correspondences between Innis and Marx in their treatment of time and space. In *Grundrisse*, Marx notes: "[C]apital by its nature drives beyond every spatial barrier. Thus the creation of the physical conditions of exchange – of the means of communication and transport – the annihilation of space by time – becomes an extraordinary necessity for it ... Thus, while capital must on one side strive to tear down every spatial barrier to intercourse, i.e. to exchange, and conquer the whole world for its market, it strives on the other side to annihilate this space with time, i.e. to reduce to a minimum the time spent in motion from one place to another" (in Smith 1991, 93).

For Innis, as for Marx, time succumbs to space in response to the imperializing capacities of the communication and information technologies accompanying the expansion of international commerce and trade. His emphasis on this point, and his study of ancient and modern history through the conceptual lens of technology and media bias, remind us how much the emergent imperialism of the modern age was based on increasingly covert economic and technological strategies for colonizing space. The classic imperialistic practices of the European "Age of Empire" had reached a state of traumatic crisis during the early part of the twentieth century. The very nature of imperialism was being transformed before Innis's eyes with the changing shape of global politics and the shift of imperial power to the New World. If European officers ruled the battles of the First World War with colossal arrogance, Europe's claim to the superiority of an advanced civilization lay in bloody tatters in the battlefields of Europe. A survivor of that catastrophic slaughter, in the face of which every form of human confidence would suffer, Innis was alert to the replacement of one economy of power by a new type, still predicated on the colonization of time by space, but characterized, as Said puts it, by "the privileged role of culture in the modern imperial experience" (1993, 5).

Obviously this is a cultural imperialism of a new sort. *I Love Lucy* does not look at all like the contemptuous arrogance of a European who assumes that imperial rule and cultural superiority are one and the same thing (though both may convey the assumption of universal value – one concerning truth and beauty, the other, fun and freedom). Stuart Hall describes this shift as:

[the emergence of a] new type of globalization [which] is not English, it is American. In cultural terms, the new kind of globalization has to do with a new form of global mass culture, very different from that associated with English identity, and the cultural identities associated with the nation-state in an earlier phase. Global mass culture is dominated by the modern means of cultural production, dominated by the image which crosses and re-crosses linguistic frontiers much more rapidly and more easily, and which speaks across languages in a much more immediate way ... One might think of satellite television as the prime example. Not because it is the only example but because you could not understand satellite television without understanding its grounding in a particular advanced national economy and culture and yet its whole purpose is precisely that it cannot be limited any longer by national boundaries. (1991, 27)

If this analysis echoes Innis's thoughts on newspapers and the mass media, I quote it only to emphasize how much Innis recognized and anticipated these new strategies of globalization. By 1900, commentators were already predicting the rapid elimination of distance, cultural difference, and national boundaries. Because the technologies were so new, these commentators forefront the technologies themselves.

Writing half a century later, Innis makes this shift of emphasis explicit. The connection and contrast between British and American imperialism have little to do with cultural representation; they are rooted in the complex cumulative impact of cultural technologies, whose manifestation in content is only part of their effects. Carey dates the emergence of this new era with the rise of the telegraph. This innovation enables information to be separated from human bodies, so that henceforth it is possible to traverse (and subsequently control) a range of sites by exporting messages – telegraphs, airwaves, databases, satellite beams, and so on – rather than armies (Carey 1989). Like paper and books, these new carriers extend the reach and potential impact of monopolies of knowledge over broader expanses of space. Unlike paper and books, they are impervious to linguistic or national borders – a characteristic that is increasingly part of their mandate and design.

This new expansionism still aims to produce and to capitalize space but this process now takes different form. Rather than setting out to conquer unclaimed, autonomous, or otherwise occupied spaces around the globe, empires now expand their domain through the recolonization of already produced spaces, by means of the recommodification of services, urban renewal, biogenetic and space research, continuous software updating, the influx of new entertainment and cultural technologies.

A major effect of this shift is that American political leaders and citizens can thereby view themselves not as members of an imperial and thus more advanced civilization, as had their European predecessors, but rather as "a righter of wrongs around the world, in pursuit of tyranny, in defence of freedom no matter the place or cost" (Said's words). It is not hard to conjure up the pleasures and compulsions of writing on the margin of that text. However, it is becoming much more difficult to determine what or where the margin is.

APORIAS OF UNEVEN DEVELOPMENT

The history of modern imperialism has been described above as the history of time succumbing to space. In this narrative local cultures and knowledge forms are uprooted, fragmented, and replaced by the space-levelling, distance-abolishing, rapidly changing dissemination of information via electronic media. Yet as this discussion has suggested, contemporary or "post-industrial" imperialism also involves a different, albeit related process in which space succumbs to the continuous recommodification of time. The ongoing differentiation of space that we associate with the concept of margins thus coexists with the growing equalization of space that we associate with globalization. As Neil Smith points out, both processes are a necessary part of uneven development, whereby different regions of the world (and within them, different social groups and cultural economies) are differentially empowered by global trade (1991, 97–130).

The continuing differentiation of space that produces margins is both an originary foundation and a geopolitical result of the global division of labour, wherein some regions provide natural resources (or, more contemporaneously, technological resources such as telecommunications hardware and silicon chips) to other regions, which thereby reproduce their own advantages in wealth and power. This is the process of differentiation that Innis had in mind when he placed the production of staples at the heart of Canadian economic history. While globalization (or, less euphemistically, transnational capitalism) continues to produce inequitable difference, there is also an unending, always-incomplete process of capitalization that works to make regions interchangeable through what Smith calls the equalization of space.[8] This process "equalizes" by subjecting local markets, industrial processes and commodities, patterns of urban growth, sciences and technologies, narratives and fantasies, forests and rivers, and so on to parallel competitive processes of innovation and exploitation. This does not mean that every nation, region, and city (not to mention gender, class, and ethnicity) will – or can – achieve equitable levels of wealth and autonomy. Nor does it imply that difference among nations or regions disappears. It does mean, however, that subjects on the margin experience both processes simultaneously – one compels the palpable differentiation of a space, and the other compels its functional equalization with other spaces in the globe.

This is the spatial configuration of what Apparadurai calls the "central tension" of global culture – that between cultural homogenization and cultural heterogenization, with all their singular complexities (1990, 295). Chatterjee locates a similar dynamic at the very heart of colonial societies, which he analyses under the rubric of the "rule of colonial difference" (1993, 26). Nationalist nation-states seek to emphasize cultural differences between colonizer and colonized, he argues, so as to be able to declare sovereignty over the "inner domain of national life." At the same time, in the "outer" domains of economy, administration, and law, nationalism fights to "erase the marks of colonial difference." The creation of sameness and of difference can occur interdependently; since Canada is a peculiar, modern, post-technology sort of colony, this conflict is imbedded in the very body of the culture, as well as in that of the economy.[9] For nearly a century, communication technologies have been the site of both difference-making and difference-abolishing policies and instruments. Government and corporate interests have employed strategies that variously encourage and sabotage the goal of cultural difference. Such strategies are inextricably bound to emergent technologies and their paradoxical effects. A government apparatus that once evoked national difference to justify the spatial expansion of communication technologies later evoked the inexorable drive of the global information revolution to further the same end.[10] The often-disruptive process of negotiation between these dynamics forms what D. Massey calls the "power-geometry" of contemporary globalization, whereby space becomes a "complex web of relations of domination and subordination, of solidarity and cooperation" (1994, 265).

The complex duality of this process finds a parallel in the technologies that effect it. For they, like the institutional trajectories that frame them, simultaneously produce and abolish difference in their subjects. At least that is the hope of marginal cultures that take them up to tell their own stories or to advance their own local purposes. In this sense, analogous with Foucault's association of knowledge and power, Innis's framework depicts technology as part of a complex and powerful apparatus that both generates and selectively administers or withholds power. Since communication media influence the forms of social organization that are possible, "competition for new means of communication [is] a principal axis of the competitive struggle" (Carey 1968,

273). Marginal groups must both resist and depend on the cultural technologies that bring them to awareness of themselves as margins. For spatially defined margins such as Canada, or Canada's own peripheries in the east and the north, the meanings of place are also subject to this ambivalent conflict.

NATURAL DIFFERENCES

The concept of "equalization of spaces" has an easy set of visual referents: the "golden arches," Hollywood, Sony, automated bank machines, cars, computers, and the internet. This aspect of globalization depends on the ability to free the profitable capacities of a particular location from its physical or geographical specificities. Differentiation, in contrast, involves learning new ways to derive profit from spatial or geographical difference. Here too images spring readily to mind: lakes and snowy mountains, animals and trees, beaches and monuments (so long as they appear ancient and unchanged, like mountains) in various parts of the world.

As we are so often reminded, the wealth of nations now depends less on sovereignty over natural resources (except in tourist zones) and more on access to information and information technologies. In traditional modernization theory, regional disparities are potentially abolished by this change. Any countries can have microchips, if they manage development properly, and so any nation can join the First or at least the Second World.

The flawed logic here lies in presupposing that it is the originary presence of natural resources (fish, lumber, ivory, uranium, beaches) that produced a marginal national economy dependent on them to the advantage of other interests and the exclusion of other economic activities. If geography and nature account for marginality, then technological development – the transcendence of nature – will, it is thought, transform that status. Canadian experience makes this claim dubious at best. We need to demolish both propositions in this hypothesis – not only because Innis has (wrongly, I think) been accused of being a geographical determinist, but, more important, because this demolition has implications for thinking about nature and technology in relation to marginal spaces.

Neither the discovery of natural resources nor the presence of the colonist explorers and settlers who discovered them was a fortuitous event in the colonies of Europe. The "age of discovery" betrayed its medieval origins by endowing far-off places with extraordinary cosmological and magical powers. When travellers reached the New World, their encounter was shaped by a readiness to find a natural paradise suffused with both abundant riches and savage wilderness (Helms 1988, 224–6).[11] By the eighteenth century, when Jesuits and entrepreneurs were travelling up the St Lawrence and setting out to cross the Canadian Shield, the powerful, magical qualities projected onto the inhabitants of these newly discovered worlds had been taken over by the travellers themselves. Eighteenth-century travellers found themselves candidates for immortality as "'second creators' of distant worlds which for them were newly established and newly regarded not only with fear and fantasy, but also with the confident superiority of men, who, now God-like as much as God-fearing, having conquered the ocean with their bravery, skills, and intelligence, believed they could conquer whatever else they encountered" (260). This association of exploration and conquest was conveniently reinforced by more worldly incentives. In 1817, frustrated with the failure of previous expeditions, the British Admiralty offered twenty thousand pounds (sterling) to the discoverer of the Northwest Passage. Successive expeditions did much to popularize the vision of the Canadian north as a rich but dangerous place requiring great heroism and perspicacity to conquer (Shields 1991, 175).

What they encountered was fish (mainly cod), fur (mainly beaver), lumber, and, briefly, gold. These, as we saw above, were exported back to Europe in exchange for manufactured goods, which enabled settlers (Innis uses the less romantic term "migrants") to maintain "the cultural traits of a civilization ... [with] the least possible depreciation" (Innis 1995, 4). This pattern of trade came to dominate the economic, spatial, and administrative shape of Canada as a colonial nation, or what Innis termed a "staple economy" – a concept that requires our closer attention. In the same text, Innis writes:

The economic history of Canada has been dominated by the discrepancy between the centre and the margin of western civilization. Energy has been directed toward the exploitation of staple products and the tendency has been cumulative. The raw material supplied to the mother country stimulated manufacturers of the finished product and also of the products which were in demand in the colony. Large-scale production of raw materials was encouraged by improvement of technique of production, of marketing, and of transport as well as by improvement in the manufacture of the finished product. As a consequence, energy in the colony was drawn into the production of the staple commodity both directly and indirectly ... Agriculture, industry, transportation, trade, finance and governmental activities tend to become subordinate to the production of the staple for a more highly specialized manufacturing community. (5)

Innis's famous "staples theory" has engendered a long debate concerning the nature of Canadian political economy and the place of natural resources in it. The theory has been criticized for two types of determinism: geographical, in which nature determines trade and economic patterns; and economic, in which economic patterns shape politics. If staples theory is indeed a marriage of these two types of determinism, then it deserves critique as a reductionist and pessimistic view of Canada's politics, history, and potential future. Where colonial exploitation is naturalized through reference to nature ("as though every cod holds the seeds of its own commodity and labour market"[12]) then Canada's landscape and resources become one with their marginal economic status.

But this is not Innis's argument. Criticizing it on this ground reifies the role of nature in order to reject Innis's more complex paradigm *and* nature's more partial effectivity. In passages such as the following, Innis provides a more subtle analysis of the relationship among geographical, administrative, economic, and political factors:

The fur trade left a framework for the later Dominion ... Into the moulds of the commercial period, set by successive heavier and cheaper commodities, and determined by geographic factors, such as the St. Lawrence River and the Precambrian formation; by cultural considerations, such as the English and French languages; by technology, such as the canoe and the raft; by business organization, such as the Northwest Company and Liverpool timber firms; and by political institutions peculiar to France and England, were poured the rivers of iron and steel in the form of steamships and railways which hardened into modern capitalism. (1995, 72)

Nature and geography are not absent here, but they are mediated by economic, political, and technological forces such as boats and trains. While there is no denying Canada's physical nature (everyone knows that it's large, gorgeous, and cold), this difference, this nature, like any biological trait – human gender or race, for instance – exists in a social setting whose power dynamics determine its meanings and effects. It's not trees that create colonialism, but how trees are traded. Of course trees can be traded in many ways. Representations and myths of landscape have also contributed to the production of Canada's marginal identity. In the tree-filled, uninhabited landscapes dominating its favourite paintings and postcards, Canada appears as a wilderness whose pristine nature counterposes a civilization that is presumably elsewhere. In these representations, the economic and technological factors contributing to Canada's formation are transformed into what Rob Shields terms an "imaginary geography," through which mountains, lakes, and beavers are identified with national history, values, and sentiments (1991, 29). Historians, writers and artists, and the tourism industry have all colluded with colonial history by contributing to the image of Canada as a wilderness, variously welcoming, rich, and forbidding, but always "Other," whose destiny is defined by – and limited to – its beauty, wildness, and natural wealth (182–3).[13] In this mythos, economic development becomes either the sacrilegious plundering or the inevitable outcome of what nature has to offer.

In the latter view, Canada's economic development continues to be shaped by its importance as provider of natural resources. The problem arises not from patterns of economic imbalance or political subservience associated with this role, but from the anticipated limits of the natural resources themselves. Canadian policy advisers drew attention to this potential crisis in a recent discussion of the shift from resource to technology export. Their words help to demolish the second flawed proposition in the modernization hypothesis: that technologies eliminate dependence. They argue that only the expansion of "high technology sectors" can compensate for anticipated crises in the export of natural resources, which remains Canada's major source of wealth (Industry, Science and Technology Canada 1990, 1). But Canada devotes proportionately fewer funds to research and development than any other nation in the G-7 group of allied Western nations. "Assuming that Canadian industrial R&D is affected by the country's economic structure," the aforementioned study observes, "the heavy reliance on resource-based industries seems to be the major reason for Canadian industry's apparent lack of propensity to perform R&D" (5).[14]

In other words, Canada's already-produced position of relative dependence – its "natural" role as a deindustrialized marginal space – shapes its move into high technology in such a way as to perpetuate its role as a marginal economy. Technological investment and innovation cannot in themselves transform Canada from a marginal to a powerful First World economy, for they reproduce the very relationship they claim to transcend. While government publicity now presents Canada as a technologically sophisticated nation, celebrating its achievements in telecommunications and aerospace optical technologies – most recently, with a billboard campaign featuring photographs of Canadarm, Canada's contribution to NASA space exploration, to mark the anniversary of Canada's flag – such achievement does little to alter Canada's deindustrialized, branch-plant economy or its submission to the geopolitics of transnational capital.[15] The country may be technically and economically "advanced" in its use of communication technologies, and its means of production and consumption may partake of late-twentieth-century technicality. None the less, it remains a strategically underdeveloped economy in relation to the overall structure of global industry. Like less-developed nations, it is unable to consume what it produces or to produce what it consumes.

The nagging question that surrounds this representation is how well we understand its relationship to the territoriality known as Canada. Like our policy advisers, we are predisposed to read these portraits of technological innovation and economic growth in relation to a homogeneous understanding of the territorial/economic space of the nation-state. Yet that space is being fractured and fissured by worldwide, increasingly interdependent changes in finance, communication systems, and industrial growth. Is it still appropriate or useful to represent a national entity as an object of natural history? Given new patterns of "post-industrial" marginalization, is marginality still a valid *spatial* concept?

TIME AND SPACE REVISITED

We are now witnessing a dramatic restructuring of social space in which the meaning of space is ever more thoroughly intertwined with its social and geopolitical context. Globalizing technology creates ever greater integration among nations, among industries, and within/between technology and science. This process leads to a radical destabilization of place, or what Innis would call the displacement of time by space-biased technologies, leading to the rise of supranational formations, ranging from Sony to Greenpeace; to new patterns of cultural and natural colonization; and to shifting strategies of representation among communities identified with particular locales. Geopolitical strategies enacted through media and information technology are working to unravel space and place. Many observers now believe that global communications and information technologies have effectively abolished centre–margin relationships, if not difference in general.

The idea that media abolish centre–margin relations was enthusiastically advocated by McLuhan in the 1960s and 1970s. While print and roads centralize, he writes, electronic media decentralize. "Departmental sovereignties have melted away as rapidly as national sovereignties under conditions of electric speed," he maintains in *Understanding Media* (1964b) (without the ambivalence we feel about these meltings and the circumstances that surround them). "Obsession with the older patterns of mechanical, one-way expansion from centres to margins is no longer relevant to our electric world. Electricity does not centralize, but decentralizes. It is like the difference between a railway system and an electric grid system: the one requires railheads and big urban centres. Electric power, equally available in the farmhouse and the Executive Suite, permits any place to be a centre, and does not require large aggregations" (1964b, 47).

Let's not even talk about McLuhan's wishful thinking. Notice how much speed figures here as an agent of spatial transformation. Through instantaneously shared experience, margins are eliminated and everyone shares equally in the wealth of the global village. McLuhan elaborates this idea in a subsequent restatement. "The wheel and the road are centralizers because they accelerate up to a point that ships cannot. But acceleration beyond a certain point, when it occurs by means of the automobile and the plane, creates decentralism in the midst of the older centralism. This is the origin of the urban chaos of our time. The wheel, pushed beyond a certain intensity of movement, no longer centralizes. All electric forms whatsoever have a decentralizing effect, cutting across the older mechanical patterns like a bagpipe in a symphony" (1964b, 167).

For McLuhan the rapidity of electronic communication abolishes both distance and the hierarchical relations produced in its administration. Speed permits every place to be the centre of the universe. His argument on the growing autonomy of users bears some similarity to audience research in the 1980s, which sought to demonstrate that every television audience makes its own meanings, employs television or other media as instruments of independence or resistance to tradition and authority, and thereby retains control over its own semantic and political space. However, McLuhan's thesis has nothing to do with content, interpretation, or politics and everything to do with technological acceleration and the abolition of distance.

In an early essay comparing McLuhan and Innis, James Carey makes a suggestive observation. "If in fact the spatial bias of contemporary media does lead to a progressive reduction of regional variation within nations and transnational variation between nations," he says, "one must not assume that differences between groups are being obliterated as some mass society theorists characterize the process of homogenization ... I am suggesting that the axis of diversity shifts from a spatial or structural dimension to a temporal or generational dimension" (1968, 298). Writing in the late 1960s, Carey emphasizes generational conflict as the most emphatic manifestation of this difference. Today the generation gap seems almost quaint, so much has it been surpassed by innovation and differentiation in technical knowledge, use, vocabulary, and psychic investments. Time is no longer easily apprehended in relation to biological categories, or historical ones either. That does not mean that such categories are useless. To newer generations, Ursula Franklin observes, changed relationships among individuals, groups, cities, nations, and the globe may seem normal or inevitable. Unless people are incited to remember the different constellations of place and identity that preceded them, and to contemplate the way the restructuring of time and space arises not from inevitable technological change but from agencies of power and control, no one will question the inevitability of their reordering (Franklin 1992, 13 and passim).[16]

Innis's research suggests that empires collapse when their rulers' struggle for dominance overreaches itself, destroying the balance in politics, space, and time that makes a culture viable. The conquest of time or space ultimately sabotages the ruling groups seeking to master them. Emergent groups struggle for power through the use of countering technologies and means of communication. In this manner space-biased authority ascended and overruled time-biased authority with the rise of the printing press and the birth of modern capitalism. These developments led to the collapse of the church and ruling aristocracy and the rise of the nation-state. Under the aegis of the new empire, the technological mastery of space extended beyond the possibility of balance between space and time, and ultimately beyond the empire's capacity to maintain control over cultures within its reach. Writing on the telegraph, Carey observes that its dynamic expansionism created a tension "between the capability to expand and the capacity to rule" (1989, 212). The now-dominant space bias overreaches its own effectiveness and begins to be subsumed in a new paradigm, which both extends and sabotages it – speed.

As Paul Virilio delights in reminding us, temporal acceleration now permeates society at every level. "Today we are beginning to realize that systems of telecommunication do not merely confine *extension*, but that, in the transmission of messages and images, they also eradicate *duration* or delay." We recognize this: it is none other than the colonization of time by space. Virilio adds: "After the crisis of 'integral' spatial dimensions, which gave increased importance to 'fractional' dimensions, we might be witnessing, in short, the crisis of the temporal dimension of the present moment ... The speed of exposure of time-light should allow us to reinterpret the 'present' or this 'real instant' that is (lest we forget) the space-time of a real action facilitated by electronic machines" (1993, 3, 7).

In response to the capacities of these machines, the fragmenting–integrating production of space under capitalism has met its limits; its logic is not abandoned, but subsumed by the fragmenting-integrating recommodification of time. Like Carey, Virilio implies that marginality is becoming a temporal rather than a spatial relationship. Virilio seems to envisage the crisis of space-time as a chronological sequence rather than as an exacerbated ordering of spatio-temporal resources. The implication, in any case, is that margins and centres must continuously reconstitute themselves in an endlessly shifting, mobile, unstable process of electronically mediated flux. The centre cannot hold, as we are seeing with the American empire, though military and economic policies have not entirely abandoned this function.

Have the hierarchical production and differentiation of space been abolished then? What about space at the margins? "Throughout history," Lefebvre reminds us,

centralities have always eventually disappeared – some displaced, some exploded, some subverted. They have perished sometimes on account of their excesses – through "saturation" – and sometimes on account of their shortcomings, the chief among which, the tendency to expel dissident elements, has a backlash effect ... The interplay between centre and periphery is thus highly complex. It mobilizes both logic and dialectics, and is hence doubly determined...

This must emphatically not be taken as implying that contradictions and conflicts *in* space (deriving from time) have disappeared. They are still present, along with what they imply, along with the strategies and tactics to which they give rise, and along, in particular, with the class conflicts that flow from them. The contradictions *of* space, however, envelop historical contradictions, presuppose them, superimpose themselves upon them, carry them to a higher level, and amplify them in the process of reproducing them. Once this displacement has been effected, the new contradictions may tend to attract all the attention, diverting interest to themselves and seeming to crowd out or even absorb the old conflicts. This impression is false, however ... The production of things *in* space has not disappeared – and neither have the questions it raises ... in face of the production of space (1990, 333-334)

I take this to mean that however much these new technologies appear to efface spatial differences in favour of new techniques for the conquest/mobilization of time, we find the latter always inscribed onto the history of the former – as evidenced by Canadian technological R&D. Yet we should not underestimate the capability of these same technologies to undermine and destabilize entrenched modes of authority and power. That is an important part of their purpose and effect. Nation-states are undermined by global corporations; corporate structures, by speculation and mergers (if not as yet by home offices or internet); conventional types of knowledge by uncertainty and the threat of imminent displacement. Centres shift, margins create their own peripheries. Marginality becomes increasingly contingent, transitory, and complex, involving temporal as well as spatial relations. The race for technological supremacy paradoxically undermines the authority of every rule. Yet margins do not disappear, any more than power does. When we find that conjecture receiving too much attention, we should recall that less than ten percent of the world's population own telephones. In disregarding such details, today's technotopian culture has produced one of the more exclusive utopias in the history of Western thought.

Innis's challenge to the techno/populist optimism of contemporary thought may help to account for his invisibility in the corpus of transnational theory. Let us conclude with a summary of his work's implications for these discussions. Innis focuses on the capacities of imperial power to dispossess communities of their cultures and their history. His emphasis on the mechanization of knowledge reminds us that he apprehends colonization – or the colonial "production of space" – as a dispossession of history, of time, and of the resources of memory and knowledge as well as space in the traditional territorial sense. It is precisely the drive to expand and conquer space that leads to the debilitating hyperfragmentation of time, to what Innis calls the obsessive present-mindedness of contemporary culture. In the shadow of this drive, many forms of knowledge become marginal: history, myth, and oral tradition (when not suitable for publication); all "non-rational" forms of knowledge, whether of the body or of the spirit; or even, as my introductory comments suggest, critical political economy, which, like these others, offers an opportunity to scholars at the centre(s) to reflect on their complicity in an imperializing apparatus. This is where social and cultural resistance emerges to counterpoise the hypermodernizing logic of capital expansion. In Canadian spaces this resistance often involves a "conservative" slowing or "feminization" of social and narrative temporalities.

Strangely, Innis, unlike McLuhan, failed to include the cultures of any Native peoples in his discussion of oral tradition. Indeed he overlooks all local cultures or practices in his account. Innis theorizes place as a social and economic entity but takes into account no living place in particular. The technologies that produce his centres and margins never encounter the everyday lives, the complex technologically and geographically mediated power dynamics, the lively vestiges of myth and memory, the diverse imaginative activities of real men and women. It is this omission, not his attention to geography and technology as agents of history, that exposes him to the charge of determinism and reductionism. Nevertheless his work offers useful insights for cultural theory and practice. His resistance to the industrialization of knowledge and the "penetrative powers" of capital, and his hybrid inflections of anti-imperialism, anti-liberalism, cultural and topological conservatism, scepticism, and ambivalence towards technology and power, remain a powerful presence in Canadian cultural critique. In directing our attention to the materiality of communication processes, and their complex contexts and effects, he has endowed Canadian scholarship with a relentless "common sense" awareness of the economic and technological foundations of all cultural possibilities.

The analysis of communication technology as mediator between culture and power points to the need to evolve and defend a plurality of communication technologies working together as vehicles for memory, dialogue, technological autonomy, and the capacity for reflective critique – all endangered species in the new imperium. In this picture no single technology can achieve political democracy or ontological balance. Rather than celebrating or condemning the capacities of specific technologies, this paradigm suggests that we seek a better balance among space- and time-biased technologies and knowledge forms. By defending the material foundations for reflection, dialogue, and difference, we lay the foundation for resistance to all monopolies of knowledge and power. Such resistance is located not in particular identities, or modes of representation either, national or otherwise, but in reclaiming communication as a practice of dialogue and emplacement that shapes and is shaped by the exigencies of power.

This suggests that we define the "margin" as any site that enables communities to employ cultural technologies as counter-hegemonic cultural tools. Such spaces are today subject to vicious assault. The recommodification of information and experience, the erosion of non-commercial spaces, and the triumph of reactionary mercantile politics in the organization of cultural production have become part of the ongoing production of space, which implicates communities at every scale. These processes continue to produce centres and margins. These are not always clearly boundable places, as in the early days of the railway, but concern the disposition of space in its widest sense.

David Harvey argues that power derives from the ability to turn space into place. Following Foucault, he sees space as a "metaphor for a site or container of power which usually constrains but sometimes liberates processes *of becoming*" (1989, 213). Cultural technologies play an important role in this process of constraint and liberation. They shape the material communicative practices that order and facilitate the production of space – of people, meanings, and things in space – as a repository of social meaning and possibility. To extrapolate once more from Innis's thought, the hope for the democratization of this process lies in a multiplicity of communication sites; in their relative autonomy from commercial and political imperatives; their right to be slow and introspective, even dark and sentimental, as well as fast, canny, and pragmatic; and so, finally, in the preservation of reflection, dialogue, history, and the inconvenience of diverse oral cultures against technocratic appropriation and the consequent ontological dispossession of both space and time. This was, and remains, marginal thought at its best.

NOTES

1 Shields cites here Jameson (1984) and Michel de Certeau (1984).

2 The same trading patterns emerged in Australia, which began to export wool to Britain in the early nineteenth century. "Australia now had a clear function in the world. Into its colonies flowed capital, labour and technology, accompanied by the transfer of institutions, knowledge and resources. Most of these came from Britain. Out of the colonies flowed exports of foodstuffs and raw materials. Most of them went to Britain. Many of the other colonies within the British Empire developed a similar pattern" (Todd 1995, 4).

3 For commentaries on the effects of this historical context on Innis's work, see Melody, Salter, and Heyer, eds., 1981, 23; Angus 1993, 22; and Stamps 1995, 44. All describe Innis's "bitter awakening" serving under British military officers during the First World War.

4 Spengler (1926) *Decline of the West*. Spengler argues here that the modern era is characterized by the restless striving of the Faustian soul and is inherently temporal, possessing an "unsurpassably intense Will to the Future." Cf. Kern (1983, 105). Innis cites this work in "Industrialism and Cultural Values" (in 1995, 316) and "A Plea for Time" (in 1951a). He writes: "What Spengler has called the Faustian West is a result of living mentally and historically and is in contrast with other important civilizations which are 'ahistoric'" (1995, 378).

5 Innis addresses this concern in "The Mechanization of Knowledge" (in 1951a; 1995) and "A Plea for Time" (in 1951a; cf. Angus 1993).

6 Cf. Berland 1998b for connections and divergences between Massey and Innis.

7 Susan R. Brooker-Gross (1985) offers an Innisian reading of this.

8 "In constant opposition to the tendency toward differentiation, this tendency toward equalization, and the resulting contradiction, are the more concrete determinants of uneven development. This contradiction is resolved historically in the concrete pattern of uneven development." Neil Smith (1991) notes that this dichotomous process is evident in the levelling of the quality of working life, in the levelling of the urban–rural dichotomy, and in "the transformations of nature into a universal means of production" (114).

9 For a study of such contradictory cultural formation cf. Berland 1998a.

10 For the authoritative history of this conflict/collusion see Babe 1990. Babe makes this particular argument regarding the reversal of national sovereignty objectives (252–6).

11 Helms (1988) notes: "A form of paradise already held Western connotations prior to the discoveries, but the attribution of wilderness and its qualities to the West was new and clearly part of the effort to create and

identify a new cosmological locale" (226). Tracing the same history in a
more worldly context, Steven Greenblatt (1991) reminds us of the powerful association of wonder and greed with which Columbus met – and
wrote of – the New World.

12 Acland (chapter 13) summarizes the argument put forward by Robin
Neill (1981).

13 Shields (1991) cites an essay by the influential historian W.L. Morton
(1970): "[T]he ultimate and the comprehensive meaning of Canadian
history is to be found where there has been no Canadian history: in the
north" (183).

14 Significantly, this is not the case with electronics, aerospace, and computer industries, all areas of expertise that Canada has developed without
damage to its branch-plant relationship to u.s. industry. Todd (1995)
describes a comparable gap in research bridging scientific knowledge and
technological innovation in nineteenth-century Australia. Agents of local
science were active in "the process of assimilation of new technologies
into local production systems," she writes. "What they were not generally doing was carrying out research aimed at direct solution of technological problems by means of domestic research activity ... Whether
through lack of interest or lack of confidence, the ready availability of
overseas technology seems indeed to have pre-empted, or displaced, local
research programs aimed at development of new home-grown technologies to solve an acknowledged industry problem" (224–5). She concludes
that Australia's willingness to appropriate and choose technological
options from diverse sources contributed to its growing technological
sovereignty, if not independence; that its full achievement of this goal has
been blocked by its failure to achieve critical mass in the dynamic interaction between receivers and producers, or "firms, industries, sectors and
colonies"; and that dependency theory explains much, but not all, of the
structural imbalance of Australian science and technology.

15 See Babe 1990 and Berland 1996 for further discussion of satellites and
the Canadian space industry.

16 Franklin (1992) associates memory, community, and resistance on the
one hand, and globalization, amnesia, and passivity on the other hand, in
terms that are quite reminiscent of Innis's work.

16 Postmodern Themes in Innis's Works

RAY CHARRON

Harold Innis may be considered a "radical conservative" (Parker 1977, 553) or a moderate thinker advocating "balance and proportion" and thereby falling somewhere between George Grant's pessimism and the uncritical optimism of a Marshall McLuhan (Kroker 1984, 87–124). Such interpretations reflect the general understanding of Innis's work within the vanguard of communications studies. They suggest that, unlike his writings in economic history, his work in communication studies has inspired little in the way of controversy.

Over the years, this uncritical acceptance has slowly developed into a cult of personality (Aitken 1977, 96), which, while flattering to Innis's memory, has nevertheless hindered the full development of his efforts. It also implies that his views can be comfortably located within a context of predictability that Innis consistently rejected. He believed that such an approach to intellectual life marked the end of genuine thought. Patterson's conclusion – that it is "ironic that admirers of Innis have assimilated his thought to conventional patterns he was breaking away from" (Patterson 1990, 173) – should encourage us to interpret Innis in ways that depart from the conventional views dominating Innisian scholarship. A helpful starting-point is Carey's remark that the challenge offered by Innis's work "is the attempt to apply and extend some of his major ideas by interpreting them within the context of concrete periods" (Carey 1981, 87–8). With these insights as a guide, I would like to present an alternative interpretation of Innis to illustrate the richness and contemporary relevance of his deliberations.

Postmodern theorists pursue a wide variety of projects from many different perspectives (Rosenau 1991, 14–17). While recognizing this diversity, I suggest that many of the epistemological concerns developed by such diverse postmodern commentators as Derrida, Rorty, Lyotard, and Baudrillard either are clearly present in Innis's work or can be extrapolated from insights that are implied but remain undeveloped by Innis himself. However, in order to establish the connections involved, we must first situate the basic problem within the historical context from which it sprang. Let me therefore begin by providing this focus.

POSTMODERNISM AND THE INTELLECTUAL TRADITION OF THE WEST

Postmodernism Defined

Despite its more superficial manifestations, postmodernism is a very serious epistemological movement directed against the definition of rationality that characterizes modernism and which has its origins in the scientific discoveries of the sixteenth, seventeenth and eighteenth centuries. Crowley describes the intellectual climate of this period as one in which science "rather than metaphysics arises as a master idea that directs the conceptualization of thought, representation and action" (Crowley 1981, 237). This change in perspective is defined by the procedures of modern science – data gathering, experimentation, classification, quantification, and prediction. Its practitioners assumed that the astounding discoveries achieved by this use of human reason as it studied the physical universe would be repeated as it applied itself to social structures and institutions with the objective of freeing humankind from the many afflictions that prevented it from realizing its full potential. This particular interpretation of rationality would later be called "instrumental reason" and would gradually eclipse all competing views to become, in our time, "one of the most prestigious forms of reason in our culture, exemplified by mathematical thinking, or other types of formal calculation" (Taylor 1991, 102).

However, as time passed, the uneasy feeling developed in some quarters that there was something drastically wrong with instrumental reason. Postmodernism attempts to explain, evaluate, and suggest alternatives to this critical derailment. Yet postmodernism, while it clearly reacts against the modern definition of rationality, also maintains that instrumental reason's most damaging manifestations are predictable outcomes of concepts that were introduced into Western thought at its very beginning, thereby making the real problem as ancient as the tradition that provided the context for its development and disastrous social manifestation.

The Problem

The basic issue is well articulated by Lyotard. In *The Postmodern Explained* (1992) he tells us that the modern definition of rationality collapsed with the tragic death camps of the Second World War. The brutality that caused such a catastrophe was the result of much more than an isolated historical expression of human perversion. It was certainly that. In addition, however, there was something powerful, sinister, and even dreadful that was hidden from view.

The death camps could operate "successfully" only if the evil of human intentionality was directly assisted by the achievements of modern science and its related technologies, from the construction of the ghastly ovens and the use of modern chemicals, to the organizational efficiencies of modern managerial techniques, logistics, and other forms of control. To Lyotard, this shameful use of modern reason demonstrates that "the project of modernity ... has not been forsaken or forgotten but destroyed, 'liquidated'" (18). If such a use of human reason is rational, then what could conceivably be defined as irrational? Thus, to Lyotard, Auschwitz "is the crime opening postmodernity ... How could the grand narratives of legitimation still have credibility in these circumstances?" (19).

Thus Lyotard uses the term "Auschwitz" to illustrate the collapse and total moral bankruptcy of the West's definition of rationality (78). In so doing he is representative of the general postmodern interpretation of the West's definition and application of rationality. But the horrors of the twentieth century, he argues, are the predictable social manifestations of a type of intellectual and moral decadence that has always characterized Western society, thereby making ours an intellectual tradition that is deeply and tragically flawed at its very roots.

To Derrida, the fatal flaw consists in the series of oppositional concepts that were introduced into our intellectual tradition by Plato (Derrida 1982, 151). These binary oppositions provided a metaphysical foundation to intellectual inquiry that has systematically excluded competing interpretations of reality. In examining the same epistemological problem, Rorty (1980) devotes most of his efforts in *Philosophy and the Mirror of Nature* to describing the futility of the traditional epistemological belief that privileges a theory of representations. Thus, while they develop their individual views on a variety of issues, the same general epistemological concerns motivate Lyotard, Derrida, and Rorty to share the conclusion that we must confront a basic interpretation of knowledge that stretches back in our history to the time of the Greeks.

Innis's View of the Same Question

Like the postmodern theorists, Innis speculates from a historical basis. Like them, he believed that there was something fundamentally wrong with the West's interpretation of reality at its inception, which progressively deteriorated as one century followed another. This historical context is apparent in *The Bias Of Communication* (1984), where he identifies the cause of the excellence of Greek culture as its ability to strike the necessary balance between (his celebrated concepts of) space and time (64, 68). The balance in question involves the requirements of the secular forms of technological, political, and economic domination (space) vis-à-vis the demands of philosophy, ethics, history, tradition, and culture (time). However, Innis notes that this period of unparalleled excellence was brief before the seeds of intellectual decline were deeply and permanently inserted within the very heart of that tradition. He identifies the beginning of the decline from excellence with a thinker whom many would consider to possess the most powerful and wide-ranging intellect in human history – Aristotle.

It is well known that in their respective philosophical deliberations Plato and Aristotle reached very different conclusions. This, according to Innis, was not the problem. The real difficulty was the fundamentally different ways in which both thinkers articulated and transmitted their speculations. It was Innis's understanding of the oral tradition that Plato, via his spokesperson Socrates, relied on the spoken word and the human interaction of debate, in which final answers rarely surfaced. Plato's inconclusiveness was his strong point; his search was much more important than any final answer. It is for this reason that Innis concludes that Socrates "was the last great product and exponent of the oral tradition" and that the *Dialogues of Plato* were superb ways of preserving the effectiveness and power of the spoken word by means of writing (Innis 1986, 60). Aristotle, in contrast, communicated via the written word, reflecting impeccable logic, systematic exposition, and textual organization and clarity. Most important, he was communicating what he thought to be the truth of all the subjects he discussed. He did not debate; he instructed the reader in "truth." This, to Innis, was a fatal error. He saw the replacement of the oral tradition of Socrates and Plato by the written exposition of Aristotle as the beginning of the end.

The basic problem of the replacement of the oral tradition with the written was the purpose that motivated intellectual investigation as well as its expression. The inconclusiveness and open-endedness of the Socratic dialectic gave way to the finality and definitiveness of the one-way conversation, in which one who "knows" transmits knowledge to those who do not "know." It was Aristotle's emphasis on writing and the arrogant certainty of writing's purpose that "destroyed a civilization based on the oral tradition." The destructive force initiated by Aristotle has consistently gained momentum as the centuries passed and in so doing increasingly threatened "to destroy the spirit of Western man" (Innis 1986, 61). To Innis this deeply embedded historical flaw came to maturity well before the Nazi death camps mentioned by Lyotard. The relevant social, technological, and epistemological conditions were in place at the beginning of the twentieth century. It is at this historical juncture that Western civilization collapsed (Innis 1946, 94), along with its associated epistemological underpinnings.

As one whose ideas lay behind this collapse, Aristotle made his critical mistake in using writing to create "grooves which determine the channels of thought of readers and later writers" (Innis 1984, 11). Since they are clearly defined and narrowly focused pathways, such grooves are necessarily exclusionary. They reinforce themselves as they systematically exclude alternative possibilities. In their focused limitation, they require that we understand our reality by excluding perspectives that do not conform to their predetermined requirements. When this epistemological context exists within a society that is dominated by the secular concerns of space-directed technology, the capacity to understand is both predictable and severely limited. Certain problems, possibilities, and perspectives will be automatically excluded from consideration because they fail to fit in the interpretive grooves of a space-informed consciousness. Thus Innis's time-related issues receive no serious consideration in the public discourse, and so "the balance between time and space has been seriously disturbed with disastrous consequences to Western civilization" (76).

Consequently, when Innis maintains that our modern technological society has "enormously increased the difficulties of thought," he is not suggesting that we do not think (Innis 1946, vii). His point is rather that we think only about certain things in certain, prescribed ways – ways contrary to the balanced perspective required of genuine thought. This impoverished intellectual context negates the positive potential of the vast array of perceived improvements in communication technology, transforming them into forces that "have made understanding more difficult" (Innis 1984, 31). The immensely diverse data that inundate us are all restricted to space-directed issues and thereby actively prevent us from developing "a sustained philosophical approach" (Innis 1946, xvi).

Our industrial, commercial, technological society therefore exerts a destructively subtle epistemological influence. It determines the way we think yet does not provide us with the perspective required to assess its own real impact (Innis 1946, xvi). And this is the very epistemological condition that has caused so many civilizations to pass into oblivion. Innis was convinced that we should take this historical lesson very seriously, since there is no reason to suppose that our civilization can escape this devastating truth. Thus does Innis connect the continuation of our civilization with the clear necessity for a renewed epistemology. "The conditions of freedom of thought are in danger of being destroyed by science, technology and the mechanization of knowledge, and with them, Western civilization" (Innis 1984, 190).

Innis thought that we were enjoying a false sense of comfort in narrow specializations, accumulation of data, and confidence in technological solutions. While this barrage of information produces a society that has "all the answers and none of the questions" (Innis 1946, 128), it results in an intellectual narrowness that is fundamentally intolerant. Thus, says Innis, "we have learned fanaticism," and though we are comfortable in our confinement, "thought has been paralyzed" (127–8). Accordingly, the urgent task facing contemporary society is to recognize the intellectual dangers that it faces and then introduce an epistemology of liberation. Consequently: "The first essential task is to see and break through the chains of modern civilization which have been created by modern science" (vii). Recapturing a sense of time is necessary if we are to avoid disaster.

SOME COMMON THEMES

The Postmodern Concern with Language

Jacques Derrida shared Innis's insight concerning the need to free ourselves of crippling intellectual impediments. He also subscribed to Innis's view that one of the basic difficulties to overcome was the tendency of the written word to restrict our understanding. Innis had warned us of the dangers of the "grooves of thought" that writing established, and Derrida focuses on this concern in his *Of Grammatology* (1976) and *Writing and Difference* (1978). These works examine the epistemological repercussions associated with the "finality" and "close-endedness" of the type of writing that Innis considered so dangerous. While Innis's solution was to substitute the flexibility of the oral tradition for the limitations of the written tradition, Derrida proposes a far different approach. He suggests that we should use the written word to undermine its traditional forms of expression. Traditional writing should be attacked by a more creative exercise of writing. However, like Innis, he recognizes the power of writing to resist attempts to undermine its historical use and mission. Written words can be replaced only by other written words, and therein lies the problem. Innis believed that this replacement could not be achieved, hence the need for the oral tradition. Derrida disagrees and introduces his concepts of "difference" and "deconstruction" to accomplish this important objective.

The same concern with the traditional use of writing is apparent with Rorty, who tells us that the means used to explain our reality has been language as "a theory of representations which stand in privileged relations to reality" (Rorty 1980, 182). The result has been a rigid interpretive framework yielding an unresponsive, ahistorical permanence to human inquiry (157). The West's attempt to define human rationality as "knowing" or "becoming" or somehow "mirroring" the substance of things must be set aside in favour of what he calls "hermeneutics," understood "as a project of edification," which means "finding new, better, more interesting more fruitful ways of speaking" (360). Echoing Innis, Rorty concludes that our principle task is to escape from the confines of traditional language and "to keep the conversation going rather than to find objective truth" (377).

The epistemological problems that Innis detected and related to Aristotle's "grooves of thought" are also reaffirmed by Lyotard, who considers all intellectual systems claiming finality, universality, and close-endedness to fall within the general category of "meta-narrative," the obvious historical failure of which signals the beginning of postmodernism. Since Innis rejected the Aristotelian meta-narrative, one can assume that he would be receptive to Lyotard's rejection of all totalizing systems. Both men share the view that such systems are all suspect because of their close-endedness and their claims of objectivity and universality. In both instances the mutual distrust of totalizing systems of thought serves as a common departure point for some very original speculation.

A Rejection of Metaphysics

Metaphysics has been of foundational significance in the development of the West's intellectual tradition, acting as a driving force behind Greek, medieval, and much of modern speculation. Any serious meditation simply had to consider it. Though this historical concern is neither seen nor implied in Innis's work,[1] three relevant points involve his concept of time and its relationship to the oral tradition.

First, Innis was not the least bit interested in Platonic metaphysics or in any other metaphysical system. To interpret him as being a Platonic idealist would be seriously to misinterpret him (di Norcia 1990, 353). Second, Innis was interested more in the questions posed in the Platonic dialogues than in the answers provided. He believed that the dialogues dealt with the great issues of human existence: the relationship between individual and state, the nature of knowledge and virtue, the institutions required for the full development of citizens, and the education of the young. To Innis these were the critical questions that each generation should ask in the light of its own concerns and knowledge. Third, he was interested in Socrates as the personification of a specific method of intellectual inquiry – namely, dialectics. Consequently, Innis valued the oral tradition and, by association, Socrates' concept of time because of the role of dialectics as a method of intellectual investigation for some crucial issues. In advocating a reintroduction of time into contemporary society, Innis was also advising us to reinvent a type of social dialogue that has long disappeared from public discourse.

We get a more precise idea of this type of inquiry when he discusses his views of education in *The Bias Of Communication* (1984). Here he tells us that we must de-emphasize data and specialization and renew the teaching of character, as understood in ancient Greece. "We should, then, be concerned like the Greeks with making men, not with overwhelming them by facts disseminated with paper and ink, film, radio and television" (203–4). In addition, "We have neglected the philosophical problems of the West and have not realized that the Greeks were fundamentally concerned with the training of character" (Innis 1979, 385).

Innis is here suggesting that we reintroduce certain values into our society. He believed that this was necessary in order to provide the young with the resources of intellect and character to regain control over the unchallenged march of the technological-industrial-commercial juggernaut, which was constantly advancing without intelligent guidance and direction. Yet, while recognizing the significance of Greek values, Innis remained completely indifferent to the Greek conviction that an ethical or a social system had to be based on metaphysical principles. From his perspective metaphysics was superfluous.

Though all the postmodern theorists would share Innis's opinion on this issue, those interested in the foundation of ethics believe that metaphysical speculation has been so centred that it cannot be ignored but must be directly confronted. One of the basic purposes of Derrida's work is to demonstrate the degree to which metaphysics has negatively influenced Western thought and to argue that our future epistemological well-being is contingent on the total eradication of metaphysical speculation. To this effect he notes, "[I]t is necessary to seek new concepts and new modes, an *economy* escaping this system of metaphysical oppositions" (Derrida 1978, 19). Derrida is representative of the postmodern view in his conclusion that we must rid ourselves of this impediment if we hope to experience the variety and richness of meaning.

The same opposition to metaphysics is evident in Lyotard's *The Post-modern Condition* (1989). His dismissal of the great meta-narratives of Western thought is a rejection of all the metaphysical systems that have claimed objectivity and universality. Similarly, in his *Philosophy and the Mirror of Nature* (1980), Rorty advises us to "free ourselves from the notion that philosophy must center around the discovery of a permanent framework for inquiry" (380). Even though Innis and the postmodern theorists share the same view of metaphysics, postmodernism actively opposes metaphysics, while Innis simply passes it by. In a somewhat similar manner, his emphasis on dialectical inquiry places Innis firmly within the postmodern perspective, since his understanding of it suggests a reliance on the postmodern concepts of community and diversity.

The Concept of Community

Innis recommended the oral tradition's dialectical search for truth because of its open-endedness and human interaction. What standards could Innis possibly invoke to provide standards to settle public controversies? Though he does not directly address this question, the fact that he clearly rejected universal and permanent standards suggests that the only viable alternative would be the postmodern concept of "community." This is the concept that acts as final arbiter in Rorty's pragmatism and in Lyotard's language games and according to Fish in *Is There a Text in This Class?* (1980), decides what does or does not constitute literature (10). It is the standard emanating from the free and open exchange of views among interested and competent individuals. The social application of the concept of community provides us with a second postmodern concept – diversity, or multiplicity.

The explicit recognition of these two concepts confers an analytical thoroughness and clarity of exposition that is in keeping with both the spirit and much of the letter of Innis' efforts. For example, there is no doubt that he would support Lyotard's conclusion that the truth value of certain statements is subject "to the collective approval of a group of persons who are competent on an equal basis" (1989, 24). In clarifying Innis's work in this manner, one can detect a genuine similarity of spirit and purpose between Innis and postmodernism, which can be further developed by extending this method to other issues.

A Common Pragmatism

The Socratic dialectic recommended by Innis is intended to achieve a definition of truth approved by the participants in the conversation. As noted above, Innis regarded the quest as being more important than a final answer. Rorty similarly emphasizes the search as he notes that the critical element is "the infinite *striving for* truth over 'all of Truth'" (1980, 377). Continuing to reflect Innis's understanding of the intellectual life, Rorty underlines "conversation as the ultimate context within which knowledge is to be understood" (389). And again, like Innis, Rorty favours the Platonic dialectic, so long as one need not subscribe to either the questions or the answers that preoccupied Greek civilization. "The fact that we can continue the conversation Plato began without discussing the topics Plato wanted discussed, illustrates the difference between treating philosophy as a voice in a conversation and treating it as a subject ... a field of professional inquiry" (391).

We can here see that there is no divergence between Innis and Rorty on this issue. Indeed, one can even consider Rorty's well-known pragmatism as central to Innis's understanding of what constitutes effective public discourse, as di Norcia in fact does. "Like John Dewey, Innis was concerned with the concrete conditions of human knowledge, freedom and action" (di Norcia 1990, 351). Both Innis and Rorty offer a realism and concreteness unencumbered by the necessity of locating or justifying one's thinking within a predetermined, abstract context. It is rather a matter of rendering communal decisions in order to resolve particular problems.

The Inconclusiveness of the Text

Innis's lack of analysis and supporting documentation for many of his major conclusions has been widely commented on. *Empire and Communication* (1986) is simply a series of conclusions, in which entire civilizations are evaluated in a few paragraphs or a few pages. By traditional standards of scholarship, Innis's conclusions remain unjustified and are simply his personal opinions on very complicated questions. However, complying with accepted academic standards was not uppermost in Innis's mind. That he was both aware of these requirements and had mastered them as few others had is admirably demonstrated by his work in economic history. In consciously departing from tradition in *Empire and Communication*, he seems to have introduced a decidely postmodern approach to the transmission of knowledge.

For example, understanding *Empire and Communication* requires active engagement with the text. The reader must supplement the meaning suggested in the book with his or her own understanding of the issues being discussed. As Wernick suggests, the reader must "do precisely what Innis himself was not prepared to entertain: systematize his categories and reflect on their inter-connected logic" (1986, 148). One must establish a partnership with Innis in what rapidly becomes a mutual search for understanding, and this, as is well known, is one of the central postmodern themes. It is no accident that there is no final, definitive interpretation to *Empire and Communication*. If Innis's style is considered in this manner, the intellectual leaps for which he is so well known become more understandable. As with postmodern writers, his expository style is an invitation to share an adventure of personal discovery in which both parties reject definitive answers. Rather than fearing different and even contradictory interpretations of a text, Innis and postmodernism actively encourage this very difference. To both, only diverse opinions can produce the quality of dialogue that encourages genuine insight. Yet, while recognizing the optimism underlying this intellectual openness, we should be aware of the pessimistic and even tragic note that lurks just beneath the surface of both perspectives.

A Deep Sense of Pessimism

The pessimism I am referring to is not confined to the interpretation of a particular issue, specific historical period, or individual theme. Rather it is general in nature and provides an ever-present background against which all issues are considered. It reflects deep concern with our inability to direct intelligently the many forces that constitute our social whole, to order a society that is developing in active opposition to real and substantial human development. Both Innis and postmodernism warn us of the dangers associated with the gigantic, self-sustaining social dynamic, which possesses its unique nature, power, needs, and self-imposed logic. It is this social colossus that is dictating the choices that humans are to make. To use Innis's terminology, things are not simply out of balance; they are totally and dangerously out of control. It is not an overstatement to say, as Whitaker does, that Innis "saw the fate of modern civilization as catastrophic" (1983, 823).

Both Innis and much postmodern speculation do not believe that human agency as it currently manifests itself has either the will or the capacity to reverse this devastating trend. Innis doubts that the values of time can be introduced into a society whose key institutions actively oppose the type of balance that would ensue, and so we will not develop the intellectual or moral resources to withstand the impositions of this technological/industrial/commercial juggernaut. We have simply been overrun. Similarly, Baudrillard concludes that social redemption is impossible, since our society is now a "gigantic simulacrum – not unreal, but a simulacrum, never again exchanging for what is real, but exchanging in itself, in an uninterrupted circuit without reference or circumference" (1983, 11). How can there be constructive action when "it is now impossible to isolate the process of the real, or to prove the real" (41)?

It may well be that Innis would disagree with much of Baudrillard's diagnosis. Yet I suspect that he would be genuinely sympathetic to Baudrillard's pessimistic view. Innis warned us of this danger some fifty years ago, and he believed that things would only get worse unless we struck a balance between space- and time-related issues. If Innis concluded then that "the tragedy of modern culture has arisen as inventions in commercialism have destroyed a sense of time" (1984, 85–6), the conditions he describes have clearly intensified.

In effect, Baudrillard is providing us with his interpretation of the type of society that Innis feared was developing. One can certainly debate the extent to which Innis would support his social diagnosis, but the issue does not seem significant. Both would attribute the dehumanization of contemporary life to the same general reasons. Innis would find no satisfaction in discovering that his predictions were right after all.

A VERY SIGNIFICANT DIFFERENCE

Let me now briefly touch on one of the major differences between Innis and postmodernism. In advocating a return to the Socratic dialectic of the oral tradition, Innis is recommending a solution that would be universally rejected by postmodern thought. The latter insists that the epistemological problems we must resolve are directly caused by the oppositional concepts introduced by Socrates via Plato. To postmodernism, these conflicting concepts provided the intellectual framework that supported all subsequent Western speculation and are thus the concepts that we must escape. Consequently, from the postmodern perspective, Innis's advocacy of the oral tradition offers no possibility of resolving our current problems. Rather than relying on any traditional means, the postmoderns recommend that we create new concepts with new meanings and, in freeing ourselves from the intellectual tyranny of the past, actively expand our epistemological horizons.

Such a difference of opinion naturally stimulates vigorous debate, in which Innis would no doubt be a valued contributor were he here to do so. His motivation would lie in his conviction that human progress requires that each generation participate in the adventure of intellectual discovery in terms that reflected its particular historical reality and deepest concerns, including a critical assessment of answers provided by tradition. Innis would certainly defend his position with enthusiasm and could well draw some hope from the debate itself, for it would be this social dialectic that would ensure that the spirit of his much-loved oral tradition was thriving and already in place.

NOTE

1 Innis did not directly deal with the subject of metaphysics as a formal discipline. He was concerned with some issues that may well be considered metaphysical questions but was interested in their verbal, oral, open-ended investigation as represented in the Platonic dialogues rather than a closed-ended, finished system as in Aristotle.

17 The Bias of Space Revisited: The Internet and the Information Highway through Women's Eyes

HEATHER MENZIES

Innis's insights on communication are useful in critically assessing the global networks of digital communication associated with the internet and the information highway.[1] They are particularly helpful in questioning whether marginalized groups that have been innovators here can use the new media to break existing monopolies of knowledge and power associated with commercial capitalism. They are equally useful in considering an alternative possibility: a reconsolidation of the bias of space in global corporate networks of "flexible accumulation," in which the erstwhile citizens of a revised democracy movement become so many teleworkers and teleconsumers in virtual workplaces and shopping malls plugged into the centre of the new economy. What Innis called "the penetrative powers of the price system" could soon enclose almost every aspect of public existence in the global information networks of the digital new economy.

This chapter looks critically at some of the grassroots popularizations of the internet that have gone on in the 1980s and 1990s to see whether the internet might represent the breakthrough of a new world order based not on domination and exclusion but on cooperation, inclusion, and sustainable diversity. It also compares this vision to developments associated more with the information highway and the new digital economy. Focusing on women's experience, I question whether "marginal" groups are able to break existing monopolies of knowledge and communication using the new technology or whether they are in danger of being recolonized in the sense that Jody Berland talks about above in chapter 15. I use two sets of Innisian concepts here: the bias of space and of time, and how these connect to communication; and structures of communication and monopolies of knowledge associated with them.

When the Innu of Davis Inlet used the internet to break an official news blackout and send out word of their standoff with the RCMP and the Newfoundland government in September 1994, they were fulfilling one of Harold Innis's propositions.[2] Innis predicted that a new medium of communication will often be appropriated by people on the margins of established authority and used to break the monopolies of knowledge that are so central to its hegemony.[3] The pattern is demonstrated in the penny press and the English democracy movement of the late eighteenth Century and when the monopoly of the Catholic church (maintained through its control of parchment texts hand-written by select scribes, in Latin) was broken by a new commercial and civil society using the printing press and vernacular language as its media of communication and knowledge. One can note the beginnings of a similar break from established (now, commercial) patterns in the early days of film, radio, and even the telephone and telegraph. In Canada, particularly in areas away from central control and scrutiny, the telegraph was used as much to communicate local information as it was for official business (Lawrence 1990, 53). In film, Ruby Grierson took cameras and microphones to the working poor and produced participative documentaries, in which people told their own stories with their own words and images (Nelson 1988, 72). For the first twenty years or so of radio, Canadian broadcasting was entirely the work of amateurs communicating among themselves (Peers 1969, 5). In telephony, switchboard operators opened up this technology to support personal communication within communities and even some ad-hoc community broadcasts.

But it is clear too that every new communications technology in the modern era has, in its dominant forms, served to extend the bias of space – that is, the control over space, militarily and administratively but especially commercially – by commoditizing it. Witness the big newspaper chains, mega-buck Hollywood movies and distribution systems, and commercial radio and television. It has also brought us to the brink of pay-per-bit (of information or access time) for telephones and related one-to-one communications (Mosco 1989). In other words, those social and cultural activities developed by popular culture and the population at large in the developmental stages of communications technologies have tended to be appropriated, or reappropriated, by corporations and supportive state regulatory institutions in the service of commercial economies and related systems of knowledge.

Innis once summarized the history of modern Western civilization as a monopoly of time followed by a monopoly of space (Innis 1984, 64). In the Middle Ages, when the church held sway, its bias was towards the spiritual concerns of time, rather than the material concerns of space. For Innis, "time" incuded sacred concerns with eternity plus more general concerns about tradition, continuity, conservation, and permanence. For all the contemporary talk about a postmodern information society, Innis's ideas would suggest that a real test of change is whether the social movements using the internet in the 1990s can truly retool the technology to serve the bias of time – not just at the innovation stage and at the end-user level of intertextual rhetoric, but at the stage of institutionalized technological development and the enabling infrastructures associated with it,[4] not just at the level of language games, but at the material level of structures that determine who gets to speak about what and who referees and designs the game plan.

Innis also reminds us that the bias of space – towards fast, space-binding communication – is inherently biased towards the kind of monopoly-scale, centrally controlled structures of communication on which it materially depends. The bias of communication tends to be fulfilled in global-scale systems of commercial communication – something that can be offset only by public policy. As well, American communication scholar James Carey extended Innis's ideas about remote versus intimate communication (long-distance versus short-distance communication) with the cogent insight that the bias of these systems is towards a deepening of disparities between centre and margin, a consolidation of authority in a few remote centres, and the erosion of expressive complexity and of the capacity for intimate ("proximate") relations, with every scale-up in speed and distance (Carey 1975, 32).

THE INTERNET AND
ITS COMMUNITY PRACTITIONERS

The internet was created by a strongly space-biased institution: the u.s. Department of Defense. But it was strategically designed (in 1969) as a self-governing collection of information nodes (rather than a centrally controlled system), so that it could withstand the destruction of any particular site. This decentred design has been a key to its growth along decidedly un-space-biased dimensions. Participating research scientists began using it for other than official business. They broke ranks, broke out of their institutional boundaries. They began communicating horizontally with colleagues, friends, and kindred spirits in various causes such as the environment. These people in turn reached out to others. And so it went, to the point that the internet has entered popular mythology as a wild and wonderful community of communities, with no one in control, and everyone free to use it as they see fit, though with a macho hacker individualism setting a distinct, and distinctly dominating tone (with sexual harassment a recurring subtext for women), throughout (Spender 1995, 210).

The WELL out of San Francisco was started by the publishers of the *Whole Earth Catalogue* and is considered by some the prototype for community ""freenets. It is also part of a larger network of networks, called the Association for Progressive Computing, with nodes in the United States, Canada (the Web, in Toronto), England (GreenNet, in London), Scandinavia, Nicaragua (niconet), and Brazil (alternex) (Shade 1994, 53–69).

Community nets (formerly called "freenets") represent a fascinating mini-renaissance in community communications. Defined as community-based, not-for-profit computer information networks (Weston 1993, 15), they also represent some of the first efforts to move beyond simply appropriating existing network technology. Participants are actually designing their own systems around local community communications goals and values.[5] By 1995, there were fourteen freenets in Canada and dozens more in the United States, New Zealand, and Germany, with the numbers growing exponentially. In Ottawa, the National Capital Freenet, launched in 1992, had more than 27,000 registered users by 1995, including over one hundred local and national organizations, such as the Ottawa Psychiatric Survivors Alliance, the La Leche League, the Saw Video Co-op, the Canadian Environmental Network, plus various news services and discussion forums on economic development.

All in all, they tend to fit what James Carey has defined as a community-building "ritual" model of communication, as compared to the dominant "transmission" model of communication (Carey 1989 15). There is a distinct sense of Innis's time-bias differentiation here too. While the transmission model moves as much information as fast and efficiently as possible, the ritual model sees communication as social bonding. The former is geared to transporting commodities and operates largely through the private sector; the latter, supported mostly by the public sector, is geared to community building and culture.

Community nets, however, are all subsidized. In Ottawa, for instance, the freenet piggybacks on the computer system of Carleton University. In Toronto, Rogers Cable (Rogers Communication) began subsidizing the launch of a community net through donations of equipment and space worth an estimated $7,000 a month. In the United States, the Corporation for Public Broadcasting, in partnership with U.S. West, awarded $1.4 million to support twelve community networking projects in the early 1990s. These initiatives, seen within the larger context of government "downsizing" and public-spending cuts, would suggest that they are all at risk of being enclosed by the larger infrastructures on which they depend. And many of these service providers – Rogers Communication, for example – are prime exemplars of the transmission model of communication. Strongly aligned to the space bias of communication, they treat content not as conversation and reciprocal community building, but as information commodities and service transactions.

Solinet

Within the internet, electronic networking is also being used by labour groups, women's groups, gays, lesbians, and bisexuals, and Native and racial-minority groups for internal communication and for solidarity and coalition building among them.

Solinet is a computer conferencing and networking system developed by the Canadian Union of Public Employees (CUPE) since 1985. Significantly, too, it is also owned by the union (Belanger 1994, 18–24). Over the years, membership has expanded to include other unions and other groups (including the Web, alternative news services, and Action Canada Network) plus individuals outside the union movement. Solinet also features an electronic library of research documents, a weekly news service called "Soli-notes," electronic mail, and other types of administrative support. Marc Belanger, the principal designer and promoter of this network, has expressed hope that it can evolve into a global network, grounded in locally owned computer systems associated either entirely with the labour movement or with other social movements. But in a conversation in late 1994, he worried at the "fast-forwarding" of technological change towards a second and third generation of multimedia, icon-driven networking (the World Wide Web), which might push even the technologically progressive CUPE system into a state of relative underdevelopment. It risks being marginalized, but not necessarily by the structures of internet service providers, as the infrastructure and overall system service are taken over by the private sector. It risks being marginalized by high "production values" and related skills standards that elsewhere helped give the Hollywood production model a virtual monopoly in film and television entertainment.

Women's Networks

Women's experience with electronic networking (including the Internet) adds new reason for concern, while attesting to the groundswell of knowledge, commitment, and material investment that is developing around this non-commercial, democratic model of communication. Canadian communication scholar Ellen Balka, who has done some of the best research in this area (Balka 1997), began her investigation by checking out women's first use of the internet in the mid-1980s. Net.women, she found, was dominated by the men involved (Balka 1993, 7). Since then, women have become a presence on the net, but largely by creating their own spaces within it. Many use it only for personal or shared electronic mail. Many groups, however, have created their own mini-networks of shared discussion use groups and electronic mail list servers. The Women's Bulletin Board in New York and the Femail Mailing List developed in the mid-1980s along these lines. The latter is both an electronic-mail system and discussion forum, offering the women who make up 75 per cent of the membership, "a sense of community as well as access to solutions to day-to-day problems" (Balka 1991, 360).

Since then, there has been a flowering of initiatives, ranging from self-help and research to resource sharing and organizing. For instance, the Breast Cancer List is run out of Memorial University in St John's, and PAR-L, the policy, action, and research list, out of the University of New Brunswick in Fredericton. Developed out of a conference call sparked by the impending demise of the Canadian Advisory Council on the Status of Women, PAR-L was launched on 8 March 1995 as a bilingual, moderated list "for developing, conducting and distributing women-centred research in a multi-disciplinary context" (Balka 1997, 51).

However, Balka also found that participation in these systems is reproducing inequalities among women and may even be exacerbating them. Studying computer use among women's groups in Newfoundland in the early 1990s, Balka found that while the majority had a computer or access to one, most lacked the technology required to network electronically (Balka 1994). There was a sharp differential between those groups with paid staff and those running entirely on voluntary labour – 88 per cent of those with paid staff had access to computers, compared to 51 per cent of those without it. As well, many with "access" to electronic mail did not have their own address but piggybacked on an existing one. Like the 40 per cent of women's groups that did not own a computer but only had access to one, they are vulnerable to losing that access. But equally important, they are less able to control the evolution of the electronic networking available through those technologies. The technologies can easily structure dependence and under-development. For instance, she has found that if groups lack a computer guru – someone who will champion the process of computer networking within an organization, and the building and sharing of skills that this involves – many rely on outsiders' expertise, often that of a male friend, and become dependent on this support (Balka 1997, 93).

Others have echoed Balka's concerns about electronic networking producing new inequalities through the new communication practices that it introduces. Reflecting critically on her experience with electronic networking while serving on the board of the Canadian Research Institute for the Advancement of Women (CRIAW), Marilyn Assheton-Smith questioned whether electronic networking delivered more effective group decision making or only an illusion of the real thing (Assheton-Smith 1988). It might deliver presidential-style "consultation," she suggested. "But to the extent that we are attempting to recreate the decision-making" as feminist process, "in which all participate until there is a resolution of differences based on something other than power, we have much work to do." She wondered whether problems of power and authority might simply become "more transparent" through technologically mediated communications than they are in face-to-face meetings.

Networking may move away from a modest, flat-fee access rate towards either a higher base rate or more of a pay-per-service and -transaction basis, as was rumoured to be imminent late in 1996 (Sandberg and Weber 1996, C2). If that happens, the commodity-intensification bias of the organizational structures could exacerbate the bias already inherent within the cryptic, fast-forward medium, along the lines detailed by Carey – namely, steady erosion of proximate relations and conversational complexity, on which friendship and solidarity rest. "The personal is political" might well be turned on its head, with fast, space-binding communication networks colonizing women's groups with their grammar of metered conversational moments.

Meanwhile, on the other horizon, the activities and players associated with the information-highway version of electronic networks are poised to merge with recent, more commercial developments on the internet, with profound consequences for the marginal groups trying to use the internet to redistribute the power of communications, knowledge, and decision making in society.

THE INFORMATION HIGHWAY: AXIS OF THE GLOBAL DIGITAL ECONOMY

Despite the hype that portrayed the information highway as glitzy multi-media, this network of more clearly commercial corporate networks can best be understood in terms of the technological restructuring associated with globalization (Menzies 1996, 7).[6] Its infrastructure of interconnecting networks is becoming the axis of the new economy – the site where business deals are forged, where work is dispatched, and where "flexible accumulation" is calculated and managed. The term, information highway, was coined by u.s. Vice-President Al Gore in 1994, when he introduced his $2-billion-a-year National Information Infrastructure Program, a sequel to his 1980s High Performance Computing Act, geared to retooling u.s. industry with super-fast computers and networks "to enable this country to leapfrog the Japanese" (Coy 1991). As in Canada, where the federal government launched a similar information-infrastructure boosting program in 1994 (through a largely private-sector consortium called CANARIE, discussed below), "economic renewal" has been the priority. From the outset, too, the focus has been on business, not on multi-media marketing, distribution, or even teleshopping. Industry Canada's (1994) *The Canadian Information Highway: Building Canada's Information and Communications Infrastructure* was unequivocal: "The key to competitiveness will be the ability of firms to develop, acquire and adapt ... the tools that will be available on and through the information highway" (8).

The highway metaphor (which Gore actually recycled from his senator grandfather's initiative to build a network of superhighways across the u.s. in the 1950s) might be comforting in its familiarity. However, it's highly misleading. It suggests just another line of communication running by outside the institutions of people's lives, when in fact this electronic highway is running right through them and transforming the very ground they stand on. With computerization, much of the information underpinning work and the management of work is being digitized. With networking – i.e., combining computers with communications – all those data and all that managerial control can then be shifted away from grounded institutions into the high-capacity networks of the information highway. It can be deinstitutionalized from bricks and mortar and fixed geography, and it can be reinstitutionalized in the global networks of the information-highway infrastructure. It can go global. Where in the 1980s, electronic networks permitted the routine global flow of capital, in the 1990s networks are permitting the routine global flow of work and everything related to it.

Work can be contracted out through a new global and local division of labour constituted through at-home teleworkers and call centres, through "agile" factories, labs, home and satellite offices, and workshops. Once they are plugged into the information highway, all these production modules (and people) can be managed remotely through the networked organizational structures of virtual corporations, virtual colleges and universities, and virtual hospitals and government departments. The highway's networks provide a ubiquitous operating environment through which any physical place – from high-rise apartment to suburban basement or garage and any car or truck – can become a virtual workplace or a customer-service and delivery site, at any moment in time. (And it can be deleted just as fast.)

With the information highway signalling the network-integration phase of a computerized restructuring that dates from the 1970s, the industrial paradigm is shifting. National machine-based economies are being restructured into a global post-industrial systems economy. It is an economy dominated by global-scale corporations, particularly in the financial-information, computer-information, and communication businesses, which can exploit the highway network as a "unified system" of production, marketing distribution, and consumption (Goldman 1993, 110).

What is emerging in this global systems economy is a variation on a lego set, with interchangeable production units operating on a standardized set of pay and performance criteria, where investments and contracts can be activated at a press-enter cue, and terminated just as fast. It is a game plan being actively promoted in the United States by a government-industry think tank called the Agility Forum. Founded in the late 1980s with funding from the U.S. Defense Department, the forum has brought together senior executives from the major military industrial suppliers, plus the major companies in computers, communications, and the auto industry.

The Forum's publications do not talk about monopoly capitalism having reached an omega point through the virtualizing infrastructures of the highway networks, where monopoly corporations, cartels, and conglomerates vanish as structures altogether. They do not say that the invisible electronic structures of the virtual corporation and "federated ... virtual enterprises" (Goldman 1993, 27) are the perfect vehicle for the kind of "flexible accumulation" that David Harvey (1990) describes as capitalism's "solution" to its crisis tendencies – whereby "the financial system has achieved a degree of autonomy from real production unprecedented in capitalism's history" (194). Instead, they mildly predict that virtual joint ventures will become "routine" (Goldman 1993, 5), with one dissolving today and a different one formed tomorrow, and many happening simultaneously, linking different parts of different corporations in parallel research, product-development, and other product-cycle activities for different periods of time. The alliances – called "the new intimacy" between "erstwhile competitors" (Davidow and Malone 1992, 140) – represent what they expect will be "the dominant world industrial order of the 21st. Century" (Goldman 1993, 1). These alliances are made possible by "streamlined legal practices," "standardized interfaces," and "pervasive connectivity" (Goldman 1994, 41) through the increasingly standardized networking systems that the forum is promoting, including a customized express lane on the information highway, called the Factory America Network.

Integrating the Agile Virtual Enterprise (Asava and Engwall 1994) offers a game plan for streamlining everything from technology and legal protocols to modules of people and their skills – a global "contingent labour force" – so that technological and human modules can be plugged into any collaborative combination for work along the information highway at minimal start-up costs to the company involved. The game plan also calls for more and better computer "metrics," so that each corporate module's "value-added" contribution, or each individual's hourly performance, can be measured for "value-based compensation" (17) and profit sharing. It also envisages further deregulation – a relaxing of anti-trust laws, minimum-wage, and equal-employment standards and a fragmentation of product liability so that every participating production unit shares the "liability risk" (26).

This lego set of costlessly interchangeable global production units operating entirely on its own corporate rules has all the markings of a perpetual-motion machine. It is also a fully realized monopoly of space, with real people and places, and all the related concerns of time – time as human experience and personal plus shared identity, time as memory, continuity, conservation, and tradition – handily deleted from the screen.

THE INTERNET IN CONTEXT:
STRUCTURAL MONOPOLIES AND
MONOPOLIES OF KNOWLEDGE

This, I would argue, is the larger context in which the democratizing initiatives on the internet must be critically examined. It can be argued that the internet has developed into a more time-oriented communitarian model of communication practice, while the information highway is clearly associated with the transmission model and the commercial, market-controlling bias of space in the modern era. In the absence of a clear and meaningful policy commitment towards a mixed-model approach to communication in the era of instant digital connectivity, however, it also seems clear that in the late 1990s the commercial, transmission model was poised to enclose the internet as an alternative infrastructure, retooling and/or containing it as a niche within the larger commercial sphere, rather like Community Access Cable.[7] Since the early 1990s, more and more corporations – from

America Online to Microsoft to Bell and AT&T – have started offering internet access on a commercial basis. As well, more and more corporations have moved onto the internet, either sponsoring the graphics version of the internet – the World Wide Web – or marketing their goods, services, and name through web sites of their own. Systems providers, such as Rogers, sell services such as Cablelink-Work to support home-based tele-work. And the home-based workforce – one manifestation of the new "contingent labour force" – is growing with the proliferation of 1-800 numbers, and so on, with everything from customer service to sales and service-support provided on line.

The 1991 Canadian census noted a 40 per cent increase (since 1981) in the number of people reporting the home as their primary place of work. After farming, three of the top three occupational groups were clerical, sales, and service – all traditionally female job ghettos. Furthermore, the majority were making less than $20,000 per year. A sizeable minority were making less than $10,000, which is not enough to support a single person, let alone a family. The trends suggest a growing number of women reconfined to the home as their primary sphere of existence, and isolated from each other as well.

Meanwhile, the Canadian federal government has been actively promoting business use of the internet, both through its own departmental initiatives and beyond. One publication noted that "even if it's not a mainstream access and service-delivery mechanism today, the Internet or something like it will certainly be the way business will be done in the not-too-distant future" (Treasury Board Secretariat 1995, 9).

The corporate presence also overshadowed the internet as governments began privatizing management of the internet infrastructure, while subsidizing business in upgrading it to accommodate routinely massive volumes of data, including multi-media. In Canada, a consortium of mostly private companies called the Canadian Network for the Advancement of Research, Industry and Education (CANARIE) was given this mandate. It has responsibility for dispensing the millions of dollars that Ottawa has allocated for upgrading the infrastructure and building on it – $26 million in the start-up phase alone. Of CANARIE's nineteen founding members, only the University of British Columbia and the Canadian Institute for Advanced Research came from outside the corporate sector. Though membership later expanded to include most of the universities in the country, it was the original group – including Bell, Canada Trust, Hewlett Packard, IBM, Newbridge, Northern Telecom, Stentor Resource Centre, Unisys, Unitel – that in 1993 laid down the by-laws of the association. This included a minimum annual CANARIE membership fee of $2,500 – a price of admission which has largely excluded from the policy-making process women's groups, unions, and other groups associated with the communitarian model of communication and the values associated with Innis's bias of time.

Key policy developments in the 1990s – including a revision of the federal Telecommunications Act in 1993 and the deliberations of the federal, industry-dominated Information Highway Advisory Council – marked a shift of public policy away from a mixed, public–private-sector approach towards near-total control by the private sector and "market forces."

Together, all these developments suggest that the infrastructures of digital communication through which women's groups, unions, and community networks are pursuing their particular networking goals will increasingly be corporate systems operated on a cost-recovery or outright commercial basis. And increasingly, too, they will be the same infrastructures, the same media environment through which these people earn their daily bread. And as Innis understood, once the bias of communication has been built into the structures of communication, particularly in the form of large, monopoly-scale structures, they strongly bias what message can be communicated. In this case, it would appear to be "business as usual."

It is impossible to predict what effect this bias will have on the grass-roots communication and coalition-building initiatives reviewed in this chapter. Certainly the mega-billion dollar scale of some of the multimedia mergers and players operating in this field is cause for concern. (Think of Time-Warner/Turner Broadcasting, Westinghouse/ABC, Microsoft, and the host of joint-ventures in which Microsoft is involved.)

Innis's ideas about monopolies of knowledge offer some helpful analytical tools – for example, in naming the prerequisite for a monopoly, and related dependence, to exist in the first place. A monopoly can emerge only where people are dependent on an external source of supply – here, equitable, easy access to long-distance communication, as opposed to short-distance, face-to-face communication, which people can furnish themselves by foot and by mouth. Then, as James Carey has pointed out, there are three dimensions through which monopolies of knowledge operate: physical, structural and cultural (Carey 1975, 38–45).

Physically, a monopoly of knowledge and related knowledge-producing communication emerges when some media can move information faster than others. Not only do instant global communications accomplish this, but there is mounting evidence that networked electronic communication is setting a new, faster pace for getting things done. Decision-making rates have gone up by a thousand percent and more (Menzies 1993, 794). In industry, decreasing response times for developing new goods and services and getting them to market has become a new basis for business competitiveness and for goods and services as virtual goods and services (Davidow and Malone 1992, 47).

Even by the early 1990s, electronic communication had introduced new problems to feminist organizations such as CRIAW. In addition to the relative exclusion of francophones because the system functioned only in English, Assheton-Smith (1988) found: "In general, communication was enhanced in the organization for those on electronic mail, (but) making those not on it comparatively more sharply disadvantaged than they would have been if we had all to rely on telephones and airmail" (5).

However, physical monopolies of knowledge operate both within organizations and between them, and this is potentially more troublesome. If government increases its reliance on electronic communication for policy-making consultation with public-interest groups, women's and other community groups will have to keep pace with the latest technology and the turnaround times it offers (and implicitly demands). Those groups who cannot keep up are in danger of being completely left out of the democratic process, and left in the dark.

They could also lose touch with each other. This problem relates to the structural aspects of monopolies of knowledge. Structurally, a monopoly of knowledge determines where information is stored, how it is structured and packaged, and by whom. Applied to community groups using the internet for community and coalition building, this structural dimension highlights the need to ensure a ubiquitous public space in the network infrastructures so that different groups – particularly low-budget groups such as those in the women's movement, the labour movement, gays and lesbians, and anti-racist movements, whose communication goals usually have little to do with commerce – can be in touch with each other easily and at no additional cost. There is a real danger that in the absence of substantial policy commitments (as opposed to the rhetoric of commitment that has emerged from IHAC) to an inclusive public network, through which public-interest organizations can have ready, easy access to each other, these groups may become isolated in their special-issue ghettos, unable to do the larger work of coalition building to redefine and redirect the public agenda.

The last of the three ways in which monopolies of knowledge and communication work is through a cultural monopoly of knowledge. The most subtle of the three, it also offers the deepest critical insight into the possibilities (or limitations) of communication as community building within the increasingly commercial infrastructures of electronic communication. A cultural monopoly operates through the control of the things thought about (what is framed into the picture as real and relevant versus what is framed out as beside the point) and of the things thought with (the terms of reference and the mental maps through which those who select and police these terms define the social reality (Carey 1975, 45). To my mind, these precepts represent a useful material detailing of how hegemony operates. In short, the ability to communicate in this high-speed medium, the ability to speak in its hypertext language and apply its multi-media grammar is emerging as the new basis for monopolizing knowledge and the knowledge-producing process.

Those who cannot speak the language, those who can't keep pace with the trends, are marginalized and silenced. But so is all the communication that cannot be assimilated into its fast, abbreviated communication media. Equally, there is the conditioning effect as more and more people, particularly women as teleworkers, become isolated from each other in computer-defined work environments, in call centres, or at home. Electronic communication could subtly consolidate a computer-mediated context as the most familiar – even the most real – social environment for taking care of business in every sense of the word.

Yet electronic communication does not put people in touch with each other, except indirectly. It puts machines in touch with each other. "Cyberspace communities are made up of units of information, not of people" (Sivanandan 1996, 10). It is a simulated extension of people's minds, but very much disembodied. Furthermore, that extension is further abstracted by the standardized iconography of alphabet and punctuation, plus the protocols of internet addresses. As A. Sivanandan (1996) commented, reflecting on the use by the Zapatista, the Palestinian and other marginalized groups of faxes and the internet to break monopolies of communication and advance their cause, "The leadership became even more remote from the uprising; they had the information, but not the feel" (10).

The bias of communication comes home at this cultural level: in the subtle erosion of expressive humanity as communication is disengaged and disembodied from the intimate bonds of conversation and dialogue with people known as whole people, and then as it is speeded up for instant global feedback. Yet intimate, trust-building communication – the stuff of social bonding, community building, and solidarity – requires face-to-face meetings, body language and gesture and eye contact, and community building over time. And it requires the habit of community building in other areas of life – such as at work, through daily give-and-take with colleagues. This can no longer be assumed in a world where more and more people work in isolation from each other and where more and more compete with each other for internet job postings. They compete anonymously with each other in what I call the new reserve army of the self-employed, otherwise known as the "contingent labour force."

This erosion of communication as community and social bonds deserves committed research and reflection. This could signal the ultimate colonizing effect of the all-pervasive networks of communication; where everything comes down to production and consumption, everything is reducible to metered motions. Meanwhile, these tentative insights suggest the need for caution and for groups interested in community and coalition building to avoid being left with no option except electronic networking.

A PLEA FOR TIME

I agree with Andrew Wernick where, in chapter 14, above, he emphasizes oral culture as the site for regaining a sense of time as continuity, in the context of actual lived experience. As Innis made explicitly clear, "the oral tradition implies the spirit but writing and printing are inherently materialistic" (Innis 1984, 130). It is clear too that the culture of Canada's First Peoples has survived via the oral culture. Much the same can be said about the culture that women share, in all its rich diversity. And it is true as well about a labour culture.[8] The integrity of those cultures and of those communities rests squarely on the oral tradition. The oral tradition has sustained them.

By comparison, the time operating in much of information economy, the information highway, and discussions about them is linear time. It is time transformed into a function of space. It is commoditized time and technological time. It is the infinitely optimized time of microchips' capacity doubling every two years, and the incessant redoubling of efforts to fill that communication capacity with information packets zipping back and forth everywhere around the world. Inside the global information networks, technological time is a dynamo keeping everyone on the run: too busy to know themselves, except as "anxious objects" strung out in cyberspace (McLuhan 1968, 24).

To know yourself on your own terms, and to possess that personal knowledge fully enough to express it, require taking one's time, coming back to the body and one's own particular body of experience (Brossard 1988, 50). This is one of the truths behind the feminist slogan "the personal is political" and a prime reason for the emphasis on process in feminist communication. Face-to-face dialogue, or what Innis has also called "short-distance communication," facilitates this.

The more distance and speed are added, however, the more the integrity of that knowing is threatened. As mentioned above, the bias of fast, long-distance communication strips language of its expressive capacity, shifts authority to more distant centres, and blunts the capacity of proximate relations (Carey 1975, 32).

The conclusion can perhaps be expressed as a proposition. If women's groups, union locals, and environmental, peace, First Nations, and racial-minority groups can network together through the internet, they can perhaps use the technology to break the corporatist monopoly operating within both the global political economy and even the global village of the public mind. But they will succeed only if their networks remain grounded in face-to-face communications within their particular communities and if their community building through the internet is an extension of that community-based communication, not a substitute for it. The integrity of their agency depends on their remaining grounded in direct, oral communication, where everyone can take their time to think and speak for themselves on their own terms.

This, I think, would be Innis's plea for time in the 1990s.

AFTERWORD

I want to end by revisiting the group I mentioned at the beginning – the Innu of Davis Inlet – because I want to emphasize the disappearance of First Peoples from this chapter, and also my tacit participation in their removal. I helped make them disappear because I relied largely on written texts in my research, and I found nothing about First Nations' use of electronic communication in the journals, books, and reports I looked at. Then, when I tried to contact the people of Davis Inlet, plus the one other Native person I know who is involved in local electronic networking, I got nowhere. They did not or could not get back to me. And I was too busy (or could not be bothered) to go to them, there, in the so-called marginal regions, when they did not return my phone calls or where they did not have a phone or e-mail address for me to try in the first place. The deadline for publishing this book, and my desire to be included, drove me to forget them.

NOTES

1 I wish to thank Ellen Balka, Jody Berland, and Liora Salter for wonderfully helpful comments on an earlier draft.
2 On 4 September, the Newfoundland government had excluded all news media from Davis Inlet as they prepared forcibly to reintroduce the rule

of (its) law to that remote and beleaguered Native community. But the people used internet to bypass the established knowledge channels by going straight to the people with their story. They posted a "help" message on internet's discussion group, alt.native, warning that "this will be Oka II but worse." I got the message when it was picked up by the *Ottawa Citizen* and printed it on page 1 (8 Sept. 1994).

3 The dictionary defines hegemony as "supreme leadership," from the Greek for "leader." But Gramsci's elaboration of it as a more generalized climate of control is more appropriate in today's wrap-around information environment. "It thus constitutes a sense of reality for most people in the society, a sense of absolute reality over experienced reality – beyond which it is very difficult for most members of society to move, in most areas of their lives" (quoted in Williams 1980).

4 Ursula Franklin makes this helpful distinction between the playful, innovative-tool stage of technological development and the more mature phases of rigid infrastructures and operating systems.

5 I am grateful to Ellen Balka for emphasizing this distinction, in her comments on an earlier draft of this chapter, and for sharing her considerable research in this area with me.

6 Much of the material, particularly for this section of the chapter, is drawn from Menzies (1996). This is its central argument.

7 For a history of the containment of community-access cable within the dominant commercial model, see Goldberg 1990.

8 Bruce Roberts, Canadian Auto Workers, told me in a personal conversation in 1995: "[T]he labour movement is an oral culture."

18 Early Innis and the Post-Massey Era in Canadian Culture

KEVIN DOWLER

Reflecting on the Report of the Royal Commission on National Development in the Arts, Letters and Sciences (Massey Report) of 1951 (Canada 1951), Harold Innis (1952a, 15) wrote that "the overwhelming pressure of mechanization in the newspaper and the magazine has led to the creation of vast monopolies of communication. Their entrenched positions involve a continuous, systematic, ruthless destruction of elements of permanence essential to cultural activity." The net effect of mechanization was, in Innis's terms, to upset the balance between space and time in favour of space and therefore to erode the historical continuity necessary for the production of culture.

For Innis, as well as for the members of the Massey Commission, the destruction of culture and civilization appeared imminent, primarily as an effect of the spread of American mass media and mass culture. Canada, however, according to Innis, was in a unique position to counteract this impending disaster: "By attempting constructive efforts to explore the cultural possibilities of various media of communication and to develop them along lines free from commercialism, Canadians might make a contribution to the cultural life of the United States" (Innis 1952a, 20). Canada therefore is situated in such a way that it could mitigate the deleterious effects of mass communications on culture. As Innis wrote in another essay in the same volume, "The conservative power of monopolies of knowledge compels the development of technological revolutions in the media of communication in the marginal areas" (1952a, 78). Canada, on the margin between the empires of Europe and the United States, becomes the privileged site for innovation.

The price of exploring the cultural potential of media free from commercialism, however, is state involvement. In the absence of private capital, only the state can secure the conditions under which cultural production and innovation can flourish. This at least was the opinion of the Massey Report in regard to Canada and seemed to be that of Innis as well. The state would create the conditions hospitable to the production of culture that would counterbalance the corrosive effects of American mass media.

It thus appears that preservation of culture requires that one form of centre–margin relations give way to another – a shift in power centres from private capital to the state. This is consistent with the historical development of Canada, particularly in terms of its security interests vis-à-vis the United States. This consistency lies in the persistent weakness of private capital in Canada and the need for state intervention to secure the well-being of the nation. This is certainly the case, as Innis's early work demonstrates, for the development of the communications and transport infrastructure necessary for national development and defence. As I argue below, it is also the case for the development of Canadian culture. It is therefore towards the early work of Innis that I turn in order to explain the logic of government intervention in the cultural realm.

As Maria Tippett (1986, 557) has argued, Canadian cultural history most often "consists of a series of specialized studies focused on particular fields of cultural activity, the development of which can be understood without the necessity of paying much attention to the process by which and the context within which the work in those fields came into being." I wish to argue that by looking at Innis's early work, particularly on government ownership, we can begin to understand the context in which cultural activity takes place in Canada. I start with Innis's investigation of the initial stages of Canada's development. I next examine the utility of this work with regard to an analysis of the development of Canadian culture. I then present a brief case study of the emergence of Canadian independent video as an illustration of how Innis's work can help in resolving certain contradictions that appear in the study of Canadian culture. Finally, I return to the implications of Innis's early work for the study of Canadian cultural development.

GOVERNMENT OWNERSHIP AS MOTIF

Government involvement in the economic activities of Canada begins at the very beginning. As Innis notes in *The Fur Trade in Canada* (1930, 406), "The relation of the government of Canada to general economic growth has been unique. The heavy expenditures on trans-

port improvements, including railways and canals, have involved government grants, subsidies and guaranties to an exceptional degree."
Government involvement in the development of the transportation
infrastructure was not gratuitous but rather the outcome of private
interests' failure to complete projects. As Robin Neill (1981, 149) has
remarked, "The weakness of private capital has been the occasion of
government involvement in canals and railways. Indeed, part of the
economic significance of 1867 can be found in the need to centralise
the railway debts of the colonies." According to Innis (1956a), this
goes back even further to the Act of Union, when an "energetic canal
policy ... begun as a private enterprise" could not find adequate capital
and therefore "necessitated purchase by the government" (68). Eventually, as Innis points out (1933), "Confederation became an effective
credit institution with the demands for long-term securities which
accompanied the spread of industrialism especially as shown in transportation" (19).

In the vacuum created by the failure of private interests, government
intervened with various financial instruments to ensure completion of
the transportation system. Arguably – which goes to Innis's point
regarding Canada's uniqueness – government took up the tasks of civil
society through its enlarged role in economic affairs. Indeed, according
to Innis, this involvement required reorganization of the political structure in order to achieve a nation-wide transportation system: "To build
canals and improve the St. Lawrence system, and to build railways ...
necessitated reorganization of the political structure," and "dependence on the Canadian political structure ... to carry out these vast projects involved ... government ownership" (1956a, 229).

Innis's early work reveals that the "uniqueness" of the Canadian
state lies in extensive government intervention, which put into place a
"tradition" of government ownership that "became an important
factor in later developments" (1956a, 68). Innis states: "Government
ownership is the legitimate child of government support of private
enterprise in the construction of railways in Canada. It is the result of
a policy directed toward building a nation in the northern part of
North America" (1933, 48). The policy dimension brought out in this
latter citation indicates that government intervention served not only
economic goals, but also security interests and the consolidation of the
space of the state.

Ironically, the attempts to consolidate the Canadian state through
space-binding technologies generated further dependence, because the
transportation system is bi-directional – it aided not only exports of the
staples on which the economy was based but also the import of manufactured goods. On this point, Innis quotes Alexander Galt's report on

the Reciprocity Treaty with the United States: "All these improvements [to transport] have been undertaken with the twofold object of diminishing the cost to the consumer of what he imports, and of increasing the *net* result of the labour of the country" (1956a, 71). The two-way structure, though it may make exports more profitable, also lays the nation open to the influx of less expensive foreign manufactured goods – made cheaper by the very system used to distribute them. Thus the net effect of improvements is further dependence on foreign commodities.

This contradiction – government construction of a transportation system for security reasons, which undermines that very goal – is the first instance of what Gordon Laxer (1985, 94) has called "aborted development," particularly with regard to defence: "Instead of a strategic logic leading to the build-up of a Canadian-owned armaments and engineering sector, the strategic question in Canada was fought over territory. The CPR was rushed into construction because the American government had explicit designs to annex Western Canada ... Such is the logic of the strategic question." As a common carrier, the railway effectively undermined the reason for which it was built: in attempting to establish sovereignty and security through mere presence, it allowed imports to inhibit the development of indigenous industrial capacity and thereby erode its status as an instrument of national security.

What Innis describes as Canada's uniqueness involves both dependence on government intervention and ownership for economic and security aims and the undermining, in terms of the net effect of this intervention, of the very aims of economic and defence policy. If we were to consider Innis's work conventionally – early economic history and later media studies – his early work uncovers the crucial position of government in Canada's development, and the later work, the extent of penetration of foreign commodities, particularly American mass culture, via the communication and transportation system on which the nation was founded. In his later work, Innis discovers that the only remaining form of defence against the fully dependent state he describes in his early studies is culture.

CULTURE AND SPACE

A nation such as Canada that comes into being through the space-binding effect of its communications system remains empty except for the structure of that system itself. As Maurice Charland (1986, 197) writes, "Canada is valorized as a nation because it is the product of technological achievement." However, this valorization "cannot but offer the empty experience of mediation." Technology qua technology, as Charland notes, is not sufficient – despite its status as foundational

myth – to solve the question of nationhood, for the space that technology brings into being generates a further crisis: "This vision of a
nation is bankrupt, however, because it provides no substance or commonality for the *polis* except communication itself. As a consequence,
... (Anglophone) Canada has no defense against the power of the
American culture industry" (198). According to Charland, this has
made Canada into an "absent nation." The empty shell of space
created by communications technology is ultimately filled with foreign
content – in other words, American mass culture.

The extent to which the question of space looms large in relation to
culture can be seen in the Massey Report (Canada 1951). In a chapter
entitled "The Forces of Geography," the report emphasizes the vitality
and diversity of Canadian life: "Canadian civilization is all the stronger
for its sincere and unaffected regionalism" (12). This regional diversity,
however, is also problematic, because "the isolations of this vast country
exert their price." The price of isolation was an absence of unity and uniformity with regard to a pan-Canadian culture and identity. The
problem, for the commission, was how to link this diversity into a supra-
regional whole, presumably into a whole that would replace "unaffected
regionalism" with a more cosmopolitan cultural sophistication.

The report's solution to national weakness was to bring the regions
into the mainstream through national cultural programs: "In a country
such as ours where many people are remote from the national capital
and from other large centres of population, it is of obvious importance
to extend to them as far as may be possible the services of the national
institutions in Ottawa" (12). In this way, government would tie the
nation together through a communications and a cultural infrastructure. The stimulation of culture on a national basis through centrally
administered agencies and institutions, would permit construction of a
specifically Canadian culture and counter-balance the deleterious
effects of American mass culture.

The Massey Report itself was the fruit of extensive lobbying demanding that the government take up a role in both administering and the
administration of culture. Despite concerns over government control of
culture (cf. Litt 1992, 103–5 passim), there were demands for a cultural
policy and an institution or institutions that would provide direct
subsidy for cultural production. It is here that the "weakness of private
capital" marks the moment of recurrence of government intervention.
Similar to the circumstances of Confederation, when a central government was formed to act as a "credit institution" (as Innis put it) to
finance the construction of transportation and communication networks
in the absence of private initiative, the "problem" of culture was likewise
to be solved by government, through its financing of cultural activity.

It was again the marked absence of a civil society, both as an economic agent and as the "mobile interface between government and governed" (Gordon 1991, 34), that created the conditions for government investment in the production of culture. The demand that the government intervene was itself indicative of the inability of private interests to develop the requisite institutions. If culture were to be Canadian, the government would have to build it.

Given a "tradition" of government ownership and sponsorship, it is no surprise that government, as with transportation, would be asked to underwrite cultural production. However, it could not do so directly, in order to avoid the possibility or even the perception of government interference. The solution was, and remains, a structure of agencies that would administer culture on behalf of, and at a distance from, the federal government.

In effect, such agencies would perform the function of an absent civil society. To the extent that they are held at a distance from both the civil service and the legislative branch – either through reporting procedures or through the use of the "arm's-length principle" – these agencies operate as the "mobile interface" between the government and citizens. This simulated civil society would become the basis for a specifically Canadian culture.

The problematic of space, once thought to be solved through the construction of a communications and transportation apparatus, re-emerges in culture. The communications apparatus, though it binds together the material space of the nation for the purposes of sovereignty, also facilitates importation of foreign culture. Space, relocated in the symbolic realm, thus reasserts itself as the problem of binding the nation together through a shared sense of specificity that exists beyond the mere physical contours of the nation. The solution to Charland's "absent nation" would be a Canadian culture brought about through centrally administered programs delivered by federal agencies. From this perspective, culture functions not only as a "time-binding" mechanism but also as a way to capture the space of the symbolic realm and to overcome the deficiencies engendered by economic dependence and the penetrative capacities of modern communications technologies. Culture thus acts as a security mechanism to compensate for dependence in other areas and to secure the continued existence of the Canadian state.

CULTURE AND SECURITY

In the view of the Massey Report, dire consequences would result from governmental inaction regarding cultural production. The probable outcome would be a slide into barbarism which would take one of two equally unappealing forms – anarchy (as in Matthew Arnold's contrast of culture and anarchy)[1] or the overwhelming of the Canadian state by American mass culture. "[A] vast and disproportionate amount of material coming from a single alien source [the United States] may stifle rather than stimulate our own creative effort; and passively accepted without any standards of comparison, this may weaken critical faculties. We are now spending millions to maintain a national independence which would be nothing but an empty shell without a vigorous and distinctive cultural life" (Canada 1951, 18). The reference to the empty shell indicates the degree to which the commission understood implicitly that the maintenance and defence of brute space are by themselves insufficient. Culture would provide the necessary bulwark to construct a strong nation with all its critical faculties intact and to ward off the potentially harmful effects of a creeping continentalism, in the form of American mass culture.

It is here, with concerns over American culture on the airwaves and in the classroom, that the underlying logic of the cultural apparatus emerges: the security of the Canadian state. The function of culture would be to inculcate in Canadian citizens a sense of culture that would be both civilizing and – as a consequence – distinct from the United States. The Canadian state's formal entry into the production of culture marks the moment when government shifts from preoccupation with territory, defined through the communications apparatus, to the use of culture as a disciplinary regime to ensure the distinctive, and therefore defensible, character of the Canadian state.

In the terms set out by the Massey Report, culture constitutes a form of defence against both internal and external threats. Indeed, recent concerns raised over federal multicultural policies constitute yet another instance of the potential threat that culture can represent to the internal order and security of the state. These concerns are in turn indicative of the "threats" that have preoccupied the security apparatus in Canada since Confederation.[2]

Normally, the task of constructing culture would be left to private interests. In Canada, however, the absence or weakness of private interests and an underdeveloped civil society have virtually compelled the state to take up a direct role in most, if not all, areas of society. The dominance of government regulation suggests that Canada has been unable to perform the type of devolution of certain powers onto the private sector consistent with the formation of a strong civil society (cf. Burchell 1991).

The turn towards culture potentially marks the moment when the Canadian state creates a simulated civil society on its own behalf. The tactic employed is the creation of the conditions of self-regulation through establishment of semi-autonomous cultural agencies. As a security apparatus, the agencies operate as forms of discipline and surveillance to fend off the imminent collapse and ensure the continuing existence of the state. The central problematic of liberal governance – the simultaneous ordering of the individual and of the whole (cf. Foucault 1991) – is to be solved through the regimen of culture. Each individual sustains a cultural identity through the process of *Bildung*, or self-actualization, organized by the pedagogical strategies delivered via centralized national programs, and, collectively, a pan-Canadian culture by virtue of the uniformity provided by cultural agencies offering nation-wide programs.

The inculcation of a national identity through a cultural apparatus is then turned towards the maintenance of national security. Culture itself becomes the prop whereby to rationalize maintenance of that spatio-political entity. As the Massey Report (Canada 1951, 274) points out: "If we as a nation are concerned with the problem of defence, what, we may ask ourselves, are we defending? We are defending civilisation, our share of it, our contribution to it. The things with which our inquiry deals are the elements which give civilisation its character and meaning. It would be paradoxical to defend something which we are unwilling to strengthen and enrich, and which we even allow to decline." It would indeed be paradoxical to defend an empty space. As a result, culture, if it does not readily appear, must be constructed to meet the political objective of policing the actual borders and what Wark (1992, 162) refers to as the "metaphysical" frontier of the state, against both external and internal threats to national security.

Many years later, Bernard Ostry (1978, 41) made a similar claim, though he linked it to military aims: "The bearing of culture on morale was well understood in Canadian military circles. If a man was to risk his life for his country, he needed to know what his country was and to have some feeling for it ... For years the Department of National Defence was alone among federal departments in developing a conscious, consistent, and imaginative cultural policy and providing the funds to make it work." As Ostry (5) points out, "Perhaps only the armed forces have understood from the start the importance of developing a sense of identity and the connection of culture with morale and community relations." This places culture squarely within the context of defence interests and clearly indicates the significant link between culture and national security. The willingness of the Department of National Defence to develop an "imaginative" cultural policy and to provide funding suggests that it alone, until the advent of the Massey Commission, understood the crucial relationship between security, culture, and national interests.

MARGINALITY AND CULTURAL PRACTICE

It is within the context of government ownership, a weak civil society, and a desire for security against American mass culture that cultural practices in Canada emerge. Having sketched the conditions within which Canadian culture has developed, we can proceed with a historical analysis of specific cultural practices and fields.

I want to turn to a brief study of the emergence of independent video. I have chosen video since it appears to meet the criteria of being both a technological medium and a marginal practice and is thus ideally placed as the locus of "technological revolutions in the media of communication," which Innis claimed would occur at the margin. This is doubly the case for Canada, since video represents a marginal practice emerging in a marginal nation. The broader historical narrative of its emergence internationally privileges it as a form of revolutionary practice at the margin of broadcast television and art, and the various histories of Canadian independent video are similarly utopian.

In the late 1960s, the early discussions regarding the introduction of the video portapak emerged within what Martha Rosler (1986, 242) called a "utopian moment" – the convergence of social movements of the period with access to (and criticism of) mass media technologies. "Many of these early users," Rosler writes, "saw themselves as carrying out an act of profound social criticism, criticism specifically directed at the domination of groups and individuals epitomised by broadcast television – and perhaps all of mainstream Western industrial and technological society. This act of criticism was itself carried out through a technological medium, one whose potential for interactive and multi-sided communication ironically appeared boundless." Liora Salter (1981, 193) has commented: "Innis believed that creative, expressive use of a small format media could offset the alienating impact of mass media." Video thus appears to be an example of the innovative use of technology to which Innis was referring. The very medium of domination itself would be transformed through its use as a tool of criticism.

Almost magically, portable video emerged at the moment it was most needed to counteract the effects that video itself had apparently created. This happy convergence of the desire for social transformation and the technology to express it was, however, problematic, since independent video as a practice rests somewhere between the institutions of art and television and remains marginalized in relation to both. This is what Rosler means when she writes that the potential for communication "ironically appeared boundless" – its apparent boundlessness has in fact reinforced its marginal status.

Canada has continued to see itself since the early 1970s, as being at the forefront of what Salter called "community media." As the Canada Council (1974, 126) reported to the Secretary of State in 1974, "Canada became – and remains – one of the most dynamic and internationally raved-about video producing countries." This perception of Canada's position fits well within an ironic conception, considering that production of independent video has had virtually no impact on either broadcasting practices or art institutions in this country. Community media form a "hinterland," as Salter has suggested, but although engaged in rebellion against empire they are also its product. It is this contradiction that requires some elaboration. What Salter and others have failed to recognize is that in Canada this activity "from the margin" is centrally funded and the product of social, economic, and cultural policies emerging from the very centre of empire. The history of independent video practices in Canada is in this sense puzzling. It appears to be consistent with the notion that creative expression occurs on the margin, but the conditions under which video practices emerged in this country speak more of the colonization of the margin by the centre. If, however, we consider its emergence within the "tradition" of government intervention, this contradiction appears less mystifying.

Unlike most traditional art forms, the entry costs for access to video technologies were (and continue to be) prohibitive for most individuals. Introduced in the mid-1960s, the one-half-inch reel portapak was the first video technology accessible to non-technical persons, though its cost was still quite substantial. Its emergence suggested the possibility of restoring the subjectivity lost through centralized, one-way forms of mass communication. Against television, video was seen as a tool that might liberate the potential of video hidden within the mass media; using video would be an act of empowerment by taking up the very technology that appeared most disempowering. Video would be the mirror machine par excellence, and getting oneself "on television" would mark the installation of the audience as subject, as both viewer and viewed (cf. Marchessault 1995).

This utopian discourse has to be seen, however, against the actual circumstances of independent video development in Canada. Though the discourse of independent video may have been an interesting and mobilizing fantasy emerging from reflection on the possibilities of the medium in the abstract, actual use of video technologies in Canada has depended on federal initiatives. Access to equipment was the product of various federal programs of the late 1960s and early 1970s aimed primarily at either social or economic goals. The Local Initiatives Program (LIP), Opportunities for Youth (OFY), Local Employment Assistance Program (LEAP), and Challenge for Change/Societé nouvelle were just

some of the federal programs administered by the Department of Man-
power and the Secretary of State that stimulated the initial development
of video practices in Canada. They made funding available for practitioners to acquire and maintain the new video technologies.

In addition to providing money for equipment, these programs also
provided the policy framework under which video would develop.
Aside from their economic aims, these programs were directed at supporting the goals of the Liberal federal government's cultural initiatives. Their goals were not, however, as straightforward as they might
seem. Though ostensibly aimed at cultural diversity, they had hidden
features. First, in the wake of the October crisis of 1970, they had a
mandate to foster tolerance and unity, as well as (in some minds) diver-
sions for youth away from potentially socially destructive activity.
"Such programs," writes Sara Diamond (1991, 63), "were symptomatic of the liberal struggle to institutionalize marginal sources of
dissent." Second, the failure of the private sector to steer the economy,
and thereby guarantee some measure of social peace, prompted
massive federal intervention, partly through the programs mentioned.
Third, with the withering away of funding by the mid-1970s, Secretary
of State used various organizations created under these programs to
exert greater control over the Canada Council and to move it closer to
the aims of the federal government (Dowler 1995, 37–8).

Independent video, though its practices rested to a large extent on a
utopian discourse, emerged in a period marked by attempts at consolidating federal control over cultural policy and its programs. This is
made abundantly clear in a set of notes from a meeting between Prime
Minister Pierre Trudeau and then Canada Council Director Peter
Dwyer. As Dwyer wrote, "[T]he Prime Minister said that he could see
no reason why the Canada Council should be exempted from the
current general government requirement that expenditures of public
funds should be directed to the present needs of our society."[3] This
reminds us that government helps direct cultural practices, and that the
state may place security interests ahead of innovation. In this case,
Trudeau was particularly worried about the continued funding of
artists who had embraced Quebec separatism and seemed willing to
put national security ahead of "artistic merit" (the council's criterion).

The status of independent video as a cultural practice has been
further complicated by the emergence of culture as a primary economic
activity in Canada. The development of economic policy with regard
to the "cultural industries" has – and continues – to put further pressure on the purely cultural innovation envisioned by Innis. This transformation has been noted by Woodrow et al. (1980, 65), who write:
"The department [of Communications] is coming to be perceived more

as a science-based unit promoting the increasingly important aspect of Canada's overall industrial strategy and less as a culture-oriented unit responsible for managing the instruments whereby Canadian identity is shaped." Here we see the further erosion of cultural autonomy as culture itself is increasingly the object of industrial and economic state planning.

This in turn has generated further inter-agency conflicts, particularly over the distribution of resources for such things as video, and the consequent necessity (especially in the case of the Canada Council) to distinguish between purely "cultural" and "industrial" applications of new media and communications technologies. It also potentially marks the moment when the possibility of cultural innovation free from the pressures of the marketplace, as embodied in both the Massey Report and in Innis's reflections on it, collapses in the face of the government's desire to see culture pay for itself and, as the resource economy withers away, to see culture as the new staple destined for export markets.

INNIS AND THE STUDY OF CULTURE

If, however, the necessity for distinctions arises when discussing practices, all the institutions (both private and public) concerned with either cultural or industrial mandates are united at the level of economic arrangements in relation to the Canadian state. These two areas – industry and culture – if conceptually distinct, share the various forms of public-sector subsidy and administration by agencies and regulatory bodies. Both industry and culture have developed under the more or less direct supervision of the public sector. The failure of the private sector to create an adequate infrastructure for cultural production has warranted intervention of the federal government, both to stimulate growth in the "cultural industries" and to foster "artistic excellence." The further expansion of communication media, for both industrial and cultural purposes, has been underwritten primarily by the federal government. If anything, the margin here cannot be viewed as a source of dissent. Rather, protest takes the form of a *demand* – that government step in, in this case to support cultural production.

Culture, however, has become more than simply a counter-strategy to economic dependence. It has evolved from a purely defence-oriented security apparatus into a basis for economic self-sufficiency. Once culture becomes an economic component and industry and culture converge, a distinction appears between "pure" culture and industrially organized forms of cultural production. As culture becomes increasingly viewed through the optic of economy, its former status as the locus of the construction of identity must be renegotiated. The rationalization of culture in effect marks the foray into economic self-sufficiency via culture's function as security. Culture takes on a new role, along with its residual role as a security apparatus. As described above, "pure" culture was stimulated for the purposes of bolstering security to compensate for a colonized economy. Culture has now also become the means to achieve economic independence; thus its original function as the signature of Canadian distinctiveness is put to further use within the economic realm. The problem of "aborted development" in the industrial sector is to be overcome through the adaptation of cultural production for the economic self-sufficiency of the nation.

To the extent that government support remains crucial for cultural practices in general, we face a paradox. To explore the "cultural possibilities" of communication media requires, in the absence of the institutions of civil society and freedom from commercial imperatives, extensive state involvement. Arguably the innovative possibilities ascribed to Canadian cultural practices at the margin can occur only as the product of the consolidation of a core–periphery relation organized by the state. Thus dependence is reconstituted at another level: freeing cultural activities from market considerations results in reliance on the state. This dependence is, however, as we have seen, consistent with the history of Canada itself and constitutes what Innis referred to as Canada's "unique" circumstances of development.

Our foray into Innis's work on government ownership thus proves relevant to the study of the development of Canadian culture. Consistent intervention of government into the economy of early Canada put in place a precedent that created the conditions for later intervention into culture. Though it is common to consider Innis's later work as the locus of his development of a discussion of culture, the early economic studies uncover a set of circumstances unique to Canadian national development that recur with regard to culture. The nation-building processes that Innis discovers installed with the initial formation of the dominion become the bases for subsequent development, in both the economic and cultural spheres.

Presumably, it was Innis's understanding of how these initial factors of Canadian nation-building had led to economic catastrophe that provoked him to comment on the Massey Report. The "plea for time" that occupies his later thought is based on an understanding of the effects of the communication system he argued was constitutive of Canada itself. Much as the system initially provided the mechanism for importation of manufactured goods from, and creation of economic dependence on, Western Europe, it evolved into one geared towards the influx of cultural goods from the United States and hence cultural dependence.

Innis clearly grasped the relation between defence and culture. In *The Bias of Communication* (1951a, 33), he wrote that "the capacity to concentrate on intense cultural activity during a short period of time and to mobilise intellectual resources over a vast territory assumes to an important extent the development of an armed force to a high state of efficiency." This had clearly not been the case in Canada, as was shown by Laxer's discussion of underdevelopment, and had resulted in the cultural underdevelopment that the Massey Commission was supposed to address. What Innis recognized was that the communication system itself, despite its bi-directional flow, was the essential component in the construction of a culture as a security apparatus. What he did not foresee was the transformation of Canadian culture into a component of a strategy for economic self-reliance. The innovative capacities for cultural activity he detected in Canada's marginality have been eroded in the shift from culture as the production of identity to culture as an industrial enterprise. As an economic exercise, the production of culture actively erases regional and national identity.

Of course, the culture that the Massey Commission (and Innis as well) had in mind was not Canadian anyway. Hidden behind the argument for innovation lurked another "monopoly of knowledge" in the form of the aesthetic traditions of Greece and western Europe. To counterpoise that tradition with an emergent American monopoly would not produce a Canadian culture either, but merely an ersatz classical tradition, or at worst an effete aestheticism. It was not enough for the Massey Report (Canada 1951, 107) to insist that the regions should be bound together by national programs – the geography of Canada would no longer provide the mainstay for the construction of Canadian art: "Modern Canadian painting can no longer exploit the novelty of the Canadian landscape. Our young abstract painters are being judged in exactly the same footing as are the abstract painters of other countries."

Here the question of geography, or rather its erasure, looms large. We can detect the emergence of an aesthetic internationalism in which the specificities of indigenous cultural production give way to a trans-national set of criteria for aesthetic and cultural production. Regional practices take a back seat to international aesthetic norms. This in turn suggests that Canada's cultural producers are looking for a way out from under their marginal status – seeking to produce cultural goods that engage aesthetic problems that transcend national boundaries. The very specificity of Canadianism, found chiefly in representations of the landscape, is to be abandoned for an

international perspective in which Canada can takes its place alongside other nations.

The problem we are confronted with here, however, is the absence of
research on the flow and circulation of aesthetic ideas and norms. We
have certainly witnessed the internationalization of aesthetic practices,
much as we are now seeing the same thing happen in trade, but very
little information exists as to how these practices penetrate regions and
how they replace indigenous production. What is noticeable is the profound *absence* of geography: for the Massey Commission, geography
represented an impediment to the transformation of Canada from a
provincial to a cosmopolitan society along aesthetic lines. The sense of
place is reduced to a set of idiosyncratic patterns that, if they appear at
all, only mediate in a weak manner what is clearly an international
form. Regional identity is itself mediated by the circulation of supra-
regional practices.

In effect, the rationalization of "pure" cultural production occurs
along much the same lines as that of the cultural industries, particularly as concerns erasure of local, regional, and national indices. The
net result is the subordination of any specificity in regard to Canada in
favour of a set of trans-national criteria that govern the production of
both mass-market and fine-art cultural goods. In the end, this displacement of Canada renders Innis's plea highly problematical. It does
not, however, undermine the value of Innis's work to the understanding of Canadian cultural development, as has been demonstrated
above. Though Innis may not have been able to predict the ironic
outcome for culture entailed in his discovery of the unique conditions
of Canadian development, his contribution nevertheless remains
crucial. It is armed with the knowledge of Canada's distinctiveness,
given to us by Innis, that we can begin to trace out the peculiarities that
have driven Canada's culture in the direction it has taken.

NOTES

1 As Paul Litt (1992, 100) writes of the Massey Commission: "The
   members of the culture lobby were indebted to Arnold for more than just
   inspiring quotations; their views echoed his on a number of fundamental
   points."
2 As Westley Wark (1992) notes, the years between 1865 and 1870 marked
   "the first stage in the evolution of a Canadian security intelligence system
   and reveals some of the early dimensions of a national insecurity state. A
   clandestine watch on the frontier, and on foreign troublemakers within
   Canada, was institutionalized" (161). By 1939 "[a]n insecure internal

frontier opened up, geographically located in the west, metaphysically located in the racial tension between Canadians of British origin and the new Central European immigrants" (2).

3 Peter Dwyer, "Notes on a Conversation with the Prime Minister on February 24, 1970," National Archives, Ottawa, RG 63, File 1378.

19 The Dilettante's Dilemma: Speaking for the Arts in Canadian Cultural Policy

ALISON BEALE

There is no metaphor here.
We are aware of the heat of the water, coldness of the rain,
smell of mud in certain sections that farts
when you step on it, mud never walked on
so you can't breathe, my God you can't breathe this air
and you swim fast your feet off the silt of history
that was there when the logs went
leaping down for the Rathburn Timber Company
when those who stole logs had to leap
right out of the country if caught.

– Michael Ondaatje 1989, 63

To us it is no dilettante work, no sleek officiality; it is sheer
rough death and earnest.

– Thomas Carlyle 1891

THE DOMINION OF UNREASON

Plato wanted to exclude poets from his republic because of the damage
they do to reason. What does it mean for us that Canadians are faced
by poets every time they turn a corner or look in a mirror. Poets (Margaret Atwood, Michael Ondaatje) are the public face of the country,
poets have infiltrated the law and government (Frank Scott, Gérald
Godin). Musical poets are on MuchMusic (Leonard Cohen, Joni
Mitchell). Poets make politics of private experience and will not keep

their bodies out of public affairs (Evelyn Lau, Nicole Brossard). But Platonists are not so easily foiled. If they cannot keep the poets down they can keep their poetry out. For is not Art the antithesis of Culture? "Is there something in our culture that kills art? And *should* art be killed? And is there something in our art that kills culture?" (Kroetsch 1993, 179).

Is art the antithesis of culture? In cultural policies it frequently is. The distinction is generally made between culture as a way or ways of life particular to peoples and nations and art, which is a set of activities chosen according to elite and traditional values for support and promotion by the state. Does our culture kill art? It does its best. It drives out all sign of unbalanced, obsessive interest in expression, and the practice and mastery of extravagant, unproductive skills in most of us and isolates the rest in their genius. Should art be killed? If it is not, our culture cannot be sustained. Is there something in our art that kills culture? Yes, because art must kill the thing it lives on in order to make its own life. This is true for good art and bad art.

Considering the danger that art poses to society, it is remarkable that so much is allowed to survive. It has been suggested that cultural policy is "totalising and modernising" and "deeply implicated in agendas of cultural nationalism" (Volkering 1994, 18). Certainly, consistent with modernism, policy has attempted to apply reason to an artistic process of breaking up the past in order to make the future. The Massey Report (Canada 1951), the foundation of contemporary cultural policies in Canada, quotes St Augustine: "A nation is an association of reasonable beings united in a peaceful sharing of the things they cherish" (quoted in Litt 1992, 210).[1] The report emphasized the role of the arts in maintaining a healthy public sphere, one in which a critical and historically informed citizenry sharing a legacy of values could employ reason to determine its collective future. It also established the principle that in Canada, because of "market failure" and the problem of geography, only the state could ensure the survival of the arts and, by extension, of democracy itself.

Here I argue that while many, including artists, subscribe to the view that art is the antithesis of reason rather than its guarantee, reason, or at least the false reason of administrators, is not the enemy of art. The enemy is the limited, decorative, or emblematic version of the arts that is entertained in the formation of policy. Art is feared for its potential for directness rather than because it is trivial embellishment or distraction. Everything possible has been done in Canada to eliminate poetry from the language of cultural policy, not because this language is indirect and allusive, or will create, as Plato feared, a frenzy of emotion, but precisely because, as Ondaatje's poem says, "there is no metaphor here."

At the end of 1994, the Canada Council set about developing a new strategic plan in order to be equipped for financial cuts anticipated in the February 1995 federal Budget. The process of consultation with the arts community was compromised by the hasty and late delivery of invitations and workbooks to the arts communities in various cities and by the ensuing perception that the "consultation" was a charade, a feeble public relations device. The budget cuts were coming anyway. The process was boycotted in Montreal and heavily criticized by artists elsewhere.

What is striking is that these protests had not arisen before and that for so many years the official representatives of the arts communities have played the game – that is, learned the jargon of economics and sincerely or not acknowledged the superior wisdom of consultants, political scientists, and economists at the management of the arts. Members of the arts community, which includes as broad a range of political views as can be found in any profession or "interest group" in Canada, have contributed through omission and commission to the muffling of their own voices. How has this come about?

INVENTING THE LANGUAGE OF
CULTURAL POLICY

Maria Tippett's *Making Culture* (1990) shows that Canadian artists and arts organizations were active from the early nineteenth century in promoting the idea of *organized* arts activity that would benefit the community as a whole. Various rationales were put forward by advocates of the arts, such as the benefit to a new nation of learning its own history, the easier absorption of immigrants into Canadian society, and the arts as a part of the education for citizenship, or British subjecthood. In Tippett's book it also becomes clear that this conservative community agenda was poor preparation for more serious commitment to the arts. Canadian art students in Paris in the 1920s were unprepared by their provincial teachers to understand the language of impressionism, let alone contemporary European trends. Canadian composers were reviled in Toronto papers for the cacophonous compositions their training in the United States produced. The effects of the worthy but unpassionate training available at home is famously symptomatized by Emily Carr's nervous collapse in Europe.

None the less, education in the arts deserves more attention in the history of Canadian cultural policy. From Victorian times and right through the era of the Aird Commission on broadcasting (1928–29) and the Massey Commission (1949–51) a practical knowledge of the arts was regarded as an essential part of the school curriculum and as part of citizenship. This practical knowledge, it was believed, intro-duced the child to the cultural heritage of the colonial society, formed character, and taught discipline. It had little to do with romantic and modernist ideas of self-expression, which is not to say that it was sup-posed to be unpleasurable. As one Canadian architectural critic sug-gests in a back-handed account of present public apathy in the face of postmodern pastiche in architecture, there were some advantages in the teaching of sol-fa and sight-singing, drawing, reciting, and (in this case) Western art history, including the orders of classical architecture (Boddy 1994). All these elements were included in the high school or normal school curriculum earlier in this century. They created a public with a common body of knowledge, prepared to participate as critical amateurs and audiences in the developing arts in the country. The results were Eurocentric, elitist, and conservative, but they were also universal within the public education systems and were oriented to an applied and not merely passive acquaintance with the culture they advocated.

It pays to look closely as well at the ways in which the arts were promoted for public support, and by whom. Little attention has been paid to class and gender in arts patronage and participation in Canada or to who speaks for the arts and in what language. I have already suggested that in order to enter into public discourse, the arts have had to come draped in ulterior motives. The curriculum and culture I described above were advocated because they would improve the individual morally and would make of Canada a "civi-lized" model among nations in the British Empire. Publicly funded education made it possible to open such activities beyond the indi-vidual patrons and private societies that sustained the performing and fine arts until well into this century. Even at a time when most financial support for the arts and arts teaching came from the private Carnegie, Guggenheim, and Rockefeller foundations, most of their gifts were filtered, through public educational institutions in Canada, from schools to universities. As was to be the case in the early years of the Canada Council, support for individual artists, as opposed to institutional education, training, and touring, was minimal from these sources (Beale 1993).

In the 1940s, the Massey Commission built on the educational dis-course that had created a space where the interests of the state in forming the citizen could be both realized and acceptably rationalized. Its report articulated the idea that cultural training provided the only resistance – an inoculation – against American popular culture. Its attitude towards this culture was complex. It displayed cultural elitism and anti-imperial nationalism, but also a fear that popular culture allowed no place for critical thought. Fear of the "mass" as anti-rational had its roots in the experience of fascism in the immediate past (Second World War), and in the contemporary context of the Cold War and anti-communist hysteria. The Massey Report institutionalized cultural policy not only as a rational activity in itself, building on the legacy of education, but as protection for the capacity for rational debate essential to democracy.

The major representative body of Canadian artists, the Federation of Canadian Artists (FCA), had made recommendations to the House of Commons Committee on Reconstruction and Re-establishment (1942) whose members were, with one notable exception, in sympathy with the subsequent recommendations of the Massey Commission: "The Artist's Brief ... was commended by the Committee and by the press for its highly organized and humanitarian thrust. Its recommendations included the need for a federal cultural agency and the establishment of a network of community art centres. A final section itemized problems that should receive government attention, including, interestingly, copyright concerns, Canadian content, decentralization and multiculturalism" (MacLachlan 1992, 28).

Canadian artists departed from what was to become government policy. The FCA had recommended from its inception that Canada should develop community arts centres. Several speakers at the meeting that led to formation of the FCA – the Kingston Conference of 1941 – had noted that in wartime "the need for art in the community life is greater than it has been at any other time" and had urged that artists be integrated into society, not enshrined (or embalmed) as protégés of an elite: "While wealthy entrepreneurs collected European old masters, living artists were marginalized" (MacLachlan 1992, 27).

Cracks in the surface of artistic unity appear at this point. For if practising artists were articulating a left-wing populism and nationalism, their counterparts in the curatorial establishment were opposed to the community centre plan and to decentralization. Their fears for the National Gallery and the major provincial galleries in the face of "competition" from community arts centres were to prove unfounded, however, since the apparent elitism and symbolism of cultural palaces was one with which government was vastly more comfortable. It is doubtful that the choice (if choice it ever was) between the two models was an economic one and far more probable that the idea of community arts centres lacked "recognition" and advocacy as a concept within government and the arts establishment. Indeed, there would have been no necessary contradiction in supporting both. In hindsight, however, Dot Tuer suggests convincingly that this recommendation is

a lost possibility and that the institutions we do have have become naturalized as the only ways of publicly supporting the arts: "That the
community arts proposal was completely lost in the historical shuffle,
however, does suggest the degree to which the recommendations which
emerged from the [Massey] Report have historically overdetermined
our imagination of the past and impoverished our vision of the future"
(Tuer 1992, 34).

The absence of artists from the Massey Commission, despite its
mandate for "the Arts, Letters and Sciences," has of course been criticized. Paul Litt (1992) has responded to the criticism in a way that
glosses over this absence but also sets the stage for his and others' subsequent damning of an undifferentiated cultural-academic elite represented by the commission: "[T]his [lack of artists] was understandable
since the commission was not officially intended to concern itself
directly with the arts. Most of the commissioners were friends-of-gov-
ernment insiders who belonged to the same quasi-academic cultural
elite and were more concerned about national culture than the arts per
se. Since the commission was founded to protect and advance the
favourite causes of the elite, it is not surprising that its composition
reflected its origins and purposes" (1992, 35).

However, it is useful to emphasize the composition of the commission. There were no artists; the commissioners were all academics,
apart from Vincent Massey himself and the engineer Arthur Surveyer,
who had academic colleagues involved with him in developing science
and technology research in Canada. The group was not just academic,
but firmly ensconced in the academic elite, with the exception of Hilda
Neatby, who held the same cultural views but was marginalized both
as a woman and as a westerner.

I would argue that in the specific case of community arts versus flagship cultural palaces, such a group was predisposed to arguments in
favour of the scholarly, curatorial function of such institutions and the
hierarchy of knowledge they maintain. While the commissioners may
have claimed at times to speak for Art, they did so in a way constrained
by their professional affiliations and in a context where education and
educational institutions were accredited representatives of the public
interest in a way in which artists themselves were not.

When the Massey Commission had reported, Canadian newspapers
joined in "a ritualistic opening protest prior to a more thoughtful consideration of the commission's proposals." The protest emphasized
"high brows and long hairs" and the usual line, "that the academics
responsible for the report, being academics, were out of touch with
reality" (224–5). With this exception, however, most of the criticism
aimed at the commission and at the model of elite cultural nationalism

it represents has been directed at artists and at the arts. The academics responsible for the policy went relatively unscathed.

REASON OVER PASSION

[*Reason over Passion* is the title of both a film (1967–69) and a quilt by Joyce Wieland in which she mocks the sceptical Enlightenment rationality that was the key to Pierre Trudeau's self-presentation and with which he succeeded in provoking "sentimental" leftists.]

The second area of divergence between representatives of artists and the Massey Commission is to be found in the artists' manifesto created in Quebec and known as *Refus Global* (1948). While the government of Quebec strongly resisted Massey Report recommendations as infringing on provincial powers, a small but articulate contingent of artists in several fields fought on another front by publishing this manifesto, which was concerned with freedom of expression, emotion, abstraction, and individuality. The values that it put forward were anathema to a repressed Catholic society and an authoritarian government and antithetical to the Reason, Augustinian and secular, that so strongly marked the Massey Commission. From the perspective of art historians, the *refus* represents just one example of the convergence of some early-twentieth-century aesthetic philosophies in another provincial context. Similar results of the meeting of the avant-garde and provincial cultures have been repeated elsewhere in Canada and in other former European colonies. This artistic manifesto and its role in the Quiet Revolution are still significant for us in Quebec and the rest of Canada.

The *Refus Global* declared:

[O]ur duty is simple: To break definitively with all conventions of society and its utilitarian spirit! We refuse to live knowingly at less than our spiritual and physical potential; refuse to close our eyes to the vices and confidence tricks perpetuated in the guise of learning, favour, or gratitude; refuse to be ghettoes in an ivory tower, well-fortified but to easy to ignore; refuse to remain silent – do with us what you will, but you shall hear us; refuse to make a deal with la gloire and its attendant honours: stigmata of malice, unawareness of servility; refuse to serve and be used for such ends; refuse all intention, evil weapon of reason – down with them, to second place!

Make way for magic! Make way for objective mysteries! Make way for love! Make way for necessities! (MacLachlan 1992, 30)

Though mysticism, anti-rationalism, and the romantic view of the artist had been articulated before in Canadian society, this is the first political statement to challenge the orthodoxies, "distinct" but (in terms of their attachment to rationality and education) quite similar, of English- and French-speaking Canada. But it is not quite correct to suggest that Paul-Émile Borduas was "echoing" Walter Abell, who at the Kingston Conference had argued that North American society was culturally undemocratic. The Quebec artists in this instance were less concerned with democratizing the arts via community centres than with freedom of expression (including freedom from the censorship of church and State) and recognition for aesthetic principles that challenged provincial orthodoxies, especially representational and high-minded ideals in art. This is explicit in their "refusal" to have the arts used as the vehicle for transmitting conformist and conservative nationalist values.

It is doubtful that the *refus* had any impact on cultural policy as part of the Canadian artists' campaign for public subsidy.[2] Whereas there are many examples of Canadian artists in the 1950s and 1960s adopting aesthetic positions similar to those of the Automatistes, the representatives of artists such as the Canadian Conference for the Arts tended to collaborate with government programs for the arts tied to nationalism, pedagogy, and prestige. The twin claims of cultural policy-makers – that the project of policy is rational, and that its ulterior motive is the reinforcement of rationality in the population – have not been challenged by artists in their collective voice. Deconstruction as a practice in the arts and in arts criticism is well-established, and complex critiques and reformulations of Reason can be found in feminist literatures and in the discussion, after Jürgen Habermas, of the public sphere. But the pursuit of this knowledge, which is also developed in the work of artists of all kinds, has not been applied to policy.

TWO SOLITUDES

When it became clear with the election of a Liberal federal government in 1993 that the Social Sciences and Humanities Research Council of Canada was not going to be merged with the Canada Council, there was relief in both the artistic and academic communities. The academic and artistic interpretations of the government's decision were complementary. Both reflect a perception of the low status of the arts. The academics worried that their research would be downgraded by association, and the artists anticipated that their concerns would become secondary to academic interests. Though the merger is now in abeyance, it is clear that most academics no longer enjoy the esteem in which they were once held by governments seeking advice on cultural matters. Academics have continued to work in this area, but as mechanics and hired hands rather than as formulators of principle. Distinctions are made among academics, such that a historian such as Hilda Neatby would no longer be called on to compose the main chapters of a key policy report. The language of economics has taken over.

"And so the snake entered the paradise of academic interest in economics" (Innis 1995, 66). Harold Innis's portmanteau essay "The Penetrative Powers of the Price System on New World States" is pertinent to this discussion in a number of ways. His arguments trace the establishment of the capitalist system in a global context through the trade between the centres and peripheries of the European empires. He shows how statistics and the predictability of prices, which were essential to this trade, became further entrenched in practice and in economic thought as a result. Innis also demonstrates the effects of the price system on government, war, and diplomacy, first replacing the ancient rules and values on which they were based with its own, and then making them its instruments. The early history of Canada becomes an illustration of his case, as he traces the role of prices in the fur trade, and later the role of the state as an instrument of monopoly capitalism in banking and transportation as well as through the fixing or prices during wars.

The most dramatic success of the price system and the most profound, for Innis, is in fragmenting knowledge and introducing a hierarchy of knowledge in which the calculation of price has become the most prestigious. In Canada the establishment of this hierarchy was well under way in the 1940s before the Massey Commission insisted that there were other, older values. Though, as I noted above, its report has been both celebrated and denounced for attempting to set a "high-toned" agenda for Canadian culture, and as having succeeded in that goal, it may be time to revisit both assessments. Rather than inventing the paternalistic relationship of education to the arts, the Massey Report might be said to have been the last significant formulation of this lopsided partnership. It certainly is the last assertion of extra-economic justifications for state intervention in research and the arts. The report follows in a long trail of governors general, social philosophers, and philanthropic foundations who articulated the same principles and objectives, clearly situating the arts within a pedagogical and institutional framework.

And the agenda set by the report needs to be separated into its parts. Certainly the institutions that it established and the administration of funding (with the emphasis on institutional funding), as well as the public funding of university research, have been enduring legacies. But this philosophy as reflected in the report faded from view in the following decades. From the 1960s on the role of the arts in enhancing the quality of life (for consumers), the prestige and value of real estate in cities and smaller communities, and the benefit to the economy of the skills and technological capacity linked to arts production were emphasized in our cultural policies. Artists and academics, each in their own way, have adapted to this shift from the pedagogical to the economic.

THE ARTISTS

A description of Canadian Artist Representation/Front des artistes canadiens (CARFAC), established in 1967, suggests an overwhelmingly narrow orientation. CARFAC was to act as a union would, in the interests of artists, to achieve copyright recognition, standardized working conditions, and a national system of rental and user fees to which galleries in Canada would have to adhere (MacLachlan 1992, 30–1). Such an organization is legitimately concerned with protecting the interests of its members, but this in a context where the parameters have already been set by others. The Association of National Non-Profit Artists' centres (ANNPAC), founded in 1976, appears to echo the 1940s proposals for community-based arts, but it too is more narrowly conceived, intended to protect artists from some of the effects of the market system.

The American artist Martha Rosler (1994) has suggested that there was good faith in the development after the 1960s of these "artists' spaces" (and other cooperative ventures in the performing arts and film/video), though actual programs for developing contact with community audiences were rare: "These 'artists' spaces' were therefore thought of as more democratic, more related to the grass roots, than museums and market-oriented galleries. The concept of the art world as a system was just then being developed, and thinking about such matters as communicative acts or messages in art, about audiences, or about government aims in giving grants, was often not clearly articulated" (56). What was important was the development of an alternative place – an idea that continues to be reborn with such inventions as the gallery as a neutral space or "liminal zone" (McMaster 1993–94, 9).[3]

Rosler, however, is convinced that, as Innis would say, the Price System has transformed the "art world." This is not only a question of the commodification of the arts. A paradigm shift has taken place, and the overcoming of the distinction between a product and its advertisement – a significant process, which Innis in his paper on the price

system examines in the marketing of printed materials and the radio –
now appears in the arts: "Most artists no longer seek to make works
that evade representation and commodification or that will not, in the
case of video and film, be shown on television ... In fact the art world
has been called a branch of the entertainment industry ... It may be
more apt to think of the art world as a branch of the fashion industry
because of its characteristic ability to turn substance into style, a
maneuver accompanied by timidity and groupthink masquerading as
bold new moves" (1994, 57).

Within this new paradigm, the Canadian critic Clive Robertson
prefers to identify what he calls the "relativizing of cultural
autonomies" – the "individual artists, artist formations, and art institutions [in a] web of dysfunctional relationships," reflecting their different roles and abilities to achieve independence within the market
system. Despite some critical autonomy, the components of the system
end up competing with one another for grants, for legitimacy, and for
the right to define norms within their field. Unlike Rosler, Robertson
(1993) sees the chief enemy as part of the art system, and not the larger
economic system: "In each of these spheres of production – criticism,
history, exhibition, and education – critical agendas and counter practices were conceived and articulated in an effort to combat dysfunc-
tionalities that had developed within the contemporary art system.
However the politics of autonomy as it affects more recently formed
organizations which represent individual artists or artist collectives and
cooperatives are often counteracted by the maneuverings of liberal
institutions" (12, 15). Certainly, more protest has been directed against
liberal institutions such as the major galleries and the Canada Council
than at the "system."

THE ACADEMICS

Like the "Art System," the "Academic System" has its competing
autonomies after research dollars and prestige. Though research into
such sectors as publishing, film, and television is now strongly marked
by the Canadian political economy tradition,[4] one which understands
cultural policy as one of the (weak) regulatory instruments of a Canadian state which compromised by being an instrument of international
capital, the reflexivity of scholarship goes only so far. Economists, sta-
tisticians, and pollsters have brought their expertise to bear on cultural
policy, motivated by hostility to public subsidy of the arts, by the desire
to increase the marketability of the arts, and by the desire to prove that
Canadians, after all, would choose Canadian if given the choice,
respectively. The language shared by all these contributors to the

debate is economic, if occasionally critically so. The agenda of government, which is to implement the recent free trade agreements while maintaining cultural production in Canada, is confused in a traditional manner, for traditional reasons, though preoccupied by the deregulation of the distribution of cultural goods.

While we academics outside economics have become very clever about cultural policy, we remain insufficiently reflexive about the knowledge we bring to bear on cultural issues. We continue to use our skills of political-economic analysis to understand the place of culture and cultural production in relation to the Canadian state and market. We do not argue, as Innis did, that the economic system and the kinds of knowledge we use are embedded as part of our culture.

Our reflexivity is incomplete because of course it is not the price system that is determinant, but rather the power relations between us. The relationship of producers to the market – political and economic relationships – become naturalized in staple-producing societies, just as they do in advanced industrial or deindustrializing, free-trading service economies. Innis's critique is directed at the bias always present when "monopolies of knowledge" deflect attention from the construction of these social relations and build instead an apparently seamless epistemology.

Innis has been described as both an economic and a technological determinist. But his economic determinism is composed in equal parts of recognition of the history and power of our present economic system and the way in which it has imposed the alchemy of the price system on our worldviews. To paraphrase a favourite quotation of Innis's, potatoes, verses, Greek, and rice are similar as commodities only because they are treated as such. We are deluded if we believe that some process has stripped away their inherent characteristics or the way in which they are produced, and even more so when we base our policies on the this illusion. His despair over the movement of political economy towards economics and econometrics led Innis to argue that it was the humanists in the universities who would be capable of truly innovative work in the social sciences and who in their research would restore the economic to its rightful place as part of a culture (Beale 1993).

This is where the arts have something to teach us. In the discussion of artist-run centres we can see that considerable insight has been gained by artists and critics working in "alternative" settings into the relationship among production, distribution, and consumption, the kinds of work and ideas that are produced, and (to a lesser extent) the kinds of audiences that are created. None the less this knowledge itself is both self-restrained and ghettoized: if it appears in "alternative" magazines, it is in order to champion one sector against another semi-autonomous sector, such as the major public galleries. If this is a self-imposed limitation within the organized arts sectors (and even the limited history I have sketched here seems to indicate that it is), that is no reason for others not to take up some of the ideas that are represented. The themes that Innis explored in his later work on monopolies of knowledge and the bias of communication are among those most frequently tackled by Canadian artists, who are concerned about the hegemony of the centre(s), unequal rights to speak and represent, and the problem of control and creativity in using new technologies. A few artists even pose an alternative to their own collective alternative organizations, by seeking to bypass altogether in some experiments the commodification and restricted circulation of their work.

Finally, to return to my opening remarks. It is neither Romantic nor anti-Rational to suggest that cultural policy, in its early elitist liberal-humanist phase or in its late elitist economistic and political economic phase, has avoided the directness, creativity, and viscerality of experience of the arts. Academics occasionally treat artists as *idiots savants*, and artists occasionally play along. My suggestion is that in so doing we conspire to suppress knowledge, ways of thinking and experiencing, of making meaning, that can transcend the very limited intellectual repertoire we have chosen. That the arts are feared is part of the Romantic legacy in which the arts are the antithesis of society. But this fear of the arts exists also because anything so intimate as the cycle of destruction and creativity involved in the arts is a reminder of mortality, of nature, and of the arbitrariness of our social arrangements.

NOTES

1 It takes nothing away from Michael Dorland's (1994) accurate critique of Marshall McLuhan's Pound-like "flight into the cosmos of the technological Pentecost of universal understanding and unity" (53) to sympathize with the outburst in McLuhan's "Counterblast" (1969): "Oh BLAST the MASSEY REPORT damp cultural igloo ... [t]he cringing flunkey spirit of Canadian culture, its/servant-quarter snobbishness/resentments/ignorance /penury."

2 Paul-Émile Borduas was dismissed by a senior government official from his job with the École du meuble – "deemed unfit to instruct the young."

3 McMaster's article concerns an installation he was invited to design at the Museum of Anthropology in Vancouver. McMaster, a Native artist, used popular representations of "Indians" to examine the politics of identity and invited audiences to sacrifice their own tourist trinkets and

trashy images of Indians in a "Cultural Amnesty" as part of this exhibition.

4 See the work of Marc Raboy, Ted Magder, Richard Collins, and Michael Dorland. The special issue "Cultural Development in an Open Economy," *Canadian Journal of Communication*, 19 no. 3/4 (1994), contains studies and overviews from several perspectives.

20 An Index of Power: Innis, Aesthetics, and Technology

KIM SAWCHUK

Mechanization has emphasized complexity and confusion; it has been responsible for monopolies in the field of knowledge; and it becomes extremely important to any civilization, if it is not to succumb to the influence of this monopoly of knowledge, to make some critical survey and report. The conditions of freedom of thought are in danger of being destroyed by science, technology, and the mechanization of knowledge, and with them, Western civilization.
– Harold Innis 1951a, 190

CONTACT POINTS[1]

Harold Innis never penned an essay uniquely dedicated to aesthetics, but his historical studies of the social implications of communications technology indicate a definite interest in cultural practices such as literature, sculpture, painting, music, and, most prominently, architecture.[2] As in his work on communications, Innis divides the arts into those dependent on the eye, such as painting, sculpture, and drawing, and those dependent on the ear, such as poetry and music. He did not separate the arts from science and technology but rather stressed their many points of contact as well as their mutual connection to the circulation of power. For example, Innis cryptically jotted down: "Science linked to technology in arts" (1980, 61). And, in "Industrialization and Cultural Values" (in Innis 1991) he commented: "Cultural activity, evident in architecture and sculpture, capable of impressing peoples over a wide area, is designed to emphasize prestige. It becomes an index of power" (133).

None of these remarks reveals a full-fledged aesthetic theory latent in Innis's work, but his thoughts on the relationship of technology to communication and culture are directly pertinent to contemporary aesthetic issues. I work from fragments of references to art and culture found in *Empire and Communications* (1950), *The Bias of Communications* (1951a), and *The Idea File* (1980), connecting these thoughts to better-known themes in his work.

This rereading of Innis is instigated by my own research into artists' projects from the postwar era that employ technological means of reproduction in their representational practices – specifically, those fashioned by Canadian feminist artists. Admittedly, Innis only hints at the exclusion of women from philosophy and religion throughout *The Idea File* by allying women with vernacular and thus implicitly putting them in an oppositional relationship to these forms of power (1980, 8, 5). Nevertheless, his work in communications, particularly his historical accounts of the space and time biases of various communications media and its resultant organization of monopolies of knowledge, are germane to this discourse. While theorists such as Jean Baudrillard, Walter Benjamin, Marshall McLuhan, and Paul Virilio have great currency in contemporary art practice, Innis has had little impact in this realm, except for Arthur Kroker's (1984) reading of Innis vis-à-vis Canadian art in *Technology and the Canadian Mind*.[3] I remain convinced that his ideas can contribute much to the analysis of art, particularly those works sharing my own preoccupation with electronic technologies.

Innis writes that the traces of a cultural proclivity towards space or time, indeed the ways in which a culture orders both space and time, are imprinted in the artistic artifacts of a given epoch and society: "The changing position of spatial organization became apparent not only in relation to political structure but also to art" (1991, 109). In short, Innis's intuition concerning the social role of art rests neither on modernist notions of art as spirit nor on the romantic notion of art as the product of the individual creative genius. Instead, Innis connected art to the world in very material ways. If Innis presents us with a method, or approach to art that can be seen as having value for our situation, it is in his work on communications technologies. His descriptions of the relationship between technological forms and the content of these forms speak critically to our media-saturated environment, as well as to the media-based art of our times.

Before continuing with Innis, I wish to take stock of the current vocabulary used in relation to media-based art. "Multi-media" is the most common term. While originally it signified use of several media – photography, with dance, with slide projection, and so on – in the presentation of the arts, it now commonly refers to the blending of audio and visual means of communication within the confines of the computer. "Electronic art" is any musical work, visual image, or sculpture that is based on electronic circuitry. "Computer art" or "computer-integrated media" covers everything from computer graphics to art that allows the viewer to interact with the work via the hardware and software. "Digital art" designates the way in which information is stored and encoded. "Media arts" are the collective disciplines that deploy any new media. "Interactive art" implies works that are not merely to be gazed on or contemplated but touched. "Hypermedia" describes works that use hypertext software to link together information in a database. "Network art" designates art that is produced for use specifically on line. "Virtual art" is concerned with the immersion of the viewer into the space of representation with the use of virtual-reality goggles and gloves.

Given this multiplicity of possible configurations, institutions have adopted terms such as "new media" (Canada Council) and "open media" (Fine Arts, Concordia University) to capture the shifting nature of art in the age of cybernetic systems. It is not my intention to police these boundaries nor to explore and link these diverse practices to Innis in some grand synthesis. Rather, I wish to indicate the many points of articulation among technology, the arts, and Harold Innis. What then can be said about this horizon of cultural projects from an Innisian purview?

CRITICAL DISCOURSES AND THE POLITICS OF FORM

Note that Innis's position was one of great scepticism towards the claims that mechanization would bring progress and that science was linked exclusively to reason. Like his mentor Graham Wallas, Innis was critical of "the idolatry of the pulpit and the laboratory" (1991, 191). His concepts of space and time articulated a theory of power for both realms: hierarchical (temporal, religious, based in the oral tradition) and decentralized (spatial, secular, based on the eye). Nevertheless, because of the predominance of scientific thought in his own time, Innis directed his most barbed criticisms towards this branch of knowledge, not religion.

He blatantly expressed his support for the "oral tradition, particularly as reflected in Greek civilization." This included art forms that were based on orality, such as music and poetry (190). In Innis's estimation, "creative thought was dependent on the oral tradition and conditions favorable to it were gradually disappearing with the mechanization of knowledge." Oral communication, which he conceived of as communication between two flesh-and-blood human beings occupying proximic space, achieved a balance between feeling and human action that has been lost. "The oral tradition involves personal contact and a consideration of the feelings of others, and it is in sharp contrast with the cruelty of mechanized communication" (191).

At times, this concern with our "present-mindedness," his "plea for time," and his somewhat formulaic assessment of their dialectical interplay arguably make him a cultural conservative – pointing to some of the theoretical weaknesses and political pitfalls of his theory. He argued against adult education in Manitoba, because he did not believe that the educational system was training its pupils to "choose the facts and make their own decisions" but was a method of propaganda in democratic countries (203). Internal transformation of the education system was impossible because its spread was dependent on communicative forms, such as textbooks, that standardize knowledge. For Innis, only opposition to standardized knowledge could restore the balance in a society severely tilted towards the domination of space and territory.

Given this emphasis on direct forms of cultural exchange outside mediated relations, his position on culture is amodern: outside, even opposed to modernity. His bias towards the Greeks causes him to play down the dynamics of power in this culture and in situations of direct human contact. He acknowledges, but underestimates, the extra-discursive conditions, the gender or class relations, at play in rhetoric and speech. Innis's faith in oral communication also assumes that there are no internal contradictions to mechanized forms of communication: the internet, for example, and its diverse functions, from e-mail to chat lines, are a fusion of the real-time experience of a conversation at a distance in a textual form and delayed communication. As such, this and many other forms of contemporary communication do not neatly fit into his dialectic.

Despite this position, and my objections to his thinking in some of these areas, Innis's "amodernism" remains pertinent to this history and to art practices that take new media as their subject and means. His work on communication systems maintains that the media we use to communicate are not simply ways to further our contact with each other but give rise to distinct forms of social organization. As such they are connected to social power. This is an important reminder when so much of the discourse on new technology is imbued with the rhetoric of the electronic sublime – the belief that these technologies will solve our economic and social problems or allow to come to fruition the democratic aspirations of the Enlightenment. Innis does not share the classically modernist belief in technology as progress. Furthermore, his work incites us to be wary of this prevalent utopianism.

One finds progressive claims for interactive forms of communications not only in the popular press but in the arts. Post-McLuhanite philosopher of technology Derrick de Kerckhove (1995) echoes this claim. He exhorts artists and designers to fashion "intelligible and livable technological environments," which he terms "enlightened design." Enlightened design is technology put to service "with the greater good and in the larger reach of people" (59). Ironically, de Kerkhove's approach makes broad, sweeping generalizations that place the origins of digital technology in the alphabet. He ascribes a profound determinism to the media, while tempering this determinism with a faith in the artist and designer to redeem whatever utopian potential can be awakened in these technologies. Artists and theorists such as de Kerckhove suggest that cultural producers can redeem the secular utopian potential of technology.[4] But what is "enlightened design"? How would it result in different patterns of work and play? Do computers allow for conductivity or control? Or is it even impossible to determine which? How would "enlightened design" change this?

I remain suspicious about McLuhanite renderings of technology, but I do share this idea with them: passively accepting the existence or technology is no longer an option for late-twentieth-century North Americans. If artists create work that addresses our interpolation into these systems, so much the better. And, while I do not accept Innis's prescription for tempering our spatial bias with a temporal one, I do agree with his diagnosis of the problem. Time has been managed into infinitesimally smaller units of measurement and calculation to maximize speed and hence productivity. Ultra-rapid, ultra-light computing machines increase our connectivity and hence the potential for control on a global level.

Technology indeed transforms patterns of perception. Here, Innis's work on technology can be compared with that of Walter Benjamin. Benjamin wrote: "The manner in which human sense perception is organized, the medium in which it is accomplished, is determined not only by nature but by historical circumstance as well" (1994, 528). In a beautiful passage in "The Problem of Space" (in Innis 1991) Innis describes the transformations of design on vases in Athens and Attica between 900 and 700 BC from geometric forms to narrative pictorial scenes. Innis demonstrates similar insights into the organization of sense perception: "The ear and the concern with time began to have its influence on the arts concerned with the eye and space. The painter attempted to create an impression of a single scene in which time was not fixed but transitory and in which several actions took place at the same time. In the fifth century this device was rapidly displaced by a method emphasizing the unity of space and time and in the fourth century a single action represented in a picture became dominant" (110). For Innis and Benjamin, among others, technology is not the determinant, final cause in an Aristotelian sense, but it does play an active, fundamental role in influencing the patterns and practices of perception and human interaction.

Both Innis and Benjamin observe the replacement of the religious function of art by a political one. They agree that this loss of a sacred function did have some progressive effects but remain aware that when art is no longer based on ritual, it is based on politics and is confronted with a whole new set of problems (Benjamin 1994, 529). Writing with the experience of the Second World War and fascism still fresh in their minds, they nuance this concern with the observation that while art could become political, politics should not become art.

I now return to Innis's use of the term "index," for I find it richly suggestive. Art works, according to Innis, are indexical because they are commissioned to emphasize the prestige of those in power. He shows how they incorporate the technological developments of an epoch or empire, employing these in multiple ways: the clay used by the Sumerians as writing tablets was also a construction material; (1986, 27) "transformation in the quality of paper – from papyrus to parchment to linen and experiments in types of ink all contributed to the growth of the printing press, commercialism and the spread of the vernacular" (1991, 52). In Europe, painters used oil as a base for paint, a development later taken over by printers (1986, 143).

Reflecting on concerns that seem to echo Innis, media artist Francesc Torres observes: "[A]rtists have consistently, not accidentally, worked with the tools of their time. There has been a correlation between technological development and art making throughout history; inventions such as oil paint and linen canvas were agents of change comparable to the emergence of chemically, and later electronically based image-making" (1990, 208). Innis suggests that materials have distinct properties that give rise to similar patterns of space, structure, rhythm and composition. Different materials demand, as Ursula Franklin (1992) noted of the casting of Chinese bronzes, distinct patterns of organization and work towards compliance, control, or cooperation. These relations are sedimented into the artifacts. Every art work tells a story of its creation.

I find Innis's thinking on the materiality of the form prescient – particularly his idea that because artists and the builders of culture often employ the same materials, art objects can be studied – albeit with a certain amount of caution – to reveal, at a micro level, tendencies in operation at a macroscopic level. Contemporary art then does not just represent the impact of technology back on us. More profoundly, when art is composed with the tools of the day, on a formal level it objectifies or gives shape to the patterns of social organization that are part of a lived world.

To his credit, Innis was not superficially causal in his understanding of this relationship. He insisted that we be aware of "the extraordinary, perhaps insuperable, difficulty of assessing the quality of a culture of which we are a part or of assessing the quality of a culture of which we are not a part" (1991, 132). He was clearly aware that while cultural products can reflect conditions within a culture, they never perfectly mirror them. Innis's views resonate in the writings of contemporary theorist Bill Nichols (1988). Nichols maintains that cultural forms give "concrete embodiment to the relation we have to existing conditions to a dominant mode of production and the various relations of production it sustains" (23). It is at this point that aesthetics and communication meet philosophy and politics. Herein lies Harold Innis's greatest potential for the study of art and technology – the politics of the form.

While I am in accord with many of Innis's theoretical presuppositions, my method differs for reading these patterns of organization as they are inscribed within art. If his footnotes and references in his texts are any indication, Innis seems to have relied heavily on the secondary sources from other historians such as M.A. Murray, Henri Frankfurt, and W.F. Albright, rather than spending time with objects in museums and galleries or speaking with living artists. Innis's general approach to theory was synthetic, and hence his reading and interpretations of visual art, music, and architecture were inclined towards sketching the overall patterns and writing "big history," a tendency that is Hegelian in its influence, if not impetus. He actively contemplated this stance in *The Idea File*: "Importance of broad generalization as an approach to civilization and its study – avoids discouragement of details and emphasizes unity of approach" (1980, 59). I, in contrast, am wholly concerned with confronting specific art works, discussing the ideas embodied in them by their creators, and placing these findings within their political, historical, and social context.

It is the details produced within specific art practices, the structural relations designed into the work, not simply their collective metaphorical statements about the danger of this or that technology, that indicate larger patterns. In the spirit of Innis, my research and choices are guided by curiosity and intuition. I seek the possibility of a contact, through conversation and coffee with artists. My primary interest is in "locally produced" feminist art, often created at the margins of the traditional art world and in response to its practices. The analysis that follows is not really a textual analysis, focusing on the plane of expression, but a close formal reading of particular artists' projects that gets at the content by paying particular attention to the politics of form. My question is not merely what is represented, but how it is represented, how it is given concrete material embodiment in a work.

Canadian feminist media artists Nell Tenhaaf and Kathy Kennedy both have used hypertext technologies in several projects. They have fashioned media arts projects that operate as pointers not only to Innis but to the circulation of economic, political, and gender-based power in a system of neo-cybernetic capitalism.[5] Their art practices directly engage themselves with technological tools that trace their lineage back to military and political interests, realms traditionally seen as outside the purview of women. Employing the hardware and software of our so-called information society to explore the limits of these technologies may seem paradoxical, or foolish, from an orthodox Innisian perspective. But these artists are not out to provide examples of "enlightened design" in order to redeem contemporary technology. Both deploy a strategy of strategic insertion that demonstrates the paradoxes of the technology and the limits and possibilities of these systems. Their approach is not dialectical oppositionality, but a subtle unravelling of effects. To requote Innis: "it becomes extremely important to any civilization, if it is not to succumb to the influence of this monopoly of knowledge, to make some critical survey and report" (1991, 190). Consider these art works as two such critical reports.

TWO CRITICAL REPORTS

Nell Tenhaaf: Expert Systems and Monopolies of Knowledge

The cultural values of an industrial society are not the cultural values of other societies. The equation of ethical values between cultures is possibly more difficult than the equation of other values...

– Harold Innis (1951a, 133)

Innis expressed suspicion of the centralizing and standardizing tendencies of information gathering that were beginning to be apparent in the late 1940s. He suggested that precursors dated back to the construction of libraries and the work of scribes, who occupied "a strategic position in centralized bureaucracies" in earlier eras (135). Unlike civilizations with a strong oral tradition, libraries, as repositories of cultural knowledge, bypassed or weakened the possibility of uniting people by cultivating a shared memory. In *Empire and Communications* he offered the sardonic assessment that "much is preserved when little is written and little is preserved when much is written" (1986, 6). Libraries, in Innis's assessment, "became a great instrument of imperial power and set an example which has influenced the history of the West until the present time" (1991, 135)

But it was not just the sheer quantity of information that could be gathered in libraries that frightened and fascinated Innis. It was the *format* in which it was being presented that also worried him. He warned of the "constant danger of building up of monopoly of knowledge in terms of material, – manuscripts, books, and libraries – leading to revolt on fringes of new techniques" (1980, 76). Archives, Innis insinuated, give a sense of continuity; but he wondered about the obsession with preservation. "Culturally, we are stressing accumulation, rather than synthesis" (223). The reason, he believed, was that "reading is quicker than listening and concentrated individual thought than verbal exposition or counter exposition of arguments" (1991, 191). Speed is more important than content or ethics. Innis's trepidation about even his own scholarly profession echoes in other works: for Innis, forms of writing and recording are not connected to the preservation of history. Their primary function is the expansion of power across geographical space.

Nell Tenhaaf is a Montreal artist whose multi-media installations have used photographs, computer-generated graphics, and video and slide projections, along with painting, drawing, and sculpture. In a vein similar to that explored by Innis, the character of knowledge under present possibilities for unlimited information storage and speedy, if not instantaneous retrieval has been at the heart of her work. In the 1980s Tenhaaf persuaded officials in the Canadian Department of Communications (DOC) to let her participate in the Telidon field trials. This emerging hypertextual technology would allow access to various databases, which the DOC hoped might have wide commercial applications.[6] Her work in this area is a precursor of the hypermedia formats – for example, so-called interactive CD-ROMs – proliferating today.

Briefly, hypermedia are computer-software programs that allow the writer, and sometimes the reader, to construct individual blocks of information (as text, sound, or image) and make links among them. The experience of reading, or navigating, a hypertext consists of "movements" through numerous paths that, depending on the choices made, may lead to a host of distinct outcomes. For many, hypertext is essentially nonsequential writing. Hypermedia, along with other forms of non-sequential reading or writing, are characterized by a particular spatial and temporal dimension related to the way a computer organizes information. As David Gelertner explains in *Mirror Worlds: Or How to Put the Universe in a Shoe Box* (1993), the computer has two functions: storage (memory) and processing power (speed). Within this system space and time are "maps" and "scripts," a structure and a pathway through the structure.

Like all menu-based systems that seem to offer an array of possibilities, Tenhaaf's installations from this period query how decisions are influenced by the structural characteristics of menu-based systems. She questions whether they only seem to offer an array of possibilities or if they actually do. Like Innis, she is concerned with the type of cultural values inscribed within forms of "mechanized knowledge" – or in his terms, "the structural and moral changes produced in modern society by scientific and technological advance" (1991, 190). In *The Bias of Communication* Innis writes that science has transformed both the form and the content of knowledge: "[S]cience lives its own life not only in the mechanism which is provided to distribute knowledge but also in the sort of knowledge which will be distributed" (1991, 192).

Take, for example, Tenhaaf's computerized data base *Us and/or Them* (1983). This work combined fifty pages of text, maps, and graphics on the Cold War, gathered from various information sources, with manipulated images and graphics. Tenhaaf establishes an analogy between the binary structure of information based on a Boolean logic of "and/or" and the deadlock of an us/them, Cold War mentality. By juxtaposing information sources from the United States and the Soviet Union she produces a dichotomous pattern of blame. A subsequent work, *Shopping for Value (Systems)* (1984), investigates the implicit cultural imperialism and reveals the use of these electronic devices within a globally voracious free-market system promoting commodity culture.

Innis wondered if the "building up of information over long periods with the use of mechanical devices" was not confusing information with knowledge (i.e., the ability to synthesize information, make judgments about its relevance and establish common ethical ends) (1980, 66). Innis thought that abstract representations, such as mathematical symbols or icons, produced the "fatal tendency to make difficult matters look easy and consequently to continually emphasize information and neglect interpretation" (168). The demands of a menu system seems to do just that, compressing information into short, snappy sentences and quickly recognizable graphics, transforming the complicated process of reasoning and the need for ethical negotiation into the appearance of choice between clearly circumscribed bits of fact that are decontextualized and hence dehistoricized. Likewise, Tenhaaf's works from this period are critical of the tendency within these computer systems to reduce knowledge to information. The artist uses hypertext to construct an alternative "menu," drawing our attention to the way information is presented in this technologically mediated format.

Tenhaaf's installation "... believable, if not always true" (see Tenhaaf, 1988) elaborates on these concerns, examining the accumulation of cultural data in places such as museums and the transformation of historical memory. It encapsulates the three major cultural phenomena that Innis saw as proof of the advanced state of information stocking: "During the twentieth century machine industry has made it possible to amass enormous quantities of information evident in encyclopedias, history of civilization, and quiz programs." In "... believable, if not always true," a small bench is placed in front of a computer terminal that was in turn encased in a tomb-like structure. On a blue screen were five clichés such as "Seeing is believing" and "It's all Greek to me." The bench invites the viewer to sit and "consult" one of these sayings by "clicking" to delve further into the database. The statements that formed the initial menu were intended to place the user in a position of uncertainty about the "truth" of what was being presented.

To quote Innis: "Technologies of communication make for constant disturbances and shifts between faith and reason" (1980, 93). Tenhaaf's combination of information, graphics, riddles, and faux architecture scrambled the clear separation between belief and truth, mythology and science. The pulpit and the laboratory are linked. Databases can be "accessed" and consulted for guidance, much like the ancient oracles at Delphi and their divine precursors. Tenhaaf implies that these new technologies, if they are to function at all, rest on a great deal of faith: the information they convey may be trusted *because* it is computerized. If we click on a forward arrow we trust that the next "page" will appear.

These information registries serve other cultural functions, unexplored by this artist but relevant to any discussion of information as a commodity. Within present contexts, machines that dispense information simultaneously gather information. Innis hints that the Oracle at Delphi was really an intelligence bureau giving information about the colonies (1980, 34)

In a catalogue essay accompanying the show, Tenhaaf (1988) mused that her installation provided "an interactive encounter with received ideas" and was "intended to seduce through a sense of the familiar, and yet introduce a conceptual space for resistance to acquired knowledge" (28). She explains that knowledge in an era of seemingly unlimited information storage and transmission contains contradictory possibilities. An array of choices is presented in the form of buttons to push on a screen, but the choice is between two clearly circumscribed options. Furthermore, interactive systems seem to offer options, but the question are begged: Who writes the scripts? What link do they make? What knowledge is considered worthy of cataloguing?

New media of information may not revolutionize the content at all. As Tenhaaf suggests, the very obverse may happen, because we are fascinated with "processed imagery, encyclopedic data banks, and infinitely mutable sentences available at our fingertips," we cling to past references – our sacred cows, old habits, and established ways of thinking.

Kathy Kennedy: Space, Time and the Talkpersonals

Nell Tenhaaf's pieces inhabit primarily the gallery space, using digital images and text to examine computer-based technologies that involve the eye and the hand. Kathy Kennedy's acoustic projects amplify how these electronic systems work, taking the form of an orally based electronic medium accessible from the home. The sound artist explores how computer systems organize and commodify our emotions and feelings.

Kennedy's "Time Piece" (1994) investigates the formal structure of a voice mail system. This form of audio exchange accentuates the particular materiality of the voice. Kennedy intersects the inherent aural pleasures with the current political economy of neo-capitalist cybernetic culture. This work challenges Innis's clear division between the eye (the written) and the ear (the oral) as indices of a cultural tendency towards either space or time.

"Time piece" began with an advertisement that Kennedy placed in the "Talkpersonal" classifieds in a Montreal cultural weekly. There are two stages of communicating in this kind of personal ad (Kennedy calls it "dating"): seduction in the form of a print message, and seduction by vocal exchange. These seductions are triggered by several signs that both caller and respondent must interpret in order to be propelled into the second level of engagement: leaving a message. Readers read the messages, decide which message/person they are most interested in, dial into the voice mailbox to reach the voice, and leave a prerecorded audio message in the mailbox to arrange a date. Kennedy left a musical composition in her voice mailbox. Her message went: "*Loneliness kills, from the heart through the lips, I need a sound relationship.*" After listening to the message, respondents are invited to reply and informed that their message will become part of a further sound piece. Thus every vocal trace is a possible entry into a next stage of communication/dating; callers must decide if they will continue a "relationship" and at what level.

The cultural weekly in which Kennedy placed her ad is distributed free of charge. This is just one of the economic and space variables at work here. In the case of the "Talkpersonal" print ad you must compose your print message with up to 150 characters, while each phone message is approximately 1½ minutes. This space can be seen as a limitation or as one of the formal elements like the seventeen words in a haiku. While the ads in the paper are free, one does pay to leave and retrieve messages, and so messages were on average no longer than a minute. Communication costs money; to a certain extent, it is the phone companies that profit from such interactive projects.

The sense that you are paying for and receiving a private sanctuary is perhaps one of the key elements in the success of the "Talkpersonals," particularly for women, for whom actual physical contact can be dangerous in the present misogynist world. Because you never divulge your own phone number and respondents pay per minute, it offers a kind of protected environment in which to interact, if you can afford it. You are given a secret code that only you can use to hear the messages left in your box, and this secrecy adds to the pleasure, as does the intimacy of the phone. The medium of the phone box message system is, paradoxically, both private and private. For while everyone dials in and hears the same message, they listen to it individually on their own phones, experiencing the illusion of solitary intimacy.

Furthermore, these voice mail systems are an example of an everyday use of information organized into a hypertextual format. The compression of personal ads into items on a menu that can be reached by pressing the appropriate number on a telephone transforms the phone into a conduit, which in turn propels the user into an ever-expanding universe of information. The recombinant, recursive, non-narrative structure leads us into a dizzying, "unfixed" perspective – the disjunctive world now called "hypertext."

While such hypertextual systems are again seen as "revolutionary" and more responsive to how we function and think as humans – paratactically, through chains of associations – there is a risk that our spatial and temporal coordinates may end up collapsing into each other (Landow 1992). Time and space are neatly divided into a series of entrances and exits through the system, but instead of establishing coordinates from a fixed reference point easily controlled by the user, these virtual architectures function through repetition, substituting location for an obsessive engagement with the numbers on the machine that stand in for a place in the system. Spatially, "home" in a hypertext is not a physical place or a beginning in the traditional sense of the nar-

382 Innis and Cultural Theory

rative. "Home" or the "main menu" establishes some kind of reference point in a virtual labyrinth, with an eject button that allows you to leave the system.

As Andreas Kitzmann (1995) writes, advocates of hypertext claim that it is a liberating medium that virtually releases readers from the tyranny of the text and the oppression of authorial intent and determinism. However, he points out that this argument for hypertext's complexity and ability to induce dissipative structures rests on the assertion that complexity exists on a formal level, rather than in the expressive realm of language and meaning. He concludes: "This amounts to proclaiming hypertext's merits as residing almost exclusively within physical and spatial structures. Discounted, or at least pushed aside, are considerations of a temporal, cognitive, social and expressive nature" (5). Martin Rosenberg (1994) adds that the design and standards of such systems are contained within expressly geometric dimensions: what is significant about geometry is its function as an overbearing paradigm of regulated time and space (270).

Tenhaaf and Kennedy investigate the transformation of space and time, and the formation of monopolies of knowledge, perhaps more accurately described as "monopolies of information" today. They question the nature of interactivity and its current rhetoric, as touted in the pages of magazines from *Newsweek* to *Time*. This rhetoric posits that the new interactive technologies are inherently more democratic because they awaken passive viewers from their previous lethargy, giving them more choice, and more control over the conditions of their viewing (Leebaert 1991; Rheingold 1991). As Baudrillard would say, there is a difference between reciprocity and feedback (1981). Conversations are reciprocal when they allow you to transform set programs, and to engage with another interlocutor.

Does one engage in reciprocal relations with the screen or telephone, or does one merely involve oneself in an endless feedback loop? While computer-accessed databases are touted as interactive, they rarely allow participants to write in other options, add information, or determine the format in which choices are presented. This concept of interactivity conflates choosing with change. Further, this rhetoric of interactivity has been adopted by governments eager to promote the electronic highway as the solution to deficit problems seen to be caused by expensive social programs. Access to information is confused with the ability to make judgments and the ability to act. We can acquire information about what is wrong, but few have the capacity or the material means – the money, food, care, chemicals, or wisdom – to do anything to rectify our situation.

IN/CONCLUSIONS

As modern developments in communications have made for greater realism they have made for greater possibilities of delusion. It is curious to see scientific teaching used everywhere as a means to stifle all freedom of investigation in moral questions under a dead weight of facts.

– Harold Innis (1951a)

Innis ended "Industrialism and Cultural Values" (in 1951) with a foreboding comment: "Each civilization has its own method of suicide." He elaborated his reasons for such a dire prognosis: the "stability which characterized certain periods in earlier civilizations is not the obvious objective of this civilization." Writing in the wake of two world wars, Innis surmised that modern communications systems favoured the creation of empires that emphasized territorial expansion at the expense of duration or time. But the health of empires was not Innis's only concern.

The media of communication found within a culture play a critical role in determining the content, form, application, and dissemination of knowledge in a given social formation. Innis wrote the following note to himself: "Changes in media [are] of enormous significance to civilizations as having profound implications to religion, learning, and intellectual capacity and training" (1980, 99). Moreover, these epistemological transformations have ontological implications. Within the spatial and temporal configuration of a given epoch and empire, those in control of the monopoly of knowledge create systems that harness the senses to serve the accumulation of information and to perpetuate themselves. Innis feared that "[t]he conditions of freedom of thought are being destroyed by science, technology and the mechanization of knowledge" (1991, 190). It is within this context that he asked: "Is great art the indication of a proper balance between space and time ... ?" (1980, 251).

I have argued above against this proposition. "Great art" is not about achieving a proper balance between space and time to compensate somehow for the tendency to territorial expansion made possible by these new technologies. Proposing that great works, or civilizations, must achieve such a balance too easily serves as a justification for the empire, without a clear enough examination of its *internal* hierarchies. Focusing, as Innis does, on the ascendancy of specific religious or political elites, Innis's analysis of the large historical patterns of domination produced by different technological forms does not adequately describe specific exclusions and inequities – for example, those based on gender. The culturally inscribed absence of women from science, philosophy, and religion within Western culture is a central concern for Nell Tenhaaf. In "... believable, if not always true," she introduces viewers to the matriarchal presence in Egyptian culture, by pointing out the religious significance of the Cycladic goddess icon. In *Gramatica* and *Memory Room* she resurrects two feminine figures: Gramatica, the allegorical art of memory, and Hypatia, the fifth-century Neoplatonist philosopher murdered by Christian monks.

Despite his remarks on "great art" and his propensity for theorizing large historical patterns, Innis still provides guidance for those interested in critiquing the proliferation of information technologies in our culture and understanding their various uses by artists. As Innis himself demonstrates, one of the functions of art – and there is more than one – is to make apparent the contradictions at work in a culture, to lay bare a culture's values: we must "make some critical survey and report" (1991, 190). In making this report, Innis's work on communications emphasizes the medium and its characteristics, the materiality of the hardware of communications – from radio waves, through fibre optic cables, to the various machinic components – and the type of interactions or pathways for exchange that they set for us to negotiate.

The epoch of computer-integrated art and its palette of interconnecting devices such as monitors, computers, keyboards, video cameras, and telephones represents the ascendant artistic media of the postwar era. Innis connects these devices to the civilizations that have spawned their development. To achieve any understanding of how the art "spawned by our culture" functions requires detailed examination of the internal features of these works. The next step in this analysis, from Innis's point of view, would be to examine specific works in relation to larger issues of power. Such an analysis – which is fitting, given Innis's concern with political economy – would locate cultural production within the institutional context of arts production in Canada. It would look at the development of institutions, policies, and funding for the arts and consider transformations occurring in funding structures at bureaucratic levels within various government arts councils. Attention also would be given to the institutional support accorded to artist-run centres concerned with video production and multi-media, their internal transformations, and the nature of the projects and people they present and champion. Further, the study would require an understanding of the problems that arise in legal and political structures related to copyright, and the law in general, because of various technological evolutions. While many technologies are making copyright violations easier and easier, juridical and technological methods being developed and implemented to uphold the present copyright laws serve owners of systems of distribution, not artists.

Art proposes a way of representing back to ourselves the ways in which new monopolies of knowledge or information are being formed and operate within these larger contexts. Often it stands in contradiction to dominant trends. In reference to the use of video in contemporary installation work, Margaret Morse writes: "[E]ach installation is an experiment in the redesign of the apparatus that represents our culture to itself: a new disposition of machines that project the imagination onto the world and that store, recirculate, and display images; and a fresh orientation of the body in space and a reformulation of visual and kinesthetic experience" (1990, 155). In this way works that employ such tools can act as an "index to power" in our present age *and* point to possible reconfigurations.

NOTES

1 Thanks to Donald Goodes for his help in the reconceptualization of these ideas.

2 Innis's *Empire and Communications* (1986) and *The Idea File* (1980) are sprinkled with examples from arts and culture. Alison Beale has written of Innis's connection to various American institutions that funded the arts (1993). In *The Idea File* Innis adopts Nietzschean categories, Apollonian and Dionysian, to describe various art forms (1980, 43, 117).

3 Kroker (1984) argues that there is a particular Canadian sensibility towards technology and tradition of writing on the subject. While I have been influenced by the holy triumvirate of Grant, Innis, and McLuhan, I am equally indebted to the lesser known but important feminist writings on technology of Jeanne Randolph and Ursula Franklin.

4 Margot Lovejoy (1989) states: "If artists can liberate technology from those who own and manipulate its use for goals of power and profit, technology can be used constructively as an enlightening influence to gain new insight, to seek new meaning, to open higher levels of communication and perception" (10). While Lovejoy's reading of art and technology presents an extremely useful and comprehensive survey, her focus is on art's "reproducibility" and loss of connection to the sacred.

5 By this I mean an economic and cultural order whose ontology obliterates the boundaries between humans and machines, whose epistemology reduces knowledge to information, and whose political economy is based on information as commodity (Sawchuk 1994).

6 For a critical discussion of this technology, see Kevin Wilson 1988 and Vincent Mosco 1989.

Works Cited

Abrams, Philip. 1982. *Historical Sociology*. Ithaca, NY: Cornell University Press.

Acheson, T.W. 1972. "The National Policy and the Industrialization of the Maritimes, 1880–1910." *Acadiensis*, 1 (spring), 2–28.

– 1977. "The Maritimes and Empire Canada." In D.J. Bercuson, ed., *Canada and the Burden of Unity*, 87–114. Toronto: MacMillan.

Acland, Charles R. 1994. "National Dreams, International Encounters: The Formation of Canadian Film Culture in the 1930s." *Canadian Journal of Film Studies*, 13 no. 1, 3–26.

Acland, Charles R., and Buxton, William J. 1994. "Continentalism and Philanthropy: A Rockefeller Officer's Impressions of the Maritime Provinces." *Acadiensis*, 23 no. 2 (spring), 72–93.

– 1996. "A Neglected Milestone: Charles F. McCombs' Report on Canadian Libraries, 1941." In Peter McNally, ed., *Readings in Canadian Library History*, vol. 2, 265–74. Ottawa: Canadian Library Association.

Aitken, Hugh G.J. 1959. "The Changing Structure of the Canadian Economy." In Hugh G.J. Aitken et al., eds., *The American Economic Impact on Canada*, 3–35. Durham, NC: Duke University Press.

– 1961. *American Capital and Canadian Resources*. Cambridge, Mass.: Harvard University Press.

– 1977. "Myth and Measurement: The Innis Tradition in Economic History." *Journal of Canadian Studies*, 12 no. 5 (winter), 96–105.

Alexander, David. 1983. *Atlantic Canada and Confederation: Essays in Canadian Political Economy*. Toronto: University of Toronto Press.

Allor, Martin, and Gagnon, Michelle. 1994. *L'état de culture: généalogie discursive des politique culturelles québécoises.* Montreal: Groupe de recherche sur la citoyenneté culturelle, Concordia University.

Ames, Mary E. 1978. *Outcome Uncertain: Science and the Political Process.* Washington, DC: Communications Press, Inc.

Anderson, Benedict. 1991. *Imagined Communities.* Rev. ed. London: Verso.

Ang, Ien, and Stratton, Jon. 1996a. "Asianing Australia: Notes Toward a Critical Transnationalism in Cultural Studies." *Cultural Studies,* 10 no. 1, 16–36.

– 1996b. "A Cultural Studies without Guarantees: Response to Kuan-Hsing Chen." *Cultural Studies,* 10 no. 1, 71–77.

Angers, François-Albert. 1961. "Naissance de la pensée économique au Canada français." *Revue d'histoire de l'Amérique française,* 15 no. 2, 204–229.

– 1969. "La pensée économique d'Esdras Minville." In R. Comeau, ed., *Économie québécoise,* 465–83. Sillery: Presses de l'Université du Québec.

Angus, Ian. 1993. "Orality in the Twilight of Humanism: A Critique of the Communication Theory of Harold Innis." *Continuum,* 7 no. 1, 16–42.

Angus, Ian, and Shoesmith, Brian. 1993. "Dependency/Space/Policy: An Introduction to a Dialogue with Harold Innis." *Continuum,* 7 no. 1, 5–15.

Apparadurai, Argun. 1990. "Disjunction and Difference in the Global Cultural Economy." In M. Featherstone, ed., *Global Culture: Nationalism, Globalization and Modernity,* 295–310. London: Sage Publications.

Archibald, Bruce. 1971. "Atlantic Regional Underdevelopment and Socialism." In LaPierre et al., 1971, 103–120.

Armour, Leslie, and Trott, Elizabeth. 1981. *The Faces of Reason: An Essay on Philosophy and Culture in English Canada, 1850–1950.* Waterloo, Ont.: Wilfrid Laurier University Press.

Armstrong, Timothy J., ed. 1992. *Michel Foucault, Philosopher.* Trans. T. Armstrong. New York: Harvester Wheatsheaf.

Arnold, Matthew. 1983. *Culture and Anarchy.* First pub. 1883. New York: Chelsea House.

Asava, R.G., and Engwall, R.C. 1994. *Key Need Areas of Integrating the Agile Virtual Enterprise.* Bethlehem, Penn.: Agility Forum.

Assheton-Smith, Marilyn. 1988. "Communicating: The Feminist and Electronic Mail." Paper presented at the 12th Annual Conference of the CRIAW, 12 Nov.

Babe, Robert E. 1990. *Telecommunications in Canada.* Toronto: University of Toronto Press.

Bakker, Isabella. 1989. "The Political Economy of Gender." In Clement and Williams, ed., 1984, 99–115.

Balka, Ellen. 1991. "Womantalk Goes On-line: The Use of Computer Networks in the Context of Feminist Social Change." PhD thesis, Simon Fraser University.

- 1993. "Women's Access to On-Line Discussions about Feminism." *Electronic Journal of Communication/La Revue électronique de la communication*, 3 no. 1.
- 1997. *Computer Networking: Spinsters on the Web: Resources for Research and Action*. Ottawa: CRIAW.
Balka, Ellen, and Doucette, Laurel. 1994. "The Accessibility of Computers to Organizations Serving Women in the Province of Newfoundland." *Electronic Journal of Virtual Culture*, Special Issue on Gender, 2 no. 3 (15 July).
Barbeau, Victor. 1939a. "La bourgeoisie et la culture." In *L'avenir de notre bourgeoisie*, 57–90. Montreal: Bernard Valiquette.
- 1939. *Le ramage de mon pays*. Montreal: Bernard Valiquette.
- 1977. *La tentation du passé*. Montreal: La Presse.
Barnes, Trevor, ed. 1993. "Focus: A Geographical Appreciation of Harold A. Innis." *Canadian Geographer / Le Géographe canadien*, 37 no. 4, 352–64.
Bateson, Gregory. 1972. *Steps to an Ecology of Mind*. New York: Ballantine Books.
Baudrillard, Jean. 1981. *For a Critique of the Political Economy of the Sign*. Trans. Charles Levin. St Louis, Mo.: Telos Press.
- 1983. *Simulations*. Trans. Paul Foss, Paul Patton, and Philip Beitchman. New York: Semiotext(e).
- 1990. *Fatal Strategies: Crystal Revenge*. New York: Semiotext(e).
Beale, Alison. 1993. "Harold Innis and Canadian Cultural Policy in the 1940s." *Continuum*, 7 no. 1, 75–90.
Belanger, Marc. 1994. "SoliNet: Electronic Conferencing for the Trade Union Movement." *Cy.Rev: A Journal of Cybernetic Revolution, Sustainable Socialism and Radical Democracy* (July), 18–24.
Benjamin, Walter. 1994. "The Work of Art in the Age of Its Technical Reproducibility." In Stephen David Ross, ed., *Art and Its Significance: An Anthology of Aesthetic Theory*, 3rd ed., 526–38. New York: State University of New York Press.
Benson, Lee. 1951. "The Historical Background of Turner's Frontier Essay." *Agricultural History*, 25 no. 2, 59–82.
Berger, Carl. 1976. *The Writing of Canadian History: Aspects of English-Canadian Historical Writing since 1900*. Toronto: University of Toronto Press.
Berland, Jody. 1992. "Angels Dancing: Cultural Technologies and the Production of Space." In Lawrence Grossberg, Cary Nelson, and Paula Treichler, eds., *Cultural Studies*, 38–55. New York: Routledge.
- 1993. "On the Politics of Representing (Canadian) Culture." *Alphabet City*, 3, 58–63.
- 1996. "Mapping Space: Imaging Technologies and the Planetary Body." In S. Aronowitz, B. Martinsons, and M. Menser, eds., *Technoscience and Cyberculture*. New York: Routledge.

– 1998. "Locating Listening: Popular Music, Technological Space, Canadian Mediations." In A. Leyshon, D. Matless and G. Revill, eds., *The Place of Music: Music, Space and the Production of Place*, 29–50. New York: Guilford Press.

– 1999. "Nationalism and the Modernist Legacy: Dialogues with Innis." In J. Berland and S. Hornstein, eds., *Capital Culture: A Reader in Modernist Legacies, State Institutions and the Value(s) of Modern Art*. Montreal: McGill-Queen's University Press.

Bernier, Gérald, and Salée, Daniel. 1987. "Social Relations and Exercise of State Power in Lower Canada, 1791–1840: Elements for an Analysis." *Studies in Political Economy*, 22, 101–43.

Bickerton, James. 1990. *Nova Scotia, Ottawa and the Politics of Regional Development*. Toronto: University of Toronto Press.

Birke, Lynda. 1990. "Selling Science to the Public." *New Scientist* (18 Aug.): 40–4.

Biss (Spry), Irene. 1936. "Hydro-Electric Power." In W. Stewart Wallace, gen. ed., *Encyclopedia of Canada*, vol. 3, 224–32. Toronto: University Associates of Canada.

– 1937. "Water." In W. Stewart Wallace, gen. ed., *Encyclopedia of Canada*, vol. 6, 262–77. Toronto: University Associates of Canada.

Blain, Jean. 1972. "Économie et société en Nouvelle-France: le cheminement historiographique dans la première moitié du XXe siècle." *Revue d'histoire de l'Amérique française*, 26 no. 1, 27–9.

Boddy, Trevor. 1994. "Plastic Lion's Gate." In Paul Delaney, ed., *Vancouver: Representing the Post-Modern City*, 25–49. Vancouver: Arsenal Pulp Press.

Boismenu, G., and Drache, D. 1990. *Politique et régulation. Modèle de développement et trajectoire canadienne*. Montreal: Méridien and L'Harmattan.

Bonenfant, J.C. 1953. Review of H.A. Innis's *Changing Concepts of Time*. *Culture*, 14, 208–10.

Bouchard, Gérard (sous la direction de). 1993. *La construction d'une culture*. Quebec City: Les Presses de l'Université Laval.

Bouchette, Errol. 1977. *L'indépendance économique du Canada français*. First pub. 1906. Montreal: Les Éditions de la Presse.

Bourdieu, Pierre. 1979. *La distinction: Critique sociale du jugement*. Paris: Les Éditions de Minuit.

Bourque, G. 1970. *Classes sociales et la question nationale au Québec, 1760–1840*. Montreal: Parti Pris.

Brebner, J.B. 1953. "Review of Changing Concepts of Time." *Canadian Historical Review*, 34, 171–3.

Brooker-Gross, S.R. 1985. "The Changing Concept of Place in the News." In J. Burgess and J.R. Gold, eds., *Geography, the Media, and Popular Culture*, 63–85. Beckenham, Kent: Croom Helm.

Brooks, Stephen, and Gagnon, Alain-G. 1988. *Social Scientists and Politics in Canada: Between Clerisy and Vanguard*. Montreal: McGill-Queen's University Press.

– 1994a. *The Political Influence of Ideas*. New York: Praeger.

– 1994b. *Les spécialistes des sciences sociales et la politique au Canada: Entre l'ordre des clercs et l'avant-garde*. Montreal: Boréal.

Brossard, Nicole. 1988. *The Aerial Letter*. Trans. Marlene Wildeman. Toronto: Women's Press.

Brown, Jennifer S.H. 1980. *Strangers in Blood: Fur Trade Company Families in Indian Country*. Vancouver: University of British Columbia Press.

Brunet, Michel. 1953. "Revue des revues." *Revue d'histoire d'Amérique française*, 7 no. 2, 300–5.

– 1958. *La présence anglaise et les Canadiens*. Montreal: Beauchemin.

– 1967. "The British Conquest: Canadian Social Scientists and the Fate of the *Canadiens*." In Carl Berger, ed., *Approaches to Canadian History*, 84–98. Toronto: University of Toronto Press.

Brym, Robert J., and Sacouman, James R., eds. 1979. *Underdevelopment and Social Movements in Atlantic Canada*. Toronto: New Hogtown Press.

Brym, Robert, with Bonnie J. Fox, eds. 1989. *From Culture to Power: The Sociology of English Canada*. Toronto: Oxford University Press.

Buckley, Kenneth. 1958. "The Role of Staples Industries in Canada's Economic Development." *Journal of Economic History*, 18 (Dec.), 439–5.

Burchell, Graham. 1991. "Peculiar Interests: Civil Society and Governing 'The System of Natural Liberty.'" In Burchell, Gordon, and Miller, eds., 1991, 119–50.

Burchell, Graham, Gordon, Colin, and Miller, Peter, eds. 1991. *The Foucault Effect: Studies in Governmentality*. Chicago: University of Chicago Press.

Burke, Edmund. 1881. "A Letter to a Member of the National Assembly." First pub. 1790. In *Works*. Boston: Little Brown and Company.

– 1955. *Reflections on the Revolution in France*. First pub. 1791. New York: Bobbs-Merrill.

Buxton, William J. 1997. "Time, Space and the Place of Universities in Western Civilization: Harold Innis's Plea." *International Journal of Canadian Studies*, 15 (spring), 37–48.

– 1998a. *American Philanthropy and Canadian Libraries: The Politics of Knowledge and Information*. Montreal: McGill University, Graduate School of Information and Library Studies and the Centre for Research on Canadian Cultural Industries and Institutions.

– 1998b. "Harold Innis's Excavation of Modernity: The Newspaper Industry, Communications, and the Decline of Public Life." *Canadian Journal of Communications*, 12 no. 2, 321–39.

Cadigan, Sean. 1995. *Hope and Deception in Conception Bay: Merchant–Settler Relations in Newfoundland, 1785–1855*. Toronto: University of Toronto Press.

Campbell, Sandra. 1995. "From Romantic History to Communications Theory: Lorne Pierce as Publisher of C.W. Jefferys and Harold Innis." *Journal of Canadian Studies / Revue d'études canadiennes*, 30 no. 3 (fall), 91–116.

Canada. 1940. Royal Commission on the Relationship between the Dominion and the Provinces. (Rowell-Sirois Commission) *Report*. 3 vols. Ottawa: King's Printer.

Canada. 1943. Advisory Committee on Reconstruction. *Report on Social Security for Canada* (Marsh Report). Prepared by Dr Leonard C. Marsh. Ottawa: E. Cloutier, Printer to the King.

Canada. 1951. Royal Commission on National Development in the Arts, Letters, and Sciences (Massey Commission, or Massey-Lévesque Commission). *Report*. Ottawa: King's Printer.

Canada. 1968. Task Force on the Structure of Canadian Industry. *Foreign Ownership and the Structure of Canadian Industry* (Watkins Report). Ottawa: Queen's Printer.

Canada Council. 1974. "Position Paper on Film and Video." *Policy Agenda*, 216.

Canadian Broadcasting Corporation (CBC). 1994. The Legacy of Harold Innis. Broadcast on CBC Radio, 6, 13, and 20 December.

Canadian Historical Association (CHA). 1940–41. *Annual Report*.

– Symposium. 1941. "The Social Sciences in the Post-War World." *Canadian Historical Review*, 22 no. 2 (June), 117–32.

Careless, J.M.S. 1954. "Frontierism, Metropolitanism, and Canadian History." *Canadian Historical Review*, 35 (March), 1–21.

– 1969. "Aspects of Metropolitanism in Atlantic Canada." In Mason Wade, ed., *Regionalism in the Canadian Community 1867–1967*, 117–29. Toronto: University of Toronto Press.

Carey, James W. 1967. "Harold Adams Innis and Marshall McLuhan." *Antioch Review* (spring), 5–39.

– 1968. "Harold Adams Innis and Marshall McLuhan." In R. Rosenthal, ed., *McLuhan Pro and Con*, 290–308. Baltimore: Penguin.

– 1975. "Canadian Communication Theory: Extensions and Interpretations of Harold Innis." In G.J. Robinson and D. Theall, eds., *Studies in Canadian Communications*, 27–59. Montreal: Graduate Programme in Communications, McGill University.

– 1981. "Culture, Geography, and Communications: The Work of Harold Innis in an American Context." In Melody, Salter, and Heyer, eds., 1981, 73–91.

– 1989. *Communication as Culture: Essays on Media and Society*. Boston: Unwin Hyman.

– 1993a. "Everything That Rises Must Diverge." In Philip Gaunt, ed., *Beyond Agendas: New Directions in Communication Research*, 171–184. Westport, Conn.: Greenwood Press.

– 1993b. "May You Live in Interesting Times." *Australian Journal of Communications*, 20 no. 3, l–12.

– 1996. "The Chicago School and the History of Mass Communication Research." In E. Dennis and E. Wartell, eds., *American Mass Communication Research: The Remembered Past*, 21–38. Mahwah, NJ: Lawrence Erlbaum Publishers.

Carlyle, Thomas. 1891. "Heroes." In *OED Compact Edition*, under "dilettante."

Cassirer, Ernst. 1960. *The Problem of Knowledge: Philosophy, Science, and History since Hegel*. New Haven, Conn.: Yale University Press.

Caves, Richard E. and Holton, Richard H. 1959. *The Canadian Economy: Prospect and Retrospect*. Cambridge, Mass.: Harvard University Press.

Charland, Maurice. 1986. "Technological Nationalism." *Canadian Journal of Political and Social Theory*, 10 nos. 1–2, 196–220.

Charlton, Bruce. 1990. "The Perils of Popular Science." *New Scientist*, 127 (18 Aug.), 36–40.

Chatterjee, Partha. 1993. *The Nation and Its Fragments: Colonial and Postcolonial Histories*. Princeton, NJ: Princeton University Press.

Chen, Kuan-Hsing. 1996. "Not Yet the Postcolonial Era: The (Super) Nation-State and Transnationalism of Cultural Studies: Response to Ang and Stratton." *Cultural Studies*, 10 no. 1, 37–70.

Chevalier, Louis. 1984. *Classes laborieuses et classes dangereuses à Paris pendant la première moitié du XIXe siècle*. Paris: Hachette. First pub. 1978.

Christian, William. 1977a. "Harold Innis as Political Theorist." *Canadian Journal of Political Science*, 10 no. 1 (March), 21–42.

– 1977b. "The Inquisition of Nationalism." *Journal of Canadian Studies*, 12 no. 5 (winter), 52–77.

– 1980. Preface in Innis 1980.

Chubin, Daryl. 1993. "Front Page Science: Positive Effects of Negative Images." *Biosciences*, 43, no. 5, 334–6.

Clark, S.D. 1975. "Sociology in Canada: An Historical Overview." *Canadian Journal of Sociology*, 1 no. 2, 225–34.

Claval, Paul. 1974. "Architecture sociale, culture et géographie au Québec: un essai d'interprétation historique." *Annales de géographie*, 83 no. 843, 394–419.

Clement, Wallace, and Williams, Glen, eds. 1989. *The New Canadian Political Economy*. Montreal: McGill-Queen's University Press.

Clow, Michael. 1984. "Politics and Uneven Capitalist Development: The Maritime Challenge to the Study of Canadian Political Economy." *Studies in Political Economy*, 14 (summer), 117–140.

– 1985. "Situating a Classic: Saunders Revisited." *Acadiensis*, 15 no. 1 (autumn), 145–152.

Cohen, Jean, and Arato, Andrew. 1992. *Civil Society and Political Theory*. Cambridge, Mass.: MIT Press.

Cohen, Marjorie Griffin. 1988. *Women's Work, Markets, and Economic Development in Nineteenth-Century Ontario*. Toronto: University of Toronto Press.

Coleman, William. 1984. *The Independence Movement in Quebec: 1945–1980*. Toronto: University of Toronto Press.

Cole, Arthur. 1959. *Business Enterprise in Its Social Setting*. Cambridge, Mass.: Harvard University Press.

Collins, Richard. 1986. "The Metaphor of Dependency and Canadian Communication: The Legacy of Harold Innis." *Canadian Journal of Communication*, 12 no. 1, 1–18.

Comor, Edward. 1994. "Harold Innis's Dialectical Triad." *Journal of Canadian Studies / Revue d'études canadiennes*, 29 no. 2 (summer), 111–27.

Connelly, M. Patricia, and Armstrong, Pat. 1992. Introduction to Patricia M. Connelly and Pat Armstrong, eds. *Feminism in Action: Studies in Political Economy*. Toronto: Canadian Scholars Press.

Connelly, M. Patricia, and MacDonald, Martha. 1983. "Women's Work: Domestic and Wage Labour in a Nova Scotia Community." *Studies in Political Economy*, no. 10 (winter), 45–72.

Continuum: The Australian Journal of Media and Culture. 1993. "Dependency/Space/Policy: A Dialogue with Harold A. Innis." 7 no. 10.

Cooley, Charles H. 1927. *Life and the Student*. New York: Alfred A. Knopf.

Cooper, Tom. 1977. "The Unknown Innis." *Journal of Canadian Studies*, 12 no. 5 (winter), 114–17.

– 1979. "Pioneers in Communication: The Lives and Thoughts of Harold Innis and Marshall McLuhan." PhD dissertation, University of Toronto.

Corrigan, Philip, and Sayer, Derek. 1985. *The Great Arch*. London: Basil Blackwell.

Couture, Claude. 1991. *Le mythe de la modernisation du Québec: des années 1930 à la révolution tranquille*. Montreal: Méridien.

Cox, Robert W. 1995. "Civilizations: Encounters and Transformations." *Studies in Political Economy*, 47 (summer), 7–31.

Coy, Peter. 1991. "How Do You Build an Information Highway?" *Business Week*, 16 Sept.

Creighton, Donald. 1952. "Harold Adams Innis, 1894–1952." *Canadian Historical Review*, 33 no. 4 (Dec.), 405–6.

– 1957. *Harold Adams Innis: Portrait of a Scholar.* Toronto: University of Toronto Press.

– 1981. "Harold Innis: An Appraisal." In Melody, Salter and Heyer, eds., 1981, 13–26.

Cronan, William. 1991. *Nature's Metropolis.* New York: W.W. Norton.

Crowley, David. 1981. "Harold Innis and the Modern Perspective Of Communications." In Melody, Salter and Heyer, eds., 1981, 235–46.

Curtis, Bruce. 1992. *True Government by Choice Men? Inspection, Education, and State Formation in Canada.* Toronto: University of Toronto Press.

Czitrom, Daniel. 1982. *Media and the American Mind: From Morse to McLuhan.* Chapel Hill: University of North Carolina Press.

Dahl, Cheryl. 1989. "On Scholarship and the Universities: The Thought of Harold Innis." Paper for the Canadian Communication Association, Quebec City.

Darnton, John. 1994. "UN Faces Staggering Refugee Crisis." *Globe and Mail*, 9 Aug., A1.

Davidow, W., and Malone, M. 1992. *The Virtual Corporation: Structuring and Revitalizing the Corporation for the Twenty-first Century.* New York: HarperCollins.

Dawson, Carl A. 1934. *The Settlement of the Peace River Country: A Study of a Pioneer Area.* Toronto: MacMillan.

– 1936. *Group Settlement.* Toronto: MacMillan.

Dawson, Carl A., and Younge, Eva R. 1940. *Pioneering in the Prairie Provinces: The Social Side of the Settlement Process.* Toronto: MacMillan.

de Certeau, Michel. 1984. *The Practice of Everyday Life.* Trans. Stephen Rendall. Berkeley: University of California Press.

de Ferro, Maria Cristina Rojas. 1994. "A Political Economy of Violence: Nineteenth Century Colombia." PhD thesis, Carleton University.

de Kerckhove, Derrick. 1995. "Design, Interactivity and the Production of Meaning." *Public*, 11, 56–9.

Delage, Denys. 1985. *Le pays renversé: Amérindiens et Européens en Amérique du Nord-Est, 1600–1664.* Montreal: Boréal.

Derrida, Jacques. 1976. *Of Grammatology.* Trans. Gayatri Chakravorty Spivak. Baltimore: Johns Hopkins University Press.

– 1978. *Writing and Difference.* Trans. Alan Bass. Chicago: University Of Chicago Press.

– 1982. *Margins of Philosophy.* Trans. Alan Bass. Chicago: University Of Chicago Press

Descombes, V. 1980. *Modern French Philosophy.* Trans. L. Scott-Fox and J.M. Harding. Cambridge: Cambridge University Press.

Dewey, John. 1916. *Democracy and Education: An Introduction to the Philosophy of Education.* New York: Macmillan.

– 1927. *The Public and Its Problems.* New York: Henry Holt.

Diamond, Sara. 1991. "Daring Documents: The Practical Aesthetics of Early Vancouver Video." In Stan Douglas, ed., *Vancouver Anthology: The Institutional Politics of Art,* 47–83. Vancouver: Talon.

di Norcia, Vincent. 1990. "Communication, Time and Power: An Innisian View." *Canadian Journal of Political Science,* 23 no. 2 (June), 337–57.

Dion, Léon. 1987. *À la recherche du Québec.* Quebec City: Les Presses de l'Université Laval.

– 1993. *Les intellectuels et le temps de Duplessis.* Quebec City: Les Presses de l'Université Laval.

Dorland, Michael. 1994. "Ressentiment and the Canadian Mind: Innis McLuhan, Grant." In Jessica Bradley and Lesley Johnstone, eds., *Sightlines: Reading Contemporary Canadian Art,* 40–65. Montreal: Artextes Editions.

Dowler, Kevin. 1995. "Interstitial Aesthetics and the Politics of Video at the Canada Council." In Janine Marchessault, ed., *Video in the Age of Identity,* 35–50. Toronto and Montreal: YYZ and Centre for Research on Canadian Cultural Industries and Institutions.

Drache, Daniel. 1969. "Harold Innis: A Canadian Nationalist." *Journal of Canadian Studies,* 4 no. 2, 7–12.

– 1976. "Rediscovering Canadian Political Economy." *Journal of Canadian Studies,* 11 no. 3, 3–18.

– 1977. "Stapleization: A Theory of Canadian Capitalist Development." In Craig Heron, ed., *Imperialism, Nationalism and Canada,* 15–33. Toronto: New Hogtown Press.

– 1978. "Rediscovering Canadian Political Economy." In W. Clement and D. Drache, eds., *A Practical Guide to Canadian Political Economy,* 1–53. Toronto: Lorimer.

– 1982. "Harold Innis and Canadian Capitalist Development." *Canadian Journal of Political and Social Theory,* 6 nos. 1–2 (winter/spring), 35–60.

– 1983. "The Crisis of Canadian Political Economy: Dependency Theory versus the New Orthodoxy." *Canadian Journal of Political and Social Theory,* 7 no. 3, 25–49.

– 1995. Introduction to *Staples, Markets and Cultural Change: Selected Essays,* ed. D. Drache. Montreal: McGill-Queen's University Press.

Drummond, Ian M. 1983. *Political Economy at the University of Toronto: A History of the Department, 1888–1982.* Toronto. Faculty of Arts and Science, University of Toronto.

– 1987. "Innis, Harold Adams (1894–1952)." In John Eatwell, Murray Milgate and Peter Newman, eds., *The New Palgrave: A Dictionary of Economics,* vol. 2, 857–8. London: MacMillan.

Dudley, Leonard M. 1995. "Space, Time, Number: Harold A. Innis as Evolutionary Theorist." *Canadian Journal of Economics / Revue canadienne d'économie*, 28 no. 4a (Nov.), 754–69.

Dumont, Fernand. 1962. "L'étude systématique de la société globale canadienne-française." In Fernand Dumont and Yves Martin, eds., *Situation de la recherche sur le Canada français*, 277–92. Quebec City: Les Presses de l'Université Laval.

– 1993. *Genèse de la société québécoise.* Montreal: Boréal.

Dunbar, Gary S. 1985. "Harold Innis and Canadian Geography." *Canadian Geographer*, 29 no. 2 (summer), 159–64.

Duncan, Hugh D. 1965. *Culture and Democracy: The Struggle for Form in Society and Architecture in Chicago and the Middle West during the Life and Times of Louis H. Sullivan.* Totowa, NJ: Bedminster Press.

Easterbrook, W.T. 1953a. With V.W. Bladen and J.H. Willits. "Harold Adams Innis, 1894–1952." *American Economic Review*, 43 no. 1 (March), 1–15.

– 1953b. "Innis and Economics." *Canadian Journal of Economics and Political Science*, 2 no. 3 (Aug.), 291–303.

– 1960. "Problems in the Relationship of Communication and Economic History." *Journal of Economic History*, 20 no. 4 (Dec.), 559–65.

Eccles, W.J. 1979. "A Belated Review of Harold Adams Innis, *The Fur Trade in Canada.*" *Canadian Historical Review*, 60 no. 4, 419–41.

– 1987. *Essays on New France.* New York: Oxford University Press.

Eckert, Allan. 1983. *The Gateway to Empire.* New York: Little Brown.

Elkins, Stanley, and McKitrick, Eric. 1954. "A Meaning for Turner's Frontier, Part I." *Political Science Quarterly*, 69 no. 3, 321–53.

Evenden, Matthew D. 1998. "Harold Innis, the Arctic Survey, and the Politics of Social Science during the Second World War. *Canadian Historical Review*, 79 no. 1, 36–67.

Fanon, Frantz. 1961. *Les damnés de la terre:* Paris: Maspero.

Faris, Ron. 1975. *The Passionate Educators: Voluntary Associations and the Struggle for Control of Adult Educational Broadcasting in Canada, 1919–1952.* Toronto: Peter Martin.

Farrell, Thomas B. 1993. *Norms of Rhetorical Culture.* London: Yale University Press.

Faucher, Albert. 1953. "Harold Adams Innis, 1894–1952." *Revue de l'Université Laval*, 8, 88–95.

– 1970. *Histoire économique et unité canadienne.* Montreal: Fides.

– 1973. *Québec en Amérique au XIXème siècle.* Montreal: Fides.

– ed. 1988. *Cinquante ans de sciences sociales à l'Université Laval: l'histoire de la Faculté des sciences sociales (1938–1988).* Sainte-Foy, Que.: Faculté des sciences sociales de l'Université Laval.

– 1989. "Interview" (by Gilles Paquet). In G. Paquet, ed., *La pensée économique au Québec français. Témoignages et perspectives*, 83–9. Montreal: Association canadienne française pour l'avancement des sciences.

Faucher, A., and Lamontagne, R. 1953. "History of Industrial Development." In J.C. Falardeau, ed., *Essays on Contemporary Quebec*, 23–37. Quebec City: Les Presses de l'Université Laval.

Fay, C.R., and Innis, H.A.. 1930. "The Maritime Provinces." In *The Cambridge History of the British Empire*, vol. 6, 659–71. Cambridge: Cambridge University Press.

Feagin, Joe R. 1989. "Arenas of Conflict: Zoning and Land Use Reform in Critical Political-Economic Perspective." In Charles M. Haar and Jerold S. Kaydon, eds., *Zoning and the American Dream: Promises Still to Keep*, 73–100. Chicago and Washington, DC: Planners Press and American Planning Association.

Ferguson, Barry. 1993. *Remaking Liberalism: The Intellectual Legacy of Adam Shortt, O.D. Skelton, W.C. Clark and W.A. Mackintosh, 1890–1925*. Montreal: McGill-Queen's University Press.

Ferguson, Barry, and Owram, Doug. 1980–81. "Social Scientists and Public Policy from the 1920s through World War II." *Journal of Canadian Studies / Revue d'études canadiennes*, 5 no. 4 (winter), 3–17.

Feyerabend, Paul. 1978. *Science in a Free Society*. London: New Left Books.

Figgis, John N. 1900. *Churches in the Modern State*. London: Oxford University Press.

Fish, Stanley. 1980. *Is There a Text in This Class? The Authority of Interpretive Communities*. Cambridge, Mass.: Harvard University Press.

Fisher, Donald. 1985. "An Experiment in Boundary Work: Rockefeller Philanthropy and Social Research at McGill in the 1930s." Unpublished paper, University of British Columbia, Vancouver.

– 1991. *The Social Sciences in Canada: Fifty Years of National Activity by the Social Science Federation of Canada*. Waterloo: Wilfrid Laurier University Press.

– 1993. *Fundamental Development of the Social Sciences: Rockefeller Philanthropy and the United States Social Science Research Council*. Ann Arbor: University of Michigan Press.

Forbes, E.R. 1977. "Misguided Symmetry: The Destruction of Regional Transportation Policy for the Maritimes." In D.J. Bercuson, ed., *Canada and the Burden of Unity*, 60–86. Toronto: MacMillan.

– 1981. "In Search of a Post-Confederation Maritime Historiography 1900–1967." In D.J. Bercuson and P.A. Buckner, eds., *Eastern and Western Perspectives*, 47–68. Toronto: University of Toronto Press.

Fortin, Pierre. 1984. "La recherche économique dans les universités du Québec français: les sources de ruptures avec le passé et les défis de l'avenir." In Georges-Henri Lévesque et al., eds., *Continuité et rupture: Les sciences sociales au Québec*, 161–71. Montreal: Les Presses de l'Université de Montréal.

Foucault, Michel. 1981. "Omnes et Singulatim: Towards a Criticism of Political Reason." In Sterling McMurrin, ed., *The Tanner Lectures on Human Values*, vol. 2, 223–54. Salt Lake City: University of Utah Press.

– 1991. "Governmentality" In Burchell, Gordon and Miller, eds., 1991, 87–104.

Fournier, Marcel. 1986. *L'entrée dans la modernité: science, culture et société au Québec*. Montreal: Les Éditions Albert Saint-Martin.

Fournier, Marcel, and Maheu, Louis. 1975. "Nationalismes et nationalisation du champ scientifique québécois." *Sociologie et sociétés*, 7 no. 2, 89–114.

Fowke, Vernon C. 1957. *The National Policy and the Wheat Economy*. Toronto: University of Toronto Press.

Fox, Bonnie J. 1989. "The Feminist Challenge: A Reconsideration of Social Inequality and Economic Development." In Brym and Fox, eds., 1989, 120–6.

Franklin, Ursula. 1992. *The Real World of Technology*. Toronto: House of Anansi.

Gagnon, Alain-G., and Montcalm, MaryBeth. 1984. "Economic Peripheralization and Quebec Unrest." In A.G. Gagnon ed., *Quebec State and Society*, 15–30. Toronto: Methuen.

– 1990. *Quebec: Beyond the Quiet Revolution*. Toronto: Nelson Canada.

Gagnon, Nicole. 1988. "Le Département de sociologie, 1943–1970." In Faucher, ed., 1988, 75–130.

Garigue, Philippe. 1958. "Avant-propos." In *Études sur le Canada français*, 5–16. Montreal:. Faculté des sciences sociales, économiques et politiques, Université de Montréal.

Gauvreau, Michael. 1996. "Baptist Religion and the Social Science of Harold Innis." *Canadian Historical Review*, 76 no. 2, 161–204.

Geertz, Clifford. 1973. *The Interpretation of Cultures*. New York: Basic Books.

– 1983. *Local Knowledge*. New York: Basic Books.

Geiger, Seth, and Newhagen, John. 1993. "Revealing the Black Box: Information Processing and Media Effects." *Journal of Communication*, 43 no. 4 (autumn), 42–50.

Gelentner, David. 1991. *Mirror Worlds or How the Clay Software Puts the Universe in a Shoe Box: How It Will Happen and What It Will Mean*. London: Oxford University Press.

Gieryn, Thomas F. 1983. "Boundary-Work and the Demarcation of Science from Non-Science: Strains and Interests in Professional Ideologies of Scientists." *American Sociological Review*, 48, 781–95.

Gingras, Yves. 1994. *Pour l'avancement des sciences. Histoire de l'ACFAS, 1923–1993*. Montreal: Boréal.

Goetzmann, William H., ed. 1973. *The American Hegelians: An Intellectual Episode in the History of Western America*. New York: Cornell University Press.

Goldberg, Kim. 1990. *The Barefoot Channel: Community Television as a Tool for Social Change*. Vancouver: New Star Books.

Goldman, Steven. 1993. *Agile Manufacturing: A New Production Paradigm for Society*. Bethlehem, Penn.: Agility Forum.

Gordon, Colin. 1991. "Government Rationality: An Introduction." In Burchell, Gordon, and Miller, eds., 1991, 1–50.

Gramsci, Antonio. 1957. *The Modern Prince and Other Writings*. London: Lawrence and Wishart.

– 1971. *Selections from the Prison Notebooks*. Ed. and trans. Q. Hoare and G. Nowell Smith. New York: International Publishers.

Grant, Hugh M. 1981. "One Step Forward, Two Steps Back: Innis, Eccles, and the Canadian Fur Trade." *Canadian Historical Review*, 62 no. 3, 504–21.

Greenblatt, Stephen. 1991. *Marvellous Possessions: The Wonder of the New World*. Chicago: University of Chicago Press.

Greer, Allan, and Radforth, Ian, eds. 1992. *Colonial Leviathan: State Formation in Mid-Nineteenth Century Canada*. Toronto: University of Toronto Press.

Gregory, Derek. 1994. *Geographical Imaginations*. Oxford: Blackwell.

Grey, John. 1989. *Liberalism: Essays in Poltical Philosophy*. London: Routledge.

Grossberg, Lawrence. 1993. "Cultural Studies and/in New Worlds." *Critical Studies in Mass Communication*, 10, 1–22.

Gwyn, Sandra. 1992. *Tapestry of War: A Private View of Canadians in the Great War*. Toronto: HarperCollins.

Habermas, Jürgen. 1983. "Modernity: An Incomplete Project." In H. Foster, ed., *The Anti-aesthetic: Essays on Postmodern Culture*, 3–15. New York: Bay Press.

– 1989. *The Structural Transformation of the Public Sphere: An Inquiry into a Category of Bourgeois Society*. Trans. Thomas Burger. Cambridge, Mass.: MIT Press.

Hall, Stuart. 1985. "Signification, Representation, Ideology: Althusser and the Post-Structuralist Debates." *Critical Studies in Mass Communication*, 2 no. 2, 91–114.

– 1991. "The Local and the Global: Globalization and Ethnicity," In A. King, ed., *Culture, Globalization and the World-System*, 19–41. Binghamton, NY: MacMillan and SUNY.

Hamilton, Roberta, and Barrett, Michèle. 1986. *The Politics of Diversity: Feminism, Marxism and Nationalism.* London: Verso.

Haraway, Donna. 1991. *Simians, Cyborgs and Women: The Reinvention of Nature.* London: Routledge.

Hardt, Hanno. 1992. *Critical Communication Studies: Communication, History and Theory in America.* New York: Routledge.

"Harold Innis and Intellectual Practice for the New Century: Interdisciplinary and Critical Studies." 1994. Conference held at Concordia University, Montreal, 13–15 Oct.

Harp, John, and Curtis, James E.. 1971. "Linguistic Communities and Sociology: Data from the Canadian Case." In J.E. Gallagher and Ronald D. Lambert, *Social Process and Institutions: The Canadian Case*, 57–70. Montreal: Holt, Rinehart and Winston.

Hartley, John. 1992. *The Politics of Pictures: The Creation of the Public in the Age of Popular Media.* New York: Routledge.

Harvey, David. 1990. *The Condition of Postmodernity: An Enquiry into the Origins of Cultural Change.* Cambridge, Mass.: Blackwell.

Harvey, Pierre. 1976. "Les idées économiques d'Esdras Minville des débuts à la maturité (1923–1936)." *L'Action nationale*, 65 nos. 9–10, 627–42.

– 1994. *Histoire de l'École des Hautes Études Commerciales de Montréal*, tome 1, *1887–1926.* Montreal: Québec/Amérique–Presses des HÉC.

Hastings, James, ed. 1912. *Encyclopedia of Religion and Ethics.* Vol. 5. Edinburgh: T. & T. Clark.

Havelock, Eric. 1963. *Preface to Plato.* Cambridge, Mass.: Belknap Press of Harvard University Press.

– 1981. "Harold Innis: A Man of His Times." *ET cetera* (fall), 242–54.

– 1982. *Harold A. Innis: A Memoir.* Toronto: Harold Innis Foundation, University of Toronto.

Hayek, Friedrich A. von. 1960. *The Constitution of Liberty.* Chicago, Regnery.

Hayes, Donald P. 1992. "The Growing Inaccessibility of Science." *Nature*, 356, 739–40.

Hayles, N. Katherine. 1993. "The Seductions of Cyberspace." In Verena Andermatt Conley, ed., *Rethinking Technologies*, 173–190. Minneapolis: University of Minnesota Press.

Heintzman, Ralph. 1977. "Quebec and the Empire of the St. Lawrence." *Journal of Canadian Studies*, 12 no. 5 (winter), 1–2.

Helmes-Hayes, Richard. 1985. "Images of Inequality in Early Canadian Sociology, 1922–1965." PhD dissertation, University of Toronto.

Helms, Mary W. 1988. *Ulysses' Sail: An Ethnographic Odyssey of Power, Knowledge, and Geographical Distance.* Princeton, NJ: Princeton University Press.

Henriques, Fernando. 1974. *Children of Caliban: Miscegenation.* London: Secker and Warburg.

Herbst, Jürgen. 1965. *The German Historical School in American Scholarship: A Study in the Transfer of Culture.* Ithaca, NY: Cornell University Press.

Heyer, Paul. 1981. "Innis and the History of Communication: Antecedents, Parallels, and Unsuspected Biases." In Melody, Salter and Heyer, eds., 1981, 247–59.

Higonnet, Margaret, Jenson, Jane, Michel, Sonya, and Weitz, Margaret, eds. 1987. *Behind the Lines: Gender and the Two World Wars.* New Haven, Conn: Yale University Press.

Hilgarten, Stephen. 1990. "The Dominant View of Popularization: Conceptual Problems, Political Uses." *Social Studies of Science,* 20, 519–39.

Hiller, H.H. 1982. *Society and Change: S.D. Clark and the Development of Canadian Sociology.* Toronto: University of Toronto Press.

Hopkin, Karen 1993. "Improving the Public Understanding of Science and Technology." *Science,* 259 (29 Jan.), 697.

House, J.D., ed. 1986. *Fish versus Oil: Resources and Rural Development in North Atlantic Societies.* St John's: Institute for Social and Economic Research, Memorial University.

Hughes, Everett. 1943a. *French Canada in Transition.* Chicago: University of Chicago Press.

– 1943b. "Programme de recherches sociales pour le Québec." *Cahiers de l'École des sciences sociales, politiques et économiques de Laval,* 2 no. 4, 41.

– 1972. *Rencontre de deux mondes: la crise d'industrialisation du Canada français.* Préface et traduction de Jean-Charles Falardeau. First pub. 1945. Montreal: Boréal.

Hume, David. 1903. "Of the Independence of Parliament." First pub. 1753. In *Essays: Moral, Political, and Literary.* London: Henry Frowde.

– 1965. *A Treatise of Human Nature.* First pub. 1745. Oxford: Clarendon Press.

– 1979. *An Inquiry Concerning Human Understanding.* Ed. Charles W. Hendel. Indianapolis, Ind.: Bobbs-Merrill Educational Publishing.

Hutcheson, John. 1978. *Dominance and Dependency: Liberalism and National Policies in the North Atlantic Triangle.* Toronto: McClelland and Stewart.

Industry Canada. 1994. *The Canadian Information Highway: Building Canada's Information and Communications Infrastructure.* Ottawa: Supply and Services Canada.

Industry, Science and Technology Canada. 1990. *Science and Technology Economic Analysis Review.* Ottawa: Supply and Services Canada.

Innis, Donald. 1953. "Comment on H. Innis." *American Economic Review*, 43 no. 1 (March), 22–5.

Innis, Harold A. n.d. "A History of Communications: An Incomplete and Unrevised Manuscript." Microfiche Collection, MacLennan Library, McGill University.

– 1923. *A History of the Canadian Pacific Railway.* London: P.S. King and Son Ltd.

– ed. 1929. *Select Documents in Canadian Economic History, 1497–1783.* Vol. 1. Toronto: University of Toronto Press.

– 1930. *The Fur Trade in Canada: An Introduction to Canadian Economic History.* New Haven, Conn.: Yale University Press.

– 1931. "An Introduction to the Economic History of the Maritimes." *Annual Report of the Canadian Historical Association*, 166–84.

– 1933. *Problems of Staple Production in Canada.* Toronto: Ryerson Press.

– 1934. Introduction to Part I of Innis and Plumptre, eds., 1934.

– See Nova Scotia 1934.

– 1935. "The Role of Intelligence: Some Further Notes." *Canadian Journal of Economics and Political Science*, 1, 280–7.

– 1936a. "Discussion in the Social Sciences." *Dalhousie Review*, 15 no. 4 (Jan.), 401–13.

– 1936b. *Settlement and the Mining Frontier.* Vol. 9, pt. 2 of *Canadian Frontiers of Settlement Series*. Toronto: MacMillian Company of Canada Ltd.

– 1937a. "Editorial Introduction." In J.A. Ruddick, W.M. Drummond, R.E. English, and J.E. Latimer, *The Dairy Industry in Canada*, v–xxvi. The Relations of Canada and the United States Series.

– 1937b. "The Pulp-and-Paper Industry." In *The Encyclopedia of Canada*, 5, 176–85. Toronto: University Associates of Canada.

– 1940a. *The Cod Fisheries: The History of an International Economy.* Relations of Canada and the United States Series. New Haven, Conn.: Yale University Press.

– 1940b. "Review of the Rowell-Sirois Report." *Canadian Journal of Economics and Political Science*, 6, 562–71.

– 1942. "The Newspaper in Economic Development." Journal of Economic History, 2 (Dec.), 1–33.

– 1944. "On the Economic Significance of Culture." *Journal of Economic History*, 4, 80–97.

– 1945. "Geography and Nationalism: A Discussion." *Geographical Review*, 35, 305.

– 1946. *Political Economy in the Modern State.* Toronto: Ryerson Press.

– 1950. *Empire and Communications.* Oxford: Clarendon Press.

– 1951a. *The Bias of Communication.* Includes "A Plea for Time." Toronto: University of Toronto.

– 1951b. "Modern Industrialism and Human Values: Industrialism and Cultural Values." *American Economic Review*, 41, 201–9.

– 1952a. *Changing Concepts of Time*. Toronto: University of Toronto Press.

– 1952b. *The Strategy of Culture*. Toronto: University of Toronto Press.

– 1953. "The Decline in the Efficiency of Instruments Essential in Equilibrium." *American Economic Review*, 43 no.1 (March), 16– 22.

– 1954. *The Cod Fisheries: History of an International Economy*. Reprint of Innis 1940a. Toronto: University of Toronto Press.

– 1956a. *Essays in Canadian Economic History*. Ed. by Mary Q. Innis. Toronto: University of Toronto Press.

– 1956b. *The Fur Trade in Canada: An Introduction to Canadian Economic History*. Rev. ed. of Innis 1930. Toronto: University of Toronto Press.

– 1964a. *The Bias of Communication*. Includes "A Plea for Time." Reprint of Innis 1951a. Intro. by Marshall McLuhan. Toronto: University of Toronto Press.

– 1964b. *The Cod Fisheries: The History of an International Economy*. Reprint of Innis 1940a. Toronto: University of Toronto Press.

– 1964c. *The Fur Trade in Canada: An Introduction to Canadian Economic History*. Reprint of Innis 1930. Toronto: University of Toronto Press.

– 1972. *Empire and Communications*. Reprint of Innis 1950. Toronto: University of Toronto Press.

– 1977. "This Has Killed That." Reprint of undated address given during Second World War. *Journal of Canadian Studies*, 12 no. 5 (winter), 32–44.

– 1979. *Essays in Canadian Economic History*. Reprint of Innis 1956a. Ed. M. Innis. Toronto: University of Toronto Press.

– 1980. *The Idea File of Harold Adams Innis*. Ed. William Christian. Toronto: University of Toronto Press.

– 1982. *The Bias of Communication*. Intro. by Marshall McLuhan. Reprint of Innis 1951a. Toronto: University of Toronto Press.

– 1983. "L'oiseau de Minerve." Traduction française de R. de la Garde et L. Russo. *Communication / Information*, 5 nos. 2–3, 267–97.

– 1984. *The Bias of Communication*. Reprint of Innis 1951a. Toronto: University of Toronto Press.

– 1986. *Empire and Communications*. New ed. of Innis 1950. Ed. D. Godfrey. Toronto: Porcépic.

– 1991. *The Bias of Communication*. New ed. of Innis 1951a. Intro. by Paul Heyer and David Crowley. Toronto: University of Toronto Press.

– 1995. *Staples, Markets and Cultural Change: Selected Essays*. Ed. D. Drache. Montreal: McGill-Queen's University Press.

Innis, Harold, and Lower, A.R.M., eds. 1933. *Select Documents in Canadian Economic History, 1783–1885*. Vol. 2. Toronto: University of Toronto Press.

Innis, Harold A., and Plumptre, A.F.W., eds. 1934. *The Canadian Economy and Its Problems: Papers and Proceedings of Study Groups of Members of the Canadian Institute of International Affairs 1933–1934.* Toronto: Canadian Institute of International Affairs.

Innis, Harold A., and Ratz, Betty. 1936. "Labour." In *The Encyclopedia of Canada*, vol. 3, 353–64. Toronto: University Associates of Canada.

Innis, Mary Quayle. 1954. *An Economic History of Canada.* Toronto: The Ryerson Press.

– ed. 1966. *The Clear Spirit: Twenty Canadian Women and Their Times.* Toronto: University of Toronto Press.

Irving, Allan. 1986. "Leonard Marsh and the McGill Social Science Research Project." *Journal of Canadian Studies / Revue d'études canadiennes*, 21 no. 2, 6–25.

Jameson, Frederic. 1984. "Postmodernism, or the Cultural Logic of Late Capitalism." *New Left Review*, 146, 53–92.

Jenson, Jane. 1995. "The Costs of Political Elitism." In C.E.S. Franks et al., eds., *Canada's Century: Governance in a Maturing Society*, 217–37. Montreal: McGill-Queen's University Press.

Jhally, Sut. 1993. "Communications and the Materialist Conception of History." *Continuum*, 7 no. 1, 161–82.

Johnson, Richard. 1986. "What Is Cultural Studies Anyway?" *Social Text*, 16 no. 6, 38–80.

Johnston, Charles M. 1976. *McMaster University*, Vol. I, *The Toronto Years.* Toronto: University of Toronto Press.

Jones Report. See Nova Scotia 1934.

Journal of Canadian Studies. 1977. Special issue on Innis. 12 no. 5 (winter).

Kant, Immanuel. 1970. *Political Writings.* Ed. H. Reiss. Cambridge: Cambridge University Press.

– 1982. *Immanuel Kant's Critique of Pure Reason.* Trans. Norman Kemp Smith. London: MacMillan Press Ltd.

Keane, John, ed. 1988. *Civil Society and the State: New European Perspectives.* London: Verso.

Keith, Michael, and Pile, Steve, eds. 1993. *Place and the Politics of Identity.* London: Routledge.

Kern, S. 1983. *The Culture of Time and Space, 1880–1918.* Cambridge, Mass.: Harvard University Press.

Kitzmann, Andreas. 1995. "Hypertext and the Tyranny of the System." Convergence and Transformations Paper, McGill University, May.

Kristeva, Julia. 1986. "Women's Time." In Toril Moi, ed., *The Julia Kristeva Reader*, 187–213. New York: Columbia University Press.

Kroetsch, Robert. 1993. "The Artist and Postmodern Cultural Policies." In Evan Alderson, Robin Blaser, and Harold Coward, eds., *Reflections on*

Cultural Policy: Past Present and Future, 173–81. Waterloo, Ont.: Wilfrid Laurier University Press and Calgary Institute for the Humanities.

Kroker, Arthur. 1984. *Technology and the Canadian Mind: Innis / McLuhan / Grant*. Montreal: New World Perspectives.

Kuhns, William. 1971. *The Post Industrial Prophets: Interpretations of Technology*. New York: Weybright and Talley.

Lamarche, Yves. 1975. "Le champ intellectuel et la structure de ses positions: l'exemple de la Société Royale du Canada." *Sociologie et Sociétés*, 7 no.1, 143–54.

Lamarre, Jean. 1993. *Le devenir de la nation québécoise selon Maurice Séguin, Guy Frégault et Michel Brunet, 1944–1969*. Sillery, Que.: Les Éditions du Septentrion.

Lamont, Michèle. 1984. "Les rapports politiques au sein du mouvement des femmes au Québec." *Politique*, 5, 75–107.

Lamontagne, Maurice. 1948. "Quebec: Rich Resources for Industry." *Public Affairs*, 11 (Dec.), 256–62.

– 1954. *Le fédéralisme canadien: évolution et problèmes*. Quebec: Les Presses de l'Université Laval.

Lanctôt, Gustave. 1942. *Situation politique de l'Église canadienne*. Vol. 1. "Servitudes de l'Église sous le régime français." Montreal: Ducharme.

– 1971. *L'administration de la Nouvelle France*. Montreal: Éditions du Jour.

Landow, George. 1992. *Hypertext: The Convergence of Contemporary Critical Theory and Technology*. Baltimore: Johns Hopkins University Press.

LaPierre, L., MacLeod, J., Taylor, C. and Young, W. 1971. *Essays on the Left: Essays in Honour of T.C. Douglas*. Toronto: McClelland and Stewart.

Lawrence, Guy. 1990. *Forty Years on the Yukon Telegraph*. Quesnel, BC: Caryall Books.

Laxer, Gordon. 1985. "The Political Economy of Aborted Development: The Canadian Case." In Robert J. Brym, ed., *The Structure of the Canadian Capitalist Class*, 67–102. Toronto, Garamond.

– 1989. *Open for Business: The Roots of Foreign Ownership in Canada*. Toronto: Oxford University Press.

Leebaert, Derek, ed. 1991. *Technology 2001: The Future of Computing and Communications*. Cambridge, Mass.: MIT Press.

Léfebvre, Henri. 1991. *The Production of Space*. Trans. Donald Nicholson-Smith. Oxford: Basil Blackwell.

Legaré, Anne. 1980. "Heures et promesses d'un débat: les analyses de classes au Québec 1960–1980." *Les cahiers du socialisme*, 5, 60–84.

Lehrer, Keith. 1989. *Thomas Reid*. New York: Routledge.

Leiss, William. 1989. "The Myth of the Information Society." In Ian Angus and Sut Jhally, eds., *Cultural Politics in Contemporary America*, 282–98. New York: Routledge.

Lévesque, Georges-Henri, et al. 1984. *Continuité et rupture: les sciences sociales au Québec*. Montreal: Les Presses de l'Université de Montréal.

Lewenstein, B.V. 1992. "The Meaning of 'Public Understanding of Science' in the United States after World War II." *Public Understanding of Science*, 1, 45–68.

Lewis, Wyndham. 1957. *Time and Western Man*. Boston: Beacon.

Linteau, Paul-André. 1992. *Histoire de Montréal depuis la confédération*. Montreal: Boréal.

Lippman, Walter. 1922. *Public Opinion*. New York: Harcourt and Brace.

Litt, Paul. 1992. *The Muses, the Masses and the Massey Commission*. Toronto: University of Toronto Press.

Locke, John. 1947. *Two Treatises of Government*. First pub. 1690. Ed. Thomas I. Cook. New York: Hafner Press.

Longley, Ronald Stewart. 1939. *Acadia University, 1838–1938*. Wolfville, NS: Privately published.

Lovejoy, Margot. 1989. *Postmodern Currents: Art and Artists in the Age of Electronic Media*. Ann Arbor, Mich.: UMI Press.

Lower, A.R.M. 1941. "The Social Sciences in the Post-War World." *Canadian Historical Review*, 22 no. 1 (March), 1–13.

Lyotard, Jean-François. 1984. *The Postmodern Condition: A Report on Knowledge*. Trans. Geoff Bennington and Brian Massumi. Minneapolis: University Of Minnesota Press.

– 1992. *The Postmodern Explained*. Minneapolis: University of Minnesota Press.

McCallum, John. 1980. *Unequal Beginnings: Agriculture and Economic Development in Quebec and Ontario until 1870*. Toronto: University of Toronto Press.

MacIntosh, W.A. 1953. "Innis on Canadian Economic Development." *Journal of Political Economy*, 61 no. 3 (June), 185–94.

McKenzie, R.D. 1927. "The Concept of Dominance and World Organization." *American Journal of Sociology*, 33 no. 1, 28–42.

McKillop, A.B. 1979. *A Disciplined Intelligence: Critical Inquiry and Canadian Thought in the Victorian Era*. Montreal: McGill-Queen's University Press.

MacLachlan, Mary. 1992. "The Bonding of Artists, the Growth of Culture." *Proscenium* (Canadian Conference of the Arts), 1 no.1, 27–33.

McLeish, J.A.B. 1978. *A Canadian for All Seasons: The John E. Robbins Story*. Toronto: Lester and Orpen Ltd.

McLuhan, Marshall. 1953. "The Later Innis." *Queen's Quarterly*, 60, 385–94.

– 1960. "Effects of the Improvements of Communication Media." *Journal of Economic History*, 20 no. 4 (Dec.), 566–75.

– 1964a. "Intro. to Innis 1964a, vii–xvii.

– 1964b. *Understanding Media: The Extensions of Man*. New York: McGraw-Hill.

– 1969. *Counterblast*. Designed by Harley Parker. Toronto: McClelland and Stewart.

– 1982. Intro. to Innis 1982.

McLuhan, Marshall, and Parker, Harley. 1968. *Through the Vanishing Point: Space in Poetry and Painting*. New York: Harper & Row.

McMaster, Gerald. 1993–94. "Creating Spaces." *Harbour Magazine*, 3 no. 1 (winter), 8–19.

McNally, David. 1981. "Staple Theory as Commodity Fetishism: Marx, Innis and Canadian Political Economy." *Studies in Political Economy*, 6 (autumn), 35–63.

Maheu, Louis, et al. 1984. "La science au Québec francophone: aperçus sur son institutionnalisation et sur les conditions d'accès à sa pratique." *Revue canadienne de sociologie et d'anthropologie*, 21 no. 3, 247–74.

Mahon, Rianne. 1993. "The 'New' Canadian Political Economy Revisited: Production, Space, Identity." In Jane Jenson, Rianne Mahon and Manfred Bienefeld, eds., *Production, Space, Identity: Political Economy Faces the 21st Century*, 1–24. Toronto: Canadian Scholars Press.

Mallory, James R. 1954. *Social Credit and the Federal Power in Canada*. Toronto: University of Toronto Press.

Marchak, P. 1985. "Canadian Political Economy." *Canadian Review of Sociology and Anthropology*, 22, 673–709.

Marchessault, Janine. 1995. "Reflections on the Dispossessed: Video and the Challenge for Change Experiment." In Janine Marchessault, ed., *Video in the Age of Identity*, 13–25. Toronto and Montreal: YYZ and Centre for Research on Canadian Cultural Industries and Institutions.

Maroney, Heather Jon, and Luxton, Meg, eds. 1987. *Feminism and Political Economy: Women's Work and Women's Struggle*. Toronto: Methuen.

Marsh Report. See Canada, 1943.

Martin, Brian. 1991. *Scientific Knowledge in Controversy: The Social Dynamics of the Fluoridation Debate*. SUNY Series in Science, Technology and Society. Albany: State University of New York Press.

Martin, Michèle. 1997. *Victor Barbeau: pionnier de la critique culturelle journalistique*. Sainte-Foy: Les Presses de l'Université Laval.

Martin, Terence. 1961. *The Instructed Vision: Scottish Common Sense Philosophy and the Origins of American Fiction*. Bloomington, Ind.: Indiana University Press.

Marvin, Carolyn. 1988. *When Old Technologies Were New*. New York: Oxford University Press.

Marx, Karl. 1967. *Capital*. First pub. 1867. New York: International Publishers.

Massey, Doreen. 1992. "The Politics of Space/Time." *New Left Review*, 196, 65–84. Reprinted in Keith and Piles 1993, 141–61.

Massey Report, or Massey-Lévesque Report. See Canada, 1951.

Meinecke, Friedrich. 1957. *Machiavellism: The Doctrine of Raison d'État and Its Place in Modern History.* Trans. Douglas Scott. London: Routledge.

Melody, W.H. 1981. Introduction to Melody, Salter and Heyer, eds., 1981, 3–12.

Melody, William H., Salter, Liora, and Heyer, Paul, eds. 1981. *Culture, Communication and Dependency: The Tradition of H.A. Innis.* Norwood, NJ: Ablex.

Memmi, Albert. 1966. *Le portrait du colonisé: précédé du portrait du colonisateur et d'une préface de Jean-Paul Sartre.* Paris: Pauvert.

Menzies, Heather. 1993. "Information Gathering and Confidentiality: Data Bases, Monopolies of Knowledge and the Right to be Informed." In Kathleen Mahoney and Paul Mahoney, eds., *Human Rights in the Twenty-first Century: A Global Challenge*, 793–800. Amsterdam: Martinus Nijhoff.

– 1994. *By the Labour of Their Hands: The Story of Ontario Cheddar Cheese.* Kingston, Ont.: Quarry Press.

– 1996. *Whose Brave New World? The Information Highway and the New Economy.* Toronto: Between the Lines.

Merton, R. 1945. "The Sociology of Knowledge." In G. Gurvitch and W. Moore, eds., *Twentieth Century Sociology*, 366–405. New York: Philosophical Library.

Meyrowitz, Joshua. 1985. *No Sense of Place: The Impact of Electronic Media on Social Behavior.* New York : Oxford University Press.

Mills, C. Wright. 1958. *The Sociological Imagination.* New York: Simon and Schuster.

Milot, P. 1992. *Le paradigme rouge: l'avant-garde politico-littéraire des années 70.* Candiac, Que.: Les éditions Balzac.

Morse, Margaret. 1990. "Video Installation Art: The Body, the Image, and the Space in Between." In Doug Hall and Sally Jo Fifer, eds., *Illuminating Video: An Essential Guide to Video Art*, 153–67. New York: Aperture Foundation, Inc.

Morton, W.L. 1970. "The North in Canadian Historiography." *Transactions of the Royal Society of Canada*, Series IV: 8, 31-40.

Mosco, Vincent. 1989, *The Pay-Per Society: Computers and Communications in the Information Age.* Toronto: Garamond Press.

Mullins, Nicholas C. 1975. "Développement des disciplines scientifiques: origines internes et externes du changement." *Sociologie et sociétés*, 7, 133–42.

Nassehi, Armin. 1994. "No Time for Utopia: The Absence of Utopian Contents in Modern Concepts of Time." *Time and Society*, 3i, 47–78, 65.

Neill, Robin. 1967. *The Work of Harold Adams Innis: Content and Context.* Ann Arbor, Mich.: Duke University Microfilms.

– 1972. *A New Theory of Value: The Canadian Economics of H.A. Innis.* Toronto: University of Toronto Press.

– 1981. "Imperialism and the Staple Theory of Canadian Economic Development: The Historical Perspective." In Melody, Salter, and Heyer, eds., 1981, 145–53.

– 1991. *A History of Canadian Economic Thought.* New York: Routledge.

Nelkin, Dorothy. 1977. "Scientists and Professional Responsibility." *Social Studies of Science*, 7, 75–95.

– 1979. *Controversy: Politics of Technical Decisions.* Beverly Hills, Calif.: Sage.

– 1987. *Selling Science: How the Press Covers Science and Technology.* New York: W.H. Freeman.

Nelson, Joyce. 1988. *The Colonized Eye: Rethinking the Grierson Legend.* Toronto: Between the Lines Press.

Nettleship, R.L. 1906. *Memoir of Thomas Hill Green.* London: Longmans, Green and Co.

Newman, John Henry. 1996. *The Idea of the University.* First Pub. 1888. New Haven, Conn.: Yale University Press.

Nichols, Bill. 1988. "The Work of Culture in the Age of Cybernetic Systems." *Screen*, 29 no. 1, 22–46.

Nietzsche, F. 1956. *The Use and Abuse of History.* First pub. 1874. Indianapolis, Ind.: Bobbs-Merrill.

Nock, David. 1974. "History and Evolution of French Canadian Sociology." *Insurgent Sociologist*, 4 no. 4 (summer), 15–29.

Nova Scotia. 1934. Royal Commission, Provincial Economic Inquiry (Jones Commission). *Report and Complementary Report* (by H.A. Innis). Halifax: King's Printer.

Ommer, Rosemary. 1991. *From Outpost to Outport: A Structural Analysis of the Jersey–Gaspé Fishery, 1767–1886.* Montreal: McGill-Queen's University Press.

Ondaatje, Michael. 1989. "Walking to Bellrock." In *The Cinnamon Peeler: Selected Poems*, 56–70. London: Picador.

Onufrijchuk, Roman. 1993. "Introducing Innis / McLuhan Concluding." *Continuum*, 7 no. 1, 43–74.

Ostry, Bernard. 1978. *The Cultural Connection: An Essay on Culture and Government Policy in Canada.* Toronto: McClelland & Stewart.

– 1993. *The Electronic Connection: An Essential Key to Canadian's Survival.* Ottawa: Government of Canada.

Ouellet, Fernand. 1966. *Histoire économique et sociale du Québec, 1760–1850: structures et conjoncture*. Montreal: Fides.

– 1985. "La modernisation de l'historiographie et l'émergence de l'histoire sociale." *Recherches sociographiques*, 26 no. 1–2, 23.

Owram, Doug. 1986. *The Government Generation: Canadian Intellectuals and the State, 1900–1945*. Toronto: University of Toronto Press.

Pal, Leslie. 1977. "Scholarship and the Later Innis." *Journal of Canadian Studies*, 12 no. 5 (winter), 32–44.

Panitch, Leo., ed. 1977. *The Canadian State*: Toronto: University of Toronto Press.

– 1981. "Dependency and Class Formation in Canadian Political Economy." *Studies in Political Economy*, 6, 7–33.

Paquet, Gilles. 1985. "Le fruit dont l'ombre est la saveur: réflexions aventureuses sur la pensée économique au Québec." *Recherches sociographiques*, 2 no. 3, 365–97.

– 1989. "'Le fruit dont l'ombre est la saveur': Réflexions aventureuses sur la pensée économique au Québec." In G. Paquet, ed., *La pensée économique au Québec français. Témoignages et perspectives*, 329–60. Montreal: Association canadienne-française pour l'avancement des sciences.

Paquet, Gilles, and Wallot, Jean-Pierre. 1969. "Canada 1760–1850: anamorphoses et prospective." In Robert Comeau, ed., *Économie québécoise*, 255–300. Montreal: Les Cahiers de l'Université du Québec.

– 1971. "Le Bas-Canada au début du XIXe siècle: une hypothèse." *Revue d'histoire de l'Amérique française*, 25 no. 1 (June), 39–61.

Park, Robert E., and Burgess, Ernest W. 1924. *Introduction to the Science of Society*. Chicago: University of Chicago Press.

Parker, Ian. 1977. "Harold Innis, Karl Marx, and Canadian Political Economy." *Queen's Quarterly*, 84 no. 4 (winter), 545–63.

Parkman, Francis. 1888. *The Old Regime in Canada*. London: Macmillan.

Patterson. Graeme. 1990. *History and Communications: Harold Innis, Marshall McLuhan, the Interpretation of History*. Toronto: University of Toronto Press.

Peers, Frank W. 1969. *The Politics of Canadian Broadcasting, 1920–1951*. Toronto: University of Toronto Press.

Phillips, Susan. 1991. "Meaning and Structure in Social Movements: Mapping the Network of National Canadian Women's Organization." *Canadian Journal of Political Science*, 24 no.4, 755–82.

Plumptre, A.F.W. 1940. *Central Banking in the British Dominions*. Toronto: University of Toronto Press.

– 1977. *Canada's International Financial Policies, 1944–1975*. Toronto: McClelland and Stewart.

Polanyi, Karl. 1944. *The Great Transformation*. New York: Rinehart.

Prewitt, K. 1988. "The Public and Science Policy." *Science, Technology and Human Values*, 7, 5–14.

Quebec (Province). 1956. Commission royale d'enquête sur les problèmes constitutionnels, Thomas Tremblay. *Report* (Tremblay Report). Quebec.

Raboy, Marc, Bernier, Ivan, Sauvageau, Florian, and Atkinson, Dave. 1994. "Cultural Development and the Open Economy: A Democratic Issue and a Challenge to Public Policy." *Canadian Journal of Communication*, 19 nos. 3/4 (autumn), 291–315.

Rajotte, Pierre. 1991. *Les mots du pouvoir ou le pouvoir des mots*. Montreal: Hexagone.

Randall, James E., and Ironside, R. Geoff. 1996. "Communities on the Edge: An Economic Geography of Resource-Dependent Communities in Canada." *Canadian Geographer / Le Géographe canadien*, 40 no. 1, 17–35.

Randolph, Jeanne. 1991. *Psychoanalysis and Synchronized Swimming and Other Writings on Art*. Toronto: YYZ.

Rawlyk, G.A. 1969. "The Maritimes and the Canadian Community." In Mason Wade, ed., *Regionalism in the Canadian Community 1867–1967*, 100–116. Toronto: University of Toronto Press.

– 1971. "The Farmer–Labour Movement and the Failure of Socialism in Nova Scotia." In L. LaPierre et al., eds., 1971, 31–41.

Refus Global. 1948. St Hilaire: Mitrha-Mythe.

Reichardt, Jasia, ed. 1968. *Cybernetic Serendipity: The Computer and the Arts*. London: ICA.

Resnick, Philip. 1990. *The Masks of Proteus: Canadian Reflections on the State*. Montreal: McGill-Queen's University Press.

Rheingold, Howard. 1991. *Virtual Reality*. New York: Simon and Schuster.

Robertson, Clive. 1993. "Invested Interests: Competitive and Dysfunctional Autonomies within the Canadian Art System." *Fuse* (spring), 12–22.

Rocher, Guy. 1957. "The Relations between Church and State in New France during the 17th Century. A Sociological Investigation." PhD dissertation, Harvard University.

Rorty, Richard. 1979. *Philosophy and the Mirror of Nature*. Princeton, NJ: Princeton University Press.

Rosenau, Pauline Marie. 1991. *Post-Modernism and the Social Sciences: Insights, Inroads, and Intrusions*. Princeton, NJ: Princeton University Press.

Rosenberg, Martin. 1994. "Physics and Hypertext: Liberation and Complicity in Art and Pedagogy." In George Landow, ed., *Hyper/Text/Theory*, 268–98. Baltimore: Johns Hopkins Press.

Rosler, Martha. 1986. "Video Art: Shedding the Utopian Moment." In René Payant, ed., *Vidéo*, 242–51. Montreal: Artexte.

– 1994. "Place, Position, Power, Politics." In Carol Becker, ed., *The Subversive Imagination: Artists, Society, and Social Responsibility*, 55–76. New York: Routledge.

Rotstein, Abraham. 1976. "Canada: The New Nationalism." *Foreign Affairs*, 55 no. 1, 97–118.

– 1988. "The Use and Misuse of Economics in Cultural Policy." In Rowland M. Lorimer and Donald C. Wilson, eds., *Communication Canada: Issues in Broadcasting and New Technologies*, 140–56. Toronto: Kagan and Woo.

Rousseau, Jean-Jacques. 1968. *The Social Contract*. First pub. 1762. Trans. Maurice Cranston. Baltimore: Penguin.

Rowell-Sirois Report. See Canada 1940.

Rudin, Ronald. *Making History in 20th Century Quebec*. Toronto: University of Toronto Press.

Rumilly, Robert. 1967. *Histoire de l'École des hautes études commerciales de Montréal, 1907–1967*. Montreal: Beauchemin.

Rush, G.B., Christensen, E., and Malcomson, J. 1981. "Lament for a Notion: the Development of Social Science in Canada." *Canadian Review of Sociology and Anthropology*, 18 no. 4, 519–44.

Ryerson, Stanley. 1968. *Unequal Union: Confederation and the Roots of Conflict in the Canadas, 1815–1873*. Toronto: Progress Books.

Sacouman, R. James. 1981. "The 'Peripheral Maritimes' and Canada-Wide Marxist Political Economy." *Studies in Political Economy*, 6 (autumn), 135–50.

Sagan, Carl. 1989. "Why Scientists Should Popularize Science." *American Journal of Physics*, 57 no. 4, 295.

Said, Edward. 1993. *Culture and Imperialism*. New York: Vintage Books/Random House.

Saint-Germain, Maurice. 1973. *Une économie à libérer: le Québec analysé dans ses structures économiques*. Montreal: Les Presses de l'Université de Montréal.

Salée, Daniel. 1983. "L'analyse socio-politique de la société québécoise: bilan et perspectives." In G. Boismenu et al., eds., *Espace régional et nation. Pour un nouveau débat sur le Québec*, 15–49. Montreal: Boréal Express.

Sales, Arnaud, and Dumais, Lucie. 1985. "La construction sociale de l'économie québécoise." *Recherches sociographiques*, 26 no. 3, 319–60.

Salter, Liora. 1981. "'Public' and Mass Media in Canada: Dialectics in Innis' Communication Analysis." In Melody, Salter, and Heyer, eds., 1981, 193–207.

– 1988. *Mandated Science: Science and Scientists in the Making of Standards*. Dordrecht: Kluwer.

Salter, Liora, and Hearn, Allison. 1996. *Outside the Lines: Issues and Problems in Interdisciplinary Research*. Montreal: McGill-Queen's University Press.

Sandberg, Jared, and Weber, Thomas. 1996. "$19.95 Internet Access fees May Not Last Much Longer." *Wall Street Journal*. Reprinted in the *Ottawa Citizen*, 26 Dec., C2.

Saunders, S.A. 1984. *The Economic History of the Maritime Provinces*. First pub. 1939. Fredericton, NB: Acadiensis Press.

Sawchuk, Kim. 1994. "Semiotics, Cybernetics and the Ecstacy of Marketing Communications." In Douglas Kellner, *Jean Baudrillard: A Critical Reader*, 89–118. Oxford: Blackwell.

Schmidt, R. 1981. "Canadian Political Economy: A Critique." *Studies in Political Economy*, 6, 65–92.

Séguin, M. 1970. *La nation "canadienne" et l'agriculture (1760–1850)*. Montreal: Fides.

Sennett, Richard. 1970. *Families against the Cities*. Cambridge, Mass.: Harvard University Press.

Seth, Andrew. 1899. *Scottish Philosophy*. Edinburgh: William Blackwood and Sons.

Shade, Leslie Regan. 1994. "Computer Networking in Canada: From CA*net to CANARIE." *Canadian Journal of Communication*, 19 no. 1, 53–69.

Shields, Rob. 1991. *Places on the Margin: Alternative Geographies of Modernity*. London: Routledge Chapman Hall.

Shoesmith, Brian. 1993. "Introduction to Innis' 'History of Communication.'" *Continuum*, 7 no.1, 121–31.

Shore, Marlene. 1987. *The Science of Social Redemption: McGill, the Chicago School, and the Origins of Social Research in Canada*. Toronto: University of Toronto Press.

Sivanandan, A. 1996. "Heresies and Prophecies: the Social and Political Fallout of the Technological Revolution: An Interview." *Race and Class: A Journal of Black and Third World Liberation*, 37 no. 4 (April–June), 2–11.

Smith, Adam. 1931. *The Wealth of Nations*. First pub. 1776. Toronto: J.M. Dent.

– 1986. *The Wealth of Nations*. First pub. 1776. Bks. 1–3. London: Penguin Classics.

Smith, Dennis. 1991. *The Rise of Historical Sociology*. Philadelphia, Penn.: Temple University Press.

Smith, Neil. 1991. *Uneven Development: Nature, Capital and the Production of Space*. Oxford: Basil Blackwell.

Smith, Norman Kemp, ed. 1982. See Kant 1982.

Spender, Dale. 1995. *Nattering on the Net: Women, Power and Cyberspace*. Toronto: Garamond Press.

Spengler, Oswald. 1926. *The Decline of the West: Form and Actuality*. First pub. 1918. 2 vols. Trans. and notes by Charles F. Atkinson. New York: Knopf.

Spry, Irene. 1958a. "Hydro-Electric Power." *Encyclopedia Canadiana*, vol. 5. 211–22. Ottawa: Canadiana.

– 1958b. "Water Power." *Encyclopedia Canadiana*, vol. 10, 273–90. Ottawa: Canadiana.

Stamps, Judith. 1995. *Unthinking Modernity: Innis, McLuhan, and the Frankfurt School*. Montreal: McGill-Queen's University Press.

Stark, F.M. 1994. "Harold Innis and the Chicago School." *Journal of Canadian Studies*, 29 no. 3, 131–45.

Stewart, Dugald. 1845. *Outlines of Moral Philosophy*. First pub. 1793. Edinburgh. McLedo and Son.

Straw, Will. 1993. "Shifting Boundaries, Lines of Descent: Cultural Studies and Institutional Realignments." In Valda Blundell, John Shepherd and Ian Taylor, eds., *Relocating Cultural Studies: Developments in Theory and Research*, 86–102. New York: Routledge.

Taussig, Michael. 1981. *The Devil and Commodity Fetishism in South America*. Chapel Hill: University of North Carolina Press.

Taylor, Charles. 1991. *The Malaise Of Modernity*. Toronto: Anansi.

Tenhaaf, Nell. 1988. "... believable, if not always true." Installation in *Siting Technology*. Walter Philips Gallery, Banff.

Thibault, Marc-Aurèle. 1988. "Le département d'économique, 1943–1987." In Faucher, ed., 1988, 131–61.

Thomas, William I. and Znaniecki, Florian. 1984. *The Polish Peasant in Europe and America*. First pub. 1918–20. Urbana: University of Illinois Press.

Thuau, Étienne. 1966. *Raison d'État et pensée politique à l'époque de Richelieu*. Paris: Colin.

Tilly, Charles. 1984. *Big Structures, Large Processes, Huge Comparisons*. New York: Russell Sage.

Timlin, Mabel F,. and Faucher, Albert. 1968. *The Social Sciences in Canada: Two Studies*. Ottawa: Social Science Research Council of Canada.

Tippett, Maria. 1986. "The Writing of English-Canadian Cultural History, 1970–85." *Canadian Historical Review*, 67 no. 4, 548–61.

– 1990. *Making Culture: English-Canadian Institutions and the Arts before the Massey Commission*. Toronto: University of Toronto Press.

Tocqueville, Alexis de. 1835. *La démocratie en Amérique*. Tome 1. Paris: Garnier-Flammarion, 1981.

– 1856. *The Old Regime and the French Revolution*. Trans. Stuart Gilbert. Garden City, NJ: Doubleday Anchor, 1955.

Todd, J. 1995. *Colonial Technology: Science and the Transfer of Innovation to Australia*. Cambridge: Cambridge University Press.

Torres, Francesc. 1990. "The Art of the Possible." In Doug Hall and Sally Jo Fifer, eds., *Illuminating Video: An Essential Guide to Video Art*, 205–9. New York: Aperture Foundation, Inc.

Treasury Board Secretariat. 1995. *The Internet: A Guide to Internet Use in the Federal Government*. Ottawa: Government of Canada.

Tremblay, Maurice. 1954. *Le fédéralisme canadien: évolutions et problèmes*. Quebec City: Les Presses de l'Université Laval.

Tremblay Report. See Quebec (Province) 1956.

Trépanier, Pierre. 1987. "Les influences leplaysiennes au Canada français, 1855–1888." *Revue d'études canadiennes*, 22 no. 1, 66–82.

Tribe, Keith. 1988. *Governing Economy: The Reformation of German Economic Discourse 1750–1840*. Cambridge: Cambridge University Press.

Trudeau, Pierre Elliott. 1956. "La Province du Québec, au moment de la grève." In P. Trudeau, ed., *La grève de l'amiante*, 1–91. Montreal: Les Éditions Cité Libre.

Tuchman, Maurice. 1971. *Art and Technology: A Report on the Art and Technology Program of the Los Angeles County Museum of Art, 1967–1971*. New York: The Viking Press.

Tuer, Dot. 1992. "The Art of Nation Building: Constructing a 'Cultural Identity' for Post-war Canada." *Parallelogramme*, 17 no. 4, 24–36.

Turgeon, Laurier. 1981. "Pour une histoire de la pêche de la morue à Marseille au XVIIIe siècle." *Histoire sociale*, 4 no. 28, 295–322.

– 1986. "Pour redécouvrir notre 16e siècle: les pêches à Terre-Neuve d'après les archives notariales de Bordeaux." *Revue d'histoire de l'Amérique française*, 39 no. 4, 523–49.

Turner, Frederick Jackson. 1920. *The Frontier in American History*. New York: H. Holt and Co.

Urwick, E.J. 1935. "The Role of Intelligence in the Social Process." *Canadian Journal of Economics and Political Science*, 1, 64–76.

Valaskakis, Gail Guthrie. 1981. "The Other Side of Empire: Contact and Communication in Southern Baffin Island." In Melody, Salter, and Heyer, eds., 1981, 209–24.

Valpy, Michael. 1994. "In Celebration of Harold Innis." *Globe and Mail*, 6 Jan., A2.

van Kirk, Sylvia. 1980. *"Many Tender Ties": Women in Fur Trade Society in Western Canada, 1670–1870*. Winnipeg: Watson and Dwyer.

Veblen, T. 1899. *The Theory of the Leisure Class*. New York: Viking.

Vipond, Mary. 1980. "The Nationalist Network: English-Canada's Intellectuals and Artists in the 1920s." *Canadian Review of Studies in Nationalism*, 8 no. 1, 32–52.

Virilio, Paul. 1977. *Speed and Politics*. Trans. M. Polizzotti. New York: Semiotext(e).

– 1993. "The Third Interval: A Critical Transition." In V.A. Conley, ed., *Rethinking Technologies*, 3–12. Minneapolis: University of Minnesota Press.

Volkering, Michael. 1994. "Death or Transfiguration: The Future for Cultural Policy in New Zealand." *Culture and Policy*, 6 no.1, 7–25.

Waite, Peter B. 1987. *Lord of Point Grey: Larry Mackenzie of UBC*. Vancouver: University of British Columbia Press.

Ward, Jane. 1953. "The Published Works of H.A. Innis." *Canadian Journal of Economics and Political Science*, 29 no. 2 (May), 233–44.

Wark, Westley. 1992. "Security Intelligence in Canada 1864–1945: The History of a 'National Insecurity State.'" In Keith Neilson and B.J.C. McKercher, eds., *Go Spy the Land: Military Intelligence in History*, 153–78. Westport, Conn.: Praeger.

Watkins, Mel H. 1963. "A Staple Theory of Economic Growth." *Canadian Journal of Economics and Political Science*, 29 no. 2 (May), 141–58.

– 1968. See Canada 1968.

– 1970. "Foreign Ownership and the Structure of Canadian Industry." In David Godfrey and Mel Watkins, eds., *Gordon to Watkins to You*, 63–83. Toronto: New Press.

– 1973. "Resources and Underdevelopment." In Robert Laxer, ed., *Canada Ltd.: The Political Economy of Dependency*, 107–126. Toronto: McClelland and Stewart.

– 1977. "The Staple Theory Revisited." *Journal of Canadian Studies*, 12 no. 5 (winter), 83–95.

– 1981. "The Staple Theory Revisited." In Melody, Salter, and Heyer, eds., 1981, 53–71.

– 1989. "The Political Economy of Growth." In Clement and Williams, eds., 1989, 16–35.

Watkins Report. See Canada 1968.

Watson, John A. 1977. "Harold Innis and Classical Scholarship." *Journal of Canadian Studies*, 12 no. 5, 45–61.

– 1981. "Marginal Man: Harold Innis Communication Works in Context." PhD dissertation, University of Toronto.

Wayland, Francis. 1870. *The Elements of Political Economy*. 2nd Ed. Boston: Gould and Lincoln.

Wernick, Andrew. 1986. "The Post-Innisian Significance of Innis." *Canadian Journal of Political and Social Theory*, 10 no. 2, 128–50.

– 1993. "American Popular Culture in Canada: Trends and Reflections." In David H. Flaherty and Frank E. Manning, eds., *The Beaver Bites Back?: American Popular Culture in Canada*, 293–302. Montreal: McGill-Queen's University Press.

Westfall, William. 1981. "The Ambivalent Verdict: Harold Innis and Canadian History." In Melody, Salter, and Heyer, eds., 1981, 37–49.

Weston, Jay. 1993. "National Capital Freenet." "Comment" submitted to the CRTC Review of Regulatory Framework (Telecom Public Notice CRTC 92–78), 25 Nov.

Whitaker, Reginald. 1983. "To Have Insight into Much and Power over Nothing: The Political Ideas of Harold Innis." *Queen's Quarterly*, 90 no. 3, 818–31.

- 1992. *A Sovereign Idea: Essays on Canada as a Democratic Community.* Montreal: McGill-Queen's University Press.

Whitley, R. 1985. "Knowledge Producers and Knowledge Acquirers." In Terry Shin and Richard Whitley, eds., *Expository Science: Forms and Functions of Popularization, Sociology of Sciences Yearbook,* vol. 9, 3–38. Dordrecht: Reidel Press; Hingham, Mass.: Kluwer.

Williams, Raymond. 1973. *The Country and the City.* London: Chatto and Windus.

- 1974. *Television: Technology and Cultural Form.* London: Fontana.

- 1980. *Problems in Materialism and Culture.* London : NLB.

Wilson, Kevin. 1988. *Technologies of Control: The New Interactive Media for the Home.* Madison: University of Wisconsin Press.

Woodrow, Brian R., Woodside, Kenneth, Wiseman, Henry, and Black, John B. 1980. *Conflict over Communications Policy: A Study of Federal-Provincial Relations and Public Policy.* Montreal: C.D. Howe Institute.

Wooster, Ann-Sargeant. 1990. "Reach Out and Touch Someone: The Romance of Interactivity." In Doug Hall and Sally Jo Fifer, eds., *Illuminating Video: An Essential Guide to Video Art,* 275–303. New York: Aperture Foundation, Inc.

Wyschogrod, Edith. 1984. *Spirit in Ashes: Hegel, Heidegger, and Man-Made Mass Death.* Chicago: University of Chicago Press.

Zerker, S. 1983. "Innis." In William Toye, ed., *The Oxford Companion to Canadian Literature,* 389–90. Toronto: Oxford University Press.

Index

postmodernism: and community, 317; concern with language in, 314–15; and dialectic, 317; and diversity, 317; epistemological concerns of, 309–10; and instrumental reason, 310–11; marginality in, 283, 303–4, 306; and metaphysics, 316–17; and the oral tradition, 320; and pessimism, 319–20; spatial bias in, 303
postmodernity: futurelessness of, 279–80; and the problematization of time, 262, 276–7
power: and centre–periphery relations, 256; and culture, 164–5; and electronic networking, 328, 372; and knowledge, 118, 164–5; result of present-mindedness, 5; as self-destructive, 58; as shaped by technology, 254, 288, 292, 296; social relations of, 184
praxis, 268, 271, 275, 278, 280
present-mindedness: counteracting, 123; effects of, on public policy, 5, 58; implications of, 35; as industrial strategy, 287; and the market, 264; as result of mechanization of culture, 246; result of space bias, 61; three determining elements of, 266; trends towards, 14; and university accountability, 122
press. See newspaper industry
La Presse (Montreal), 159, 161, 163, 167–8
Prince Edward Island, 231
propaganda: American, 38; education as, 372;

and film, 63
public expression, 69, 77–8
publishing industry, 248, 250, 264
Pullman strike, 86
pulp and paper industry, 179, 246; and American monopoly, 249, 286

Quebec, 151; church doctrine and intellectualism in, 200; development of social sciences in, 23, 212–16; and federal commissions, 215; French church in, 75–6; Innis's intellectual contemporaries in, 199–203; intellectual divisiveness in, 211, 217–20; intellectual traditions of, 209–11; methodological revolution in, 203; modernization of, 200–1, 219; nationalism in, 200–5, 211, 219; neo-Innisian failure in, 197, 204–6, 207; and the "new political economy," 203–6; as police state, 72–3; political economy in, 24; as self-contained society, 219; sociopolitical imperatives of, 200–2, 205; staples theory in, 210–11; symbolic order in, 75–6
Queen's University, 138, 149, 152; Department of Political Economy, 200

race: and centre–periphery relations, 259; and colonialism, 190; in feminist scholarship, 181; and the fur trade, 186
Radforth, Ian, 69
radio, 119–20, 237, 292; early days of, 323; and

manipulation, 36; societal context of, 266; and spatial bias, 97, 265
railway, 84–5, 262, 265, 286, 292; effect of, on local industry, 342; and frontier thesis, 95; government ownership of, 341; and rigidities, 110
raison d'état, 70
Ratz, Betty, 107
Rawls, John, 42
reason, 33, 310–11
Red River Settlement, 190
reflexivity, 268–9, 336–7, 365–6
Refus Global (1948), 361–2
Rehabilitation Committee, 145–7
Reid, Thomas, 16, 46, 50–2, 54, 60
Reith Lectures, 269
resistance, 305–6
Resnick, Philip, 69
rigidities, 108–11
Robbins, J.E., 144; on CSSRC and administrators, 149; on CSSRC autonomy, 140, 149; CSSRC boundary work of, 142–3; on CSSRC during the war, 145
Robertson, Clive, 365
Rocher, Guy, 75–6
Rockefeller Foundation, 23, 138–9, 142, 170
Rogers Cable, 325–6, 332
Rorty, Richard, 20, 84, 310; on binary opposition, 311; on communal decision-making, 318; on the epistemological consequences of writing, 315; on metaphysics, 317
Rosenberg, Martin, 382
Rosler, Martha, 347, 364
Rotstein, Abe, 10, 203
Roundtable on Science and Technology, 122

women: absence of, in
   culture, 383–4, in historical studies, 183, in
   Innis, 22, 177, 370; economic role of, 182–3,
   187–8; and electronic
   networking, 326–8

Woodrow, Brian, 349
Woodsworth, J.S., 85
Woods, Walter, 145
Woolf, Virginia, 126
writing, 34–5; and dogma-
   tism, 36; epistemological repercussions of,

312–15; invention of,
   65
Wundt, Wilhelm, 54

Young, George Paxton, 52

Znaniecki, Florian, 89